The Logic of Desire

The Logic of Desire

Aquinas on Emotion

✧

NICHOLAS E. LOMBARDO, O.P.

The Catholic University of America Press
Washington, D.C.

The paper used in this publication meets the minimum requirements of American National Standards for Information Science—Permanence of Paper for Printed Library Materials, ANSI Z39.48-1984.
∞

Library of Congress Cataloging-in-Publication Data
Lombardo, Nicholas E. (Nicholas Emerson)
The logic of desire : Aquinas on emotion / Nicholas E. Lombardo.
p. cm.
Includes bibliographical references (p.) and index.
ISBN 978-0-8132-1797-0 (pbk. : alk. paper) 1. Thomas, Aquinas, Saint, 1225?–1274. 2. Emotions. 3. Thomas, Aquinas, Saint, 1225?–1274. Summa theologica. I. Title.
B765.T54L59 2011
128'.37—dc22 2010021133

To my father, my mother, and my sister

What does a man do when he finds himself living after an age has ended and he can no longer understand himself because the theories of man of the former age no longer work and the theories of the new age are not yet known, for even the name of the new age is not known, and so everything is upside down, people feeling bad when they should feel good, good when they should feel bad?

What a man does is start afresh as if he were newly come into a new world, which in fact it is; start with what he knows for sure, look at the birds and beasts, and like a visitor from Mars newly landed on earth notice what is different about man.

Walker Percy, "The Delta Factor"

✧ ✧ ✧

More tortuous than all else is the human heart,
beyond remedy; who can understand it?
I, the Lord, alone probe the mind
and test the heart
To reward everyone according to his ways,
according to the merit of his deeds.

Jeremiah 17:9–10

Contents

Preface

Aquinas's account of emotion centers on his account of desire. In turn, it is desire that gives the *Summa theologiae* its *exitus-reditus* structure: Aquinas begins with God and then traces how creation flows from God's desire and returns to him through ours. Consequently, to follow the theme of emotion through the *Summa* is to follow the guiding principle around which Aquinas organized his most mature thought. The *Summa* is often compared to the great cathedrals of the Middle Ages for its vast structure and its comprehensive synthesis of so many component parts. Looking at the theme of desire and emotion is like stepping away from the many side chapels of the *Summa* and looking down the nave.

Desire and emotion are not just central to the structure of the *Summa:* they are central to Aquinas's project and especially his ethics. For Aquinas, ethics is nothing other than the study of human psychology insofar as it flourishes or fails to flourish. Unlike approaches that regard psychology and ethics as two distinct categories that are only occasionally concerned with each other, or perhaps extrinsically related in a calculus where psychological well-being is weighed against doing what is right, Aquinas's approach offers a refreshing synthesis of psychology and ethics. In many popular understandings, there is something paradoxical about divine commandments: God gives us desires and then commands us not to act on them. For Aquinas, there is no paradox, because God commands us *through* the desires he gives us. The commandments of divine revelation are ancillary to our natural inclinations; they are signposts to the fulfillment of desire, shorthand conclusions following from the logic of human nature.

Two extreme views about emotion seem to emerge continually in different eras of human history and sometimes side by side within the same culture. There is one view that is suspicious of human emotion and seeks to guard against it, restrain it, and prevent it from taking control. Then there is another view that exults in emotion and desire and glorifies following wherever it might lead. While most cultures and peoples settle on some middle way, it is striking how frequently the extreme views manifest themselves time and again, in all sorts of different cultural contexts. Nonetheless, it is not all that surprising. Both views have their origins in human experience: all of us at times experience the goodness of desire and emotion, and all of us at times experience how our emotions can mislead us, disrupt our inner calm, and generally cause trouble. These experiences can be so intense that we are liable to emphasize one reality at the expense of the other. Aquinas manages to avoid either extreme. He affirms the fundamental goodness of emotion even while maintaining that, in a fallen world, human affectivity is prone to distortions. In consequence, his account is of broad interest to anyone who seeks to reconcile a positive view of the human person with the empirical fact of our proclivities toward self-destructive and other-destructive behavior.

The positive role of emotion in Aquinas's theology derives in no small part from the cultural milieu of the Dominican Order to which Aquinas belonged, even apart from the influence of individual Dominicans such as his teacher Albert the Great, who had pioneered the study of Aristotle and the integration of theology with natural science. The order had grown out of an informal band of itinerant preachers devoted to defending the goodness of the material world against the dualistic beliefs of the Cathars of southern France. These origins gave Dominic and his companions an especially acute attentiveness to the goodness of creation. Insofar as they established the government and basic structure of the order, and consciously and unconsciously shaped the distinctive traits of Dominican culture, their legacy undoubtedly influenced Aquinas toward a more pronounced appreciation of creation—and thus emotion. His account of emotion, then, in part reflects the cultural dispositions of the early Dominicans. This genealogy underscores its rootedness in practical concerns and the analysis of ordinary human experience, and also helps to explain its balance and humaneness.

Aquinas reinvigorated the living intellectual tradition that he had received with a passion for rigorous analysis and a radical openness to all sources of knowledge, whether secular or religious. Today, several centuries later, his contribution to making sense of the human condition remains relevant to many contemporary concerns. It is my hope that *The Logic of Desire* will make that contribution more accessible and help to build upon it.

✧

I am grateful to many people and institutions for the role they played in bringing this book to print. Looking back at the end of a long process, I am struck by just how much I owe.

I would like to express my gratitude for the grounding in analytic philosophy that I received at Brown University, and for the exceptional theological education that I received at the Dominican House of Studies in Washington, D.C. I am particularly grateful to Lawrence Donohoo, O.P., who directed my S.T.L. thesis "Aquinas on Emotion." His guidance and feedback were invaluable. I would also like to thank Kevin White, who graciously permitted me to audit his lectures on Aquinas and the passions at the Catholic University of America.

I would like to thank Romanus Cessario, O.P., and Archbishop Augustine Di Noia, O.P., for encouraging me in the idea of turning my S.T.L. thesis into a book and helping me in the practical process of finding a publisher. Without their encouragement and assistance, it is unlikely that this book would ever have been written.

The feedback, criticism, and encouragement of many people played a crucial role in bringing this book to completion. I am especially grateful to Nicholas Ingham, O.P., who commented on every chapter of the manuscript as I was writing it. I am also grateful to Michael Sherwin, O.P., for his extensive and very helpful comments. Special thanks are owed as well to Boniface Endorf, O.P., Brian Mullady, O.P., and an anonymous reviewer for CUA Press.

I am indebted to many other people for their comments and feedback, and I would particularly like to thank Andrew Brookes, Ann Brown, Clement Burns, O.P., Sarah Coakley, Hugh Vincent Dyer, O.P., Fergus Kerr, O.P., John Baptist Ku, O.P., Thomas Joseph White, O.P., and Celia Wolf-Devine. I owe special thanks to Michele Ransil, C.D.P., for her expert proofreading, to Benedict Croell, O.P., for scanning a thesis from the Angelicum library in Rome, and to James Kruggel, my editor, for assistance above and beyond.

Finally, I would like to thank my father, my mother, and my sister, who more than anyone else made this book possible, and to whom it is dedicated, with love and affection.

Nicholas E. Lombardo, O.P.
Blackfriars, Cambridge
May 2010

The Logic of Desire

Introduction

When Thomas Aquinas finished the *Prima secundae* of the *Summa theologiae* in 1271,[1] questions 22–48 probably constituted the longest sustained discussion of the passions ever written.[2] This *Treatise on the Passions,* as questions 22–48 of the *Prima secundae* have come to be known, is the culmination of a lifetime of reflection and the centerpiece of a much larger project. Aquinas's attention to the passions spans his entire literary output, beginning with his commentary on the *Sentences* of Peter Lombard, and permeates each part of the *Summa theologiae.*[3] In the *Summa,* he thorough-

1. For a discussion of the historical origins and precise chronology of the *Summa theologiae* and Aquinas's other works, see Jean-Pierre Torrell, *Saint Thomas Aquinas,* vol. 1, *The Person and His Work,* trans. Robert Royal (Washington, D.C.: The Catholic University of America Press, 1996), esp. 146–47, 330–61. On the origins of the *Summa,* see also Leonard E. Boyle, "The Setting of the *Summa theologiae* of Saint Thomas," in *Facing History: A Different Thomas Aquinas* (Louvain-La-Neuve: Fédération Internationale des Instituts d'Études Médiévales, 2000), 65–91, and M. Michèle Mulchahey, *"First the Bow Is Bent in Study": Dominican Education before 1350* (Toronto: Pontifical Institute of Mediaeval Studies, 1998), 278–306. For an accessible introduction to the *Summa* and the history of its reception, see Jean-Pierre Torrell, *Aquinas's* Summa: *Background, Structure, and Reception* (Washington, D.C.: The Catholic University of America Press, 2005).

2. To my knowledge, the longest sustained discussion of the passions before Aquinas is found in Aristotle's *Rhetoric,* and Aristotle's treatment is neither as long nor as systematic as Aquinas's.

Paul Gondreau states that the *Treatise on the Passions* "dwarfs the only known historical precedents [for a systematic treatment of the passions], both of which Aquinas draws upon: Nemesius of Emesa's short treatise on the passions in his *De natura hominis* and, following this, John Damascene's treatise on the same in his *De fide orthodoxa* (Aristotle left us no systematic treatment of the passions)." Gondreau, "The Passions and the Moral Life: Appreciating the Originality of Aquinas," *Thomist* 71 (2007): 426. See also Paul Gondreau, *The Passions of Christ's Soul in the Theology of St. Thomas Aquinas* (Münster: Aschendorff Verlag, 2003), 106.

Servais Pinckaers writes: "To our knowledge, there does not exist in the Fathers nor in the Middle Ages a study of the human passions comparable for its length and its quality. It is a unique, classic work—and is too neglected." Servais Pinckaers, "Les passions et la morale," *Revue des sciences philosophiques et théologiques* 74 (1990): 379.

Simo Knuuttila calls it "the most extensive medieval treatise" on the passions. Simo Knuuttila, *Emotions in Ancient and Medieval Philosophy* (Oxford: Oxford University Press, 2004), 239.

3. Besides the *Summa,* the most significant places where Aquinas discusses the passions

ly integrates his discussion of the passions with his metaphysics and his account of human nature, the desire for happiness, virtue, vice, sin, and grace.[4] In its integration within such an expansive project, the *Treatise on the Passions* is without historical precedent,[5] as is the *Prima secundae* in which it is found.[6] Aquinas's account of the passions also represents an

include (listed in approximate chronological order): *Scriptum super libros Sententiarum* II 36, III 15–16, III 26–27, III 34, IV 49; *De veritate* 22.3–4, 25–26; *Summa contra gentiles* I 89–91; *Sententia libri De anima,* passim, esp. III.14; *De malo,* passim; *De virtutibus* 1.4–5, 4.1–2; *Sententia libri Ethicorum, passim,* esp. II.5. Of these, Aquinas's discussion of the passions in the *Scriptum super libros Sententiarum* and *De veritate* 25–26 are probably the most important.

4. Most studies of Aquinas on the passions focus almost exclusively on the *Treatise on the Passions* and questions 80–82 of the *Prima pars.* As a result, much work remains to be done, especially in clarifying his treatment of the passions vis-à-vis original sin, grace, and specific virtues and vices.

5. Mark Jordan argues that Aquinas's extended discussion of the passions in the *Prima secundae* constitutes a structural innovation compared to the work of his predecessors. See Mark D. Jordan, "Ideals of *Scientia moralis* and the Invention of the *Summa theologiae,*" in *Aquinas' Moral Theory: Essays in Honor of Norman Kretzmann,* ed. S. MacDonald and E. Stump (Ithaca, N.Y.: Cornell University Press, 1999), 84–90. Kevin White described the *Treatise on the Passions* as a new literary form in a philosophy lecture at the Catholic University of America.

6. Historical evidence suggests that Aquinas began writing the *Summa theologiae* to correct the casuistry prevalent in manuals for confessors and other works of moral theology. He was concerned that the moral theology taught to Dominican students and others had a skewed emphasis on vice and sin and lacked sufficient theological and anthropological context. Consequently, one of Aquinas's principal objectives in writing the *Summa* was to give a balanced foundation for the study of Christian ethics. For this reason, Leonard Boyle suggests that the *Prima secundae,* Aquinas's analysis of human actions and passions par excellence, is the heart of the *Summa theologiae.* In any case, nothing comparable to the *Prima secundae* in scope or content existed before Aquinas or during his lifetime. There are contemporary parallels to the *Secunda secundae* and its discussion of particular virtues and vices, such as the *Summa de vitiis et virtutibus* of William Peraldus, and there are parallels to the *Summa theologiae* considered as a whole, notably the *Summa theologiae* of Alexander of Hales, one of the principal models for Aquinas's work, but there are no parallels to the *Prima secundae.* See Boyle, "Setting of the *Summa*"; Torrell, *The Person and His Work,* 142–59; and Gondreau, *Passions of Christ's Soul,* 22, 45–46, 107–10.

Mark Jordan comes to a conclusion similar to Boyle's about the centrality of the *Secunda pars* to Aquinas's project. He writes: "I believe that Thomas wrote the *Summa* for the sake of the second part—that is, in order to situate the moral component of theology within a properly ordered account of the whole. Thomas undertook the writing at the end of a series of experiments in comprehensive theological composition: a first commentary on the Lombard, a projected series of Boethius commentaries, the so-called *Contra gentiles,* an abandoned *Compendium,* and the bare beginnings of a second commentary on the Lombard. Reading through these experiments, we can argue over Thomas's motives for moving from one project to another. But the largest contrast between the *Summa* and the earlier works seems to me beyond argument: it is the contrast created by the *secunda pars,* by the large and ingeniously arranged teaching of *scientia moralis* at the center of theology. Any account of the *Summa*'s purposes that fails to explain the unprecedented size and scope of the moral teaching in the work will be an inadequate account" (Jordan, "Invention of the *Summa theologiae,*" 97).

original synthesis of every major thinker available to him, particularly Aristotle, Augustine, Nemesius of Emesa, John Damascene, and his teacher, Albert the Great.[7] When his writings are considered under the rubric of emotion—a modern concept considerably broader than the ancient and medieval concept of passion—the scope of his achievement becomes even more impressive.

Nonetheless, despite renewed interest in emotion among contemporary philosophers and theologians, Aquinas's account of emotion remains neglected. Robert Solomon's anthology of classic texts on emotion, a standard philosophy textbook, does not include anything from Aquinas.[8] Martha Nussbaum gives him only cursory mention in her massive work on emotion.[9] In his book *Aquinas on Mind,* Anthony Kenny criticizes Aquinas's account of the passions as forced, derivative, and not entirely coherent, despite his great sympathy for many aspects of his thought.[10]

With 27 questions and 132 articles, the *Treatise on the Passions* is the longest treatise in the *Prima secundae* (Pinckaers, "Les passions et la morale," 379). This does not necessarily mean that Aquinas regarded his treatment of the passions as the centerpiece of the *Prima secundae* and his fundamental moral theology, but all things considered, it is possible that he did. If so, and if Boyle is right that the *Prima secundae* is the heart of the *Summa,* than the *Treatise on the Passions* may be the centerpiece of more than just Aquinas's account of emotion.

For an extended discussion of the originality and historical context of the *Secunda pars* and the relationship between the *Prima secundae* and the *Secunda secundae,* see Jordan, "Invention of the *Summa theologiae,*" 79–97.

7. For discussions of Aquinas's sources, and those he deliberately excludes, see Gondreau, *Passions of Christ's Soul,* 101–35; Mark D. Jordan, "Aquinas's Construction of a Moral Account of the Passions," *Freiburger Zeitschrift für Philosophie und Theologie* 33 (1986): 71–97; and John Patrick Reid, Introduction, notes, and appendices to *Summa theologiae,* vol. 21, *Fear and Anger* (New York: McGraw-Hill, 1968), 146–50.

8. Robert C. Solomon, *What Is an Emotion? Classic and Contemporary Readings,* 2nd ed. (New York: Oxford University Press, 2003).

9. Martha C. Nussbaum, *Upheavals of Thought: The Intelligence of Emotions* (Cambridge: Cambridge University Press, 2003). In a recent article that is sympathetic to her account of emotion, Carlo Leget expresses surprise at Nussbaum's neglect of Aquinas: "Given, however, Nussbaum's historical interest and the Aristotelian and Stoic traditions she draws upon, it is surprising that in her study hardly any attention is paid to the work of Thomas Aquinas. Aquinas's account not only belonged to the very same intellectual tradition upon which Nussbaum builds; he also composed the most extensive treatise on emotions in his day, one that has had a considerable influence on later Western thought." Carlo Leget, "Martha Nussbaum and Thomas Aquinas on the Emotions," *Theological Studies* 64 (2003): 558–81.

10. "Aquinas divides the sensory appetite into two sub-faculties: one which is the locus of affective drives, and another which is the locus of aggressive drives. It would be unprofitable to follow in detail his justification for this anatomizing; it consists largely of forced assimilation of diverse classifications made by previous philosophers and theologians. Altogether, it cannot be said that Aquinas' treatment of sensory desire is quite coherent." Anthony Kenny, *Aquinas*

Interest in Aquinas's account of emotion, however, is growing. Recent studies have made extraordinary statements about Aquinas's influence on subsequent medieval and early modern thinkers. Peter King states that Aquinas "set the agenda for later medieval discussions of the passions" such that "later thinkers could do no better than to begin with his account, even when they disagreed with it."[11] In her book, *Passion and Action: The Emotions in Seventeenth-Century Philosophy,* Susan James devotes a chapter to Aquinas. Of all the medievals, she claims, he exerted the greatest influence on early modern theorists of the passions and perhaps even eclipsed Aristotle.[12] Eileen Sweeney suggests that Descartes and Hobbes should be understood "as reacting to and constructing alternatives to Aquinas's arrangement of the passions."[13] Thomas Dixon's historical study of the categories of passion and emotion singles out Augustine and Aquinas as the two principal representatives of the Christian tradition prior to the early modern period.[14]

Furthermore, a number of analytic philosophers have offered sympathetic reconstructions and appraisals of Aquinas's understanding of the passions.[15]

---

on Mind (New York: Routledge, 1993), 63. Kenny does, however, express admiration for many aspects of Aquinas's thought, especially his philosophy of mind (ibid., preface, 1–14). Moreover, his earlier influential book on the philosophy of emotion is informed by his engagement with Aquinas. See Anthony Kenny, *Action, Emotion, and Will* (London: Routledge and Kegan Paul, 1963). Consequently, Kenny's criticism should not be interpreted as a categorical dismissal of Aquinas's account of emotion. While he seems to consider many of its significant features unworthy of much consideration, he does not deny the enduring relevance of Aquinas's philosophical anthropology to contemporary philosophy of emotion.

11. Peter King, "Late Scholastic Theories of the Passions: Controversies in the Thomist Tradition," in *Emotions and Choice from Boethius to Descartes,* ed. Henrik Lagerlund and Mikko Yrjönsuuri, Studies in the History of the Philosophy of Mind 1 (Dordrecht: Kluwer, 2002), 229.

12. "However, the Scholastic interpreter [of Aristotle] who exerted the greatest influence on early-modern theorists of the passions was undoubtedly Thomas Aquinas. His analyses of the differences between activity and passivity, alongside his description and classification of the passions of the soul, were reiterated and discussed throughout the seventeenth century, and may well have been more widely read than Aristotle's own texts." Susan James, *Passion and Action: The Emotions in Seventeenth-Century Philosophy* (Oxford: Clarendon Press, 1997), 30.

13. Eileen Sweeney, "Restructuring Desire: Aquinas, Hobbes, and Descartes on the Passions," in *Meeting of the Minds: The Relations between Medieval and Classical Modern European Philosophy,* ed. Stephen F. Brown (Turnhout, Belgium: Brepols, 1998), 215.

14. Thomas Dixon, *From Passions to Emotions: The Creation of a Secular Psychological Category* (Cambridge: Cambridge University Press, 2003), 26–61.

15. See Mark P. Drost, "Intentionality in Aquinas' Theory of the Emotions," *International Philosophical Quarterly* 31 (1991): 449–60; Robert C. Roberts, "Thomas Aquinas on the Morality of Emotions," *History of Philosophy Quarterly* 9 (1992): 287–305; Norman Kretzmann, "Philosophy of Mind," in *The Cambridge Companion to Aquinas,* ed. Norman Kretzmann and Eleonore Stump (Cambridge: Cambridge University Press, 1993), 128–59, esp. 144–46; Mark Stephen Pes-

The revival of virtue ethics inspired by Alasdair MacIntyre's *After Virtue* seems partly responsible for much of this interest, since Aquinas is one of the primary representatives of the virtue ethics tradition, and his account of the passions is closely connected to his account of virtue.[16]

There has been a similar renewal of interest in Thomist scholarship.[17] Thomist scholars have always looked to Aquinas as a primary point of refer-

---

tana, "Second Order Desires and Strength of Will," *Modern Schoolman* 72 (1996): 173–82; Peter King, "Aquinas on the Passions," in *Thomas Aquinas: Contemporary Philosophical Perspectives*, ed. Brian Davies (New York: Oxford University Press, 2002), 353–84; Claudia Eisen Murphy, "Aquinas on Our Responsibility for Our Emotions," *Medieval Philosophy and Theology* 8 (1999): 163–205; Pasnau, *Thomas Aquinas on Human Nature*, 200–64.

16. Alasdair MacIntyre, *After Virtue*, 2nd ed. (Notre Dame, Ind.: University of Notre Dame Press, 1984).

17. The following are some highlights of recent literature. In English, Gondreau, *The Passions of Christ's Soul;* Craig Titus, *Resilience and the Virtue of Fortitude: Aquinas in Dialogue with the Psychosocial Sciences* (Washington, D.C.: The Catholic University of America Press, 2006); and Kevin White, "The Passions of the Soul (Ia IIae, qq. 22–48)," in *The Ethics of Aquinas*, ed. Stephen J. Pope (Washington, D.C.: Georgetown University Press, 2002), 103–15. Titus's work deserves special mention as a pioneering attempt to integrate contemporary psychology with Aquinas's anthropology and ethics.

In French, Pinckaers, "Les passions et la morale," and Jean-Pierre Torrell, *Saint Thomas Aquinas*, vol. 2, *Spiritual Master*, trans. Robert Royal (Washington, D.C.: The Catholic University of America Press, 2003), esp. 244–65.

In Spanish, Marcos Manzanedo has written an excellent series of articles in *Studium*. His articles focus on a close textual analysis of Aquinas's work on the passions, giving special attention to the development of his thought over the course of his lifetime.

In Italian, Matteo Laghi, "Passio et 'passione' nella letteratura tomista: Riflessioni in merito allo Status Quaestionis," *Divus Thomas* (Piacenza) 103 (2000): 59–92; Constantino Marmo, "Hoc autem etsi potest tollerari: Egidio Romano e Tommaso d'Aquino sulle passioni dell'anima," in *Documenti e studi sulla tradizione filosofica medievale*, vol. 2 (Spoleto, Italy: Centro italiano di studi sull'alto Medioevo, 1991), 281–315; Italo Sciuto, "Le passioni dell'anima nel pensiero di Tommaso d'Aquino," in *Anima e corpo nella cultura medievale*, ed. C. Casagrande and S. Vecchio (Florence: Edizioni del Galluzzo, 1999), 73–93; and Antonio Stagnitta, *L'anthropologia in Tommaso d'Aquino: saggio di ricerca comparata sulle passioni e abitudini dell'uomo* (Naples: E.D.I. Editrice, 1979).

In German, Alexander Brungs, *Metaphysik der Sinnlichkeit: Das System der Passiones Animae bei Thomas von Aquin* (Halle/Saale, Germany: Hallescher Verlag, 2002), which along with Gondreau's book constitute the only monographs on Aquinas and the passions published in recent years until 2009.

Gondreau also offers a survey of Thomist scholarship on Aquinas and human affectivity (Gondreau, *The Passions of Christ's Soul*, esp. 23–25).

Three important monographs were published in 2009, too late for this study to engage with, as the manuscript was already in preparation for publication: Diana Fritz Cates, *Aquinas on the Emotions: A Religious-Ethical Inquiry* (Washington, D.C.: Georgetown University Press, 2009); Robert Miner, *Thomas Aquinas on the Passions: A Study of* Summa Theologiae, *1a2ae 22–48* (Cambridge: Cambridge University Press, 2009); and Servais Pinckaers, *Passions et Vertu* (Paris: Editiòns Parole et Silence, 2009).

ence regarding the passions; nonetheless, until the twentieth century, his treatment of them was neglected, because the centrality of the passions to his anthropology and ethics was insufficiently appreciated.[18] Since then, there has been sustained interest in the passions and an unbroken chain of scholarship, with varying degrees of attentiveness to non-Thomist philosophy and scientific psychology.[19] During the early and mid-twentieth century, the passions received relatively intense attention before passing into a period of mild neglect. The passions are now receiving more attention within Thomist circles, in large part due to the scholarship of Servais Pinckaers and Jean-Pierre Torrell, as well as the growing interest of analytic philosophers in both Aquinas and emotion. Nonetheless, Torrell notes that the *Treatise on the Passions* "has scarcely attracted the attention of moralists," and, in a paper given at the American Catholic Philosophical Association's annual meeting in 1997, Richard Mansfield suggests that "perhaps no aspect of Aquinas's moral theory has been more neglected than his treatment of the *passiones animae*."[20]

18. Gondreau, *The Passions of Christ's Soul,* 23. Neglect of Aquinas's treatment of the passions begins with Aquinas's contemporaries and immediate successors. They were more interested in his discussion of specific virtues and vices in the *Secunda secundae* than the more abstract anthropological principles found in the *Prima secundae.* The breakdown of extant manuscript copies of the *Summa* reflects their interests: the *Tertia pars* accounts for 18%, the *Prima secundae* for 20%, the *Prima pars* for 25%, and the *Secunda secundae* for 37%. It may have been the originality of the *Prima secundae* that caused it to be overlooked. Boyle opines that Aquinas's project of regrounding pastoral concerns in a comprehensive theological context went over the heads of his Dominican confreres (Boyle, "Setting of the *Summa,*" 85–86).

One of the most popular and influential guides for confessors in the Middle Ages, which was written by a Dominican and sought to popularize the moral teaching of Aquinas, quotes the *Secunda secundae* frequently but refers to the *Prima secundae* only occasionally. While this focus on the *Secunda secundae* is not surprising, considering the work's orientation toward concrete pastoral advice rather than theory, it is consistent with the supposition that even Aquinas's fellow Dominicans did not fully appreciate the relevance of the *Prima secundae,* let alone the *Treatise on the Passions,* to his overall project. See Leonard E. Boyle, "The 'Summa confessorum' of John of Freiburg and the Popularization of the Moral Teaching of St. Thomas and Some of His Contemporaries," in *Facing History: A Different Thomas Aquinas* (Louvain-La-Neuve: Fédération Internationale des Instituts d'Études Médiévales, 2000), 50.

19. Of special note is the work of two Dutch psychiatrists, Anna Terruwe and Conrad Baars, who pioneered the integration of Thomistic psychology with clinical practice. Each published numerous books. A synthesis of their mature thought can be found in Anna A. Terruwe and Conrad W. Baars, *Loving and Curing the Neurotic: A New Look at Emotional Illness* (New Rochelle, N.Y.: Arlington House, 1972). A revised version was republished in two separate volumes: *Healing the Unaffirmed* (Staten Island, N.Y.: Alba House, 1976) and *Psychic Wholeness and Healing* (Staten Island, N.Y.: Alba House, 1981).

20. Torrell, *Spiritual Master,* 259; Richard K. Mansfield, "Antecedent Passion and the Moral

Focusing on the *Summa theologiae,* this study hopes to contribute to the recovery, reconstruction, and critique of Aquinas's account of emotion in dialogue with both the Thomist tradition and contemporary analytic philosophy.[21] The orientation of this study, however, is theological, not philosophical. While much of Aquinas's account of emotion is intelligible and rigorous from a philosophical perspective, the full significance of his purely philosophical insights cannot be grasped in isolation from the theological principles that ground and contextualize his work. Furthermore, his thought extends well beyond the domain of philosophy, and a nontheological analysis cannot do it justice.

However, these caveats in no way imply that Aquinas's account of emotion is comprehensible only from the perspective of his faith and therefore of interest only to Christian theologians. Paradoxically, it is precisely his theology of creation and creation's relationship to its Creator that opens up the logical space to consider human nature on its own terms. Aquinas affirms that creation has its own integrity even while depending on God for its existence, which means that, for Aquinas, faith is not necessary to know the truth about the natural world. Faith deepens knowledge of the natural world, but it does not replace or diminish the genuine contribution of philosophical and scientific reflection in the attainment of that knowledge. Consequently, Aquinas respects the proper autonomy of philosophical investigation, and so his account of emotion is of interest to philosophers and psychologists as well as theologians, albeit to different degrees.

This monograph has been organized to suit a variety of interests. Those

Quality of Human Acts According to St. Thomas," in *Virtues and Virtue Theory: Proceedings of the American Catholic Philosophical Association* 71 (1997): 221.

21. Although the theme of affectivity figures prominently in Aquinas's writings from the beginning with his commentary on the *Sentences,* his treatment in the *Summa theologiae* dwarfs the scope and significance of his earlier writings. Questions are investigated, connections are made, and issues are contextualized in a way that he does not attempt earlier. Furthermore, with some exceptions, Aquinas shows little evidence of changing his mind in significant ways about the passions and affections over the course of his life. There are two reasons for this lack of evidence: first, he remains committed to certain basic notions from the beginning of his career, and second, the attention he gives to the theme of affectivity in the *Summa* so far eclipses his previous writings that there are often little grounds for comparison. For this reason, a close analysis of the *Summa* can reasonably claim to represent Aquinas's thought on emotion. In those rare occasions when his previous writings on the passions and affections and other relevant topics contrast significantly with his mature thought, or when they shed light on topics inadequately discussed in the *Summa,* this study adverts to them. Otherwise the *Summa* provides the principal point of reference for this study.

who are not interested in Aquinas's theology may want to focus on the first four chapters, the latter part of chapter 6, and chapter 8; those who are interested in his theology may find it necessary to read the entire book, since his theology simultaneously shapes and presupposes his philosophy.

The Category of Emotion in Contemporary Analytic Philosophy

Emotion is an ambiguous concept, even if individual emotions, such as anger, fear, desire, and joy, seem as familiar and as concrete as any phenomenon of human life. There are many reasons for this ambiguity. First, there is the intrinsic difficulty of speaking about psychological realities that cannot be seen or touched. Even the physiological dimensions of emotion can be measured only externally; in no way can one person's subjective experience of emotion be made directly accessible to another. Second, emotion has been an important psychological category only since the early nineteenth century.[22] In a relatively brief span of time, the conceptual framework of Christian psychology was secularized, and a complex vocabulary of passions, affections, and sentiments was flattened into a single word. The category of emotion now encompasses a wide range of psychological phenomena that previously had been classified by different terms. Consequently, it is difficult to isolate the defining characteristics of an emotion. As Thomas Dixon summarizes, "The over-inclusivity of 'emotion' has made it impossible for there to be any consensus about what an emotion is."[23] Third, for most of the twentieth century, Anglo-American philosophy neglected discussion of the concept of emotion—as did, ironically, academic psychology—thus precluding the possibility of much progress in its philosophical clarification.

Consequently, although we constantly invoke the category of emotion in ordinary conversation, today there is little agreement among scholars in any

22. "It is an immensely striking fact of the history of English-language psychological thought that during the period between c. 1800 and c. 1850 a wholesale change in established vocabulary occurred such that those engaged in theoretical discussions about phenomena including hope, fear, love, hate, joy, sorrow, anger and the like no longer primarily discussed the passions or affections of the soul, nor the sentiments, but almost invariably referred to 'the emotions.' This transition is as striking as if established conceptual terms such as 'reason' or 'memory' or 'imagination' or 'will' had been quite suddenly replaced by a wholly new category" (Dixon, *From Passions to Emotions*, 4). See also Amélie Oksenberg Rorty, "From Passions to Emotions and Sentiments," *Philosophy* 57 (1982): 159–72.

23. Dixon, *From Passions to Emotions*, 246.

field about its definition or extension. In practice, much writing on emotion avoids clarifying its precise definition or giving a verdict about exactly which psychological phenomena "count" as emotions. Many focus instead on topics that do not require a definitive resolution of these questions. Some philosophers think it is misguided even to attempt to define emotion, regarding it as a mistake to think that all emotions belong to the same category.[24] They suggest that we should investigate individual emotions and avoid broad claims about the category as a whole.

Nonetheless, over the past few decades, as philosophical and scientific investigation of emotion has exploded, some lines of agreement about the category of emotion have begun to emerge.[25] The story of this convergence

24. See Amélie Oksenberg Rorty, "Enough Already with Theories of Emotion," in *Thinking about Feeling: Contemporary Philosophers on Emotion*, ed. Robert C. Solomon (New York: Oxford University Press, 2004), 269–78.

Paul Griffiths goes one step further and argues that "the general concept of emotion has no role in any future psychology." Instead, he holds that "current knowledge suggests that the domain of emotion fractures into three parts," that is, "sustained pretenses, affect program response, and higher cognitive states." See Paul Griffiths, *What Emotions Really Are: The Problem of Psychological Categories* (Chicago: University of Chicago Press, 1997), 247, 14–17. As might be expected, his provocative position has elicited criticism from other philosophers. See Robert C. Roberts, *Emotions: An Essay in Aid of Moral Psychology* (Cambridge: Cambridge University Press, 2003), 14–36.

For a defense of the natural kind status of emotion, that is, of the position that the category of emotion corresponds to fault lines that exist in nature and not just our minds, see Louis C. Charland, "The Natural Kind Status of Emotion," *British Journal of the Philosophy of Science* 53 (2002): 511–37.

25. For an overview of the present state of analytic philosophy of emotion, see Ronald de Sousa, "Emotion," in the online *Stanford Encyclopedia of Philosophy* (June 2007), and Peter Goldie, "Emotion," *Philosophy Compass* 2 (2007): 928–38. The account given here has been influenced by many of their distinctions and observations.

For a collection of historic and contemporary texts on the philosophy of emotion, see Solomon's *What Is an Emotion? Classic and Contemporary Readings*. For a comprehensive overview of the philosophy of emotion and its history, with contributions from a range of scholars, see Peter Goldie, ed., *The Oxford Handbook of Philosophy of Emotion* (Oxford: Oxford University Press, 2009). For collections of representative articles from contemporary philosophers, see Solomon's *Thinking about Feeling: Contemporary Philosophers on Emotion;* Stephen Leighton, *Philosophy and the Emotions: A Reader* (Petersborough, Ont., Canada: Broadview Press, 2003); and Anthony Hatzimoysis, ed., *Philosophy and the Emotions*, Royal Institute of Philosophy Supplement 52 (Cambridge: Cambridge University Press, 2003). Although it is now dated, an influential collection of essays edited by Amélie Rorty provides a good overview of perspectives on the philosophy of emotion just when interest in the field was beginning to gather momentum. See Amélie Oksenberg Rorty, ed., *Explaining Emotions*, (Berkeley and Los Angeles: University of California Press, 1980).

For an overview of continental philosophy of emotion, see Robert C. Solomon, "Emotions in Continental Philosophy," *Philosophy Compass* 1 (2006): 413–31. For a collection of recent texts

is long and complex. It begins in the late nineteenth century when William James set the agenda for contemporary discussion of emotion with his seminal article "What Is an Emotion?" (published in 1884). He writes, "Our natural way of thinking about these standard emotions is that the mental perception of some fact excites the mental affection called the emotion, and that this latter state of mind gives rise to the bodily expression. My thesis on the contrary is that *the bodily changes follow directly the PERCEPTION of the exciting fact, and that our feeling of the same changes as they occur IS the emotion.*"[26] James's identification of emotion with bodily feeling, which has antecedents in David Hume's theory of the passions, became enormously influential.[27]

One of the first important critical responses came from Walter Cannon, a prominent scientist at Harvard and a former student of James. His research in the physiology of emotion led him to the opposite conclusion from James: that emotion is not identical to the feeling of physiological changes. He first published his critical views in 1914,[28] but returned to the subject in subsequent publications as well.[29] Nonetheless, James's identification of emotion with feeling remained dominant, partly because it was convenient to both behaviorism and logical positivism, then at the height of their influence. The reduction of emotion to nonrational physiology well suited behaviorism's purposeful avoidance of interior phenomena and logical positivism's reduction of ethics to irrational emotivism. Since emotions were held to be physiological and irrational, not many philosophers saw much point in discussing them; that was seen as better left to another discipline. In this way, the dominance of the feeling theory of emotion partly explains philosophy's neglect of emotion in the first half of the twentieth century.

Anglo-American philosophy began to shift toward a "cognitivist" ac-

on emotion from a psychological perspective, see Paul Ekman and Richard J. Davidson, eds., *The Nature of Emotion: Fundamental Questions* (New York: Oxford University Press, 1994).

26. William James, "What Is an Emotion?" *Mind* 19 (1884): 189–90. The following year, Carl Lange, a Danish psychologist, published a monograph that argued independently for the same conclusion. Consequently, this account of emotion is often known as the James-Lange theory.

27. See David Hume, *A Treatise of Human Nature,* 2.1.1.

28. Walter B. Cannon, "The Interrelations of Emotions as Suggested by Recent Physiological Researches," *American Journal of Psychology* 25 (1914): 252–82.

29. See especially Walter B. Cannon, "The James-Lange Theory of Emotions: A Critical Examination and an Alternative Theory," *American Journal of Psychology* 39 (1927): 106–24, and Walter B. Cannon, *Bodily Changes in Pain, Hunger, Fear and Rage: An Account of Recent Researches into the Function of Emotional Excitement* (New York: Appleton, 1915).

count of emotion after Errol Bedford published his article "Emotions" in 1957. In his article, Bedford contends that emotions have a cognitive dimension that theories of emotions as pure feelings cannot explain.[30] Shortly afterward, Anthony Kenny published *Action, Emotion and Will,* in which he argues that, unlike pure bodily sensations, emotions are intentional, that is, directed toward definite objects.[31] Then George Pitcher wrote an influential article deconstructing the idea of emotions as interior sensations, focusing his critique on the accounts of Hume and James.[32] At around the same time, academic psychology began to give new attention to cognition. The psychologist Magda Arnold, who had been deeply influenced by her study of Aquinas,[33] published a two-volume work on emotion that emphasized the role of what she called "cognitive appraisal."[34] Cognitivist accounts of emotion have since become dominant in both philosophy and psychology.

Prominent representatives of the cognitivist account of emotion include Robert Solomon and Martha Nussbaum. Robert Solomon maintains that emotions are judgments.[35] Martha Nussbaum has developed what she describes as a neo-Stoic "cognitive-evaluative" view, "according to which emotions are forms of evaluative judgment that ascribe to certain things and persons outside a person's own control great importance for the person's own flourishing."[36] She holds that "feeling" often accompanies emotion but is not essential to it.[37]

30. Errol Bedford, "Emotions," *Proceedings of the Aristotelian Society* 57 (1957): 281–304.

31. Anthony Kenny writes: "The most important difference between a sensation and an emotion is that emotions, unlike sensations, are essentially directed to objects." Kenny, *Action, Emotion and Will,* 60.

32. George Pitcher, "Emotion," *Mind* 74 (1965): 326–46.

33. Regarding Aquinas's influence on Magda Arnold, see Randolph R. Cornelius, "Magda Arnold's Thomistic Theory of Emotion, the Self-Ideal, and the Moral Dimension of Appraisal," *Cognition and Emotion* 20 (2006): 976–1000.

34. See Magda Arnold, *Emotion and Personality,* 2 vols. (New York: Columbia University Press, 1960). Her attentiveness to the cognitive dimension of emotion was developed further especially by Richard Lazarus. See his *Emotion and Adaptation* (New York: Oxford University Press, 1991).

35. Solomon has defended this claim for over three decades, though he acknowledges that his sense of its precise meaning has evolved. For an early articulation of his account of emotion, see Robert C. Solomon, "Emotions and Choice," *Review of Metaphysics* 28 (1973): 20–41.

36. Nussbaum, *Upheavals of Thought,* 22–23.

37. Ibid., 60. She notes, however, that there are different senses of the word "feeling" and certain nonbodily feelings might well be requisite conditions of certain emotions. She writes: "[T]here are feelings with a rich intentional content—feelings of the emptiness of one's life without a certain person, feelings of unhappy love for that person, and so forth. Feelings like these

Other philosophers regard the current emphasis on cognition as an overreaction.[38] They are especially critical of the idea that emotions necessarily involve rational judgment. Their alternative proposals are difficult to classify, because their differences are subtle and their terminology is often incommensurable. Nonetheless, alternative theories can be clustered into a handful of different categories, although the boundaries between these categories are porous, and others might plausibly classify these alternative theories in other ways.

Some authors argue for a modified version of James's theory, often called either a noncognitive or a "feeling" theory of emotion, which incorporates elements of the cognitivist critique against it. Jesse Prinz, a prominent advocate of this approach, holds that emotions are the perceptions of physiological changes. He writes that "emotions are perceptions (conscious or unconscious) of patterned changes in the body (construed inclusively)."[39] However, Prinz is more sensitive than James to the intentionality of emotion and the dependence of these physiological changes on sense perception and cognition.[40] Similarly, the neurologist Antonio Damasio defends the essential validity of James's theory of emotion and maintains that emotions are the feeling of physiological changes ("the feeling of what happens"), although he also thinks that James errs by focusing on the body to the neglect of the brain.[41] Within the discipline of psychology, noncognitivist accounts of emotion have also been advanced. In 1984, Robert Zajonc wrote an influential article challenging the cognitivist account of Richard Lazarus (who had embraced Magda Arnold's account of emotion as dependent on cognitive appraisals), in which Zajonc rejects the claim that all emotions require some kind of cognition.[42]

Another alternative to the standard cognitivist account is the perceptual

may enter into the identity conditions for some emotion; but the word 'feeling' now does not contrast without cognitive words 'perception' and 'judgment,' it is merely a terminological variant of them" (60).

38. For a critical reflection on the ascendency of cognitive accounts, see John Deigh, "Cognitivism in the Theory of Emotions," *Ethics* 104 (1994): 824–54.

39. Jesse Prinz, "Embodied Emotions," in *Thinking about Feeling: Contemporary Philosophers on Emotion,* ed. Robert C. Solomon (New York: Oxford University Press, 2004), 44–58.

40. Ibid., 54–56.

41. Antonio Damasio, *The Feeling of What Happens: Body, Emotion and the Making of Consciousness* (London: Vintage, 1999), 287–89.

42. Robert B. Zajonc, "On the Primacy of Affect," *American Psychologist* 39 (1984): 117–23.

theory of emotion. Advocates of perceptual theories are broadly sympathetic to the cognitivist critique of James, but have misgivings about some philosophers' seeming identification of emotion with higher-level cognition. Ronald de Sousa and Robert Roberts are representatives of this approach to emotion. Ronald de Sousa classifies himself as advocating a perceptual theory of emotion in which "emotions are not so much perceptions as they are ways of seeing—species of determinate patterns of salience among objects of attention, lines of inquiry, and inferential strategies."[43] Similarly, Roberts, falling somewhere between James and the cognitivist account, argues that emotions are "concern-based construals."[44]

Other philosophers view emotions primarily as feelings, but in a way different from James. Peter Goldie sees emotions as involving "feeling towards," a category of feeling distinct from nonintentional bodily feeling. For Goldie, "emotional feeling toward an object (typically toward the object of the emotion) is a feeling toward that thing as being a particular way or as having certain properties or features."[45] Michael Stocker, contrasting his position with that of certain cognitive theorists, argues that affectivity cannot be reduced to desire or reason, but constitutes its own category of psychological phenomena.[46]

Some philosophically oriented psychologists have proposed that emotions are best understood as functional: mechanisms oriented toward the satisfaction of human needs. Nico Frijda argues that emotions "exist for the sake of action."[47] They prompt us toward the satisfaction of concerns and, as such, they are "the manifestations of the individual's concern satisfaction system."[48] Frijda acknowledges that emotions can also have nonfunctional manifestations, but nonetheless emotion "may be considered

43. De Sousa, "Emotion," §6. In his book, *The Rationality of Emotion,* he argues that the emotions are not reducible to other categories and are best understood with analogies to the concepts of perception, belief, and want. See Ronald de Sousa, *The Rationality of Emotion* (Cambridge: M.I.T. Press, 1987), 19.

44. Roberts, *Emotions*, 64.

45. Peter Goldie, *The Emotions* (Oxford: Clarendon Press, 2000), 58.

46. Michael L. Stocker and Elizabeth Hegeman, *Valuing Emotions* (Cambridge: Cambridge University Press, 1996), 17–55.

47. Nico H. Frijda, "Emotions and Actions," in *Feelings and Emotions: the Amsterdam Symposium,* ed. Antony S. R. Manstead, Nico Frijda, and Agneta Fischer (Cambridge: Cambridge University Press, 2004), 170.

48. Nico H. Frijda, *The Emotions* (Cambridge: Cambridge University Press, 1986), 478.

an overall functionally adequate, useful provision even if it is not adequate or useful in all its manifestations."[49] Similarly, Keith Oatley argues that the core of an emotion is a "change of readiness" that is "normally based on an evaluation of something happening that affects important concerns," and that this evaluation "need not be made consciously."[50] Damasio's account of emotion also emphasizes emotion's role in motivating us to action.[51]

The two poles of emotion as feeling and emotion as cognition are still the principal markers of contemporary discussion in analytic philosophy, but the lines between the different understandings of emotion are becoming increasingly blurred. David Solomon has acknowledged that his earlier work did not sufficiently account for the feeling element of emotion.[52] Patricia Greenspan has made a similar acknowledgement and now argues that emotions are "feelings with evaluative thought content."[53] Prinz follows James in identifying emotions with feelings, but laments James's "failure to reckon with what can broadly be regarded as the rationality of emotions."[54] Goldie takes the idea that emotions are intentional, a hallmark of the cognitivist approach, and makes it one of the anchors of his account of emotion as intentional feeling.[55] Ben-Ze'ev, seeking to construct an account that synthesizes the various proposals on offer, argues that emotions involve feelings, motivations, and cognitive evaluations.[56]

49. Ibid., 477.

50. Keith Oatley, *Best Laid Schemes: The Psychology of the Emotions* (Cambridge: Cambridge University Press, 1992), 19–20.

51. Damasio writes: "[E]motions are *bioregulatory reactions* that aim at promoting, directly or indirectly, the sort of physiological states that secure not just survival but survival regulated into the range that we, conscious and thinking creatures, identify with *well-being.*" Antonio Damasio, "Emotions and Feelings: A Neurobiological Perspective," in *Feelings and Emotions: the Amsterdam Symposium,* ed. Antony S. R. Manstead, Nico Frijda, and Agneta Fischer (Cambridge: Cambridge University Press, 2004), 50.

52. Robert C. Solomon, "What Is a 'Cognitive Theory' of the Emotions," in *Philosophy and the Emotions,* ed. Anthony Hatzimoysis, Royal Institute of Philosophy Supplement 52 (Cambridge: Cambridge University Press, 2003): 1–18. He writes, "To put my current thinking in a nutshell, I think that a great deal of what is unhelpfully called 'affect' and 'affectivity' and is supposedly missing from cognitive accounts can be identified with the body, or what I will call (no doubt to howls of indignation) *the judgments of the body*" (14).

53. Patricia Greenspan, "Emotions, Rationality, and Mind/Body," in *Thinking about Feeling: Contemporary Philosophers on Emotion,* ed. Robert C. Solomon (New York: Oxford University Press, 2004), 133.

54. Prinz, "Embodied Emotions," 45.

55. Goldie, *The Emotions.*

56. Aaron Ben-Ze'ev, "Emotions Are Not Mere Judgments," *Philosophy and Phenomenological Research* 68 (2004): 450–57.

This brief survey suggests that, for all its diversity, contemporary analytic philosophy has been converging around some important conclusions.[57] First, emotions involve more than feeling: they also involve perception and cognition. Consequently, emotions are not intrinsically irrational, and they can reveal what is of value and point us toward what is necessary for human flourishing. Philosophers disagree about the nature of cognition, especially about whether cognition includes perception, and about whether emotion is a form of cognition (and/or perception) or merely responds to it, but they agree that emotion cannot be understood only in terms of bodily feeling. Second, at least some emotions are intentional, that is, directed toward objects. Third, emotions have great significance for ethics and the development of moral character. Many substantive disagreements remain, but there is now broad agreement that an adequate philosophy of emotion must incorporate these insights in some way.

Aquinas, Emotion, and Method

The central difficulty in reconstructing Aquinas's account of emotion is that Aquinas never wrote about emotion. He wrote about appetites, passions, affections, *habitus*, virtues, vices, grace, and many other subjects that relate to the contemporary category of emotion, but the word "emotion" has no direct parallel in the Latin vocabulary of the thirteenth century.[58] If the contemporary category of emotion were clearly defined, the absence of a direct parallel in his writings would not be a major obstacle to reconstructing his account of emotion. Aquinas's categories could be sifted and those involving emotion easily identified. But given the ambiguity and controversy surrounding emotion, it seems inadvisable to present a working definition of emotion and then apply it to Aquinas's thought. Such an approach would require an inevitably inadequate prejudgment of contemporary debate and then distort things further by viewing Aquinas through its lens.

57. The various characteristics that analytic philosophers generally agree must be addressed by any adequate philosophy of emotion are summarized in Goldie, "Emotions," 928–33; Roberts, *Emotions*, 60–64; and de Sousa, "Emotion," §12.

58. The closest etymological parallel to emotion in Latin is *motus*, or movement, which is occasionally used in a psychological context (sometimes as *motus animae*) to refer to a movement of the soul (Dixon, *From Passions to Emotions*, 39–40). It will be argued that the closest parallel in meaning is *affectus* or *affectio*, that is, affection.

The problems with a common reading of Aquinas serve as a salutary warning against jumping to conclusions about what corresponds to emotion in his writings. Since the mid-twentieth century, scholars of Aquinas writing in English frequently identify what he calls the passions of the soul (*passiones animae*) with the emotions, translating *passio* as "emotion," rather than the more literal "passion."[59] This translation is seriously misleading. While it is accurate to regard many of the passions as emotions, Aquinas also speaks of affections (*affectiones* or *affectus*) that are not passions and yet clearly correspond to the category of emotion, such as certain kinds of joy or love.[60] So the equation of passion with emotion excludes a category of psychological phenomena that should not be excluded.[61] More-

59. Many of the volumes of the Blackfriars *Summa* edited by Thomas Gilby adopt this practice. Eric D'Arcy prefaces his translation of questions 22–39 of the *Treatise on the Passions* with a detailed explanation for his choice of emotion for *passio*. See Eric D'Arcy, Introduction and notes to *Summa theologiae*, vol. 19, *The Emotions*, and vol. 20, *Pleasure* (New York: McGraw-Hill, 1967, 1975).

60. For a discussion of the category of affection in Aquinas, see chapter 3. See also Dixon, *From Passions to Emotions*, 26–61, esp. 40. Dixon's work first drew my attention to the significance of affection in Aquinas vis-à-vis the contemporary category of emotion.

61. While I am much indebted to Dixon's work for alerting me to the importance of the category of affection, there are serious problems with his reading of Aquinas. According to Dixon, the passions are involuntary, imperfect, unruly, and somewhat negative, and the affections are voluntary and generally regarded in a more positive light. While noting that the passions can be good and affections can be evil, he claims that in Aquinas's writings there is "rarely any reference to a positively virtuous passion" (48). The passions involve bodily modification and are therefore ungodly; affections, as acts of will, involve no "bodily disobedience" and are "quite godly." Moreover, the proper object of both passion and affection is "an incorporeal ideal," and improper objects are "worldly, physical and ephemeral (people, bodies, sex, money, ambition, pleasure, pain)" (56).

Dixon rightly observes that Aquinas distinguishes movements of the sense appetite from those of the rational appetite, and that for Aquinas passion and affection are different categories. But despite his partial sympathies for Augustine and Aquinas, his analysis is otherwise seriously inaccurate. His interpretation illustrates common misconceptions about Aquinas and therefore requires a response. In many ways this study as a whole will provide that response, but in the meantime, a few proleptic comments suffice.

First, Aquinas often uses the word "affection" interchangeably with the word "passion" and in such a way that bodily modification is implied. For example, he writes: "The passions of the soul are the same as the affections" (*ST* I-II 22.2). It is true that the terminology here is not entirely his own: immediately before this passage, Aquinas cites a text from *City of God*, 9.4, where Augustine equates passions with affections. Nonetheless, the point stands: Aquinas from time to time refers to the passions as affections. For other instances, see *ST* I-II 1.5, 1.7, 29.2, 60.2, 62.4 obj 3, 68.4 ad 5; *ST* II-II 60.3; *ST* III 15.4.

Second, Aquinas not only discusses virtuous passions frequently, he regards passion as essential to virtue. Regarding the necessity of passion for virtue, he writes that in God and the angels, "Good operation [of faculties] in God and the angels is entirely without passion, because

over, Aquinas also writes about a category called the passions of the body (*passiones corporalis*) that encompasses phenomena that we would hesitate to describe as emotions, such as itches, pangs, hunger, and thirst. Consequently, when Aquinas refers to "passions" without further qualification, he can be referring to passions of the body or to a set of passions that includes both passions of the body and passions of the soul. In light of these sorts of observations about the nonidentity of emotion and passion, much recent scholarship on Aquinas makes a point of translating *passio* as "passion" rather than "emotion."[62]

There are two reasons for this common misreading of Aquinas. First, it is often assumed that emotion necessarily involves physiological change, a view that is more tenuous than is sometimes realized. This assumption sets up a seeming correspondence between the category of emotion and the category of passion, which by Aquinas's explicit definition always involve

it does not involve a body, but good operation in man is with passion, because it involves the contribution of a body" (*ST* I-II 59.5 ad 3). Moreover, he takes the controversial position, contrary to Bonaventure, that virtue is seated in the sense appetite, and not only the intellect and the will, thus strongly emphasizing the possibility of virtuous passions. The *Treatise on the Passions* does not refer to virtuous or vicious passions as much as other sections of the *Summa*, but that is because it is specifically focused on passions considered apart from questions of morality. The presumption that underlies the *Treatise* is that the passions are good in their sheer existence and by their nature incline us toward happiness and moral excellence. The questions on virtue that follow the *Treatise* frequently discuss virtuous passion. Aquinas does not have a negative or undervaluing estimation of the passions. One of the more remarkable aspects of his account is precisely his positive and balanced appraisal of the *passiones animae*.

Lastly, Aquinas does not hold that the only proper objects of the passions are incorporeal ideals. Virtuous passions may well respond to abstract ideals, either by being shaped by rational considerations or by sharing by overflow in the affections of the will. Similarly, the affections of the will may rejoice or sorrow virtuously in sense objects (see *ST* I-II 31.3, 34.1, 34.4).

62. Gondreau argues for this approach to translating Aquinas and also gives an overview of recent scholarship on this topic in both English and French (Gondreau, *Passions of Christ's Soul*, 30–33). Other contemporary discussions of the terminology of passion and emotion include: Leget, "Nussbaum and Aquinas," 571–75; Stephen Loughlin, "Similarities and Differences between Human and Animal Emotion in Aquinas's Thought," *Thomist* 65 (2001): 45n1; Shawn D. Floyd, "Aquinas on Emotion: A Response to Some Recent Interpretations," *History of Philosophy Quarterly* 15 (1998): 161–75; Daniel Westberg, "Emotion and God: A Reply to Michael Sarot," *Thomist* 60 (1996): 112–15; Eisen Murphy, "Responsibility for Our Emotions," 165–68. Finally, Dixon's entire monograph constitutes a sustained argument against the tendency to equate *passio animae* with emotion.

Some analytic philosophers object to identifying passion with emotion for another reason: they object to the implied attribution of passivity to emotion. But this objection is difficult to sustain. For a discussion of this objection and a nuanced explication of the passive dimension of emotion, see Robert M. Gordon, *The Structure of Emotions: Investigations in Cognitive Philosophy* (Cambridge: Cambridge University Press, 1987), 110–27.

the body. Second, the distinctions Aquinas makes between the categories of passion and affection are easy to miss, and the tendency in the secondary literature to focus almost exclusively on questions 80–82 of the *Prima pars* and questions 22–48 of the *Prima secundae* makes it even easier, since there are not many explicit references to the category of affection in these sections. But when it is not assumed that emotion always involves physiological change, and when it is not assumed that Aquinas always categorizes particular emotions such as love and joy as passions of the soul, the mistake of identifying our contemporary category of emotion with his category of the passions of the soul becomes more avoidable.

Rather than constructing a definition of emotion and then applying it to Aquinas, or making the hasty identification of the emotions with the *passiones animae,* a more promising approach to the reconstruction of Aquinas's account of emotion is to see what Aquinas has to say about the particular psychological phenomena that we typically identify as emotions. Analytic philosophers seem to make use of a similar approach when they talk to each other about emotion across different philosophical systems: they share a common presumption that a certain set of psychological phenomena are indisputably gestured toward by the word "emotion" (e.g., joy, sadness, anger, fear, etc.). This common presumption makes it possible for them to converse intelligibly even when they disagree about the nature of emotion, or when they disagree about whether certain psychological phenomena should be classified as emotions.

This study, then, will focus on Aquinas's discussion of those psychological phenomena that we typically identify as emotions. It will not assume from the outset any particular definition of emotion or any correspondence between Aquinas's categories and the category of emotion. The adoption of this method does not imply despair of finding a category in Aquinas that is functionally equivalent to the category of emotion. Just the opposite: a strong case can be made for conceptual correspondence between emotion and his category of affection. However, this reading of Aquinas is necessarily tentative and controversial, and it requires taking positions on certain matters debated by contemporary philosophers. Its merits, moreover, can only be established after the necessary evidence has been provided by a thorough examination of Aquinas on his own terms. Consequently, it is better to avoid injecting this proposed equivalence between affection and emotion into the actual reconstruction of Aquinas's account of emotion, and only afterward make a case for it. This approach minimizes the possibility of distortion, especially for those who disagree with this reading of Aquinas, while also engaging the question of how Aquinas's thought can be brought to bear on the contemporary discussion of emotion.

With these considerations in mind, this study will adopt a twofold strategy in its presentation of Aquinas's account of emotion. First, the bulk of this study will follow Aquinas over the widest possible range of psychological phenomena that might plausibly correspond to ordinary language use of the word "emotion" (e.g., realities such as joy, sadness, anger, desire, and jealousy, as well as moods and emotional dispositions), as well as the larger context in which he discusses these phenomena. The shape and geography of his categories will be followed closely, and the category of emotion will be avoided entirely. This first section aims to reconstruct his system on its own terms and to probe its internal coherence in dialogue with both analytic and Thomist secondary literature on Aquinas.

Second, the final two chapters of this study will provide a preliminary discussion of Aquinas's account of emotion vis-à-vis contemporary philosophy and theology. Chapter 8 will propose that Aquinas's category of affection should be considered a close conceptual equivalent to the contemporary category of emotion, while granting that analytic philosophers with a more cognitivist understanding of emotion might balk at this identification. Then it will provide a preliminary evaluation of Aquinas's account of emotion—with emotion now understood as conceptually equivalent to affection—and note some of its strengths and weaknesses. Finally, chapter 9 will suggest some ways that Aquinas's thought might be applied to certain topics in the theology of emotion.

This two-part structure separates the analysis of Aquinas from the evaluation of Aquinas's relevance to contemporary discussion of emotion, thus preventing any controversy or deficiency in the evaluation from spoiling the analysis. In this way, I hope that this study will better serve the interests of a variety of readers, and, especially through the second section, help to make the contemporary relevance of Aquinas's account of emotion more widely appreciated.

CHAPTER 1

The Passions of the Soul

"Passion," writes Aquinas, "is a movement of the sense appetite caused by imagining good or evil."[1] This pithy definition, borrowed from John Damascene and replete with Aristotelian terminology, summarizes his understanding of the passions of the soul. A passion is a physiological and psychological response to the apprehension of a sensible good or a sensible evil, that is, an object that is known through the senses, and judged to be either good or evil.[2] There are two important moments in the structure of passion: the apprehension of an object, and then the passion itself, in which the object acts upon the sense appetite through this apprehension and elicits its movement from the sense appetite. This chapter will discuss Aquinas's account of the passions and their essential dependence on cognition, clarifying his use of Aristotelian terminology when necessary.

1. *ST* I-II 22.3. See also John Damascene, *De fide orthodoxa* 2.22. The translations of the *Summa theologiae* given in this study are my own. I have been particularly concerned to make Aquinas accessible for those without much familiarity with Aristotelian terminology while also staying close to the Latin text. In translating I have measured my work against the two complete English translations of the *Summa theologiae,* the English Dominican translation finished in 1920 and then the Blackfriars translation finished in 1980, consulting them frequently to assist my own translating and to make sure of its accuracy. Those interested in a more literal translation of the *Summa* should consult the English Dominican translation; those interested in a more literary, but less precise, translation, with facing Latin pages, should consult the Blackfriars translation.

2. When he discusses the passions, Aquinas often refers to the object of a passion without any qualifier such as "sensible." It is simply an object, or a good, or an evil. However, it is evident that, for Aquinas, the proper object of the sense appetite is a sensible object. First, in his view that sense appetite responds to sense cognition (see especially *ST* I 81.1), Aquinas makes plain that the objects of sense appetite are known through sense cognition, and thus must be sensible. Second, Aquinas specifies the object of concupiscible passions as "a straightforward sensible good or evil," and the object of irascible passions as "a good or evil that is arduous or difficult" (*ST* I-II 23.1; see also *ST* I-II 46.3). While Aquinas does not explicitly describe the object of irascible passion as sensible here, it is evident from the context that it is not just an arduous good or evil, but an arduous sensible good or evil. Hence both sorts of passions have sensible objects, according to Aquinas.

Apprehension and Intentionality

According to Aquinas, there are two kinds of cognition: sense cognition and intellectual cognition, and each pertains to different aspects of the world. Sense cognition pertains to the material aspects of reality, and intellectual cognition pertains to the immaterial aspects of reality by abstracting what is universal about material things.[3] Aquinas's identification of two different kinds of cognition does not imply that they function independently; it is a structural clarification, and they should be understood as usually simultaneous and mutually interpenetrating.[4] The kind of apprehension that elicits passion is more than sheer perception. It involves both kinds of cognition and includes shaping the perception into a coherent object from an undifferentiated blur of data, and some evaluation of the sensible object vis-à-vis the subject. Aquinas refers to the sense perception of an object combined with cognitive evaluation of its relevance to the subject's interests as an "intention" (*intentio*).[5] Such apprehension does not grasp the sensible object directly, but

---

It is important to note that concepts and abstract ideals can elicit a response from the sense appetite, insofar as they involve sensible characteristics in the subject's apprehension of them. For a discussion of this aspect of his account, see chap. 3.

3. See *ST* I 78, 79. For a discussion of sensory cognition in light of analytic epistemological concerns, see Paul A. Macdonald Jr., "Direct Realism and Aquinas's Account of Sensory Cognition," *Thomist* 71 (2007): 343–78.

4. Claudia Eisen Murphy offers an illuminating discussion of the relationship between cognition and passion to which I am indebted. (See Eisen Murphy, "Responsibility for Our Emotions," 166–73.) In the course of her discussion, she offers this analysis of the relationship between sensory cognition and intellectual cognition: "Sensory cognition is cognition (ranging from perception to memory to imagination to very primitive forms of comparison and inference) of the sensible qualities of particular objects insofar as they can affect the external senses. Intellective cognition, on the other hand, cognizes common features of particular objects (insofar as they are common), and abstracts them into concepts which can apply to more than one particular thing. . . . Most, if not all of our conscious cognitions are the product of both sensory *and* intellective cognition. (I cognize this piece of paper—recognize it as such—by perceiving its sensory properties, abstracting from them, and applying the appropriate concepts to them.)" (169).

5. Since intentionality has a very specific meaning in contemporary phenomenology, it may seem anachronistic to suggest that Aquinas employed a similar concept. Nonetheless, it is not far-fetched: Franz Brentano launched the contemporary discussion of intentionality from his recovery of *intentionalitas*, a technical term in currency in the late Middle Ages. He had been deeply influenced by Aristotle and Aquinas in many areas of philosophical psychology and was broadly familiar with Scholastic philosophy. See Dermot Moran, *Introduction to Phenomenology* (London: Routledge, 2000), 43, 45, 47–52, esp. n80.

Furthermore, based on his study of Aquinas, Drost also concludes that he had something akin to the contemporary idea of intentionality: "I believe . . . that Aquinas did have the concept of an intentional object and this is evinced by his descriptions of emotional experiences" (Drost, "Intentionality in Aquinas," 449). See also Anthony J. Lisska, "Medieval Theories of Intentionality:

rather through the intention of the object: "The apprehensive power is not drawn to a thing according to what the thing is in itself; instead the apprehensive power knows it according to the intention of the thing."[6] This is not to say that the subject apprehends a miniature mental image of the object and not the object itself. Aquinas would maintain that the subject apprehends the object itself through the intention. He is not trapped in the Cartesian dilemma of getting from the mind to the real world, because the apprehension of the object connects directly to the object itself, and not just to a mental construct that could exist without external reality.[7] Similarly, after the subject apprehends an object as desirable via an intention, passion is evoked and draws the subject to the actual object itself, not to a mental image.[8] One may see something beautiful that elicits desire, but one then seeks not a mental image of this beautiful object, but rather the object itself.

Aquinas outlines a logical progression from raw sense data to the formation of an intention. This logical progression should not be understood as

---

From Aquinas to Brentano and Beyond," in *Analytical Thomism: Traditions in Dialogue*, ed. Craig Paterson and Matthew S. Pugh (Burlington, Vt.: Ashgate, 2006). For an excellent summary of the meaning of intentionality in contemporary phenomenology, see Robert Sokolowski, "Intentionality," in *Introduction to Phenomenology* (Cambridge: Cambridge University Press, 2000), 8–16.

6. *ST* I-II 22.2.

7. For helpful discussions of the direct realism of Aquinas's account of perception, see D'Arcy, Notes to *Summa*, 10–11; Kenny, *Aquinas on Mind*, 35; and Macdonald, "Direct Realism and Sensory Cognition," 352–78. For an analysis of Aquinas that argues for the opposite view, namely, that his account is not a form of direct realism, see Claude Panaccio, "Aquinas on Intellectual Representation," in *Ancient and Medieval Theories of Intentionality*, ed. Dominik Perler (Leiden: Brill, 2001), 185–201.

Kenny compares Aquinas to some modern theories of perception as follows: "The way in which Aquinas' intentionality theory can cast philosophical light on the nature of perception is best understood if we contrast it with a different philosophical theory, the representational theory of perception. According to some philosophers, in sense-experience we do not directly observe objects or properties in the external world; the immediate objects of our experience are sense-data, private objects of which we have infallible knowledge, and from which we make more or less dubious inferences to the real nature of external objects and properties. In Aquinas' theory there are no intermediaries like sense-data which come between perceiver and perceived. In sensation the sense-faculty does not come in contact with a likeness of the sense-object. Instead, it becomes itself like the sense-object, by taking on the sense-object's form; but it takes on the form not physically, but intentionally. This is summed up by Aquinas in a slogan which he takes over from Aristotle: the sense-faculty in operation is identical with the sense-object in action (*Sensus in actu est sensibile in actu*)" (Kenny, *Aquinas on Mind*, 35).

8. "Through the appetitive power the soul is directed toward things as they are in themselves" (*ST* I-II 22.2). Aquinas distinguishes the roles of cognition and appetite as follows: "The operation of the apprehensive power reaches its fulfillment when what is apprehended is in the one apprehending, while the operation of the appetitive power reaches its fulfillment when the one desiring is inclined toward the desirable thing" (*ST* I 81.1).

a chronological progression; the formation of an intention typically occurs simultaneously with perception. Sense knowledge is first received through the five external senses, each sense being "a kind of passive power which naturally responds to exterior sense objects."[9] The raw sense data obtained through the five external senses are cognized with the assistance of four internal senses, namely, the common sense (*sensus communis*), fantasy (*phantasia*) or imagination (*imaginatio*),[10] the estimative power (*vis aestimativa*), and the memorative power (*vis memorativa*) or memory (*memoria*).[11] The common sense synthesizes the raw sense data of the external senses, and any raw images produced by the imagination from memories of past sense perception, into a coherent whole.[12] The common sense thus assembles the various elements of sense perception—for instance, that an object is sweet to the taste and white to the eyes—into a synthesis that includes the contributions of the different external and internal senses.

Synthesized perceptions are simultaneously colored by an evaluation of these perceptions vis-à-vis the interests of the perceiver, and thus formed into intentions. The apprehension of intentions occurs through the estimative power, the power that colors perception with some evaluation of it.[13] Nonhuman animals perceive intentions only by natural instinct (*naturalus instinctus*),[14] and so their power of estimation is called the natural estimative power (*aestimativa naturalis*).[15] Humans apprehend intentions by the cogita-

9. *ST* I 78.3.

10. Aquinas notes that Avicenna distinguishes between *phantasia* and imagination, classifying them as two separate faculties. Aquinas, however, does not: for Aquinas, both terms refer to the same faculty. See *ST* I 78.4. For a study of the faculty of *phantasia* in Aquinas, see Dorothea Frede, "Aquinas on *Phantasia*," in *Ancient and Medieval Theories of Intentionality*, ed. Dominik Perler (Leiden: Brill, 2001), 155–83. See also Robert E. Brennan, "The Thomistic Concept of the Imagination," *New Scholasticism* 15 (1941): 149–61.

11. For an overview of the internal senses in Aquinas and a survey of what was then recent scholarship, see J. A. Gasson, "The Internal Senses—Functions or Powers? Part I," *Thomist* 26 (1963): 1–14, and Magda B. Arnold, "The Internal Senses—Functions or Powers? Part II," *Thomist* 26 (1963): 15–34.

12. *ST* I 78.4 *ad* 2.

13. *ST* I 78.4.

14. Aquinas's concept of natural instinct should not be misunderstood as constituting a single unitary faculty; it is "a combination of external and internal cognitions, of appetites and local movements of all kinds." In animals, the estimative power plays a crucial role in instinctual behavior, but it is not to be identified with instinct itself. See Julien Peghaire, "A Forgotten Sense, the Cogitative, according to St. Thomas Aquinas," *Modern Schoolman* 20 (1943): 228. See also Gasson, "The Internal Senses," 7.

15. *ST* I 78.4, 81.3.

tive power (*vis cogitativa*) or particular reason (*ratio particularis*), a power that judges concrete particulars through a process of comparison.[16] Unlike universal reason, which involves intellectual cognition, the realm of thought where universals are abstracted from concrete particulars, particular reason is not an immaterial power. In fact, employing the best thirteenth-century medical knowledge available to him, Aquinas assigns particular reason to a bodily organ located in the middle of the head, a claim that seems to derive from Islamic physicians.[17] However, despite its corporeality and its independence from universal reason, particular reason is nonetheless somewhat governable by universal reason.[18]

Aquinas arrives at the concept of intention in order to explain how the passions operate. He notes how sheep perceive wolves as dangerous and fear them, and he concludes that it is not simply perception that inspires passion, but perception colored by evaluation.[19] From the fact that animals apprehend intentions, Aquinas concludes that there must be some sort of estimative power for judging the relevance of what is perceived to the interests of the perceiver.

Intentions are stored by memory (*memoria*), which Aquinas calls a treasury (*thesaurus*) of these intentions. Both animals and humans store intentions in their memories, but animals cannot call them to mind at will, nor do their intentions have any rational content, since they are shaped by instinct rather than reason. Since animals have memory even without an immaterial intellect, their memory is a bodily power, but human memory involves the intellect as well as the body.[20]

The concept of intention—that is, perception colored by cognitive evaluation—is necessary to maintain the coherence of Aquinas's object-centered

16. Aquinas does not use the terms *vis cogitativa* and *ratio particularis* with great frequency, and so exactly what Aquinas means by them, especially in how they relate to the other terms that he uses to talk about cognition, is difficult to say. The most thorough study of the *vis cogitativa* remains Peghaire's study. For some more recent attempts to clarify how these terms function within Aquinas's understanding of cognition, see Kenny, *Aquinas on Mind*, 37, and Pasnau, *Aquinas on Human Nature*, 253–56.

17. Gasson, "Internal Senses," 4.

18. *ST* I 78.4, 81.3. Universal reason's guidance of particular reason is discussed in chap. 4.

19. "A sheep flees when it sees a wolf coming, not because the wolf's colors or shape are jarring, but because the wolf is a natural enemy. Similarly the bird collects chaff, not because the chaff pleases the bird's senses, but because it is useful for building a nest. It is necessary, therefore, that animals perceive intentions which are not perceived by an exterior sense" (*ST* I 78.4).

20. *ST* I 78.4, 79.6–7.

account of the passions. Otherwise, his account would require that the same object always elicit the same passion, and clearly this is not the case. When we are hungry, we perceive an apple as something desirable; when we are full, or when we know that the apple has been poisoned or flavored with something unpleasant, we do not perceive the apple as something desirable.[21] It is not the perception of an object per se that elicits passion, but the perception of an object grasped under a certain aspect. Furthermore, the concept of intention is necessary in Aquinas's account to explain how memories shape the passions. After we eat several apples from the same basket, and find them all flavorless and mealy despite a beautiful appearance, the sight of another such apple would not elicit desire, because the perception of their beautiful appearance has been shaped into a different type of intention by our memory of previous experiences. The distinction between objects as they are in themselves and objects as they are apprehended through intentions, that is, the distinction between material objects and formal objects, allows Aquinas to account for memory-dependent variances in passion.

After the apprehension of an object, the sense appetite may respond with a passion, that is, a movement of the sense appetite. In order to understand these movements of the sense appetite, it is first necessary to turn to the metaphysics of appetite.

The Metaphysics of Appetite

The concept of appetite is central to Aquinas's anthropology. It is also central to his metaphysics, and he builds the former from the latter: the placement of the questions on man in the *Summa theologiae* after the questions on God and creation reflects a deliberate choice to ground human psychology in metaphysical principles.[22] Consequently, to appreciate fully his

21. Aquinas makes the same point with a very similar example: "The lower appetitive power does not naturally tend to anything until after that thing is presented to it under the aspect of its proper object, as is clear from what has been said. Since it is in the power of reason to present one and the same thing under different aspects, a particular sort of food, for instance, as delicious or as deadly, reason is able to move sensuality to different objects." *De veritate* 25.4 ad 4, trans. Robert W. Schmidt (Chicago: Henry Regnery, 1954).

22. For a discussion of how Aquinas's metaphysics provides the framework for his anthropology and his strong affirmation of the goodness of human nature, see John F. Wippel, "Meta-

account of human appetite, it is necessary to respect Aquinas's pedagogy and begin with his metaphysics.

The theme of appetite runs through the entire *Summa theologiae.*[23] In its most generic sense, appetite (*appetitus*) is the principle in being that aims toward what is perfective or completing. "Appetite," Aquinas writes, "is nothing other than an inclination toward something, something that is both similar and suited to that which desires it."[24] It directs being toward its *telos,*[25] that is, its perfection and completion. As such, appetite is an essential constituent of anything that exists. Consequently, for Aquinas, all being is ecstatic.[26]

---

physical Foundations for Christian Humanism in Thomas Aquinas," in *Proceedings of the International Congress on Christian Humanism in the Third Millennium: The Perspective of Thomas Aquinas: 21–25 September 2003* (Vatican City: Pontificia Academia Sancti Thomae Aquinatis, 2004), 101–18. For a discussion of the connections between his metaphysics and his ethics, see Jan A. Aertsen, "Thomas Aquinas on the Good: The Relation between Metaphysics and Ethics," in *Aquinas' Moral Theory: Essays in Honor of Norman Kretzmann,* ed. S. MacDonald and E. Stump (Ithaca, N.Y.: Cornell University Press, 1999), 235–53.

23. Lawrence Donohoo argues that the prominent status of appetite in the thought of Aquinas has received insufficient attention. See Lawrence J. Donohoo, "The Nature of Desire" (STL Thesis, Dominican House of Studies, Washington, D.C., 1989), 1–15. His thesis offers an overview of appetite in Aquinas, and I am indebted to it for calling my attention to the importance of this theme in Aquinas's writings.

24. *ST* I-II 8.1.

25. Aquinas uses the Latin word *finis,* not its Greek cognate *telos,* but for various reasons this study has opted to use primarily *telos* rather than *finis* or "end" (the English equivalent of *finis*). In ancient Greek, *telos* has a simultaneous double meaning: it indicates both what a thing aims at and its completion and perfection. In other words, it has a sense not only of a terminal destination, but also of the perfective completion of a nature according to its own inner ontological trajectory. Hence it is particularly suited to express the metaphysical concept of that to which an appetite strives.

In Aquinas's writings, *finis* has multiple meanings. It can mean "end, limit, conclusion" with synonyms *extremitas, extremum, terminus, ultimatum,* or it can mean "aim, purpose" with synonyms *causa finalis, terminus.* Consequently, *finis* can refer to the end to which a nature tends by virtue of its ontological structure, that is, its *telos,* or it can refer to, say, an objective chosen by a rational creature that is not intrinsic to its natural inclinations and that may, in fact, be opposed to them (as in the case of sin). Its meaning must be determined from context, and it does not always serve as a synonym to *telos.* Furthermore, while Aquinas often employs *finis* in contexts that imply the same functional characteristics as *telos,* as much of his teleology is drawn directly from Aristotle, the word *finis* does not inherently imply the same sense of a nature's perfection. Similarly, the English word "end" is unsatisfactory because it has many possible meanings and thus fails to emphasize the highly specific meaning that is implied in this context.

Lastly, analytic philosophers have lately become more interested in the concept of teleology, and so the use of the word *telos* in English-language philosophy is not uncommon and can be relied upon to summon the desired associations.

See Roy J. Deferrari, M. Inviolata Barry, and Ignatius McGuiness, *A Lexicon of St. Thomas Aquinas* (Washington, D.C.: The Catholic University of America Press, 1948), 424–26.

26. G. J. McAleer, *Ecstatic Morality and Sexual Politics: A Catholic and Antitotalitarian Theory of the Body* (New York: Fordham University Press, 2005), 13–33.

Appetite first emerges in the discussion of being and goodness in question 5 of the *Prima pars*. In this question, Aquinas maintains that everything is good insofar as it exists, and vice versa.[27] "Being" and "goodness" are convertible terms that denote the same reality, although the words signify different concepts and different aspects of that reality.[28] To distinguish between them, he introduces the concept of appetite. He describes goodness as that which evokes appetite: to be good is to be appetible, that is, desirable.[29] The implications of this definition are startling. Appetite is inextricably linked to being and goodness.[30] Also, appetite is not just good in itself; appetibility, that is, desirability, is the defining characteristic of goodness.[31] The goodness of appetite is bound up with the goodness of being. This positive evaluation of appetite permeates his appraisal of human appetite, as will be discussed later.

The convertibility of "being" and "goodness" means that creation is good—not just because God created it, but because being, any kind of being, is necessarily good. "God loves everything that exists," Aquinas writes,

27. *ST* I 5.1. In this article, Aquinas quotes Augustine's pithy maxim from *De doctrina Christiana* 1.32: *"inquantum sumus boni sumus,"* or "inasmuch as we exist, we are good." For a collection of essays on the question of the relationship between being and good from an analytic perspective, with particular reference to Aquinas, see Scott MacDonald, ed., *Being and Goodness: The Concept of the Good in Metaphysics and Philosophical Theology* (Ithaca: Cornell University Press, 1991).

28. For an exposition of Aquinas on the convertibility of being and goodness, see Jan A. Aertsen, "The Convertibility of Being and Good in St. Thomas Aquinas," *New Scholasticism* 59 (1985): 449–70. For a survey of contemporary and medieval objections to the idea that everything that exists is good, see Jan A. Aertsen, *Medieval Philosophy and the Transcendentals: The Case of Thomas Aquinas* (New York: E. J. Brill, 1996), 290–91, 306–14.

29. "The reason something is good is that it is desirable. . . . Goodness and being are the same in actuality, but goodness as such involves the idea of desirability while being as such does not" (*ST* I 5.1).

30. It follows that any *telos* or end is good, and vice versa. If something is perfective and therefore desirable, it is good; if something is good, it must be an end insofar as it is desirable. Aertsen succinctly describes their relationship as follows: "'Good' is something desirable and thus it becomes the end of the appetite. 'Good' has the aspect of a final cause. Conversely, the end has, because it is desirable, the aspect of 'good.' Therefore, [writes Aquinas], '"Good" and "end" have the same nature, since the good is that which all desire'" (Aertsen, "Convertibility of Being," 466–67; *Sententia super Metaphysicam* II.4).

31. It is important to note that the good is good not simply because it is desired. Rather, the fact that something is desired is the principal clue that it is good. "The definition [of the good in terms of appetite] does not mean to say that something is good because it is desired but rather the converse: something is desired because it is good. Through the effect, in this case the appetite, the cause is manifested, that is, the good. The nature of the good is such that it is appetible" (Aertsen, *Medieval Philosophy and the Transcendentals,* 300).

"because everything that exists, insofar as it exists, is good."[32] The perfection of anything is also good, he continues, and (we can infer) so too must be the appetite that inclines it toward that perfection.[33] In God's plan, creation is inherently dynamic: created imperfect and permeated with appetite, it cannot help moving toward its perfection.[34] Without appetite, there would not be this dynamic movement, and creation would not move toward its perfection. Instead, creation would stagnate. Appetite is not just intrinsically good; it is integral to creation's inherent dynamism.

Since God is being and goodness in the fullest sense, and since appetite is inextricably bound up in both being and goodness, it is unsurprising that Aquinas maintains that there is something analogous to created appetite in God.[35] There is one important qualification. Appetite aims toward what is perfective or completing. Sometimes it strives toward an unattained *telos;* at other times it rests in an attained *telos*. However, God lacks for nothing, and so the divine appetite never strives toward an unattained *telos*. Appetite is present in God only as an inclination toward a good already possessed.[36] Appetite involves passivity in created things, because created things have the potential to become something other than what they already are, but not in God, because God cannot become something other than what God already is.

Aquinas identifies appetite in God with the divine will, defining the divine will as a kind of appetite, namely, intellectual appetite (*appetitus intellectivus*).[37] Intellectual appetite inclines toward unqualified and unlimited goodness.[38] Only God's own being can satisfy the divine will, so God necessarily wills his own goodness, but he can also will other contingent goods if

32. *ST* I 20.2. Aquinas holds that even the demons are not evil by nature: as fallen angels, their inmost nature remains good despite their freely chosen malice (*ST* I 63.4).

33. *ST* I 20.2.

34. For a discussion of creation's teleological orientation, especially of Aquinas's claim that all things have some sort of end or *telos*, see Norman Kretzmann, "The Metaphysics of Providence: Aquinas's Natural Theology in *Summa contra gentiles* III," *Medieval Philosophy and Theology* 9 (2000): 91–183, esp. 104–26.

35. For a study of Aquinas's account of appetite in God, see Donohoo, "Nature of Desire," 89–116.

36. "In us the will belongs to the appetitive part, which although named from desiring does not only desire what it does not have: it also loves what it has and delights in it. And this is how will is in God, because God's will always has the good which is its object, that is, his own essence" (*ST* I 19.1 ad 2). See also *De veritate*, 23.1 ad 8.

37. See *ST* I 19–20, esp. 19.1 and 20.1 ad 1.

38. *ST* I 59.1. See also *ST* I 19.3, 82.1–3; *ST* I-II 2.7–8, 5.8.

he chooses.[39] In the operations of the divine appetite, Aquinas posits something in God analogous to the human experience of love and joy (the movement of the divine will toward some good and the resting of the divine will in the possession of some good, respectively), as will be discussed later in greater depth.[40] Furthermore, Aquinas argues that God is an utter unity of pure being, entirely simple and without the composition of parts.[41] There may seem to be distinctions between the different powers and operations we attribute to God, but there can be no difference between them as they actually exist in God. Consequently, the divine essence is identical with the divine will and its operations.[42] Aquinas identifies God with appetite and its inherent dynamism. Since God is also the exemplar of all perfections found in creation, and since men and women are created in the image and likeness of God, this conclusion says much about the place that Aquinas assigns to appetite in his understanding of creation and the human person.[43]

Appetite plays a central role in the Neoplatonic *exitus-reditus* theme of creation flowing from God and then back to him, a theme that structures Aquinas's entire theology of creation (as well as the *Summa theologiae*).[44] According to this view, first, God is the source of creation, both as its Creator and as the exemplar of all perfections found in created things, and then, creation is oriented back to God and ordered to the manifestation of God's goodness.[45] God is glorified in the sheer fact of God's gratuitous creation, in the goodness of every created being, and in the appetite of created things toward their perfection. Above all, God is glorified in rational creatures, whose intellectual appetites draw them to seek God as the unlimited Good

39. *ST* I 19.2–3, 19.10.

40. *ST* I 20.1.

41. *ST* I 3.2–7.

42. *ST* I 19.1, 20.1. Similarly, the divine essence is identical with the divine intellect and the divine act of understanding (*ST* I 14.4).

43. Aquinas teases out the implications of being created in the image and likeness of God in *ST* I 93. This question affirms in yet another way the goodness of the human person and, by extension, human appetite, especially the human will. For a study of the *Imago Dei* in the anthropology of Aquinas, see Torrell, *Spiritual Master,* 105–32, and J. Augustine Di Noia, "Imago Dei–Imago Christi: The Theological Foundations of Christian Humanism," in *Proceedings of the International Congress on Christian Humanism in the Third Millenium: The Perspective of Thomas Aquinas: 21–25 September 2003* (Vatican City: Pontificia Academia Sancti Thomae Aquinatis, 2004), 19–30.

44. For a discussion of the *exitus-reditus* structure of the *Summa,* see Marie-Dominique Chenu, *Toward Understanding Saint Thomas,* trans. A.-M. Landry and D. Hughes (New York: Macmillan, 1968), 297–322. See also Torrell, *Aquinas's* Summa, 17–62.

45. *ST* I 44.3–4, 65.2.

that they cannot but desire (yet can still decide not to choose). Appetite is the engine driving the *exitus-reditus:* both in the divine *exitus,* since it flows from an act of God's will, and in the creaturely *reditus,* since appetite motivates creation to return to God.

Aquinas's account of evil also illuminates his view of created appetite. Following Augustine, Aquinas defines evil as a privation of goodness.[46] He distinguishes between two different kinds of evil (*malum*): physical evil and moral evil. Physical evil is nonmoral and refers to material loss or corruption, as when something material passes from existence. Physical evil in general, though not necessarily in any given instance, is willed by God insofar as it makes the movement from imperfection to perfection possible in the realm of material things. Moral evil is found only in rational creatures and consists in the voluntary choice of something disordered and contrary to one's *telos.* This kind of evil is never willed by God.[47]

Both physical and moral evil are defined vis-à-vis appetite. Aquinas maintains that evil is the effect of something good being impeded from the completion of "its natural and due disposition" (*sua naturali debita dispositione*)—a claim that implicitly defines evil in terms of appetite, insofar as a thing's disposition manifests its appetite.[48] Hence evil can be defined not just as a privation of goodness, but also as a frustration of appetite and the consequent disintegration of being, insofar as evil blocks appetite from attaining its natural *telos.* This metaphysical opposition between appetite and evil has implications for the moral reliability of appetite in human action, insofar as appetite, by pointing the way to human nature's completion, also points the way to moral goodness, as will be discussed in more depth in chapter 4.

46. *ST* I 48.1. For a discussion about the classical doctrine of evil as privation, see the recent exchange between Patrick Lee and John F. Crosby. Patrick Lee, "The Goodness of Creation, Evil, and Christian Teaching," *Thomist* 64 (2000): 239–70; John F. Crosby, "Is All Evil Really Only Privation?" *Proceedings of the American Catholic Philosophical Association* 75 (2001): 197–210; Patrick Lee, "Evil as Such Is a Privation: A Reply to John Crosby," *American Catholic Philosophical Quarterly* 81 (2007): 469–88; and John F. Crosby, "Doubts about the Privation Theory That Will Not Go Away: Response to Patrick Lee," *American Catholic Philosophical Quarterly* 81 (2007): 489–505.

47. Aquinas discusses the metaphysics of evil in *ST* I 48–49. For his treatment of the metaphysics of moral evil, see especially *ST* I 48.5–6, 49.1 ad 3, 49.2.

48. *ST* I 49.1. See also *De malo* 1.1–3, and especially *De malo* 1.1, where Aquinas discusses the relationship of evil to *appetitus.*

Apprehension and the Passivity of Created Appetite

Created appetite does not generate movement toward its *telos* by itself. It is a "passive power,"[49] and, as such, it is a tendency toward something that nonetheless requires an external trigger before generating movement. It is an inclination and a power to act when certain objects come into view. Aquinas identifies three kinds of appetites in creation: natural appetite, sense appetite, and the will (also called the intellectual or rational appetite).[50] Each responds to a different kind of desirable object, and each is distinguished by the kind of knowledge, or lack thereof, required for an object to act upon it. Once activated, each appetite moves being toward perfection in its own way.

> Some things are inclined toward a good only by natural disposition, without cognition, such as plants and inanimate objects. And this sort of inclination toward a good is called natural appetite. Other things are inclined toward a good with some amount of cognition; not that they apprehend the good as good, they apprehend only some particular good, just as the senses apprehend sweet and white and the like. The inclination that follows this sort of cognition is called the sense appetite. Still other things are inclined to a good with the cognition proper to the intellect, and these things know the good as good. These things are most perfectly inclined toward the good. . . . And this inclination is called the will.[51]

In this passage, the three appetites are defined according to the objects toward which they tend. Appetite necessarily inclines toward the kind of object suitable to itself, driving toward a specific kind of completion relentlessly and reliably, and therefore the species of appetite can be distinguished by the kind of object desired, that is, by *telos*.[52] For Aquinas, the sort of

49. *ST* I 80.2.

50. For a discussion of created appetite in Aquinas, see William A. Wallace, "Appetition and Emotion," in *The Modeling of Nature: Philosophy of Science and Philosophy of Nature in Synthesis* (Washington, D.C.: The Catholic University of America Press, 1996), 174–180. For a discussion of the rational appetite, see David Gallagher, "Thomas Aquinas on the Will as Rational Appetite," *Journal of the History of Philosophy* 29 (1991): 559–84.

51. *ST* I 59.1. Aquinas further distinguishes natural appetite from sense appetite in *ST* I 80.1 and sense appetite from intellectual appetite in *ST* I 80.2.

52. *ST* I 80.1 ad 3; *ST* I 80.2. The inclusion of natural appetite in the same category as sense appetite and intellectual appetite sits uneasily with contemporary science. Kenny, for instance, is critical of this teleological understanding of noncognitive agents (Kenny, *Aquinas on Mind*, 61). However, Aquinas's account of the universality of appetite constitutes a philosophical and

knowledge to which an appetite responds, or lack thereof, is its most salient feature, and accordingly, he divides created appetite into the three appetites discussed above.

Aquinas is most interested in the appetites that require some kind of apprehension. Sometimes he even defines appetite with reference to apprehension, even though natural appetite would seem to be excluded by such a definition.[53] He writes, "Appetitive power is a passive power (*potentia passiva*) which is naturally moved by what is apprehended."[54] Appetite is passive insofar as it is "acted upon" by objects via apprehension; it is a power insofar as appetite acts in response to the apprehended objects. Without apprehension, appetite remains dormant. Once the object toward which an appetite inclines is apprehended, the appetite responds and moves toward

---

theological position that contemporary physics does not engage or contradict. It is a philosophically interesting attempt to find metaphysical commonality in disparate aspects of reality that cannot be easily dismissed. But regardless of the merits of his position, Aquinas's classification of physical tendencies as a form of appetite draws attention to the central place of appetite in his metaphysics, as well as his conviction that every created thing is internally oriented by appetite toward its *telos*.

53. See *ST* I 80.2. The natural appetite does not follow apprehension as do the sense appetite and the intellectual appetite (*ST* I 78.1 ad 3; see also *ST* I-II 8.1). Rather "natural appetite is an inclination following on physical form [*formam naturalem*]" (*ST* I 81.2). So it is not clear why Aquinas defines appetite in *ST* I 80.2 in a way that excludes natural appetite. When pressed, it seems that he would not want to retain apprehension as an absolutely necessary feature of appetite at the expense of excluding natural appetite. It is possible, though, that he might insist on it: elsewhere he argues that natural appetite is not without its cognitive dimension insofar as it inclines objects according to God's knowledge. He writes: "Natural objects desire that which is suited to their nature, not through their own knowledge, but through the knowledge of the Author of nature" (*ST* I-II 26.1). See also *ST* I 6.1 ad 2, 103.1 ad 1; *ST* I-II 27.2 ad 3.

54. *ST* I 80.2. After 1270, Aquinas avoids referring to the will as a passive power, seemingly due to the condemnations of the bishop of Paris in 1270. These condemnations anathematize the description of free choice (*liberum arbitrium*) as a passive power, and even though the condemnations do not touch on whether the will is a passive power, Aquinas seems to avoid applying such language to the will afterward. Nonetheless, Aquinas does not refrain from implicitly describing the will as a passive power. For example, see *ST* I-II 18.2 ad 3, which describes appetite as intrinsically passive, albeit in a qualified sense, in a way that clearly includes the will (Sherwin, *By Knowledge and By Love*, 96–97). On the essential continuity of Aquinas's position regarding the will's passivity, see also Daniel Westberg, "Did Aquinas Change His Mind about the Will?" *Thomist* 58 (1994): 41–60.

The text of the condemnations of 1270 can be found in Latin in H. Denifle and A. Chatelain, *Chartularium universitatis parisiensis* (Paris: Frairs Delalain, 1889), 1:486–87, and in English in James Weisheipl, *Friar Thomas d'Aquino*, 2nd ed. (Washington, D.C.: The Catholic University of America Press, 1983), 273. For the historical context, see John F. Wippel, "The Condemnations of 1270 and 1277 at Paris," *Journal of Medieval and Renaissance Studies* 7 (1977): 169–201, and François-Xavier Putallaz, *Insolente liberté: controversies et condamnations au XIIIe siècle* (Paris: Cerf, 1995). See Sherwin, *By Knowledge and By Love*, 96n126.

it. There are two kinds of cognition, sense cognition and intellectual cognition, and accordingly there are two kinds of cognition-dependent appetites. Sense appetite operates in response to sense cognition, and intellectual appetite operates in response to intellectual cognition.

There is a hierarchy among the appetites based on the degree of cognition on which they depend. The rational and sense appetites surpass natural appetite because they imply cognition and voluntary engagement. The rational appetite surpasses the sense appetite because it inclines toward unqualified and unlimited goodness[55] and not just sense goods, although it can also seek sense goods. Most importantly, the rational appetite shares an essential similarity with God's appetite,[56] and, with its orientation toward infinite good, it has the capacity to love and enjoy God. This ranking is not based on distrust or disdain for the material, but on the metaphysical principle that superior knowledge correlates with a superior capacity for engagement with being. Those appetites that incline toward greater goods or a more profound appreciation of being are superior to others. For instance, the casual cigar smoker might enjoy a superb Cuban cigar, but the cigar connoisseur appreciates it more because of his greater knowledge. Similarly, animals cannot enjoy good food as much as we can: they can appreciate food only on a sensible level, but we can appreciate food—and the social contexts in which it is consumed—on many levels.

Appetite in the Human Person

As with the rest of creation, appetite drives us toward our *telos,* which consists of partial happiness in this life and union with God and complete happiness in the next.[57] We are more complicated than any other kind of being because we have all three kinds of appetites. Inanimate and vegetative beings have natural appetites; animals have both natural and sense appetites; and God and the angels have intellectual appetites. Only we have all three. When they are operative, they influence and sometimes compete with each other, as when they incline us toward mutually incompatible goods. It is this conflux of different appetites that makes us complicated. Nonethe-

55. *ST* I 59.1. See also *ST* I 19.3, 82.1–3; *ST* I-II 2.7–8, 5.8.

56. See *ST* I 93 (esp. 93.3, 93.6–7).

57. See *ST* I-II 1–5. For a comparison of Aquinas's concept of appetite with Freud's libido, see George Cottier, "«Libido» de Freud et «appetitus» de saint Thomas," in *L'anthropologie de saint Thomas,* ed. N. A. Luyten (Fribourg: Éditions Universitaires, 1974), 91–123.

less, despite the difficulties that sometimes arise from their interactions, each moves us toward our perfection; each is necessary for human flourishing; each is a God-given inner compass oriented toward happiness; none can be ignored without cost.

Passion: A Movement of the Sense Appetite

The sense appetite inclines us toward goods that are apprehended through sense cognition, and in this way directs us toward certain aspects of our *telos*. A passion is nothing other than the movement of the sense appetite, a passive power, from dormancy to act, in response to the apprehension of an object to which the sense appetite is inclined.[58] There are thus two aspects of a passion: receptivity to a sensible object's stimulation—apprehension of an intention being a necessary precondition for a passion[59]—and movement toward some *telos*. The perceptive and cognitive faculties "present" the finished product of an intention to the sense appetite, and if the intention corresponds to its capacities and inclinations, the sense appetite is triggered and a passion results.

Passion as Receptivity

Passion (*passio*) has a wide range of equivocal meanings in ancient and medieval philosophy and theology, as does its Greek cognate, *pathos*. The word is most commonly used to refer to the passions of the soul, but the passions of the soul constitute only one species of passion. More generally, passion signifies passivity and the "act" of being acted upon. It refers especially to suffering, that is, to ways of being acted upon that are unpleasant because they somehow rub against natural tendencies and inclinations.

Cognizant of the ambiguities surrounding the word, Aquinas attempts to clarify matters by rehearsing its various meanings in multiple places in the *Summa theologiae*.[60] The most relevant and thorough discussion is at the beginning of the *Treatise on the Passions*, where Aquinas analyzes three uses of the Latin word *pati* (to suffer or undergo), the verb form of *passio*:

58. See *ST* I-II 22.2–3, 41.1, 45.2.

59. For passion's dependence on apprehension, see *ST* I-II 17.7, 45.4, 62.4, 75.2, 77.1, and for its specific dependence on the apprehension of intentions, see *ST* I 78.4, 81.2–3; and esp. *ST* I-II 22.2.

60. *ST* I 79.2, 97.2; *ST* I-II 22.1, 41.1.

First, in a general way, all receiving is passion [*pati*], even when nothing is lost, and so it could be said that the air "undergoes" when it is illuminated. However, this kind of passion is more about *being perfected* than *undergoing*. Second, passion properly means that something is received while something else is lost. This happens in two ways. When something is lost that is not suitable to a thing, just as when the body of an animal is made healthy, it is called "passion" because the animal's body receives health and sickness is removed. In another way, sometimes the opposite happens: getting sick is called "passion" because weakness is received and health is lost. This last case is what is most properly called passion.[61]

Passion, then, is the "act" of being acted upon. It implies the potential to be actualized and thus perfected. Insofar as this potential is bound up in the tendency toward something not yet attained, it also implies a metaphysical deficiency.[62] Just as the term "appetite" encompasses many kinds of inclination, and not just the sense appetite, the term "passion" encompasses many kinds of receptivity. Others had distinguished passion's various meanings before,[63] but Aquinas synthesizes these various meanings into a coherent unity. He also organizes them into a hierarchy of ascending specificity: passion as reception of a quality, passion as reception of a quality in place of another, and passion as reception of an inferior quality in place of another. By doing so, he puts the more negative connotations of passion in a context that lessens their significance.

Then Aquinas applies the three senses of passion outlined above to the powers of the soul:

Passion can be in the soul in each of these three ways. Regarding the first sort of passion, which involves only reception, Aristotle says that sensing and understanding are a kind of passion. The sort of passion that involves loss always involves bodily change. Passion in this stricter sense is not in the soul except insofar as the composite of body and soul undergoes it. But here again there is a distinction: when the bodily change is for the worse, it is even more strictly passion than when the bodily change is for the better. Hence sorrow is more strictly a passion than rejoicing.[64]

61. *ST* I-II 22.1.

62. *ST* I-II 22.2 ad 1.

63. In his discussion of the passions, John Damascene also writes about the equivocal meanings of *pathos*. See *De fide orthodoxa* 2.22.

64. *ST* I-II 22.1.

The primary attribute of the passions qua passion is their aspect of receptivity. Passion in a stricter and more idiosyncratic sense also involves suffering, and so, according to this schema, sorrow is more properly a passion than joy. This specification, however, does not do much work in Aquinas's system. He does affirm that passion in the strictest sense refers to suffering, and occasionally points out that certain passions are more strictly passions because they involve suffering or the experience of something contrary to nature's most basic inclinations,[65] but this is a linguistic clarification, not a philosophical claim. For Aquinas, love, not sorrow or fear, is the most paradigmatic of the passions. Although he says sorrow and fear are more strictly passions than love and joy, he singles out love as the first of the passions and the source of all the rest.[66] Furthermore, in his discussion of love, Aquinas observes: "The term 'passion' denotes the effect produced in a thing when it is acted upon by some agent," without noting that, in its most strict sense, passion requires suffering.[67] This text seems to supply his actual working definition of passion.

Nonetheless, some interpret the passages discussed above as evidence of a negative view of the passions.[68] When interpreted properly, the same texts show the opposite. First, although he accepts the common meaning of the word "passion" established by centuries of pagan and Christian thinkers (which was more a fact of language than a philosophical axiom), Aquinas subtly shifts its connotation in favor of a more positive signification. By laying out the various meanings of passion side by side, as he does repeat-

65. *ST* I-II 22.1, 35.1, 41.1. Contemporary use of the word "emotion" seems to involve similar negative associations. While the word "emotion" usually has a neutral connotation, in ordinary language use, we say that someone is emotional if overcome with sorrow or fear or anger—all of which imply something negative—but not so much if filled with joy or energy or hope. We say that someone is emotional when joyful to the point of tears, but even here some latent negative association remains, since such joy implies the loss of self-control and even something phenomenologically similar to sorrow.

66. *ST* I-II 25.2–3.

67. *ST* I-II 26.2.

68. For example, Dixon, who interprets Augustine as having a negative view of the passions, writes: "So Aquinas' passions (*passiones animae*) were conceived, at one level, simply as special cases of the fundamental state of being acted upon (*passio*). This is significant since this category of passion was essentially a negative one. . . . Passion, for Aquinas, implied imperfection. . . . So, while taking a different, Aristotelian basis for his definition of the passions, Aquinas came to endorse a theory of the passions that was similar to Augustine's, and equally negative. For both these theologians the passions were signs of deficiency and imperfection, and were contrasted unfavourably with the cognitive powers of the soul" (Dixon, *From Passions to Emotions*, 41–42).

edly,[69] Aquinas stresses the possible positive connotations of passion and minimizes the negative.[70] In the end, he locates passion's defining characteristic in receptivity rather than suffering.

Second, although Aquinas says that passion indicates deficiency (*defectus*), in the context of his metaphysics, or indeed any Aristotelian metaphysics, "deficiency" and "imperfection" are technical terms that do not necessarily have negative connotations. For Aquinas, something can be imperfect and deficient with respect to its ultimate *telos*, or compared to God, but nonetheless entirely intact and morally praiseworthy. Furthermore, imperfection and deficiency in the Aristotelian sense creates the space for movement, dynamism, and some of the more outstanding forms of creaturely excellence. The rational creature is the most dramatic instance of this principle. Unless the rational creature is imperfect—that is, not yet brought to the completion of its being—before it begins to make choices, there would be no room for it to shape its own identity. Lastly, according to Aquinas, God is the only being that does not need anything; every other being is deficient and imperfect insofar as it is dependent on God and other beings. The modern proclivity to interpret dependence as inherently negative can obscure the neutrality of "deficiency" and "imperfection" in Aquinas's metaphysics.

Passion as Movement toward a *Telos*

Unlike many other forms of passion, the passions of the soul involve more than the experience of being acted upon by some agent; they also move their subject toward its *telos*.[71] As movements of an appetitive power, they are both

69. *ST* I 79.2, 97.2; *ST* I-II 22.1, 41.1. Two of the three meanings Aquinas gives for *passio* have positive or neutral connotations.

70. Sweeney seems to interpret Aquinas's use of the word *passio* in the same way. She suggests that in the *Summa* he employs a rhetorical strategy that downplays the negative connotations of *passio* even while acknowledging them: "Aquinas begins pessimistically, taking passion in its most proper sense as the *loss* of what is natural and the receiving of what is not; hence sorrow is more a passion than joy (I-II ST 22, 1). He then works through the next 24 questions to construct an account which emphasizes just the opposite, converting the reader to a vision of the passions as forces for good, moving away from seeing them as a detriment or something to be merely tolerated or controlled" (Sweeney, "Restructuring Desire," 220).

71. For a discussion of Aquinas's use of the metaphor of physical movement to describe psychological events, see James, *Passion and Action*, 62–63; Gondreau, *Passions of Christ's Soul*, 209–10; Knuuttila, *Emotions*, 249–51; and especially Carlo Leget, "Moral Theology Upside Down: Aquinas' Treatise *de passionibus animae* Considered through the Lens of Its Spatial Metaphors," in *Jaarboek Thomas Instituut 1999* (Utrecht: Thomas Instituut, 2000), 101–26.

passive and active, not just one or the other.[72] For example, the sense appetite has the capacity to be acted upon by the apprehension of something beautiful (the passive dimension of passion), one consequence of which is that the subject may come to desire the beautiful (the active dimension of passion). The words "passion" and "movement" refer to the same reality, but each emphasizes different aspects. The former emphasizes being acted upon; the latter emphasizes moving in such a way that the perfection of the subject is advanced or safeguarded.

Aquinas's account of the passions cannot be understood without reference to both their active dimension and their passive dimension, but their active dimension is primary and more central to his account. Although the sense appetite encompasses the capacity to enjoy (or suffer) present sensible objects, it is principally an inclination toward sensible objects, irrespective of whether they are already possessed or not. "Sense appetite," Aquinas writes, "is an inclination responding to sense apprehension (*apprehensionem sensitivam*)."[73] So too are the passions that are its movements. "An act of an appetitive power is a kind of inclination,"[74] and the passions, insofar as they are acts of the sense appetite, are inclinations toward sensible objects. The primary function of the passions is not to allow sensible objects to act upon us, although of course they do that, but to incline us toward the perfection of our nature. Aquinas's view that the passions are *movements,* rather than *qualities,* was a minority position in his lifetime—Albert the Great among others disagreed with it—and remained a minority position after Aquinas's death.[75] His commitment to an unpopular position

72. "Appetite both moves and is moved" (*ST* I 80.2).

73. *ST* I 81.2.

74. *ST* I-II 15.1.

75. Knuuttila, *Emotions,* 248–55. Disagreement among medieval thinkers about whether the passions constitute movements or qualities, or both, derives in large part from study of Aristotle's *Categories.* In his discussion of the category of quality, Aristotle first names the passions as the third genus of quality, but then he goes on to note that there are some sorts of passions that are not qualities (*Categories* 8, 9a–10a). What Aristotle seems to be getting at is the difference between moods that are more or less stable, and thus qualities, and sudden flashes of passion, which are not qualities.

The uncertainty of Aristotle's meaning is heightened by an ambiguous remark by Boethius in his commentary on the *Categories,* which leads many to interpret Aristotle as holding that the passions are always qualities (Knuuttila, *Emotions,* 237). Albert follows this line of interpretation and argues that the passions are not movements, even though John Damascene imprecisely calls them movements (*De fide orthodoxa* 2.22), but rather what are left from movements (*De bono* III

suggests that he found the analogy of movement particularly illuminating, and further indicates that seeing the passions as active expressions of the sense appetite's inclinations is more central to his conception of the passions than their passivity.

Aquinas's attribution of appetite to God also indicates that the inclination toward a *telos* is more essential to the sense appetite than its passivity, because, while he affirms that appetite is found in God, he states that passion is not. God is pure act and perfection itself; passion implies potential not yet actualized and the possibility for improvement; therefore passion cannot be found in God.[76] Passion is present only in creaturely forms of appetite. If passion were more essential to the meaning of appetite than the inclination toward a *telos,* it stands to reason that Aquinas would not have attributed appetite to God.

Nonetheless, some passions considered individually have less of the aspect of movement and consist more in the quasi-contemplative experience of some object, whether that object is perfective of nature or repugnant to it. These passions, such as pleasure and sadness, have more the character of passion (in its most generic sense) than movement (in the sense of moving somewhere) because they are dead ends; they follow the fulfillment or failure of the sense appetite to attain a certain *telos.*[77] Yet even these passions are not without an active element. Pleasure inclines the subject toward the maintenance of pleasure, and sadness inclines the subject away from the cause of the sadness. They accomplish this by communicating information

---

5.1 ad 8). Pleasure, for instance, is not itself a movement, but is left from a movement that alters the soul (*De bono* III 5.3 ad 4).

Despite Albert's position and the dominant interpretative tradition that he represents, Aquinas holds firmly to a sense of passion as movement and makes it one of the cornerstones of his account of the passions. By thus affirming the literal sense of John Damascene's definition of passion as a movement of the sense appetite, Aquinas seems to be closer to Aristotle's original meaning in the *Categories* than Albert. He also thus emphasizes the way the passions carry us toward our *telos,* whereas Albert's view of the passions as qualities implicitly emphasizes their receptivity and how they color our experience of the world.

76. *ST* I 3.1, 4.1–2, 9.1, 25.1. See also *De potentia* 2.1 ad 1. Regarding Aquinas on the absence of passion in God, see Michael Dodds, *The Unchanging God of Love: Thomas Aquinas and Contemporary Theology on Divine Immutability,* 2nd ed. (Washington, D.C.: The Catholic University of America Press, 2008).

77. Note that according to this interpretation of Aquinas, pleasure and sadness equally represent the most "passive" of the passions. Contrary to his linguistic clarification in *ST* I-II 22.1, sadness is not more passive than pleasure, with respect to the way the passions actually function in his account.

insofar as pleasure tells the subject that a *telos* has been attained and sadness indicates that it has not.[78]

Taking these resting, quasi-contemplative passions into consideration, we might say that for Aquinas, the passions paradoxically drive us toward passion, that is, toward letting the goods we desire act upon us.

The Passions and Human Flourishing

Aquinas emphatically rejects negative evaluations of the passions,[79] and the contrast between Aquinas and some earlier understandings of the passions, both pagan and Christian, is dramatic.[80] Instead of being obstacles to the *telos* of human existence, the passions are indispensable to its attainment.[81] They are psychic motors driving us toward it.[82] Numerous contemporary authors have made similar observations about the centrality of the passions to human flourishing in Aquinas.[83] The tendency toward specific objects is not an extrinsic feature of the sense appetite; the inclina-

78. Sadness, or the experience of the frustration of a given desire of the sense appetite, also inclines the human person to pursue those other desires, including desires of the intellectual appetite, that are still open to fulfillment. Hence the educative and self-transcending consequence often noted about suffering: it inclines us to consider other ways in which fulfillment is still possible despite the suffering. So, in Aquinas's account, even the frustration of appetite (or at least some kinds of frustration of appetite) ultimately moves us toward our *telos*.

79. For example, in his analysis of the Stoic understanding of passion, Aquinas writes: "The passions are not diseases or disturbances of the soul, unless they are without the moderation of reason" (*ST* I-II 24.2).

80. Aquinas distances himself from the Stoic view of the passions as intrinsically disordered in favor of the more positive Aristotelian view of the passions as good or evil, depending on whether or not they are guided by reason (see *ST* I-II 24.2). He does not reject the Stoic view outright, however. He prefers to give their view of the passions a charitable interpretation, suggesting that the difference between the Stoic and Aristotelian views of the passions is more verbal than substantial, even with Cicero's description of the passions as "disturbances of the soul" (*perturbationes animi*) in *Tusculan Disputations*, 3.4. Whatever the validity of his interpretation of Stoic doctrine, Aquinas's intellectual charity should not obscure his firm rejection of the view of the passions as intrinsically disordered.

81. The placement of the *Treatise on the Passions* shortly after questions 1–5 of the *Prima secundae* (in which happiness is laid out as the end of all human action) manifests the centrality of the passions to human flourishing in Aquinas's anthropology. For a discussion of this point, see Loughlin, "Human and Animal Emotion," 60n29, and Gondreau, *Passions of Christ's Soul*, 108.

82. The phrase "psychic motors" is taken from Conrad Baars, who uses it to describe the emotions in his Thomistic psychology. See Conrad W. Baars, *Feeling and Healing Your Emotions* (Plainsfield, N.J.: Logos International, 1979).

83. See Pinckaers, "Les passions et la morale"; Thomas Ryan, "Positive and Negative Emotions in Aquinas: Retrieving a Distorted Tradition," *Australasian Catholic Record* 78 (2001): 141–52; Paul J. Wadell, *The Primacy of Love: An Introduction to the Ethics of Thomas Aquinas* (Mahwah, NJ: Paulist Press, 1992), esp. 79–105; Simon Harak, *Virtuous Passions: The Formation*

tion toward its proper objects "belongs to the very essence of a power."[84] The receptivity of passion is an important aspect of Aquinas's account, but it does not exhaust it, and this receptivity also moves us toward sense goods and their enjoyment.

An important qualification is necessary here. Aquinas does not hold that the fundamental orientation of the passions toward human flourishing implies that each and every movement of the sense appetite reliably directs us toward our proper *telos*. The passions require the guidance of reason, especially in our fallen condition. Paradoxically, however, even when the passions prompt us to act in ways that we ultimately judge inappropriate, in their essential structure, the passions still serve the attainment of our *telos*. The passions require the guidance of reason in order to become virtuous, and thus fully conducive to human flourishing, but virtue also requires the passions. Without the passions, we would not respond to sensible objects, and without this first step toward engaging the world, human flourishing would not be possible.[85] The function of the passions is not to decide upon a course of action; the function of the passions is to respond to stimuli and prompt the human person to act according to the face value of those stimuli. Then the passions defer to the judgment of reason, because only the rational appetite can command human action, and because the sense appetite naturally tends toward conformity with reason.[86] When rational analysis concludes that acting on a certain prompting of the passions is not conducive to the attainment of our final end, the passions have not failed to offer reliable guidance: they have provided precisely the sort of first-order response and motivation that is their sphere of competence. The passions require education and the elevation of grace for optimal functioning, and various things can warp the passions and their responses to stimuli, most obviously sin and the privation of grace and all their attendant consequenc-

of Christian Character (New York: Paulist Press, 1993); Sweeney, "Restructuring Desire," esp. 218–23; and Gondreau, "The Passions and the Moral Life."

84. *ST* I-II 51.1.

85. "The moral virtues which are concerned with the passions as their proper matter cannot exist without them. The reason for this is that otherwise it would follow that moral virtue would make the sense appetite indifferent to everything. But virtue does not consist in the passions being subject to reason, apart from their own proper acts, but rather in the passions executing the command of reason through their own proper acts" (*ST* I-II 59.5). See chap. 4 for a more detailed discussion of the integral role of passion in virtue and human flourishing.

86. For more on the relationship between passion and reason, see chap. 4.

es.[87] Nonetheless, in their essential structure, the passions make a crucial contribution in guiding us toward flourishing and happiness.[88]

Aquinas's positive evaluation of the passions and their role in human flourishing pervades his analysis of particular passions. He touts the beneficial effects and inherent goodness of pleasure: it perfects actions,[89] and insensitivity to pleasure is a vice.[90] Unlike some early Christian theologians, Aquinas not only affirms that sexual intercourse was possible in the Garden of Eden, he claims that it would have been more pleasurable, since human nature would have been fully intact and the body more sensitive.[91] By contrast, his Franciscan contemporaries Alexander of Hales and Bonaventure argued that the pleasure would have been less.[92] Sorrow can be morally good because, in its inmost nature, it is ontologically good, even though it involves the suffering of an evil.[93]

Aquinas's view of passion and *telos* does not derive from philosophical reflection alone. There is a massive theological premise that is never explic-

87. For more on the effects of sin and grace on the passions, see chap. 5.

88. Gondreau expands elegantly on Aquinas's view of the passions vis-à-vis our *telos:* "That Aquinas places the treatise on the passions in the moral part of the *Summa* is surprising if we recall that the dominant *telos* of the moral life, and the governing principle of the entire *Secunda Pars,* is eternal beatitude. Indeed, at first sight one would expect Aquinas to have placed his study on the passions earlier, in the *Prima Pars,* specifically in the treatise on the human soul (qq. 75–90), whose prologue proposes to study 'the essence of the soul, its powers, and its operations' (q. 75). As movements of the sensitive appetite (a power of the soul), the emotions are certainly to be included among the soul's operations.

"But Aquinas prefers the moral life, not the more metaphysical study on the human soul, as the backdrop for his study on the emotions. Such a move allows him to drive home the point that the emotions play a necessary first step in our striving for happiness, in our attaining the end of seeing God. Although the passions incline us to the lowest kind of goods, to bodily goods, which cannot bring us complete fulfillment as rational beings, these goods do participate in goodness itself—they are, after all, 'good.' These interim lower goods remain ordered ultimately to the perfect and sufficient good (*summum bonum*), to the absolute perfection of God.

"By being inclined internally to limited bodily goods, we are already on the road, as it were, to the highest good. We are set on a trajectory, even if only in its initial stages, that has as its ultimate end point God himself. It bears insisting: the life of spiritual and moral excellence is not bereft of the enjoyment of earthly and bodily pleasures. On the contrary, such enjoyment is foundational to the life of holiness and moral perfection. The life of holiness is inclusive of our desires, not at odds with them. In a word, God wants all of us to share in beatitude, bodily desires and all, not just our 'cerebral' sides; he does not want love of him to exclude desiring and loving created earthly goods" (Gondreau, "The Passions and the Moral Life," 427–28).

89. *ST* I-II 33.4.

90. *ST* II-II 142.1.

91. *ST* I 98.2 ad 3. *Commentaria in quatuor libros Sententiarum* II 20.1.3.

92. Bonaventure, II *Sentences* 20, 1.3; Alexander of Hales, *Summa theologiae* I.2 496 (p 701–03).

93. *ST* I-II 39.1–3.

itly stated because it is so obvious: the passions carry us toward our *telos* (and therefore happiness) because they were created by a God who is trustworthy. God is the guarantor of desire. In him, there is a metaphysical basis for welcoming and trusting the passions.[94]

The Intentionality of the Passions

The dependence of the passions on the apprehension of intentions means that the passions themselves are intentional. Every passion responds to a particular intentional object, and the passions can be classified accordingly.[95] Just as the various kinds of appetite are distinguished according to what they incline toward, the passions are distinguished according to the kind of intentional object that elicits them. It is significant that the passions respond to intentional objects, rather than objects considered in themselves, that is, material objects. Without this distinction, Aquinas's account would become obscure and confusing. For instance, Susan James does not distinguish between intentional objects and material objects, and she reports difficulty in making sense of Aquinas's taxonomy of the passions. She describes Aquinas's system of distinguishing passions by their objects as "confusing" since the same object can evoke different passions, depending on the perspective of the subject.[96] Independently, Mark Drost notes the same interpretative puzzle, but concludes that Aquinas avoids incoherence precisely because he classifies passions not by material objects, but by intentional objects.[97]

There are two objects associated with a passion: the object that evokes the passion and the object it moves toward or away from. Aquinas states

94. Aristotle was able to arrive at some of these conclusions without theological premises because he sees human fulfillment as the proper operation of all the powers of the human person, and consequently the sense appetite is integral to his understanding of moral virtue. In the *De anima* he discusses the sense appetite and the passions, but his account of the passions is not as systematically related to the sense appetite as Aquinas's, and his lengthy discussion of the passions in the *Rhetoric* is more a phenomenological survey than a discussion of how they lead us toward our flourishing. For Aristotle, the passions should be moderated, not squelched, but not necessarily seen as guiding us toward fulfillment either. Aquinas's faith in a benevolent Creator provides him with theological as well as philosophical reasons to think that our passions, in their inner structure, ultimately guide us toward our *telos*, as long as they are properly moderated by reason. He has more trust in the passions and where they are inclined to take us.

95. Drost, "Intentionality in Aquinas."

96. James, *Passion and Action*, 56.

97. Drost, "Intentionality in Aquinas," 456–57.

that these two objects are one and the same. He writes, "The term 'passion' implies that the patient is drawn to something about the agent."[98] In other words, whatever causes the passion is also the object it moves toward or away from.

There are three interpretative puzzles involved in making sense of Aquinas's principle. First, Aquinas's principle speaks only of the patient being drawn to something about the agent, so how does it apply to a passion, such as fear, that involves movement away from the agent? The answer seems to be simply that Aquinas is speaking loosely, because it is cumbersome to talk about "the object that a passion moves toward or away from."

Second, does Aquinas's principle imply that the two objects of passion—the object that evokes the passion and the object it moves toward or away from—are identical only with respect to the material object, or are they also identical with respect to the intentional object? This question is more difficult to resolve. It is obvious that the material object both elicits the passion and is what the passion moves toward or away from. However, it is not so plain whether the same can be said of the intentional object. Still, Aquinas's principle must imply that the intentional objects are identical as well, since, as discussed above, with the passions, the relevant objects are not material, but intentional. Third, in his account of anger, Aquinas speaks of a twofold object: the object that evokes anger, and the object that anger seeks.[99] Is anger an exception to his principle, or is his principle operative on some deeper level even in the case of anger? The answer to this question is difficult to determine. It is enough to raise the issue here; the question of the intentionality of anger will be addressed in the next chapter.

Body, Soul, and Passion

The sense appetite and its movements, the passions, invariably involve the body.[100] Moreover, Aquinas maintains that the word "passion" in its most proper sense implies corporeality. He writes:

98. *ST* I-II 22.2. He also writes: "Passion (*pati*) describes a thing being drawn to an agent" (*ST* I-II 22.1).

99. *ST* I-II 46.2.

100. For a discussion of Aquinas's theory of the body in dialogue with a wide range of philosophers and theologians, particularly insofar as it relates to desire and especially sexual desire, see McAleer, *Ecstatic Morality and Sexual Politics.*

Passion first and foremost involves the motion of a passive power, that is, a power that is moved to act by its object (as passion is the effect of an agent). In this way, both sensing and understanding are passions. Secondly, more strictly speaking, passion is a movement of an appetitive power; and even more strictly speaking, passion is a movement of an appetitive power that involves a bodily organ and a bodily reaction.[101]

This attention to corporeality permeates his account of the passions, as when he repeatedly notes that the passions are rooted in bodily organs and necessarily involve bodily modification.[102] Aquinas locates the passions principally in the soul and describes them as *passiones animae*, "passions of the soul."[103] Nonetheless, the passions affect the soul only through the medium of the body and, therefore, in a somewhat secondary fashion.[104] Since sensing is an activity of the whole human person,[105] so too is the sense appetite that follows upon it: neither the body nor the soul is the sole subject of the passions.

In his earlier writings, such as *De veritate* 26, Aquinas distinguishes between passions of the body (*passiones corporalis*) and passions of the soul (*passiones animalis*).[106] Simply put, the passions of the body begin in the body and end in the soul, while the passions of the soul begin in the soul and end in the body.[107] Being stabbed by a knife begins in the body and penetrates the soul; being given some bad news begins in the soul and filters down to the body (perhaps leading to tears or a nervous collapse). Aquinas does not, however, employ this distinction in his discussion of the passions in the *Summa theologiae*—except when analyzing Christ's passions—and perhaps in some brief allusions in the *Secunda secundae*.[108] Furthermore,

101. *ST* I-II 41.1.

102. "The sense appetite is a material power since it is grounded in a bodily organ" (*ST* I-II 77.1 obj 3). See also *ST* I 75.3 ad 3; *ST* I-II 10.3, 22.1, 22.2 ad 3, 22.3.

103. *ST* I-II 22.1. Aquinas qualifies his account of man as a body-soul composite with the nuance that man is more properly identified with his mind than his body (*ST* I-II 29.4).

104. *ST* I-II 22.1.

105. *ST* I 75.4.

106. For a discussion of the *passio corporalis* vis-à-vis the *passio animalis*, see Marcel Sarot, "God, Emotion and Corporeality: A Thomist Perspective," *Thomist* 58 (1994): 66–71. See also Gondreau, *Passions of Christ's Soul*, 207–8, 245–57, 380–84, and Floyd, "Aquinas on Emotion," 163–64.

107. *De veritate* 26.2, 26.3 ad 9.

108. Aquinas explicitly invokes the distinction between passions of the body and passions of the soul when discussing Christ's passions in *ST* III 15.4, and it also seems operative in *ST* III

Aquinas classifies pain (*dolor*) as a passion of the soul in the *Treatise on the Passions,* but earlier, in the *Scriptum super libros Sententiarum* and the *De veritate,* he had classified it as a *passio corporalis.* Scholars disagree about the significance of this shift.[109] Since, however, Aquinas retains the terminology of *passio corporalis* in the *Tertia pars,* which was written shortly before his death, it seems clear that he never rejected its heuristic value. At the same time, his declining use of the term, and especially its absence from the *Treatise on the Passions,* seems to indicate that he came to see the distinction between *passio corporalis* and *passio animalis* to be less important than he had thought initially. The more important feature of the passions, he may have concluded, is their composite body-soul character and their responsiveness to perception and cognition, not the structural sequence in which body and soul respond to stimuli.

For Aquinas, matter is the metaphysical realm of passive potency par excellence—that is, of the capacity to be acted upon by other agents—and the bodily dimension of the passions makes their subjective experience more dramatic than that of immaterial psychological movements. For example, Aquinas explains that bodily pleasures tend to be more intense than spiritual pleasures, even though the latter are greater in themselves.[110] Sensible objects are better known to us than immaterial objects, and being better known, they tend to evoke more vehement appetitive reactions. Moreover, sensible pleasures involve the body directly in its senses, and not just by overflow, as is the case with spiritual pleasure, and so they are experienced more forcefully. Lastly, sensible pleasures can be especially dramatic when they cast out some sensible pain or discomfort, as when someone drinks a glass of water after being very thirsty.

Biology of the Passions

Aquinas devotes substantial attention to the bodily aspects of the passions whenever relevant, that is, to the physical causes and effects of plea-

46.7. Aquinas may also invoke the distinction in *ST* II-II 117.5 ad 2, where he refers to pleasures of the body in contradistinction to pleasures of the soul.

109. For a discussion of this issue, see Sarot, "God, Emotion and Corporeality," 67–70; Rémi Tittley, "La Douleur Sensible Est-Elle une Passion Corporelle ou une Passion Animale Selon Saint Thomas d'Aquin?" (Diss., University of Montreal, 1967); Howard Gil Weil, *The Dynamic Aspect of Emotions in the Philosophy of St. Thomas Aquinas* (Rome: Angelicum, 1966), 57–62; and Journet D. Kahn, "A Thomistic Theory of Emotion" (Ph.D. diss., University of Notre Dame, 1957), 28–57.

110. *ST* I-II 31.5.

sure, sorrow, fear, anger, and so on, as understood by thirteenth-century biology.[111] Like his biology, his analysis is by turns amusing, puzzling, and occasionally philosophically interesting. The sheer amount of attention given to this subject demonstrates how seriously he takes the body's role in passion. Although the *Treatise on the Passions* is ordered to his discussion of virtue and vice, he does not allow this overarching objective to narrow or distort his investigation of the passions. He is genuinely interested in making sense of how the passions work and in integrating every bit of knowledge available to him.

Two main principles emerge in his discussions of body-soul dynamics. First, the relationship between the bodily aspects of passion and the mental aspects of passion is more than accidental: the body expresses and resembles on a physical level the experience of the soul.[112] Second, bodily conditions and changes have a direct bearing on our passions, since they can make us disposed to react more or less powerfully to various stimuli. For example, Aquinas attributes differences in personality types, temperaments, and moods, in part, to bodily differences.[113] He notes that wine drives away fear and inspires hope, and he claims that it is because wine enlarges and stretches out the heart.[114] He also observes that the body can interfere with passion's responsiveness to reason and will.[115]

Animal Passions

Throughout his discussion of human passions, Aquinas has a running interest in animal passions.[116] Although he has some interest in animals in their own right, his primary interest is in how they illuminate the material dimensions of human passions. Just as angels provide a point of reference because they have an intellectual appetite, animals provide a point of reference because they have a sense appetite. Aquinas concludes that animal

111. See *ST* I-II 24.2 ad 2, 33.1, 37.2, 37.4, 38.2, 38.5, 44.1, 44.3, 44.4, 45.3, 48.2, 48.4.

112. *ST* I-II 44.1.

113. *ST* I-II 17.7 ad 2, 46.5, 51.1, 63.1, 82.4 ad 1; *ST* II-II 35.1 ad 2. Aquinas notes that psychological inclinations can vary according to differences in natural constitution, though without explicit reference to the body, in *ST* I-II 64.2, 66.1.

114. *ST* I-II 45.3. In this article, Aquinas draws on Aristotle's discussion of how animals with larger hearts are more daring, and his observation that those drinking wine become more daring, because of wine's warming effect on the heart. See Aristotle, *De partibus animalium,* III.4, 667a15.

115. *ST* I-II 17.7.

116. *ST* I 78.4, 81.2–3; *ST* I-II 11.2, 35.2 ad 3, 40.3, 46.4 ad 2, 46.5 ad 1, 46.7 ad 1, 47.2 ad 2.

passions must be located in the body since animals do not have an intellect or will, and therefore, he reasons, their human equivalents must also be located in the body. He uses this principle to help him make distinctions between the sense appetite and the intellectual appetite as they exist in humans.

The parallel between animals and humans, however, only extends so far. Aquinas holds that animals do not have passions in the fullest sense. For instance, he holds that only rational creatures can experience the full meaning of *frui* (the enjoyment that flows from an act), although animals experience something like it.[117] Humans can take pleasure in objects of any of the senses, but, according to Aquinas, animals can take pleasure only in touch.[118] Animals are disposed to species-wide tendencies regarding passion (e.g., lions are aggressive, rabbits are timid), whereas humans experience a fuller and more balanced spectrum of passions.[119] The thorniest and most interesting of the topics he raises vis-à-vis animal passion is the mechanism by which animals adjudicate between competing desires. His suggests that, in animals, natural instinct replaces the function of reason and will.[120] He argues, for example, that animals can hope for future goods by natural instinct, a passion that requires rational judgment about the future, because the Creator's rationality provides the necessary rational judgment.[121]

117. *ST* I-II 11.2.
118. *ST* I-II 35.2 ad 3.
119. *ST* I-II 46.5 ad 1.
120. *ST* I 78.4, 81.2.
121. *ST* I-II 40.3.

CHAPTER 2

The Structure of the Passions

In his treatment of the different types of elemental passions, the distinctions between them, and their inner relations, Aquinas relies on the work of many predecessors, but he also reaches a new height of sophistication. Susan James summarizes the historical achievement of Aquinas's work and his influence on subsequent thinkers as follows:

> Aquinas's analysis of the passions is far more thorough and meticulous than those of his predecessors, and is worked out with a fervent attention to detail to which none of them aspired. Rather than simply listing the principal passions, each one is examined and anatomized in best Scholastic style. In this way, the relevant sections of the *Summa* set a standard for later discussions of the subject, and established a format that endured into the seventeenth century. Long after philosophers ceased to organize their works into *quaestiones*, treatises on the passions still opened with a section on the passions in general, and followed this up with elaborate chapters on individual passions, in which interpretation is mixed with assessments of various authorities, summaries of other writers, and instructive anecdotes. Both as to form and content, the influence of Aquinas was, therefore, enormous.[1]

The foundation of his system is the classification of passions according to their objects. Passions are distinguished from each other "according to the species of their objects."[2] The kind of object that distinguishes passions is not the material object, that is, the object as it is in itself, but the formal or intentional object, that is, the object as it is apprehended through an intention. On the basis of this principle, Aquinas identifies eleven different passions from eleven different categories of intentional objects.[3] This taxonomy

1. James, *Passion and Action*, 60.

2. *ST* I-II 23.1 obj 3. See also *ST* I 77.3; *ST* I-II 23.4.

3. Aquinas's account of the structure of the passions is original to him. It first appears in

is not intended to be an inventory of every conceivable passion, but rather a catalog of the basic types: love, desire, joy, hate, aversion, sadness, hope, daring, despair, fear, and anger. The sequence of the questions in the *Treatise on the Passions* is pedagogically organized to illustrate how the various passions relate to each other, and how all of the passions are ordered to the sense appetite's inclination toward sensible goods. After discussing the passions in general (q. 22–25), Aquinas begins with love (q. 26–28), which is the font of the rest. He continues with the other passions as they flow from love, first the other concupiscible passions and then the irascible passions, and finally concludes with anger (q. 46–48), the most unusual and complex of the passions. This chapter will discuss the structure of the passions, with particular attention to clarifying the intentional object of each elemental passion.[4]

The Two Parts of the Sense Appetite

Aquinas identifies two basic categories of intentional objects and therefore two basic categories of passions. Accordingly, he divides the sense appetite into two distinct powers: the concupiscible power (*concupiscibilis*) and the irascible power (*irascibilis*).[5]

In the sensitive part of the soul there are two appetitive powers. By one the soul is simply inclined to pursue what is agreeable to the senses and to pull back

the *Scriptum super libros Sententiarum* (see especially *Sentences* III.26) and remains unmodified in later works. Nonetheless, some key aspects derive from John of La Rochelle. All of Aquinas's eleven passions, for instance, are also found in John of La Rochelle. Aquinas's originality and taxonomical innovations are in his metaphysics and the principles of classification that undergird his system. See John of La Rochelle, *Tractatus de divisione multiplici potentiarum animae*, ed. Pierre Michaud-Quantin (Paris: J. Vrin, 1964); Gondreau, *Passions of Christ's Soul*, 211–18; and Knuuttila, *Emotions*, 243.

4. Of recent scholarship on the structure of the passions and the individual characteristics of the passions, two authors merit special mention: Marcos Manzanedo and Alexander Brungs. Manzanedo has written over fifteen different articles on various aspects of Aquinas's thought on the passions. His work is particularly invaluable insofar as it reviews all of Aquinas's writings, not just the *Summa*, and gives them a close reading. The recent monograph of Alexander Brungs gives an analysis of the metaphysics of the passions in Aquinas; it is more concerned with principles than with a close reading of texts. Both are excellent resources for all of the topics raised in this chapter. For a brief overview and analysis of the structure of the passions and their relations among themselves, see King, "Aquinas on the Passions," 359–67.

5. Aquinas appropriates this division from Aristotle, Nemesius of Emesa, and John Damascene and makes it his own. He probably takes the idea of making an arduous object the defining characteristic of the irascible passions from John of La Rochelle (Knuuttila, *Emotions*, 243).

from what is harmful, and this is called the concupiscible. By the other the soul resists whatever would attack what it finds agreeable and cause harm, and this power is called the irascible. Hence the irascible power's object is called arduous, because it tends to rise above obstacles and overcome them.[6]

Aquinas makes various distinctions among the passions, but only *concupiscibilis* and *irascibilis* constitute separate powers. The concupiscible passions concern first-order desires, aversions, pleasures, and pains. The irascible passions presuppose the concupiscible passions: they are second-order desires and aversions that defend the inclinations of the concupiscible passions and evaporate when the concupiscible power attains its goals.[7] The irascible power is "a kind of defender and protector of the concupiscible power, rising against whatever gets in the way of what is agreeable, which the concupiscible power desires, and whatever threatens harm, which the concupiscible power flees. Thus all of the passions of the irascible power begin in the concupiscible passions and then terminate in them."[8]

The possibility that the same material object can generate conflicting passions is what proves the necessity of the distinction between the inclinations of the concupiscible and irascible powers: "These two inclinations cannot be reduced to a single principle. For sometimes the soul engages distressing matters, against the inclination of the concupiscible power, so that it can follow the inclination of the irascible power and battle against obstacles."[9] Other kinds of conflict are possible, as when someone desires two entrées but must choose only one. But the conflict between concupiscible and irascible passions that Aquinas mentions here is of a different order: in this case, the conflicting passions have their origins in the same object, rather than in two different objects. Aquinas reasons that the possibility of such conflict proves that there must be two different powers that respond to objects under two different aspects: the aspect of desirability in the case of

6. *ST* I 81.2.

7. *ST* I-II 23.1, 25.1, 40.1. Other scholars sometimes use similar language and talk about first-order and second-order desires, although perhaps with some differences in meaning. For a discussion of Aquinas that employs this terminology, see Pestana, "Second Order Desires and Strength of Will."

8. *ST* I 81.2. Aquinas derives some of his understanding of the concupiscible and irascible distinction from Nemesius (whom he confuses with Gregory of Nyssa) and John Damascene. He draws a particularly striking image from Nemesius: "Gregory of Nyssa says that anger is a kind of armor-bearer of desire, in that anger fights against whatever would thwart desire" (*ST* I-II 46.2 obj 1; Nemesius, *De natura hominis*, 21).

9. *ST* I 81.2.

the concupiscible power and the aspect of usefulness with respect to first-order desires in the case of the irascible power.[10] He writes, "The concupiscible power looks to goods that are pleasurable to the senses and naturally suitable, while the irascible power looks to goods that repulse and attack what is harmful."[11]

The objects of the irascible power, therefore, are the same as those of the concupiscible power, except that they are apprehended under the aspect of the arduous or difficult, and thus constitute a different sort of intentional object. He explains:

> The object of the concupiscible power is sensible good or evil simply accepted as either pleasurable or distressing. But sometimes the soul encounters difficulty or struggle in obtaining something good or in fleeing from something evil, because it is beyond its natural power to do so easily. The object of the irascible power, therefore, is this sort of good or evil considered as being arduous or difficult to either obtain or avoid.[12]

The irascible passions have their origins in the desires and aversions of the concupiscible power, and ultimately end there, coming to rest in either pleasure or sadness.[13] Because the concupiscible passions include pleasure and sadness and thus actually rest in objects, they are more diverse than the irascible passions, which only seek or avoid objects.[14] Moreover, the irascible passions are aroused exclusively in the face of some threat to desire. For this reason, Aquinas maintains that we will not experience the irascible passions in heaven and that, except for the passion of hope, Adam and Eve did not experience them in the Garden of Eden.[15]

In defining the irascible passions according to the arduous or difficult, Aquinas relegates tense to secondary importance.[16] For Aquinas, the most

10. This interpretation of the irascible power is indebted to Anna Terruwe and Conrad Baars, who evocatively refer to the concupiscible power as the pleasure appetite and the irascible power as the utility appetite.

11. *ST* I 82.5.

12. *ST* I-II 23.1. See also *ST* I-II 46.3. For a discussion of the meaning of *arduum* in Aquinas, see René Antoine Gauthier, *Magnanimité: l'idéal de la grandeur dans la philosophie païenne et dans la théologie chrétienne* (Paris: J. Vrin, 1951), 322–25.

13. *ST* I-II 23.1 ad 1, 25.1.

14. *ST* I-II 25.1.

15. *ST* I 95.2; *ST* I-II 67.1, 67.4. Aquinas also denies that there will be desire or pleasure in heaven with regard to either food or sex in *ST* I-II 67.1.

16. For a discussion of the place of tense and presence in Aquinas's account of the passions, see James, *Passion and Action,* 59–60.

defining feature of a passion is not whether its object is present or future, but whether or not it is difficult to obtain or avoid. For example, desire and hope each have an intentional object that is absent and therefore future. Nonetheless, Aquinas does not group them together in opposition to those passions that concern present objects, such as pleasure and sadness. Instead, they are distinguished from each other as being passions of the concupiscible and irascible powers respectively, thus indicating that, for Aquinas, the presence or absence of an arduous difficulty is more important than tense.

Susan James suggests that the distinction between those concupiscible and irascible passions that are oriented toward future objects amounts to a distinction between passions whose future object is expected with certainty and those whose future object is uncertain.[17] However, Aquinas never explicitly correlates the irascible passions with uncertain objects, and other texts contradict this reading of Aquinas. For example, as mentioned above, Aquinas claims that Adam could experience the passion of hope in the Garden of Eden. In this idyllic state, the objects of Adam's hope would normally be certain as well as difficult. For instance, Adam might hope to plant a vegetable garden, knowing that it would require long hours and heavy lifting, with the certain expectation that he would eventually succeed. So, for Aquinas, certain expectation would not prevent an object from being arduous.

The technical Latin terms that Aquinas uses for the two powers of the sense appetite, *concupiscibilis* and *irascibilis,* are taken from William of Moerbeke's translation of Aristotle's *epithumetike* and *thumike.*[18] These words have negative connotations in their etymological origins and associations that can obscure the meaning that Aquinas assigns them. *Concupiscentia,* the root of *concupiscibilis,* can signify lust as well as a general sort of desire. Furthermore, Augustine had coined a technical use of *concupiscentia* to describe the tendency toward sin and disordered pleasure caused by original sin, and Aquinas himself sometimes uses the word in this technical sense.[19] Consequently, the category of *concupiscibilis* has negative associations with sinful desire that are not intended. Similarly, *ira,* the passion of anger and

17. "The salient point about hope and fear is not just that they are directed to the future, but that their futurity introduces an element of uncertainty as to whether an end will be achieved or avoided which is itself a kind of obstacle or difficulty" (James, *Passion and Action,* 59).

18. D'Arcy, Introduction to *Summa,* vol. 19, xxv.

19. See *ST* I-II 85.3.

the root of *irascibilis,* also has misleading connotations. First, the passion of anger itself often has negative connotations of disorder and sin. Second, as was the norm, Aquinas uses *ira* to denote the vice of anger as well as the passion of anger. Since the passion of anger gives its name to the category of *irascibilis,* these negative associations can seem to carry over to the irascible passions.

These negative connotations are clearly not intended by Aquinas. These terms and their negative associations are simply part of his inherited vocabulary. Aquinas unequivocally presents all of the elemental passions, including the passions of desire and anger, as ontologically good in themselves and capable of being shaped by virtue, even if they are all prone to disorder in our fallen condition. Similarly, Aquinas sometimes, but not always, uses *sensualitas* in a neutral sense, as a synonym for sense appetite, though the Latin word and its English cognate "sensuality" are rife with negative connotations.[20]

The confusion escalates in English because only the negative connotations have survived for the rarely used cognates "concupiscible" and "irascible." Many contemporary scholars have proposed other translations because of these words' obscurity and their negative associations.[21] While many of these translations are more accessible and therefore preferable for general use, the sheer number of alternative proposals witnesses to their inadequacy. In order to avoid a misleading translation and to highlight the etymological origins and connections between key terms, this study will use the more traditional terminology of "concupiscible" and "irascible" as placeholders for their Latin cognates.

The Concupiscible Passions

The concupiscible passions concern the inclination to sensible goods, the repugnance to sensible evils, and the affective experience caused by either's presence (figure 2-1). Aquinas emphasizes those passions oriented toward goods (love, desire, and pleasure) more than those concerned with

20. See *ST* I 81.1, *ST* I-II 74.3.

21. Alternative translations for "concupiscible" include: desirous, impulse, mild, affective, resting, and pleasure. Alternative translations for "irascible" include: aggressive, contending, striving, and utility.

Figure 2-1. The Concupiscible Passions

Cognition of good object → love (*amor*)
- Absent good → desire (*concupiscentia*)
- Present good → pleasure (*delectatio*)

Cognition of evil object → hatred (*odium*)
- Absent evil → aversion (*fuga*) or repulsion (*abominatio*)
- Present evil → sorrow (*tristitia*) or pain (*dolor*)

evils (hate, aversion, and sorrow), demonstrating again that he is primarily interested in happiness rather than its obstacles.[22]

The passion of love (*amor*) spawns the other concupiscible passions, just as the concupiscible passions taken as a whole spawn the irascible passions. Consequently, "love is the first of the concupiscible passions."[23] Love is the response elicited by a good when it is apprehended as *conveniens*, that is, as suitable or agreeable, and it implies that there is some kind of similarity between the apprehender and the apprehended object.[24] Aquinas describes love as "complacency in something desirable" (*complacentia appetibilis*).[25] This complacency leads to desire (*concupiscentia*), an affective movement toward an object that is not possessed, and pleasure (*delectatio*), a kind of repose in an object that is possessed.[26] The essential difference

22. There are three questions on love, one on desire, and four on pleasure, versus one question on hatred, none on aversion, and five on sorrow (one of which is concerned with remedies to sorrow).

23. *ST* I-II 25.2. Aquinas draws on Augustine's articulation of love's ontological precedence. See Augustine, *City of God*, 14.7.

24. *ST* I-II 27.3, 29.1. See Sherwin, *By Knowledge and By Love*, 73–74.

25. *ST* I-II 26.2. For an extended discussion of love as complacency in Aquinas, see Frederick E. Crowe, "Complacency and Concern in the Thought of St. Thomas," *Theological Studies* 20 (1959): 1–39, 198–230, 343–82. See also Sherwin, *By Knowledge and By Love*, 64–81, and Arkadius Gudaniec, "Amore come *complacentia boni* in Tomasso d'Aquino," in *Proceedings of the International Congress on Christian Humanism in the Third Millennium: The Perspective of Thomas Aquinas: 21–25 September 2003* (Vatican City: Pontificia Academia Sancti Thomae Aquinatis, 2004), 497–504.

26. *ST* I-II 25.2, 26.2, 30.2. By common usage and Aquinas's deliberate intention, *concupiscentia*, strictly speaking, refers only to the desire for sensible goods, and is sometimes translated as "sensory desire" for that reason. Similarly, although *delectatio* does not refer exclusively to sensory pleasure, he prefers to use *delectatio* for pleasure that is bodily or sensible. Occasionally he also uses *gaudium* or (quoting Augustine in *ST* I-II 25.2) *laetitia* for sensible pleasure. For a discussion of *delectatio* in Aquinas, see L. Massara, "La «delectatio» dans la psychologie de Saint Thomas d'Aquin," *Archives de Philosophie* 27 (1964): 186–205.

between the intentional objects of desire and pleasure is best expressed as a difference between absence and presence: desire seeks an absent good and pleasure rests in a present good.[27] Sometimes Aquinas or commentators will oppose the objects in terms of present versus future, or possessed versus non-possessed, and although these distinctions are valid, strictly speaking, they can be misleading. It is not an object's temporal and spatial presence that ultimately matters, but its mental presence. A subject can take pleasure in a past or future good by thinking about it, thus making it mentally present. Also, a subject might not enjoy a present good if it is not mentally present as a good, as when some distraction spoils an otherwise pleasurable event.[28] The same clarification applies to his discussion of the other passions: it is mental presence and mental absence that matter, not tense or possession per se.[29]

In his taxonomy of the passions, while Aquinas distinguishes between present and future objects, he does not give attention to past objects, even though his account presumes that past objects can arouse the passions. His system, however, can fully accommodate them, if his distinction between presence and futurity is understood more precisely as a distinction between presence and absence. Insofar as past objects are experienced as mentally present or mentally absent through the mediation of memory, everything that applies to present or future objects also applies to past objects. Thinking about a past good might generate a combination of pleasure and desire: pleasure, insofar as the subject perceives the material object as mentally possessed and therefore present, and desire, insofar as the subject perceives the material object as absent.[30] The plausibility of applying his system to past objects in this way supports an interpretation that sees the phenomenological categories of presence and absence as more important

27. "The motivating power of a good differs according to whether it is present or absent in reality. When present, a good causes the appetite to rest in it; when, however, a good is absent, it causes the appetite to move toward it" (*ST* I-II 30.2). For a discussion of the relevance of presence and absence to Aquinas's account of desire and delight, see Drost, "Aquinas on Intentionality," 457.

28. Aquinas explicitly discusses how non-possessed goods can cause pleasure insofar as they are mentally possessed (see *ST* I-II 32.1 ad 1, 32.3, 36.2 ad 3, 48.1).

29. In his interest in the presence and absence of objects, Aquinas anticipates a major theme of contemporary phenomenology. For an overview of the topic of presence and absence, see Sokolowski, *Introduction to Phenomenology*, 33–40.

30. For Aquinas, what we would call "nostalgia" might then be understood as the simultaneous experience of multiple passions in response to the memory of a past object.

to Aquinas's understanding of passion than the metaphysical categories of past, present, and future.

Negative concupiscible passions are evoked by a repugnant object. The first of these is hatred (*odium*), which he defines as the contrary of love. Just as the object of love is a good, the object of hatred is an evil: "Love is a certain consonance of appetite with something apprehended as agreeable, while hatred is a certain dissonance of appetite with something apprehended as repulsive and harmful."[31] But hatred is not just the contrary of love; it derives from love since "nothing can be hated unless it opposes something agreeable that is loved."[32] Aquinas's account of hatred thus parallels his metaphysical account of evil as privation: the affective response of hatred is parasitic on the good, in the sense of responding to the absence of something good and lovable, rather than something entirely hateful. Hatred leads to the passion of avoidance, called aversion (*fuga*) or repulsion (*abominatio*), and then, if the evil becomes present, to the passion of resting in an evil, that is, sorrow (*tristitia*) or pain (*dolor*).[33]

There are some difficulties in understanding Aquinas's account of the passion of love. His descriptions of love are evocative but also elusive. Aquinas employs multiple phrases to characterize the passion of love:[34] affinity with (*connaturalitas*) or aptness to (*coaptatio*) some good;[35] a certain consonance (*consonantia quaedam* with something agreeable);[36] affective union (*unio affectiva*);[37] a change caused in the appetite (*immutatione appetitus*) by the appetible object;[38] movement toward good (*accessum ad bonum*);[39] complacency in some good (*complacentia boni*);[40] and complacency in something desirable (*complacentia appetitibilis*).[41] These phrases communicate a general sense of Aquinas's account of the passion of love, which seems plausible enough, considered in itself. However, because these phrases suggest features also associated with desire and pleasure,[42] it is difficult to grasp what precisely these expressions could signify concretely that would be dif-

31. *ST* I-II 29.1.
32. *ST* I-II 29.2.
33. *ST* I-II 23.2, 23.4.
34. *ST* I-II 23.4, 25.2, 26.1, 26.2, 27.1, 27.4, 28.1, 29.1, 29.2 obj 3, 32.3 ad 3.
35. *ST* I-II 27.4.
36. *ST* I-II 29.1.
37. *ST* I-II 25.2 ad 2.
38. *ST* I-II 26.2.
39. *ST* I-II 29.2 obj 3.
40. *ST* I-II 26.1.
41. *ST* I-II 26.2.
42. Sherwin similarly notes that the terms Aquinas uses to describe love convey a "dual character" that involves "incipient enjoyment, without excluding full enjoyment." Sherwin goes

ferent from the psychological phenomena already staked out by the passions of desire and pleasure and their respective striving and resting.[43]

One way to clarify Aquinas's account of love is to focus on its functional role in relation to other concupiscible passions. Aquinas specifies that love is the first inclination toward the possession of a good.[44] He writes, "The first principle of appetitive movement is love, which is the first inclination of the appetite toward the attaining of a good."[45] As an inclination toward the attaining of some good, the passion of love is a movement toward complacency in that good without actually being a movement toward the good itself. He writes: "Although love does not name an appetitive movement that tends toward something desirable, it does name an appetitive movement in which the appetite is changed by the desirable object, so that the appetite becomes complacent in the desirable object."[46] Even though love is a movement in a general sense, love is not a movement in the more specific sense of being a movement toward a good. Desire is the movement toward a good,

---

on to argue that Aquinas's choice of words underlines the role of love as "the principle of both desire and enjoyment" (Sherwin, *By Knowledge and By Love,* 78–79).

43. Although opposed to interpretations of Aquinas that emphasize love as movement, rather than love as resting in the good, Crowe acknowledges that both understandings of love are present in Aquinas's writings. He concludes that Aquinas did not sufficiently clarify his thought on the passion of love: "St. Thomas never brought these two notions into careful confrontation or worked out extensively their relations to one another, with the result that two contrasting and unintegrated lines of thought show up in a whole series of questions" (Crowe, "Complacency and Concern," 3).

44. Aquinas comes to a deeper appreciation of the importance of classifying love as an inclination (*inclinatio*) over the course of his life. H.-D. Simonin makes a case for such an evolution, contrasting, for example, *Scriptum super libros Sententiarum* III 27.1.2 and III 27.1.3, which emphasize love as the *termination* and *quietatio* of appetite, respectively, with *ST* I-II 23.4, which speaks of love as an *inclinatio.* Simonin argues that in his mature writings Aquinas emphasizes love as movement over love as rest, in part because Simonin associates *inclinatio* more with movement than rest. See H.-D. Simonin, "Autour de la solution thomiste du problem de l'amour," *Archives d'histoire doctrinale et littéraire du moyen âge* 6 (1931): 174–274, and Sherwin, *By Knowledge and By Love,* 78n67.

Sherwin sees a similar progression, agreeing with Simonin that the later Aquinas moves away from an understanding of love that emphasizes rest, and regards this development as the result of Aquinas's clarification of his understanding of the relationship between knowing and loving. He writes that in Aquinas's description of love's *complacentia* in *ST* I-II 28.2, "Aquinas now seems to recognize more clearly that the 'rest' proper to love is not inactivity, but full actuality" (Sherwin, *By Knowledge and By Love,* 77). However, Sherwin convincingly challenges Simonin's interpretation that *inclinatio* primarily signifies a motion or impulse, arguing instead that "*inclinatio* primarily signifies a *principle* of motion. It is the appetitive orientation of the appetite toward its object" (78n67).

45. *ST* I-II 36.2.

46. *ST* I-II 26.2 ad 3.

while love is an inclination or a kind of complacency, and, as such, the principle of desire and pleasure and the rest of the passions.

But even after this clarification, the distinction between love and desire remains murky. If desire is the movement toward an object, what room is there for another passion that moves from an indifferent state toward complacency in the object, without actually moving toward the object?[47] These two types of movement cannot be distinguished physically, since both are psychological forms of movement: it is not that desire involves physical movement, but love does not. Nor is it that desire involves voluntary psychic movement, but love does not, since either kind of passion can be pleasing or displeasing to the will in a specific instance. Could desire and love be distinguished by saying that desire prompts voluntary action, but love simply rests in the good without prompting voluntary action? Perhaps, but then it would be impossible to distinguish love from pleasure. Complicating the task of clarification is Aquinas's affirmation that love always coexists with either desire or pleasure.[48] Consequently, according to Aquinas, we cannot isolate love's characteristics from those of desire by imagining what it would be like to feel love without desire, insofar as it is metaphysically impossible to have such an experience.[49]

47. Knuuttila also notes ambiguities in Aquinas's account of the relationship between love, desire, and joy, especially concerning the sense in which desire is a movement. See Knuuttila, *Emotions*, 249–51.

48. Aquinas quotes Augustine with approval: "Love longing to have what it loves is desire, while love having what it loves and the benefit of it is joy" (*ST* I-II 25.2; Augustine, *City of God*, 14.7). By way of comparison, Augustine avoids the problems Aquinas encounters because, being less metaphysically oriented, he is content to define love in terms of desire and joy. For Augustine, love is a twofold passion manifested as either desire or joy, and it is not distinct from either.

49. Mark Drost interprets Aquinas differently on this point. He claims that, according to Aquinas, it is indeed possible to experience love without desire. "The ontological possibility of loving something without taking delight in it or desiring it," he writes, "is a consequence of Aquinas's understanding of the passion of love." See Mark P. Drost, "In the Realm of the Senses: Saint Thomas Aquinas on Sensory Love, Desire, and Delight," *Thomist* 59 (1995): 48.

If Drost is correct, then much of the above critique about Aquinas's handling of love and desire would collapse. However, he gives no textual evidence that Aquinas would hold that it is possible to experience love without either desire or pleasure. Drost himself acknowledges that "where there is love there typically will be delight (or desire)" (58). Furthermore, Drost gives no explanation why the "inclination" and "complacency" that he sees as essential characteristics of love cannot be understood as aspects of desire and pleasure, respectively. Without a clear, unambiguous distinction between inclination and desire, and between complacency and pleasure, it is difficult to maintain that it is ontologically possible to experience love without either desire or pleasure.

Christopher Malloy proposes the same interpretation of Aquinas given here, namely, that love is always accompanied by either desire or pleasure. He also explicitly disagrees with Drost

It is striking that Aquinas seems to have struggled to clarify the relationship between love and desire: his thought evolves over the course of his career before settling on the mature doctrine found in the *Summa*. Earlier in his life, Aquinas often places desire before love in his ordering of the passions, but the later Aquinas unequivocally ranks love before desire in the order of appetitive movements.[50] Also, in his earlier writings, Aquinas draws an analogy between love and cognition, but in his mature writings he avoids any such analogy and emphasizes that love is a movement or inclination, seemingly because he comes to think that this analogy is misleading, insofar as it blurs the line between cognition and appetite.[51] While the fact of Aquinas's evolution does not prove anything, in light of the interpretive difficulties that remain in his mature writings, it does suggest that Aquinas himself sensed that his distinction between love and desire was difficult to reconcile with some of his metaphysical principles. Aquinas's treatments of hatred and aversion manifest similar ambiguity. He defines hatred as dissonance with some evil and aversion as the movement away from the evil, but it is hard to understand how hatred could be a movement from an indifferent state toward dissonance with an object, and yet not involve any movement away from it.[52]

---

on this point. See Christopher J. Malloy, "Thomas on the Order of Love and Desire: A Development of Doctrine," *Thomist* 71 (2007): 67n6.

50. At some points in his commentary on the *Sentences*, Aquinas affirms that desire precedes love. In two passages, Aquinas holds that desire (*desiderium*), which has to do with a good not yet possessed, precedes love (*amor*), which has to do with a good that is possessed (*Scriptum super libros Sententiarum* II 1.2.1, III 26.2.3.2). Most notably, in a first draft written in his own hand, Aquinas states that desire (*concupiscentia vel desiderium*) is the "first of the concupiscible passions" and precedes the passion of love (*Scriptum super libros Sententiarum* III 26.1.3). For the text of this first draft, see P.-M. Gils, "Textes inédits de S. Thomas: Les premières rédactions du *Scriptum super Tertio Sententiarum*," *Revue des sciences philosophiques et théologiques* 46 (1962): 460. However, even in his earlier writings, there are some other places where he emphasizes the precedence of love over desire (see *Scriptum super libros Sententiarum* III 27.2.1, III 27.1.3). So his early writings are marked by some amount of ambiguity. Nonetheless, Aquinas's final position in the *Summa* is consistent and unambiguous: "desire (*desiderium*) of some thing always presupposes love (*amor*) of that thing" (*ST* I-II 27.4 ad 2). Malloy "Order of Love and Desire," 65–87.

51. In his early writings, Aquinas describes love as the reception of the form of the loved object into the appetite, and he draws an explicit analogy to how the intellect receives the form of the thing known. This invocation of form is absent from his discussion of love in the *Treatise on the Passions*, which describes love in terms of movement or inclination. For example, compare *Scriptum super libros Sententiarum* III 27.1.1 and *ST* I-II 23.4, 36.2 (Sherwin, *By Knowledge and By Love*, 64–81, and H.-D. Simonin, "Problem de l'amour," 179–84). Sherwin argues that Aquinas moved away from his earlier descriptions of love because he realized that they do not sufficiently differentiate between cognition and appetite.

52. Eric D'Arcy also questions whether the distinction between hatred and aversion has any substance (see D'Arcy, Notes to *Summa*, vol. 19, 28–29 note c).

A related puzzle is the nature of love's intentional object. The intentional object of desire is an absent good, and the intentional object of pleasure is a present good. For Aquinas, love's intentional object somehow incorporates both present and absent goods, and yet this intentional object cannot be identified with either category—otherwise love would simply be reduced to desire or pleasure, since passions are identified by their intentional object. It is difficult to imagine how love's intentional object might be defined without compromising love's status as a distinct and elemental passion. Only for love and hatred does Aquinas avoid any clarification of the nature of the intentional object vis-à-vis presence and absence; the objects of all the other passions are characterized by either presence or absence. In the article where Aquinas explains why desire is a distinct passion from either love or pleasure, we might expect some clarification about the differences in their intentional objects, especially since, in the first objection, he notes that the passions are distinguished by their objects.[53] However, Aquinas distinguishes love and desire not by object, but by the object's effect on the appetite—that is, whether the object adapts the appetite to itself or attracts the appetite to itself—and so sidesteps any clarification of the precise nature of love's intentional object. His reticence on this question highlights again the difficulty of determining exactly how love is different from desire.

The inclusion of love among the passions has intuitive appeal—if love is not a passion, what is? Moreover, the systematic unification of the passions in the passion of love has a certain elegance, as witnessed by the perennial attraction of the idea, which was first set forward by Augustine and experienced a major revival as late as in seventeenth-century philosophy.[54] And since Aquinas holds that the first movement of every appetite is the love (*amor*) proper to it,[55] his theory of appetite requires him to postulate a passion of love.

Nonetheless, the passion of love does not seem to have a function in Aquinas's account of the passions that is unequivocally distinct from the

53. *ST* I-II 30.2.

54. See Augustine, *City of God* 14.7, and James, *Passion and Action*, 6. Augustine maintains that the passions of desire, joy, fear, and sadness are different aspects of love: "For love that strives to have that which is loved is desire (*cupiditas*), just as love which has and enjoys what is loved is joy (*laetitia*); love which flees from what threatens is fear (*timor*), and if what is feared comes to pass, love that feels it is sadness (*tristitia*)."

55. Aquinas maintains that love has ontological precedence in every kind of appetite: "The first movement of the will, and of any appetitive power, is love" (*ST* I 20.1).

functions of desire and pleasure. However, even if it turns out that this ambiguity is without a satisfactory solution, and, according to Aquinas's metaphysical principles, the postulation of the passion of love cannot be justified, the absence of love from his system would not cause it to crumble.[56] The essential structure of his system can be preserved by interpreting the sense appetite itself, in place of love, as the principle of desire and pleasure. Also, the qualities Aquinas attributes to the passion of love can be interpreted as a combination of apprehension, desire, and pleasure: apprehension subsuming the attentiveness of love; desire subsuming the movement of love; and pleasure subsuming the complacency of love. The contrary passion of hate similarly might be dissolved into apprehension and the passions of aversion and sadness, with the sense appetite serving as the principle of aversion and sadness.[57] This revision accounts for all the psychological phenomena that Aquinas attributes to either love or hate and also eliminates ambiguity and redundancy from his account of the concupiscible passions.

The Irascible Passions

After analyzing each concupiscible passion in turn, Aquinas turns his attention to the irascible passions (figure 2-2). Irascible passions always involve the concupiscible passions, of which there is at least some distinct preliminary and partial awareness. For example, the fear that results from hearing a sudden noise in a dark alley is ontologically dependent on the accompanying passion of aversion. The irascible passions concern the interests of the concupiscible passions in the face of some difficulty: namely, the attainment of future goods (hope and despair), the avoidance or overcoming of future evils (daring and fear), and the elimination of present evils (anger).

The concupiscible passions are defined as concupiscible more by the

56. Drost might disagree with this analysis. He argues that the distinction between love and desire is important and crucial: "Delight intends its object as present, whereas desire intends its object as absent; but love intends its object as such. . . . [L]ove transcends the difference between desire and delight" (Drost, "Aquinas on Intentionality," 455).

57. In *ST* I-II 46.6 ad 3, Aquinas maintains that the passion of hate lasts longer than the passion of anger, because hate results from a disposition, whereas anger responds to an injury. The connection he draws between hate and disposition gives further reason to think that the sense appetite with all its inherent dispositions can account for many of the phenomena that Aquinas associates with the passion of hate.

Figure 2-2. The Irascible Passions

Cognition of arduous future good { Seems possible to obtain → hope (*spes*)
Seems impossible to obtain → despair (*desperatio*) }

Cognition of arduous future evil { Seems possible to overcome → daring (*audacia*)
Seems impossible to overcome → fear (*timor*) }

Cognition of arduous present evil with hope of overcoming → anger (*ira*)

goods that the sense appetite inclines toward than the evils it avoids. Conversely, the irascible passions are defined as irascible more by an evil (some obstacle) than by the good whose attainment it blocks or the evil whose avoidance it makes difficult. The etymology of *concupiscibilis* and *irascibilis* reflect this structural distinction, since the former's derivation from *concupiscentia* suggests an emphasis on good objects (the object of desire) and the latter's derivation from *ira* suggests an emphasis on evil objects (the object of anger). Moreover, just as Aquinas gives disproportionate attention to those concupiscible passions whose intentional objects are goods, he also gives disproportionate attention to those irascible passions whose intentional objects are evils, particularly fear and anger, thus emphasizing that evils of one kind or another are more defining of the irascible passions than goods.[58]

Unlike the concupiscible passions, the irascible passions differ not just by object (good or evil), but by direction of movement (toward or away).[59] Consequently, each irascible passion has two contraries, whereas each concupiscible passion has only one: "The irascible passions are opposed to each other in two ways. The first is the opposition of good and evil, and in this way fear is contrary to hope. The second is the opposition of approach and retreat, and in this way fear is contrary to daring and hope is contrary to despair."[60] The exception is anger, a movement toward an arduous pres-

58. There are four questions on fear, three on anger, one on daring, and one split between hope and despair.

59. *ST* I-II 23.2, 40.4.

60. *ST* I-II 45.1 ad 2.

ent evil, which has no contrary.[61] The contrary of anger would be an irascible drive toward a present good, but there could not be anything arduous about a present good, and therefore there is no such passion.[62] As with the concupiscible passions, Aquinas gives much attention to pairing the irascible passions with their contraries in the *Treatise on the Passions* and elsewhere. In his view, the passions turn on polarities, and this ordering therefore constitutes one of the principal structural (and mnemonic) elements in his systematic understanding of the passions.[63]

Aquinas begins his analysis of the irascible passions with hope (*spes*). He writes, "Hope is a movement of appetite following the apprehension of a future good that is arduous but possible to obtain. It is a straining of appetite toward this sort of object."[64] It is similar to some kinds of desire, since desire also has a future good as its object, but hope responds to a future good qua arduous. He writes: "The object of hope must be something arduous and difficult to obtain, for it is not said that one hopes for something trivial that is always in one's power to have. In this way, hope differs from the desire or longing whose object is a future good without qualification. The latter belongs to the concupiscible power, while hope belongs the irascible power."[65] Hope, then, turns on the judgment that the object is difficult but possible to attain. The cognitive evaluation of possibility is crucial: hope is not elicited by the apprehension of a good believed impossible to attain.[66] When an arduous good is judged impossible to attain, the passion of despair (*desperatio*) follows instead of hope.[67] The object of both hope and despair is a good, but the quality of the intentional object proper to each

61. *ST* I-II 23.3, 46.1 ad 2.

62. *ST* I-II 23.3–4, 25.3.

63. Aquinas follows Aristotle's enumeration of different kinds of oppositions (see Aristotle, *Metaphysics,* V.10, 1018a20). Since other pairings of the passions are possible, the way Aquinas chooses to group the passions according to oppositions, and the way he chooses to frame these oppositions, is significant. Note that, in Aquinas's system, these kinds of oppositions turn on object and movement, thus emphasizing once again the importance of these two concepts to his account of the passions.

Since the irascible passions can be contrary in two respects, they can be paired according to opposition in object (i.e., hope and daring, despair and fear) or they can be paired according to opposition in both object and movement (i.e., hope and fear, despair and daring), as he discusses in *ST* I-II 23.2. In his actual structuring of the *Summa,* he pairs them according to a common object: i.e., hope and despair are opposed responses to a good, and fear and daring are opposed responses to an evil.

64. *ST* I-II 40.2.

65. *ST* I-II 40.1.

66. *ST* I-II 40.1 ad 3, 40.5.

67. *ST* I-II 40.4.

passion varies according to the judgment of the object's attainability. The intentional object of hope is a good, an attainable arduous good, and the intentional object of despair is an evil, an unattainable arduous good. Although hope depends on the cognitive evaluation of an object as possible to obtain, Aquinas is emphatic that "hope belongs, not to the cognitive power, but to the appetitive power."[68] Hope hangs on a judgment of possibility, but consists in the desire for an arduous good. A parallel analysis applies to despair: despair hangs on a judgment of impossibility, but consists in the withdrawal from an arduous good.

After covering hope and despair, Aquinas turns to fear (*timor*).[69] Aquinas defines the object of fear as a threatening future evil not easily resisted or even irresistible.[70] Like the other passions, it derives from love, since one fears only what is contrary to something loved.[71] Fear is similar to aversion but differs because its object is difficult to avoid.[72] When the same object is judged to be conquerable, it elicits daring (*audacia*) instead. Whereas fear shrinks from a threat, daring advances and seeks to overcome it.[73] Daring and fear share the same object, but each responds to a different aspect of that object: evil as conquerable (a good) and evil as irresistible (an evil), respectively. The difference between the two passions, therefore, turns on a cognitive judgment about the object, as it does for hope and despair.

Anger (*ira*) is the fifth irascible passion and the most complex: caused by sadness, it reaches out in hope for the elimination of that sadness. It at-

68. *ST* I-II 40.2.

69. For a more detailed treatment of Aquinas's account of fear, see Stephen Loughlin, "The Complexity and Importance of *timor* in Aquinas' *Summa Theologiae*," in *Fear and Its Representations in the Middle Ages and Renaissance*, ed. Anne Scott and Cynthia Kosso (Tempe: Arizona Center for Middle Ages and Renaissance Studies Publications, 2002), 1–16.

70. *ST* I-II 41.2, 43.1. Notably, Aquinas holds that fear itself can be feared. Although he does not develop this observation, the idea of one passion having another passion as its object has interesting implications, especially after Freud, as Terruwe and Baars have shown. Aquinas also states, without explanation, that we can love love and grieve about sorrow (*ST* I-II 42.4). Similarly, in the *Secunda secundae*, Aquinas holds that in a certain sense charity can be the object of charity. Here he offers a sustained argument and explanation that seems to shed light on his undefended assertion about loving love and grieving about sorrow (see *ST* II-II 25.2). The idea that passions can have other passions as their objects takes on crucial significance in Anna Terruwe's interpretation of Freud's concept of repression from within a Thomistic framework. See Anna A. Terruwe, *The Neurosis in the Light of Rational Psychology*, trans. Conrad W. Baars (New York: P. J. Kenedy and Sons, 1960).

71. *ST* I-II 43.1; *ST* II-II 125.2.

72. Aquinas discusses the differences between *fuga* and *timor* in *ST* I-II 41.2 ad 2.

73. *ST* I-II 45.1.

tacks what frustrates desire and seeks to eliminate it.[74] Accordingly, Aquinas defines anger as the desire for revenge (*vindicta*),[75] with revenge understood in a neutral sense without negative connotations, and thus including, for instance, the elimination of some injustice against the poor. It is the only passion that has two objects: "the revenge that it desires and the person on whom it seeks revenge," a good and an evil respectively.[76] As well as having a twofold object, anger is caused by the concurrence of multiple passions, and "does not arise unless one has endured some distress and unless there is desire and hope of revenge."[77] Aquinas goes on to say that anger is "in a certain way" (*quodammodo*) composed of different passions, though he stresses that anger is composed of sadness and desire "not as parts but as causes."[78] Apparently, he means that anger is closely connected in its origins to these passions, but is itself distinct from them. Hope is also important to anger. Without the hope for revenge—for example, when facing a vastly more powerful enemy—an injury inspires not anger but only sadness.[79] Anger is also accompanied by some pleasure in anticipation of its satisfaction. Once revenge is attained, anger turns entirely to pleasure, and the deeper the injury that aroused the anger, the greater the pleasure.[80]

Following Aristotle, Aquinas specifies that anger does not respond to any kind of evil, but only to those that involve some perceived injustice against oneself.[81] He allows that there is a sense in which one can get angry at inanimate objects and nonrational creatures, like a writer getting angry at his pen or a rider at his horse. Still, injury or injustice must be perceived as somehow deliberate and rational, and directed against oneself, even if only

74. See *ST* I-II 46.2 obj 1.

75. *ST* I-II 46.4.

76. *ST* I-II 46.3. It is important to note that the objects associated with anger need not be present in a temporal sense; an object can be mentally present without being temporally present. Hence Aquinas's view of anger can accommodate the experience of becoming angry at past events or hypothetical future ones.

77. *ST* I-II 46.1. See also *ST* I-II 46.2, 46.6 obj 3.

78. *ST* I-II 46.2, 46.3 ad 3. Aquinas cites anger's mixed composition as another reason why it lacks a contrary: "Because anger is caused from contrary passions, namely hope, which is about a good, and sadness, which is about an evil, it includes in itself opposition. Consequently, it has no contrary outside itself" (*ST* I-II 46.1 ad 2).

79. *ST* I-II 45.4 ad 3, 46.1. See also *ST* I-II 23.3.

80. *ST* I-II 48.1.

81. *ST* I-II 47.2. As Kevin White pointed out in a lecture at the Catholic University of America, Aquinas constructs question 47 around Aristotle's treatment of anger in the *Rhetoric*. Each article revolves around a quotation from Aristotle in its *sed contra*. See *Rhetoric* II.2–4, II.9, 1378a–1387b.

by identification with the injured party.[82] Otherwise anger does not result.

Like the other irascible passions, anger depends on a judgment. Since anger requires hope to be anything more than sadness, and hope requires a judgment of an object's attainability, anger follows only a judgment that the desired revenge is possible. Without the judgment that a material evil can be overcome, and therefore the possibility of hope, sadness results instead of anger.[83] Aquinas need not be read too literally here: he does not mean to exclude the possibility of becoming angry in an objectively hopeless situation. His point, rather, is that those without some kind of hope, no matter how unwarranted, do not become angry, only sad. Anger also requires a judgment that the evil was deliberately willed by some other entity. Aquinas regards anger as particularly dependent on reason and devotes an entire article to discuss whether or not anger involves reason—literally, is "with reason" (*cum ratione*)—something he does with no other passion.[84] He concludes that "anger in a certain way involves reason."[85]

Aquinas maps out the chronological sequence of the irascible passions in relation to each other and to the concupiscible passions. He ranks hope as the first of the irascible passions, because it is the nearest to the passion of love,[86] and because the other irascible passions depend in some way on hope or its contrary, despair.[87] After establishing the primacy of hope among the irascible passions, he goes on to arrange all eleven passions according to their order of occurrence: "Love and hatred occur first; second, desire and aversion; third, hope and despair; fourth, fear and daring; fifth, anger; sixth and last, joy and sadness, which follow from all the passions, as it is said in Aristotle's *Ethics*—in such a way, however, that love precedes hatred, desire precedes aversion, hope precedes despair, fear precedes dar-

82. *ST* I-II 46.7 ad 1; *ST* I-II 47.1.

83. *ST* I-II 23.3. See also *ST* I-II 45.4 ad 3, 46.1. The judgment that a material object cannot be overcome can also lead to a berserk frenzy, as Nicholas Ingham noted to me, but this possibility does not present a significant problem for Aquinas. He could argue that this sort of frenzy would require the judgment, even if irrational, that berserk violence would accomplish something positive.

84. *ST* I-II 46.4.

85. *ST* I-II 46.4. Nonrational animals experience something analogous to human anger because the structure of their passions manifests the rationality of the Creator. See *ST* I-II 46.4 ad 2.

86. *ST* I-II 25.3.

87. "Daring follows on the hope of victory, and fear follows on the despair of it. Moreover anger follows on daring: for no one grows angry desiring revenge without also daring to seek it" (*ST* I-II 25.3).

ing, and joy precedes sadness."[88] Each passion is ordered toward the flourishing of the sense appetite, and each has its unique role in motivating us as we negotiate a world filled with sensible goods and sensible evils. Each of the irascible passions begins in love, and if successful, terminates in union with a desired object and thus, pleasure; if unsuccessful, it terminates in privation and thus, sadness. The description of the passions as movements facilitates the structuring of the passions according to teleology: each is a link in a chain that terminates in the attainment of goods and ultimately, if the passions are ordered properly, beatitude.[89]

The Intentionality of the Irascible Passions

There are some interpretative difficulties concerning the intentional objects of the irascible passions. Aquinas maintains that movement can be only toward a good or away from an evil, and never away from a good or toward an evil.[90] However, he defines despair as movement away from a good and daring as movement toward an evil.[91] He accounts for the seeming discrepancy by explaining that the irascible passions respond to arduous objects, and arduous objects are not simply good or evil, but also difficult to attain or avoid. Due to their complex nature, arduous objects can be grasped under different aspects, and depending on how an arduous object is apprehended, different passions result.[92] He explains:

> The arduous or difficult good considered as good attracts us and elicits the passion of hope; considered as arduous or difficult, it causes us to retreat and elicits the passion of despair. Similarly, the arduous evil considered as evil causes us to shun it and elicits the passion of fear; but it is also attractive considered as arduous, as a means to escape from subjection to evil, and thus the passion of daring tends toward it.[93]

Therefore, "despair implies movement away from a good, although not because it is good, and daring implies movement toward an evil, but again, not because it is evil."[94]

88. *ST* I-II 25.3; Aristotle, *Ethics* II.5, 1105b23.

89. For a discussion of how viewing the passions as movements affects Aquinas's account of their structure, see Knuuttila, *Emotions*, 246–47.

90. *ST* I-II 23.2, 23.4, 45.2.

91. *ST* I-II 23.2, 45.2.

92. *ST* I-II 23.2, 45.2 ad 3

93. *ST* I-II 23.2.

94. *ST* I-II 25.4 ad 3.

In the light of these texts from Aquinas, it is important to emphasize again that Aquinas's taxonomy of the irascible passions classifies the irascible passions, not according to material objects, to the objects considered as they are in themselves, but according to formal or intentional objects. Despair is elicited by a good judged to be unattainable, that is, an intentional object that is an evil, and so it prompts movement away from the intentional object. Daring is elicited by an evil judged to be conquerable, that is, an intentional object that is a good, and so it prompts movement toward the intentional object. This interpretation of Aquinas's system preserves his claim that the object that evokes a passion is the same object that the passion moves toward or away from.[95] Unless the irascible passions are classified according to their intentional objects, it would not be possible for Aquinas to preserve this axiom about relationship between passion, its object, and the direction of movement. For example, daring is related to two distinct objects, since it is evoked by a material evil (some obstacle) and moves toward a material good (victory). If Aquinas's axiom that the object that evokes a passion is the same object that the passion moves toward or away from is seen as applying to the material objects of passions, then it could not accommodate the passion of daring with its two material objects. However, daring has only a single intentional object, that is, an evil perceived to be conquerable and therefore a good, and in this sense daring moves toward the same object that evokes it. When Aquinas's axiom is seen as applying to intentional objects, and not the sheer ontological reality of the objects themselves, it can apply to the irascible passions; otherwise, it runs into intractable difficulties.

While this interpretation of the intentionality of the irascible passions solves one difficulty, it raises others in its place. Aquinas maintains that hope and daring are distinct passions: hope's object is a future good that is judged possible to attain, and daring's object is a future evil that is judged possible to overcome.[96] He also holds that daring results from hope, "for it is from hoping to overcome some threatening danger that one confronts it with daring."[97] But according to the interpretation given here, even though,

95. *ST* I-II 22.1, 22.2.

96. "Daring is about an evil to which is joined the good of victory in the estimation of the daring individual. Nonetheless, daring looks to the evil; hope looks to the accompanying good" (*ST* I-II 45.2 ad 3).

97. *ST* I-II 45.2.

in one sense, the object of daring is an evil, the *intentional* object of daring is a good: the good of overcoming an evil.[98] Consequently, hope and daring have the same sort of intentional object, that is, a good, or more specifically, an arduous future good judged possible to attain. But for hope and daring to remain distinct passions, the logic of Aquinas's system requires some intrinsic difference between their intentional objects. Aquinas's solution is that hope moves toward an object that is good in itself, whereas daring moves toward the good of overcoming an evil. However, the object's arduous quality already denotes the presence of some obstacle, and hope, like daring, necessarily moves toward the overcoming of some evil. So in the end we are left with the tenuous distinction that hope moves toward a good by overcoming an evil, while daring moves toward an evil in order to overcome it and attain some good. It is difficult to discern a real distinction between these two intentional objects: they seem to amount to the same thing. Without some sort of distinction between their intentional objects, hope and daring cannot be classified as separate passions according to the principles of Aquinas's system.[99] Still, whether or not the *principles* of his system require otherwise, Aquinas clearly regards hope and daring as distinct psychological phenomena.[100]

98. There is some ambiguity as to how Aquinas wants to define the intentional object of daring. In *ST* I-II 23.2, he describes daring's object as escaping from an evil, and in *ST* I-II 45.2 ad 3, he speaks of daring as moving toward an evil only accidentally. But in *ST* I-II 45.2, he suggests that the "good of victory" associated with daring is not the object of daring, but rather the object of the hope that necessarily accompanies daring. Daring's object, he argues, is the evil that stands in the way of victory. When pressed, it seems that Aquinas would want to maintain that the intentional object of daring is an evil, because otherwise there would little left to distinguish daring from hope. The trouble is that he also holds that the passions cannot move toward an evil considered as such, and that daring, therefore, moves toward an evil only accidentally. It is hard to see how these positions are compatible.

99. In their Thomistic appropriation of Freudian psychoanalysis, Anna Terruwe and Conrad Baars preserve Aquinas's distinctions between hope and daring and between despair and fear. Nonetheless, they tend to treat the two pairs as units: hope and daring as expressions of "energy," and despair and fear as expressions of "fear." Given that their work is based on years of clinical experience, their relative neglect of these distinctions in their appropriation of Aquinas's theory of the passions may be an indication of the distinctions' practical and theoretical irrelevance.

100. There are various ways to incorporate Aquinas's phenomenological descriptions of hope and daring into a revised taxonomy that is faithful to the metaphysical principles of his system. In one model, daring remains the affective movement toward an arduous good, and hope ceases to denote a distinct passion. Hope, instead, names a combination of concupiscible passions: desire for some absent good and pleasure in the mental presence of that same good. Another model defines hope as the movement toward an arduous future good, while daring and

There are also questions about Aquinas's treatment of despair. The intentional object of despair must be an evil, since despair moves away from its object, and movement away from an intentional object implies that the object is an evil. Despair's intentional object can be either an arduous evil or a simple, non-arduous evil. Either possibility presents difficulties. If despair's intentional object is an arduous future evil, there would be nothing to distinguish despair and fear, since fear moves away from an arduous future evil. If despair's intentional object is a simple, non-arduous evil, then there would be nothing to distinguish despair and aversion, since aversion moves way from a simple, non-arduous evil. According to the principles of Aquinas's system, therefore, it does not seem possible to maintain despair's status as a passion distinct from either fear or aversion.

There are questions about the chronological sequence of fear and despair as well. First, Aquinas says that despair causes fear and precedes fear in occurrence.[101] Later he writes that fear causes despair, even that "all despair proceeds from some fear."[102] The apparent contradiction between these statements can be interpreted in different ways.[103] It seems plausible

anger denote a movement toward the elimination of some present evil, as opposed to the elimination of some future evil that, in this interpretation, would be constitutive of the object of hope. Although this would eliminate any formal distinction between daring and anger, Anna Terruwe, for instance, argues that daring and anger are the same passion, as will be discussed below.

101. Hope and despair precede fear and daring because "hope and despair are the reason for fear and daring: for daring follows on the hope of victory, and fear follows on the despair of it" (*ST* I-II 25.3). He also writes: "just as daring is caused by hope, so fear is caused by despair" (*ST* I-II 25.4 obj 3).

102. *ST* II-II 125.2 obj 3. Although this quotation is taken from an objection, based on his response, Aquinas does not seem to question the truth of this statement. The relevant part of his response to the objection reads as follows: "Just as hope is the origin of daring, so fear is the origin of despair. Therefore, just as the moderate daring of the brave presupposes hope, so conversely despair proceeds from some kind of fear. But it is not the case that any kind of despair proceeds from just any kind of fear: each kind of despair proceeds from its own kind of fear" (*ST* II-II 125.2 ad 3). Earlier he also writes, "From fear follows despair: someone despairs from fear of the difficulty that surrounds the hoped-for good" (*ST* I-II 45.2).

103. Knuuttila also notes this contradiction. He suggests that Aquinas confuses natural precedence with the order of occurrence, and that what he really means is that fear chronologically precedes despair, but despair ontologically precedes fear, insofar as despair concerns a good rather than an evil (Knuuttila, *Emotions*, 246). Knuuttila seems correct that Aquinas uses precedence equivocally in these different contexts. However, since Aquinas sometimes suggests that despair chronologically precedes fear (*ST* I-II 25.3, 25.4 obj. 3), Knuuttila's analysis cannot stand as it is. It seems more accurate to say that Aquinas's analysis of the relationship between fear and despair is just more impressionistic than logically precise, and that his equivocation about the chronological sequence of fear and despair indicates that he has not fully conceptualized their relationship. Although Aquinas gives a lot of attention to fear (four questions), he gives

that Aquinas is describing the relationship between fear and despair from different angles and therefore, in their context, his descriptions are not intrinsically contradictory. The claim that fear can cause despair does not directly clash with the claim that despair can cause fear. Still, the unresolved tension between his different descriptions of the relationship between fear and despair suggests some underlying ambiguity. The haphazard character of his comments about the relationship between fear and despair suggests that Aquinas's primary point of reference for his account of despair (which is much less developed than his account of fear) is the phenomenology of the psychological experiences that Aquinas intuitively characterizes as despair, and not the logical implications of his metaphysical principles, despite his interest in making despair fit with the rest of his system.[104] In any case, Aquinas neglects a more obvious point: sometimes despair can lead to daring, as when Poe speaks of "the wild courage of despair" in "The Masque of the Red Death."[105]

Lastly, there are some questions about his treatment of anger. According to Aquinas, anger is unique in having two objects: the agent who evokes anger from the subject and the revenge toward which anger moves.[106] This

---

little attention to despair (only one article), and so his account of their relationship, like his account of despair, is notably less precise than other aspects of his system.

104. Aquinas seems to give prominence to the passion of despair, not because of his interest in despair qua passion—he devotes only one article to it—but in order to fill out his larger system. It balances the passion of hope and provides a parallel to theological despair, a movement of the will, which he treats in *ST* II-II 20. However, as noted here, the principles of Aquinas's system do not seem capable of sustaining the status of despair as a distinct passion. The intentional object implicit in his account of despair does not substantively differ from the intentional objects of fear and aversion. But without a distinct intentional object, despair cannot constitute a distinct passion.

How could Aquinas's account of the passion of despair be reconciled with the logic of his system? The phenomenon that Aquinas calls "despair" could be interpreted not as a distinct passion, but instead as a combination of two things: first, the passion of sadness (*tristitia*) in not being able to attain some future good, and second, the experience of the fading of the passion of hope, after its object is judged less attainable than previously thought. So despair would be the fading of hope combined with sadness in the seeming impossibility of attaining a certain good. Aquinas's account of the passions does not include an explicit discussion of the subjective experience of a passion's fading—although he does discuss how the intensity of anger and love can fade over time (see *ST* I-II 48.2 ad 2)—but this proposal fits well with the logic of his system. The passions, as temporal events, encompass intervals of time, not just discrete moments, and the analogy between passion and movement implies change. Hence the idea that the same passion might be experienced differently at different moments of its movement fits naturally with Aquinas's system.

105. This observation was suggested to me by Nicholas Ingham.

106. *ST* I-II 46.2.

claim is problematic because of his insistence elsewhere that a passion is directed toward the same object that elicits it. The exception that he makes for anger seems ad hoc.

Aquinas's view that anger is an exception to the metaphysical principles undergirding his account of the passions can be accepted at face value. Otherwise, there are two ways to revise his account of anger with a more rigorous application of his own metaphysical principles and thus maintain the inner logic of his system. One option is to view anger as the conflux of multiple passions, which is an especially reasonable interpretation, since Aquinas himself equivocates somewhat about whether multiple passions compose or merely cause anger.[107] In this interpretation, anger is a combination of sadness (*tristitia*), whose object causes anger, and daring (*audacia*), whose object is the revenge toward which anger inclines. In support of this position is the similar interpretation of Anna Terruwe: while agreeing with the broad outline of Aquinas's account of the passions, she argues that anger should be understood not as a separate passion, but as a kind of daring.[108] Such a resolution to this difficulty, however, may not do justice to our intuitive understanding of anger as a distinct type of passion. Also, Aquinas's claim that anger necessarily involves sadness is dubious. Anger is often accompanied by sadness, and both passions respond to evil objects, but sometimes anger is elicited without being either preceded or accompanied by pain or sadness.[109] For example, after hearing of an injustice, people can become angry immediately, without any preceding or accompanying sadness.

Another option is to translate the multiple objects of anger into a single intentional object: a future good that is presently arduous, that is, a future good that is attained through the elimination of a present evil.[110] This would

107. *ST* I-II 46.1–2, 46.3 ad 3, 46.6 obj 3.

108. Terruwe, *Neurosis in Light of Rational Psychology*, 18.

109. Knuuttila observes that Aquinas places anger before sadness in order of occurrence (see *ST* I-II 25.3) and that this sequence is at odds with his claim that sadness causes anger (Knuuttila, *Emotions*, 246). This contradiction may suggest that Aquinas is not entirely committed to the idea that sadness is a necessary prelude to anger. As with the ambiguity over the order of occurrence of fear and despair, it also suggests that Aquinas has not fully conceptualized anger's relationship to sadness and that his account of it is more impressionistic than logically precise.

110. The term "arduous" denotes that an object is evil with respect to the subject's capacity to attain it, or avoid it, not with respect to the object's intrinsic desirability or repulsiveness. The arduousness of an object can either complicate future movement (that is, the future attainment of a good or the future avoidance of an evil) or disrupt the subject's rest in some previously possessed good (as in the case of anger, which involves an already present evil). According to this in-

be different from the sort of obstacle associated with the other irascible passions. In the cases of hope, daring, despair, and fear, the obstacle involved is not yet present, but rather is foreseen to stand in the way of either attaining a good or avoiding an evil. This interpretation preserves the intuition that anger is its own distinct species of passion, rather than a conflux of passions. It also maintains the close connection Aquinas draws between sadness and hope, since this sort of intentional object necessarily possesses the qualities that elicit sadness and hope. In order to evoke anger, such an intentional object would necessarily include the judgment that the material evil is a threat to one's well-being and that the material evil is capable of being overcome. These are the necessary conditions for sadness and hope, respectively. Nonetheless, while such an interpretation of anger requires that anger be accompanied by hope, since the hope of achieving justice is necessary for anger, it does not require that anger involve sadness. Anger might turn to sadness if hope is lost, or it might be accompanied by sadness, but does not, by definition, imply its presence in some form or other. This interpretation of anger steers clear of Aquinas's problematic claim that anger is always preceded or accompanied by sadness, while at the same time remaining true to his fundamental metaphysical principles.

---

terpretation of anger, its intentional object is the attainment of a future good by the overcoming of a *present* evil. By contrast, the intentional objects of hope and daring concern the attainment of a future good by the overcoming of a *future* or *non-present* evil. Anger concerns a future good that is presently arduous; hope and daring concern a future good whose attainment is anticipated to be arduous.

CHAPTER 3

The Affections of the Will

For Aquinas, the category of affection denotes a class of psychological phenomena that includes both movements of the sense appetite and movements of the intellectual appetite, that is, the will. Unlike passion, affection does not necessarily imply either corporeality or passivity. Previous chapters have considered the passions, which are the affections of the sense appetite. This chapter will address the affections of the will and their interactions with the passions, a topic often neglected in studies of Aquinas's account of human affectivity.

The Category of Affection

Affection (in Latin, *affectus* and its synonym *affectio*) is never explicitly defined by Aquinas. In consequence, its meaning can be determined only by analyzing the contexts in which it is used and by scouring tangential asides for clues.[1] Typically the term serves as a synonym for the passions of the soul, or else differentiates human passions from movements of the human will or the love and joy of God and the angels.[2] In some cases, espe-

1. The idea of making a distinction between two kinds of affection goes back at least to Peter Lombard, who states that "in us affection is twofold, namely of the mind and of sensuality" (*in nobis duplex est affectus, mentis scilicet et sensualitatis*) (Peter Lombard, *Sententiae* III 17.2).

2. Aquinas discusses affection in God and the angels in numerous places. Sometimes he discusses affection only with respect to God (see *ST* I 19.11, 20, 21.3, 26); sometimes he discusses affection only with respect to the angels (see *ST* I 59.4, 60); but in the most relevant passages he discusses both simultaneously (see *ST* I 82.5 ad 1; *ST* I-II 22.3 ad 3, 31.4 ad 2, 59.5 ad 3; *ST* II-II 162.3). Three recent articles dwell extensively on this topic: Norman Kretzmann, "Aquinas on God's Joy, Love, and Liberality," *The Modern Schoolman* 72 (1995): 125–48, esp. 126–31; Westberg, "Emotion and God"; Sarot, "God, Emotion and Corporeality"; and Anastasia Scrutton, "Emotion in Augustine of Hippo and Thomas Aquinas: A Way Forward for the Im/possibility Debate?" *International Journal of Systematic Theology* 7 (2005): 169–77.

cially in his treatments of particular virtues and vices, Aquinas seems to use the category of affection in a vague way, as though he could be referring to movements of either the sense appetite or the intellectual appetite.[3]

From his scattered comments, it seems clear that all passions of the soul are affections but not all affections are passions.[4] He usually refers to those affections that are not passions negatively, calling them passionless (*sine passione*) affections or acts of the will.[5] In two places, however, Aquinas does name this kind of affection. He calls it "intellectual affection" (*intellectiva*

3. See chap. 6.

4. "It is the affections of the sense appetite that are most properly called passions of the soul," Aquinas writes, thus explicitly including the passions among the affections and implying that some affections are not passions (*ST* III 15.4).

The same point is made in a discussion of the Stoic and the Peripatetics: "Since the Stoics did not distinguish between the intellectual appetite, which is the will, and the sense appetite, which is divided into irascible and concupiscible parts, they did not distinguish, as the Peripatetics did, between the passions of the soul and other human affections, between the passions of the soul which are movements of the sense appetite and the other affections which are not passions of the soul but rather movements of the intellectual appetite, which is called the will" (*ST* I-II 59.2).

Elsewhere, Aquinas notes that mercy can be attributed to God "according to its effect, not according to the affection of passion" (*ST* I 21.3). This passage again suggests that Aquinas regards affection as a broad category that includes the passions.

Of the few who address this topic, scholars with particular expertise in the study of Aquinas unanimously interpret affection as a category that includes both the passions of the soul and the movements of the will. See Westberg, "Emotion and God," 109–21; Leget, "Nussbaum and Aquinas," 573–75; Floyd, "Aquinas on Emotion," 166–70; and Kretzmann, "God's Joy," 126–31.

Another line of interpretation originates with Susan James, who sees passion and "affect" (as she calls it) as two entirely separate categories (James, *Passion and Action,* 61–62). Thomas Dixon, who relies on James, similarly interprets passion as a category distinct from affection (Dixon, *From Passions to Emotions,* 26–61, esp. 40). Then, Anastasia Scrutton, who is aware of Dixon's work, also seems to propose a non-overlapping distinction between affection and passion (Scrutton, "Emotion in Augustine and Aquinas," 175–77).

5. For example, Aquinas describes some affections as being without passion in *ST* I 82.5 ad 1. In his commentary on Aristotle's *Ethics,* he writes: "Even among the appetitive powers the operation of the intellective appetite is not properly called passion. It does not take place with a change of a bodily organ, which is necessary to the nature of a passion properly speaking. It remains, therefore, that operations of the sensitive appetite, which are accompanied by a change of a bodily organ and which in a way draw man, should be called passions in a strict sense." *Commentary on Aristotle's Nicomachean Ethics,* trans. C. I. Litzinger (Notre Dame: Dumb Ox Books, 1993), II.5, 292.

Nonetheless, since all created appetite is a passive power, there is an element of passion and receptivity in every created appetite, including the will, as discussed in chap. 1. So when Aquinas speaks of affection without passion, he does not mean to imply the absence of any kind of receptivity or passivity, but rather the absence of that kind of passivity that is proper to the passions of the soul. For a discussion of the passivity of the will, see Sherwin, *By Knowledge and By Love,* 94–100.

affectione) in the *Summa contra gentiles.*[6] In the *Summa theologiae,* he calls it "simple affection" (*simplex affectus*), thus making the intriguing suggestion that the passions are complex affections.[7] This study will also refer to such affections as "affections of the will." Aquinas does not use this term, but it is succinctly descriptive.

Every affection of the will is a movement of the will, but it is unclear whether all movements of the will are affections. Since every movement of an appetite involves love, and since he clearly regards the will's love as a kind of affection, his system seems to require that all movements of the will are affections. If so, then everything said about affections of the will would seem to apply to movements of the will, at least under certain aspects.[8] Nonetheless, since Aquinas says so little about the category of affection, and since he seems to use the term "affection" only to describe movements of the will that are analogous to the passions in some way, it is also possible that he would reserve the term "affection" for only those phenomena that somehow resemble the subjective experience of the passions.[9] To avoid any potential misinterpretation, therefore, this study will focus on those psychological phenomena that he actually describes as affections.

6. "There are no affections with passions in God. For with intellectual affection there is no passion, only with sensible affection, as proved in Book VII of the *Physics*. But no such affection can be in God, since he is without sensible cognition, as is manifest from what was said above. Therefore in God there is not affective passion" (*Summa contra gentiles* I 89.1–2); see also Aristotle, *Physics,* VII.3, 246b20.

7. "Love, desire, and other such things can be taken in two ways. Sometimes they are taken to be passions, coming about with some upheaval in the soul. This is how they are commonly taken, and in this way they are in the sense appetite. But in another way they signify simple affection, without passion or upheaval in the soul, and acts of the will. And in this way they are attributed to angels and God" (*ST* I 82.5 ad 1).

8. In a suggestive but puzzling passage, Aquinas states that free choice (*liberum arbitrium*) consists in "the application of cognition to affection" (*De veritate* 17.1 ad 4). This phrase is difficult to interpret, because it is not clear what happens to affection after cognition is applied to it. Does it remain a kind of affection or does the application of cognition make it something that can no longer be described as such? The context of the text does not allow for a definitive answer. In any case, whether or not free choice qualifies as an affection, the passage nonetheless suggests that Aquinas would classify much of the will's activity under the category of affection.

9. In *De veritate,* Aquinas explains that souls separated from their bodies experience joy and fear after death. In the process, he makes a suggestive comment regarding acts of the will: "Joy and fear, which are passions, do not remain in the separated soul, since they take place with a bodily change. But there remain acts of the will similar to those passions [*sed remanent actus voluntatis similes illis passionibus*]" (*De veritate* 25.3 ad 7). The seeming implication of this passage is that there are some acts of the will that are *not* similar to the passions—which perhaps means that there are some acts of the will that are not affections. But Aquinas does not elaborate, and

The Structure of Intellectual Affection

Love is the first of the affections, just as love is the first of the passions, since "the first movement of the will, and of any appetitive power, is love [*amor*]."[10] As with the passions of the soul, the affections of the will respond to cognition, and in the case of the affection of love, the intellectual apprehension of a good. The intellectual affection of desire (*desiderium*) occurs when a good is absent,[11] and that kind of pleasure (*delectatio*) called joy (*gaudium*) occurs when a good is present and the will can rest in it.[12] In this way, the structure of intellectual affection parallels the structure of the concupiscible passions.[13]

The will's most basic inclination is for complete, unrestricted goodness,

---

since the *De veritate* is one of his earlier discussions of the passions, it is not possible to come to any definite conclusions regarding his mature thinking from this passage alone.

10. *ST* I 20.1. The word *amor* can refer to multiple kinds of loves, including those of inanimate objects, animals, and rational creatures, because each type of appetite has its own proper love (*ST* I-II 26.1).

11. In *ST* I-II 31.3 ad 2, Aquinas states that *desiderium* is the movement that leads to the repose of *gaudium*, just as *concupiscentia* is the movement that leads to the repose of *delectatio*. He also classifies this *desiderium* as a *concupiscentia animalis*, in contradistinction to the type of *concupiscentia* that corresponds to *delectatio*. Since *gaudium* clearly involves the movement of the will, and since the contrast between *concupiscentia animalis* and *concupiscentia* seems to indicate that the former is not a movement of the sense appetite, this particular sort of *desiderium*—the kind that corresponds to *gaudium*—is best understood as an affection of the will. (Elsewhere Aquinas uses the term *desiderium* in a generic sense, or to refer to other kinds of desire, so this classification should not be taken as having universal application.)

12. *ST* I-II 31.3.

13. There are some unresolved questions about the role of rational choice in the structure of intellectual affection. In one article, Aquinas seems to imply that the intellectual affection of love always involves rational choice. After classifying *dilectio* as a species of *amor* that implies some antecedent choice (*ST* I-II 26.3), he notes that the *amor* of the intellectual appetite and *dilectio* are one and the same thing (*ST* I-II 26.3 ad 1). This taxonomy implies that the intellectual affection of love always involves rational choice. However, this article should not be taken as his definitive statement on the relationship between rational choice and the intellectual affection of love. The article falls in the midst of his discussion of the passion of love, and his main concern is to reconcile the terminology of pseudo-Dionysius and Augustine with his own, not to analyze the intellectual affection of love.

Furthermore, there is reason to think Aquinas would want to deny that the intellectual affection of love always involves rational choice. In his discussion of Christ's affectivity, Aquinas distinguishes between *voluntas-ut-ratio* and *voluntas-ut-natura*, and thus between the sort of willing that involves rational choice and the sort of willing that does not (see *ST* III 18, 21; see also chap. 7). Clearly, then, Aquinas wants to affirm that we can desire something on the level of the will without rationally choosing it. But since love is the first movement of the will, if the intellectual affection of love necessarily involved rational choice, it would not be possible to desire anything on the level of the will without also rationally choosing it. Consequently, Aquinas's discussion of the semantics of *dilectio* should not be taken as applying without qualification to

which Aquinas equates with the inclination toward happiness and beatitude.[14] Until it is attained, this inclination generates the experience of desire. This desire is not chosen by a free act of the will. It is an instinctive drive that springs from the nature of intellectual appetite.[15] Consequently, "man is unable not to want to be happy."[16] The same applies to the angels and even to God, in the sense that God necessarily wills his own goodness.[17] Since only God is infinitely good, our desire for infinite good can be satisfied completely only by God in the beatific vision.[18] Consequently, we have a natural instinct to worship God, although it may not always be recognized as such.[19] Once we possess God in the beatific vision, the attainment of which presupposes the voluntary love of God, we cannot but continue to choose and love God, because our inclination toward happiness is so overwhelmingly satisfied.[20]

---

the intellectual affection of love. There is little indication that this one article is meant to provide a definitive analysis of the intellectual affection of love, and it creates serious problems for his account of human affectivity to suppose that it does.

This interpretation of Aquinas preserves the structure of intellectual affection from the critique given in chap. 2 regarding the passion of love. It makes it possible to distinguish between two intellectual affections that move toward the same intentional object: a first movement that does not involve rational choice, and then a second, subsequent movement that does. The passions, however, never involve rational choice (though they can be influenced by it), and so it is not possible to distinguish between them in this way.

14. *ST* I 19.3, 59.1; *ST* I-II 2.7–8, 3.8, 5.8.

15. Aquinas's attempts to make sense of Christ's prayer in the garden of Gethsemane leads him to distinguish between an instinctive will (*voluntas ut natura*) and a will shaped by rational choice (*voluntas ut ratio*) in *ST* III 18.3, as will be discussed in chap. 7. In making this distinction, Aquinas affirms that instinctual, non-chosen desires can occur on the level of the will.

16. *ST* I-II 5.4 ad 2. He also writes, "We want to be happy not by free choice (*liberum arbitrium*) but by natural instinct (*naturalis instinctus*)" (*ST* I 19.10). See also *ST* I 19.3, 82.1–2, 83.2; *ST* I-II 2.4, 5.8.

17. "God necessarily wills his own goodness, just as our will necessarily wills happiness" (*ST* I 19.3).

18. "The object of the will, that is, the human appetite, is universal goodness, goodness as such; just as the object of the intellect is universal truth, truth as such. From this it is evident that nothing can quiet man's will except universal goodness. But this is not found in anything created, but only in God, because creatures only have participated and derivative goodness. Thus only God can satisfy the human will: as it is said in Psalm 102, God satisfies your desire with good things. In God alone therefore does human happiness (*beatitudo*) consist" (*ST* I-II 2.8). See also *ST* I-II 1.7, 3.8.

Aquinas maintains that all things, inanimate as well as animate, desire God inasmuch as they desire their own proper *telos*, since all perfection shares in God's goodness: "In desiring their own proper perfections, all things desire God himself, since the perfections of all things each have a kind of likeness to divine being (*esse*)" (*ST* I 6.1 ad 2).

19. *ST* III 60.5 ad 3.

20. *ST* I-II 5.4. Similarly it is impossible to hate God once he is apprehended in his essence (*ST* II-II 34.1).

In our earthly condition, however, we are presented only with limited goods. Nothing is so irresistibly attractive that its rejection cannot also be attractive under some aspect. As a result, our wills must choose between any number of limited goods, and this, Aquinas maintains, explains the relationship between will (*voluntas*) and free choice (*liberum arbitrium*).[21] In some places Aquinas describes the will and free choice as different aspects of the same power;[22] elsewhere he calls free choice "the faculty of will and reason."[23] Both descriptions are ways of expressing his underlying view that free choice comes into play only when there is no infinitely desirable good available, and we must use our intellects and wills to decide which limited goods to pursue. The will's inclination toward infinite good, and the impossibility of finding a good that completely satisfies, is what opens up the possibility of free choice.[24] Without the will's inclination toward infinite good, we would not seek out any good, and if there were something completely satisfying that was immediately available to us, we would not choose anything else.[25]

The operations of the intellect and will are closely linked, and so too are

21. *ST* I 83. The indeterminacy of object distinguishes the sense appetite from the will: "The difference between the sense appetite and the will is that the sense appetite is determined to one particular thing by the order of nature. The will, however, is only determined by the order of nature to one general thing, which is goodness, but is not determined with respect to any particular good. And therefore it is proper to the will to choose, but not to the sense appetite, which is the only appetite in brute animals. It is on this account that brute animals are not able to choose" (*ST* I-II 13.2). See also *ST* I-II 19.3.

For analysis of the relationship between will (*voluntas*) and free choice (*liberum arbitrium*) in Aquinas, see Patrick Lee, "The Relation between Intellect and Will in Free Choice according to Aquinas and Scotus," *Thomist* 49 (1985): 321–42, and Daniel Westberg, "Did Aquinas Change His Mind about the Will?" *Thomist* 58 (1994): 41–60.

22. *ST* I 83.4. See also *ST* II-II 24.1 ad 3.

23. *ST* I-II 1.1.

24. Aquinas's account of free choice as something that emerges from unchosen desire contrasts sharply with many contemporary accounts. As Daniel Westberg notes, "the modern view of the will has shifted from the biblical and Augustinian view that incorporated affect, to a mere decision-making faculty independent of and often opposed to emotion" (Westberg, "Emotion and God," 121).

25. This understanding of the will's inclination toward the good as the condition of the possibility of freedom is drawn from the work of Servais Pinckaers, *Sources of Christian Ethics,* 327–456, and Michael Sherwin, *By Knowledge and By Love,* 18–62. Throughout his book, Sherwin takes care to defend this interpretation of Aquinas on freedom against those who argue that it implies a kind of intellectual determinism, i.e., that the intellect's apprehension of the good determines the will's choice of it. Sherwin argues that Aquinas avoids intellectual determinism because the will can influence which goods the intellect turns its attention toward, and in this way the will determines which goods it will desire (see especially 204–38).

the fundamental acts of knowing and loving.[26] The will responds to what is known, and to some extent the intellect can be directed by the will. In a few texts, Aquinas suggests that the intellect and the will together form a single principle of action, at least from a certain perspective.[27] In the *De malo*, Aquinas writes that "the intellect and the will are the active or causal source in human beings, as [Aristotle's] *De anima* says."[28] In the *Prima secundae*, Aquinas speaks of "the interior principle of a voluntary act" as a "cognitive and appetitive power," thus again implying that intellect and will can be considered as together constituting a single principle.[29] As mentioned above, Aquinas sometimes refers to free choice as "the faculty of will and reason."[30] These affirmations indicate how closely he connects the will—and therefore the affections of the will—to the intellect. His frequent use of the expressions "rational appetite" and "intellectual appetite" to refer to the will is itself highly suggestive of the dependence on intellectual cognition that Aquinas attributes to the will.[31]

The situation of the saints and angels in heaven further clarifies Aquinas's account of freedom and how it relates to knowledge and free choice. Since God is the infinite good from whom all finite goods derive their goodness, all creatures, when confronted with the apprehension of God in himself, find God irresistibly attractive. Consequently, the saints and angels in heaven cannot choose not-God, but not because they lack freedom.[32] They

26. For a thorough exposition of the mutual dependence and interpenetration of knowing and loving in Aquinas's thought, see Sherwin, *By Knowledge and By Love*.

27. Sherwin, *By Knowledge and By Love*, 39.

28. *De malo* 6, trans. Richard Regan, ed. Brian Davies (Oxford: Oxford University Press, 2001). See also Aristotle, *De anima* III.10, 433a13–18.

29. *ST* I-II 6.1 ad 1.

30. *ST* I-II 1.1.

31. Aquinas's view on the relationship between knowing and loving and how it relates to the concept of free will is complex and open to various interpretations. It is beyond the scope of this study to inquire deeply into these matters. For some recent syntheses of Aquinas's account of human action, see Daniel Westberg, *Right Practical Reason: Aristotle, Action, and Prudence in Aquinas* (Oxford: Clarendon Press, 1994); Stephen L. Brock, *Action and Conduct: Thomas Aquinas and the Theory of Action* (Edinburgh: T & T Clark, 1998); Kevin Flannery, *Acts Amid Precepts: The Aristotelian Logical Structure of Thomas Aquinas's Moral Theory* (Washington, D.C.: The Catholic University of America Press, 2001); and Michael Sherwin, *By Knowledge and By Love*.

32. Simon Gaine offers a comprehensive study of the question of freedom in heaven. After examining some contemporary challenges to the possibility of free will in heaven, and Francisco Suarez's contribution to the modern framing of this question, he considers how Aquinas, Duns Scotus, and William of Ockham attempt to explain how there might be freedom in heaven without sin. He concludes that only Aquinas provides a satisfying solution. See Simon Francis Gaine, *Will There Be Free Will in Heaven?* (London: T & T Clark, 2003).

continue to love God not out of external compulsion, but because God overwhelmingly corresponds to their inclinations and every alternative fails to be even remotely interesting.[33] Furthermore, since joy is an effect of love, and occurs when the loved good is present to the subject,[34] in heaven the saints and the angels are filled with joy precisely because they possess the God that they love.

Affection in God and the Angels

Aquinas attributes love to God on the basis of the affirmations of Scripture and his own philosophical conclusions. Since there is appetite in God, there must also be love: "Wherever there is will or appetite, there must be love, since love is the first appetitive movement, and if it were taken away everything else would go with it. It has been shown that in God there is will. Therefore it is necessary to affirm that in God there is love."[35] Similarly, since God loves himself and possesses his own being, and since God loves all his creatures and rejoices in them, God is full of joy.[36] On account of God's simplicity, we can say that God *is* love and its concomitant effect of joy. Just as he can be said to be appetite, so too can he be said to be affection: that is, love and its concomitant joy.[37]

Nevertheless God does not experience affection in the way that humans and angels do, because God is the fullness of being and lacks for nothing. God's affections are not passions, and they imply neither potentiality nor change:

33. Although no creature in heaven can choose not-God, every rational creature in heaven at some point in its existence could have chosen not-God, with the possible exception of those who died as infants. Aquinas holds that the angels exercised free choice before being admitted to the vision of God (*ST* I 62.1), and likewise humans exercise free choice on earth before being admitted to God's presence.

34. *ST* II-II 28.1.

35. *ST* I 20.1. For the same reason there must be love in the angels. See *ST* I 60.1. Another reason for locating love in God is that God as Creator and Exemplar contains in himself the fullness of all perfection and goodness found in creation. Since love is good, it must be present in some analogous form in God and not just metaphorically. For a discussion of Aquinas on analogy as a way of knowing God, see William J. Hill, *Knowing the Unknown God* (New York: Philosophical Library, 1971), 111–61, and Gregory P. Rocca, *Speaking the Incomprehensible God: Thomas Aquinas on the Interplay of Positive and Negative Theology* (Washington, D.C.: The Catholic University of America Press, 2004), 93–195.

36. See *ST* I 20.1 ad 3, 20.2, 26.4. Aquinas affirms that God is ecstatic in his love for creation, in the sense of being transported outside himself, in *ST* I 20.2 ad 1. For Aquinas on ecstasy, see *ST* I-II 28.3.

37. *ST* I 20.1, 26.1.

Therefore acts of the sense appetite, since they involve bodily change, are called passions, not acts of the will. For love and joy and pleasure, when referring to acts of the sense appetite, are passions, but when referring to acts of the intellectual appetite, they are not. It is in this latter sense that they are in God. As Aristotle says in the *Ethics,* God rejoices in an operation that is one and simple. For this reason God loves without passion.[38]

Passions like love and joy are analogously present in God, but passions that imply some imperfection, such as sadness and anger, which each imply the experience of some evil, cannot be analogously present in God; they can be only metaphorically attributed to God.[39]

Angels do not experience passions either, since they lack bodies and sense appetites. Their affections still involve passion in one of the more qualified senses of *passio,* however, because they are creatures, and as such their created appetites are passive powers directed toward goods outside themselves.[40] Furthermore, angelic natures are vulnerable to suffering, that is, passion in the strictest sense of the word, as illustrated by the demons, who share the same nature as the angels but have rejected God and suffer spiritual pain (*dolor*). This pain comes from the frustration of desire, since the demons cannot help desiring God and happiness and yet have deprived themselves of both, and from envy, since they desire the damnation of other creatures and are saddened by those creatures that are not damned.[41] Interestingly, Aquinas suggests that the demons also experience limited joys, again through acts of the will, presumably by rejoicing in such things as the perdition of a particular person.[42] For Aquinas, the capacity for joy is natural to the will; it is an intrinsic feature of intellectual appetite that survives even separation from God.

38. *ST* I 20.1 ad 1; Aristotle, *Ethics* VII.14, 1154b26. See also *ST* I 82.5 ad 1.

39. *ST* I 20.1 ad 2. Aquinas discusses the metaphorical attribution of anger to God in *ST* I 19.11. He also attributes mercy to God insofar as he acts mercifully, but not in the sense of feeling sorrow over creaturely suffering (*ST* I 21.3).

40. Their intellects also exhibit passion since they are acted upon by what informs them, whereas God knows the world in knowing his causation of it and so his knowledge does not have this aspect of passivity. For the various meanings of *passio,* see *ST* I 79.2, 97.2; *ST* I-II 22.1, 41.1. In their inclination toward unlimited goodness, the angels love themselves, other creatures, and most of all God, whom they love more than themselves because God's goodness is greater than their own (*ST* I 60.4–5). Nonetheless, angelic affection is not pure act as is divine affection, so the angels love, but it is not the case that they "are" love.

41. *ST* I 64.3.

42. *ST* I 64.3 ad 1. He also speculates that the demons experience something analogous to fear as they anticipate the final judgment (*ST* I 64.3 ad 2).

Passion and Affection in the Human Person

For Aquinas, affection in God and the angels is an important point of reference for affection in us, since we also have wills and therefore must experience something analogous to what God and the angels experience in their wills.[43] Aquinas's use of this analogy emerges most clearly in his discussion of separated souls, that is, human souls separated from their bodies after death and not yet rejoined to them in the general resurrection. The body is dead, yet the soul perdures, and "separated souls grieve and rejoice at the rewards and punishments they have."[44] He concludes that "joy and sadness are in a separated soul not in the sense appetite, but in the intellectual appetite, as with the angels."[45] The parallel with angelic affection guides his analysis only so far, however. His analysis of intellectual affections in our earthly condition and his speculation about our future condition when rejoined to our bodies in heaven synthesize reflections on animal passions, angelic affections, and what is uniquely human. According to Aquinas, our passions and intellectual affections constantly influence each other, and they are typically experienced together rather than in isolation.

As humans, we are unique in that both sensible and immaterial goods may be objects of the will's love and desire. With respect to immaterial goods, the intellectual appetite can desire such things as wisdom, and it can have affection (*affectus*) toward the things of God, an affection that involves "union with them by means of love" (*coniunctio ad ipsa per amorem*).[46] The will can also endorse the desires of the sense appetite: "whatever we desire according to nature we can also desire as a pleasure of reason, but not the other way around."[47] The will can desire or avoid objects because the will is inclined toward any and all kinds of goodness, and the sense appetite alerts it to the goodness of sensible objects. In a sense, the will shares in the sense

43. For example, consider Aquinas's discussion of spiritual pleasure: "In us there is not only a kind of pleasure that we have in common with brute animals but also a kind of pleasure that we have in common with angels. Hence Dionysius says that holy men often share in the pleasures of the angels. In us, therefore, there is not only pleasure in the sense appetite which we have in common with brute animals but also pleasure in the intellectual appetite which we have in common with angels" (*ST* I-II 31.4 ad 3; see also Dionysius, *De coelesti hierarchia* 15.9).

44. *ST* I 77.8 obj 5.

45. *ST* I 77.8 ad 5.

46. *ST* I-II 30.1 ad l; *ST* I-II 22.3 ad 1.

47. *ST* I 31.3.

appetite's pleasure by seconding it. This rational endorsement of sensible desire has been called "reduplication."[48]

The fulfillment of desire brings joy, the will's counterpart to sensible pleasure. For Aquinas, joy (*gaudium*) is not the same thing as pleasure (*delectatio*): joy is a species of pleasure.[49] Pleasure refers to both passions and intellectual affections. Joy results only from acts that follow reason, and joy does not necessarily involve bodily modification.[50] "For we take pleasure in obtaining both what we naturally desire and what we desire from reason. But the name of joy does not apply to pleasures unless they follow from reason; that is why we do not attribute joy to brute animals, but only pleasures."[51] As with desire and love, both sensible and immaterial goods may be the cause of the will's joy: "everything that can be an object of pleasure can also be an object of joy in those possessing reason."[52]

Aquinas notes that we do not always take joy in objects of pleasure, even when they are explicitly desired by the will, instead experiencing only bodily pleasure. He does not offer an explanation. Other texts, though, may help provide a sense of what his explanation would be. In his discussion of pleasure, Aquinas, citing Aristotle, defines pleasure as a movement of the soul that "sensibly" brings one to a condition appropriate to one's nature through "the presence of a good for which one has an affinity."[53] Therefore, even if a good is in harmony with one's nature, if there is no *perceptible* movement of the will, or no appreciable *improvement* of one's condition vis-à-vis one's natural inclinations, then it seems that joy does not follow. Another interpretation is that unless pleasure is perceived as addressing the

48. See Loughlin, "Human and Animal Emotion," 57–58.

49. *ST* I-II 31.3–4. Aquinas cites Avicenna in his definition of joy in *ST* I-II 31.3. See also Avicenna, *De anima* IV.5.

50. *ST* I-II 31.4 ad 2. In some places, Aquinas uses *gaudium* to refer to sensible pleasures, but this word choice seems to stem from his use of authorities who do not make a clear distinction between pleasure and joy. When not quoting others, Aquinas tends to use *gaudium* in a more specific sense than *delectatio*, in order to refer to something that involves a movement of the will. For a discussion of the difference between pleasure and joy, and the significance of this difference for Thomistic moral theology, see Servais Pinckaers, *Morality: The Catholic View*, trans. Michael Sherwin (South Bend, Ind.: St. Augustine's Press, 2001), 76–81. See also Hubert Benz, "Lust (*delectatio*) und Freude (*gaudium*) bei Thomas von Aquin," *Bochumer Philosophisches Jarbuch für Antike und Mittelalter* 7 (2002): 1–23.

51. *ST* I-II 31.3. Aquinas sometimes seems to use joy to refer to a combination of intellectual affection and passion and not just a purely intellectual affection.

52. *ST* I-II 31.3; see also *ST* I-II 31.4.

53. *ST* I-II 31.1; Aristotle, *Rhetoric* I.11, 1369b33.

will's desire for infinite good, rather than something purely on the level of the passions, it does not fully engage the will, and so joy cannot follow.

Just as joy is a species of pleasure, Aquinas writes, so too sorrow (*tristitia*) is a species of pain (*dolor*).[54] Pain can be either exterior or interior, but sorrow refers to interior pain. Exterior pain, including bodily pains, results from sense perception; interior pain results from interior apprehension but can encompass exterior pain.[55] Joy is described as a movement of the will, but sorrow is defined as an interior affection without specific reference to the will, and consequently, it is not clear whether sorrow (*tristitia*) is proper to the will in the same way as joy (*gaudium*).[56] On the one hand, in his discussion of pain, he defines joy to parallel his definition of sorrow: "only the sort of pleasure that is caused by interior apprehension is named joy."[57] This parallelism suggests that the language of interiority denotes intellectual affection. On the other hand, in the same articles, he lists the objects of both the intellect and the imagination among things that are apprehended through "interior apprehension."[58] Since the imagination is a sensory power, not an immaterial power,[59] this may be an indication that he is using "interior" in a broad, inclusive sense in these questions, and that the category of interior pain includes both passions and intellectual affections. In any case, while discussing the sacrament of penance in the *Tertia pars,* Aquinas indicates without any ambiguity that it is possible for *tristitia* to refer to an intellectual affection. He writes: "We can speak of sorrow [*dolor*] and joy in two ways. In the first way, they are passions of the sense appetite. . . . In the other way, we can speak of joy and sorrow [*tristitia*] as simple acts of the will, to which something is pleasing or displeasing."[60] After weighing these considerations, it is clear that, for Aquinas, *tristitia* can sometimes refer to an intellectual affection, even if sometimes it also refers to either a passion or an unspecified affection.[61] Part of Aquinas's ambiguity about *tristitia*

54. *ST* I-II 35.2.

55. "Whatever is repugnant to the body can be repugnant to the interior appetite, and whatever is apprehended by the senses can be apprehended by imagination and reason, but not the other way around" (*ST* I-II 35.7).

56. *ST* I-II 35.1–2, 35.7.

57. *ST* I-II 35.2.

58. *ST* I-II 35.2, 35.7.

59. *ST* I 78.4.

60. *ST* III 84.9 ad 2.

61. Rebecca Konyndyk DeYoung shares this interpretation of *tristitia:* "In general, one can also distinguish three levels of one's 'aversion to a present evil' in Aquinas's moral psychology: first, pain as aversion to bodily injury or evil; second, sadness as the passion averse to evil on the

may stem from the tension between the Vulgate's attribution of *tristitia* in its translation of *Matthew* 26:37 and his theological view that only Christ's sense appetite was affected by the suffering of his passion.[62] It seems that Aquinas is inclined to associate *tristitia* with the will, but his account of Christ's affectivity holds him back.

Natural and Nonnatural Passions

The line between passion and intellectual affection becomes murky with passions that Aquinas calls "nonnatural" (*non naturalis*) or, following Aristotle, "rational" (*cum ratione*).[63] Natural passions respond to objects that are beneficial or harmful to the physical preservation of animal nature, and they are common to animals and humans.[64] Nonnatural passions, however, are unique to humans. They respond to intentional objects that are apprehended as beneficial or harmful through a judgment of reason, and not simply because they are essential to animal nature.[65] In this way, the passions become oriented toward immaterial objects by the influence of reason and will. Aquinas's category of nonnatural passions seems to include, in principle, any kind of passion, but he mainly discusses nonnatural desire, pleasure, and fear.[66] Sometimes nonnatural passions are in harmony with

level of the sensitive appetite; and finally sorrow (in the technical sense), which is aversion (disgust, contempt) at the level of intellectual appetite (simple willing). Aquinas uses *dolor* (pain) and *tristitia* (sadness) almost interchangeably for levels one and two, but reserves the technical sense of *tristitia* to refer to level three, on account of a difference in the objects of the respective appetites (sensible objects vs. spiritual objects)." Rebecca Konyndyk DeYoung, "Resistance to the Demands of Love: Aquinas on the Vice of *Acedia*," *Thomist* 68 (2004): 182n30.

62. See *ST* III 15.4, 15.6. This interpretation was suggested to me by Michael Sherwin.

63. Aquinas delineates two senses in which a passion may be nonnatural in *ST* I-II 31.7. (See also *ST* I-II 41.3.) In one sense, nonnatural denotes the quality of being counter to rational human nature in its entirety. Morally depraved pleasure is nonnatural in this sense. In another sense, nonnatural denotes the quality of going beyond purely animal nature due to the involvement of reason. This latter sense of nonnatural is the one being discussed here and has no negative connotations. Following Aristotle, Aquinas also classifies passions that are nonnatural in this latter sense as "rational" passions (*ST* I-II 30.3, esp. ad 2; *Rhetoric* I.2, 1370a18).

64. *ST* I-II 30.3, 31.7.

65. *ST* I-II 30.3–4. See also *ST* I-II 31.3. For a discussion of the difference between natural and nonnatural passions, see Loughlin, "Human and Animal Emotion."

66. On nonnatural desire, see *ST* I-II 30.3–4; on nonnatural pleasure, see *ST* I-II 31.3, 31.7; on nonnatural fear, see *ST* I-II 41.3 (where he also talks, in passing, about nonnatural love). Aquinas also discusses anger in a similar context. Following Aristotle, Aquinas maintains that, in one sense, anger is more natural than desire, since it is more rational and therefore more proper to the human person. However, he also notes that, in another sense, desire is more natural than anger because it is more essential to our physical nature (*ST* I-II 46.5). Although his clarifications

our natural inclinations; other times they are not (though they can never be in disharmony with *all* of our natural inclinations: nonnatural passions must be in harmony with our natural inclinations to some extent for the sense appetite to have been moved to act). Nonnatural passions can become attuned even to objects that in some way are opposed to the inclinations of rational human nature, to the point that disordered appetitive inclinations become connatural (in a certain sense) to a particular individual.[67]

Aquinas gives particular attention to nonnatural desire in the *Treatise on the Passions*, and so turning to his treatment of nonnatural desire helps clarify the category of nonnatural passion more generally. Natural desire is oriented toward objects that are naturally pleasurable to the senses, while nonnatural desire is oriented toward objects that are seen as pleasurable through some rational judgment of their desirability. Nonnatural desires are not only oriented toward more abstract objects; they can also be oriented toward the goods of our animal nature, although under a different aspect. For example, the desire for a particular kind of food because it is judged especially tasty or healthy is a nonnatural desire.[68] Aquinas does not work out the details of how nonnatural desires come to be formed, but it seems that natural desires are shaped over time into nonnatural desires by a combination of reason and intellectual affection. Although sensible desire is naturally oriented toward sensually pleasurable objects, and particularly the pleasures of touch, the only kind of pleasure that Aquinas attributes to animals,[69] reason and intellectual affection over time can permeate memory and the sense appetite. They form complex mental associations between certain objects, such as money or praise, and the experience of physical pleasure, such as eating or the comfort of being held as an infant. Very quickly, a complex web of associations penetrates the sense appetite and forms many nonnatural desires. For the most part, then, with the possible exception of infants and very young children, purely natural desires are

about anger and his attempts to reconcile his system with Aristotle's terminology can be confusing, Aquinas evidently sees anger as especially open to being shaped by a rational subject into a nonnatural passion.

67. *ST* I-II 31.7. For a discussion of the notion of connaturality vis-à-vis affectivity in Aquinas, see Thomas Ryan, "Revisiting Affective Knowledge and Connaturality in Aquinas," *Theological Studies* 66 (2005): 54–55.

68. Loughlin, "Human and Animal Emotion," 57–58.

69. *ST* I-II 35.2 ad 3. The pleasures of touch seem to define natural pleasure for humans as well (See *ST* I-II 72.2).

rarely experienced.[70] The same kind of mechanism that forms nonnatural desires seems to apply to other nonnatural passions.

Aquinas never defines nonnatural desire according to its appetite of origin, and so there is some ambiguity about whether nonnatural desires are movements of the sense appetite or movements of the will. On the one hand, Aquinas's classification of nonnatural desire as *concupiscentia* strongly suggests that it is a movement of the sense appetite, since Aquinas limits the scope of *concupiscentia* to the desires of the sense appetite.[71] On the other hand, he maintains elsewhere that in a less strict sense *concupiscentia* can also denote the will's desire.[72] Moreover, the dependence of nonnatural desire on rational judgment suggests that it originates in the intellectual appetite. Also, nonnatural *concupiscentia* can be infinite,[73] a characteristic associated with desires of the will rather than of the sense appetite. Further, Aquinas describes the pleasure that follows nonnatural desire as *delectatio spiritualis,* in contradistinction to the bodily pleasures associated with touch.[74] It is not clear how to reconcile these seeming contradictory descriptions of nonnatural desire. The simplest and most plausible interpretation is that nonnatural desires involve movements of both the sense appetite and the will.[75] This same conclusion seems to apply to other nonnatural passions as well.

Overflow to the Passions

According to Aquinas, the will's loves, desires, and joys, as well as its hates, aversions, and sorrows, can spill over into the passions of the sense appetite by a kind of overflow,[76] because "it is not possible for the will to be moved intensely toward something without exciting some passion in the sense appetite."[77] He mentions specific examples. The will's desire for wisdom or other spiritual goods can spill over into the sense appetite;[78] the joy of contemplation can soothe pain felt in the senses;[79] the will's joy in an

70. Loughlin, "Human and Animal Emotion," 58.

71. *ST* I-II 30.1.

72. *ST* I-II 31.3.

73. *ST* I-II 30.4.

74. *ST* I-II 72.2.

75. His discussion of joy and spiritual pleasure is particularly suggestive of this interpretation. See *ST* I-II 31.3–4.

76. "In the powers of the soul there is an overflow from the higher to the lower. And in this way the pleasure of contemplation, which is in the superior part, overflows to mitigate even the pain that is in the senses" (*ST* I-II 38.4 ad 3).

77. *ST* I-II 77.6. See also *ST* I-II 24.3 ad 1.

78. *ST* I-II 30.1 ad 1.

79. *ST* I-II 38.4 ad 3. Wondering is also a cause of pleasure (*ST* I-II 32.8).

act of justice can redound to the passions;[80] and in heaven, after the resurrection, though beatitude consists first and foremost of the soul's vision of God,[81] the intense spiritual joy of the saints will flood their passions and bodies with a kind of overflow.[82] Like spiritual joy, spiritual sorrow can also overflow and affect the passions and the body.[83] Although Aquinas is vague about the precise mechanism of this overflow, we might plausibly reconstruct it as follows. The will first moves the intellect by the vehemence of its affections regarding some object, so that the intellect causes the particular reason to form an intentional object that engages the passions. This new intentional object then immediately prompts a response from the sense appetite.

Some scholars have criticized Aquinas's overflow theory. Robert Roberts notes that we can get emotionally aroused about "theories, injustices, betrayals, guilds, moral improvement, and the kingdom of God," but, according to Roberts, Aquinas does not allow for the passions to respond to such objects. Consequently, Roberts argues that the distinction between the sense appetite and the intellectual appetite is not sound. He criticizes Aquinas for a view of emotion that dissociates passion from rationality, and he sees this overflow theory as "an ad hoc move to save the faculty psychology."[84] This objection, however, fails to appreciate that the category of nonnatural passions allows for passionate reactions to immaterial objects. There is no need to "save" the faculty psychology by an overflow theory or any other device: the close relationship of the different powers of the soul has already been well-established by the category of nonnatural desires.[85] Moreover, Aquinas holds that we come to know immaterial concepts through phantasms (that is, a sort of interior image) of material objects,[86] and in fact explicitly denies that it is possible for our intellect to know anything without the mediation of phantasms.[87] Consequently, on Aquinas's account, even apart from

80. *ST* I-II 59.5.

81. *ST* I-II 3.8.

82. *ST* I-II 3.3, 4.5–6. Aquinas writes, "In perfect happiness the whole man is perfected and fulfilled, his lower parts by overflow from his higher parts" (*ST* I-II 3.3 ad 3).

83. *ST* I-II 37.2.

84. Roberts, "Aquinas on Morality of Emotions," 295. Mark Drost notes Roberts's criticism with some sympathy (Drost, "Aquinas on Intentionality," 459).

85. Claudia Eisen Murphy also notes and dismisses this criticism of Roberts and a similar one made by Anthony Kenny (Eisen Murphy, "Responsibility for Our Emotions," 169n16).

86. *ST* I 85.1.

87. *ST* I 84.7.

his discussion of natural and nonnatural desires, it is easy to explain why the passions respond to concepts. Since concepts are known through phantasms abstracted from material objects, they are directly related to sense experience and thus the sense appetite, and so it follows naturally that the passions might respond to the apprehension of a concept.[88]

According to Aquinas, would it be possible to experience intellectual affection without some kind of overflow to the passions, some kind of passionate involvement? Shawn Floyd grants that Aquinas makes a distinction between passions of the soul and intellectual affections, but he does not think that Aquinas would hold that we ever experience "pure" intellectual affection. Our experience of intellectual affection, he argues, is always accompanied by some corresponding passion: "acts involving the will must occur through sense appetite."[89] Contrary to Floyd, Daniel Westberg argues that according to Aquinas, we do experience passionless affections, and then defends the soundness of this view.[90]

Of these two interpretations, Westberg's seems the more plausible. On the question of Aquinas's view, there is substantial textual evidence that he does indeed hold that we can experience passionless affection, and furthermore that it constitutes a significant aspect of human experience. For example, Aquinas notes that we can have affection for divine things without experiencing bodily change.[91] The possibility of passionless affection seems important to explain human experience within Aristotelian psychology, because the will's desires are often in conflict with the passions. People often act counter to the inclinations of their passions because of other interests, indicating that the will's affections and the passions do not necessarily move in tandem. Furthermore, people often experience good and bad feelings simultaneously on seemingly different levels. For example, a soldier who is wounded while performing some heroic action may feel a combination of physical pain and sadness for the death of a companion, while simultaneously experiencing some sense of contentment for having acting heroically. It is possible to explain this combination of suffering and

88. This point was suggested to me by Michael Sherwin.

89. Floyd, "Aquinas on Emotion," 170.

90. Westberg, "Emotion and God," 112–15.

91. *ST* I-II 22.3 ad 1. In the same article, Aquinas also writes: "When love, joy, and the like are attributed to God or the angels or to our intellectual appetite, they refer to simple acts of will having similar effects to the passions of the soul that share the same name, but without passion" (*ST* I-II 22.3 ad 3). See also *ST* I-II 30.1 ad 1, 31.4, 59.2, 59.5; *ST* II-II 18.1.

contentment purely on the level of the passions and to argue that the conflicting passions are in conflict simply because they are directed to different objects. Nonetheless, this explanation is somewhat unsatisfactory, because there seems to be something different in kind between the soldier's subdued contentment in having acted heroically and his suffering.

Aquinas makes use of the category of intellectual affection to address just this question, that is, how it is possible to feel sorrow and joy at the same time. After explaining how sorrow and joy can refer to either movements of the sense appetite or acts of the will, he shows how this distinction explains why it is possible to rejoice and sorrow over the same thing: in this case, one's sins. He explains that joy and sorrow cannot be simultaneous with respect to the same aspect of the same thing, since the same aspect of the same thing cannot please and displease at the same time. However, joy and sorrow can be simultaneous in another way:

> If joy and sorrow are not concerned with the same thing under the same aspect, but rather with different things or the same thing under different aspects, there is no opposition between the joy and sadness in question. Therefore there is nothing preventing us from rejoicing and sorrowing at the same time. So when we see a just man afflicted, we are simultaneously pleased by his justice and displeased by his affliction. And in this way it is possible for someone to be displeased at having sinned but also pleased at being displeased because the displeasure is accompanied by the hope of pardon. Thus sorrow itself can be a cause for joy.[92]

Aquinas's explanation needs some clarification. On its most obvious level, it seems to explain only how the same object could arouse different passions: that one's sins inspire the passion of sadness under the aspect of evil, but also the passion of pleasure considered in relation to the hope of God's pardon. However, because he introduces this explanation by noting that joy and sorrow can refer to either movements of the sense appetite or acts of the will, it is clear that the joy in question is a movement of the will, and the sorrow is a passion. The possibility of a movement of the will coexisting with a seemingly opposed movement of the sense appetite also emerges in different discussions of fortitude. He affirms, for instance, that the brave man might experience "spiritual pleasure" (*delectatio animalis*) in his virtue, even while he also suffers "spiritually" (*animaliter*) and "bodily" (*corporaliter*).[93] These

92. *ST* III 84.9 ad 2. See also *ST* III 85.1.

93. *ST* II-II 123.8.

examples indicate that Aquinas does not think that all intellectual affections are automatically shared by the sense appetite.

However, strictly speaking, Aquinas's discussion of how it is possible to rejoice in the will while sorrowing in the passions does not address directly the question of whether humans experience purely intellectual affection. It is conceivable that the only reason that the brave man does not experience pleasure in his sense appetite, even while rejoicing in his will, is that his sensible sorrow effectively drowns out the possibility of sensible pleasure. In his discussion of the vice of anger, for instance, Aquinas affirms that the sense appetite follows the movements of the will, unless there is some obstacle.[94] So Aquinas might be willing to affirm that, as a matter of fact, intellectual affection always correlates with some movements of the sense appetite, and that the only question is whether the sense appetite mirrors the affections of the intellectual appetite, or instead drowns out their parallel passions. Nonetheless, Aquinas seems to affirm that something could generate intellectual affection without eliciting any passion, even when there is no special obstacle to its overflow.[95]

94. In humans, the passion of anger "necessarily follows from the simple movement of the will, because an inferior appetite naturally follows the movement of a superior appetite, unless there is something that obstructs it" (*ST* II-II 158.8).

95. The following passage is particularly suggestive: "The moral virtues that are not about passions, but about operations, can be without the passions (such as the virtue of justice), because through these operations the will is applied to its proper action, which is not passion. But the act of justice leads to joy, at least in the will, where joy is not a passion. If this joy is multiplied by the perfection of justice, the joy will overflow to the sense appetite, since the inferior powers follow the movements of the superior powers, as was said above. Through this sort of overflow, therefore, the more perfect the virtue, the more it causes passion" (*ST* I-II 59.5). See also *ST* I-II 22.3 ad 1.

CHAPTER 4

Passion, Reason, and Virtue

Aquinas maintains that the passions naturally obey reason and that over time reason's guidance becomes embedded in the sense appetite, manifesting itself in either virtuous or vicious passions. This chapter will lay out his account of how the passions are specified by reason and will into character traits, with particular attention to virtue.

Passion and Reason

"The movement of an appetitive power follows the act of an apprehensive power,"[1] and the passions follow the apprehension of intentional objects, as was discussed earlier.[2] This is the first way that cognition affects the passions. After the passions respond to intentional objects, reason can influence the passions either directly, by reshaping the intentions to which they respond, or indirectly, by forming rational judgments that the will executes and that somehow affect the passions in their execution.

"Born to Be Moved by Reason"

Although the passions depend on the cognitive powers, they also enjoy some autonomy. The irascible and concupiscible powers "do not obey the command of reason automatically, but have their own proper movements, by which they sometimes oppose reason."[3] This autonomy, paradoxically,

1. *ST* I-II 46.2.

2. This has an important interpretative consequence. Although Aquinas sometimes speaks of particular classes of passions as irrational, "irrational" here must be understand in the very specific sense of being directed toward objects that contradict the goods identified by right reason. Since he maintains that cognition is a necessary prerequisite for passion, he does not mean that the passions are noncognitive or independent of the mechanisms of rational thought.

3. *ST* I-II 56.4 ad 3.

is oriented toward the service of reason. According to Aquinas, the passions are inclined toward the guidance of reason.[4] "It is natural to the sense appetite to be moved by the rational appetite," or literally, "the sense appetite is born to be moved by the rational appetite" (*appetitus sensitivus natus est moveri ab appetitu rationali*).[5] Elsewhere he uses slightly stronger language and says that for the passions "it is natural to obey reason" (*natae sunt rationi obedire*).[6] He holds that it is natural for any cognition-dependent appetite, the sense appetite as well as the will, to be moved by reason and by reason's command.[7] Consequently, in humans but not in animals, the passions can be "rational by participation."[8] The natural capacity to be moved by reason does not mean that the sense appetite is like a lump of clay that can be molded passively into any shape. Rather, according to Aquinas, the sense appetite responds to reason in a way that involves its own natural dynamism. The sense appetite is oriented toward reason's guidance, but it responds to reason on its own terms. In a discussion of the difference between the passions and moral virtue, Aquinas rests part of his argument on this dynamic orientation of the sense appetite toward reason, noting that "appetite tends [*tendit*] toward conformity with reason."[9] This natural tendency of the sense appetite is compromised by original sin, because the complete subjection of the lower powers to reason is a gift of grace.[10] Nonetheless, although the passions are not completely subject to reason in humanity's fallen condition, the sense appetite still obeys reason "to some extent" (*aliqualiter*).[11] This idea—that the passions in their inner structure tend toward

4. My analysis of this aspect of Aquinas's thought and my appreciation of its significance is greatly indebted to the works of Anna Terruwe and Conrad Baars.

5. *ST* I-II 50.3 ad 3.

6. *ST* I-II 56.4. See also *ST* I-II 50.3 ad 1, 74.3; *ST* III 18.2.

7. *ST* I 81.3; *ST* I-II 53.1, 68.4.

8. For example, see *ST* I-II 56.4 ad 1, 56.6 ad 2, 60.1. The phrase is derived from Aristotle: see Aristotle, *Ethics*, I.13, 1102b13, b26, b30. See also Elisabeth Uffenheimer-Lippens, "Rationalized Passion and Passionate Rationality: Thomas Aquinas on the Relation between Reason and the Passions," *Review of Metaphysics* 56 (2003): 542–47, and Gondreau, "The Passions and the Moral Life," 435.

9. *ST* I-II 59.1. As he progresses through the *Summa*, Aquinas seems to become more emphatic about the natural tendency of the passions to look to reason for guidance.

10. *ST* I 95.1. See also *ST* I-II 85.3, where Aquinas discusses how original sin introduces disorder into the passions and thwarts their natural inclination toward virtue: "All the powers of the soul are destitute in a certain way of their proper order, by which they would be naturally ordered to virtue, and on account of this destitution nature is said to be wounded."

11. *ST* I 95.2.

the guidance of reason—is central to Aquinas's account and one of its most fascinating features.[12]

Reason and will each influence the passions in their own way, and he differentiates sharply between their respective influences.[13] Aquinas's most sustained discussion of this topic is in the *Prima pars,* question 81, article 3. He begins with reason, first summarizing the dependence of the sense appetite upon apprehension:

> In other animals, it is natural to the sense appetite to be moved by the estimative power, as when a sheep fears a wolf after judging it to be an enemy. However, as was said above, in man, in place of the estimative power, there is the cogitative power; some call it particular reason because it collates individual intentions. It follows that it is natural to man's sense appetite to be moved by particular reason.[14]

Memory and discursive reasoning continually shape and reshape particular reason's evaluation of objects, and the *intentio* of a given object varies accordingly.[15] For instance, a man sees a wolf, and his intentional grasp of the wolf includes a sense that the wolf is a threatening evil, and so fear follows. On another day, he sees the same wolf again, but this time he is carrying a

12. One might object that this account overplays Aquinas's account of the sense appetite's ordering to reason. It is one thing to say that Aquinas holds that the sense appetite is naturally susceptible to being molded by reason; it is another thing to say that Aquinas thinks that the sense appetite actually inclines toward this guidance, even if only to a limited extent. The following passage, taken from Aquinas's treatment of avarice, offers support for this objection. He writes, "Virtue is perfected according to reason, but vice is perfected according to the inclination of the sense appetite" (*ST* II-II 118.7 ad 1; see also *ST* I-II 71.2 ad 3). This passage can be read as implying that the sense appetite does not seek out the guidance of reason and that the sense appetite might passively accept reason's guidance, but it is not actually inclined toward it.

However, this passage need not be read so strictly, especially since Aquinas is writing not to define the nature of sense appetite's relation to reason, but rather to explain why avarice is a capital vice. In the light of his explicit statements about sense appetite's ordering to reason, it seems best to interpret this comment as explaining that vice perfects certain inclinations of the sense appetite, but not all of them, and that the sort of perfection characteristic of vice is accomplished at the expense of the sense appetite's inclination toward the guidance of reason. Elsewhere, for example, Aquinas notes that, since desire (*concupiscentia*) is naturally guided by reason, desire is natural to man only insofar as it follows reason. Consequently, disordered passion, precisely because it is departs from reason's guidance, is not natural to man (*ST* I-II 82.4 ad 1).

13. "The irascible and concupiscible passions obey the superior part, in which there is the intellect (or reason) and the will, in two ways: first, by obeying the reason; second, by obeying the will" (*ST* I 81.3).

14. *ST* I 81.3.

15. Aquinas discusses some examples of reason reshaping the intentions of objects and affecting passion accordingly in *ST* I-II 42.5 ad 3.

bazooka, and so his intentional grasp of the wolf does not include a sense that the wolf is a threatening evil, and, consequently, fear does not follow. Aquinas explains how particular reason is guided by universal reason as follows: "Moreover, it is natural to this particular reason to be moved and directed by universal reason, as when individual conclusions are logically derived from universal propositions. Evidently, therefore, universal reason commands the sense appetite, which is divided into the concupiscible and the irascible, and this appetite obeys."[16] Particular reason, an interior sensory power, is the faculty that evaluates sensible objects with respect to the inclinations of the sense appetite.[17] Universal reason, an immaterial power, is the locus of abstract thought, and as such it has oversight over particular reason. Its judgments, however, have to be applied by engaging particular reason; its conclusions do not penetrate particular reason automatically.

The passions obey reason, not the intellect (*intellectus*, which can also be translated as "understanding").[18] Intellect and reason are different aspects of the same cognitive power, but intellect indicates the power's capacity to understand acquired knowledge, while reason indicates the power's capacity to reason actively toward the acquisition of new knowledge.[19] Reason rather than intellect claims the obedience of the passions, because it is reason rather than intellect that applies universal principles to particular reason, and thus reshapes the intentional objects to which passion responds. "The deduction of singular conclusions from universal principles is not the work of the intellect as such but of reason. Therefore the irascible and concupiscible are better said to obey the reason than the intellect. Anyone can experience this in himself: by applying certain universal considerations, anger, fear, and other such things can be mitigated or instigated."[20] There is a missing premise in this excerpt: the "certain universal considerations" do not directly influence the passions, but rather through particular

16. *ST* I 81.3.

17. *ST* I 78.4.

18. Thomas Hibbs argues that Aquinas's concept of *intellectus*, when properly understood, anticipates contemporary developments in philosophy of mind that seek to re-appropriate Aristotle's concept of *nous*, in order to stake out the conceptual space for a richer receptivity in the act of knowing. See Thomas Hibbs, "Against a Cartesian Reading of *Intellectus* in Aquinas," *Modern Schoolman* 66 (1988): 55–69.

19. The relation of reasoning to understanding "is that of moving to resting, or of acquiring to having" (*ST* I 79.8).

20. *ST* I 81.3.

reason's evaluation of objects and formation of intentions. After universal reason has influenced particular reason, the objects are apprehended as different intentions, and modified or different passions are elicited. This does not mean that universal reason has absolute control over the passions. To the contrary, it exerts very limited influence and cannot alter the essential structure of the passions. Universal reason affects the passions only insofar as it affects how particular reason forms intentions of the objects to which they respond, and there are limits to particular reason's capacity to interpret sense perception counterfactually. No amount of reasoning can convert the apprehension of a rampaging grizzly bear into the intentional equivalent of a friendly neighborhood dog, at least for those who are remotely sane. Fear may be increased or decreased by reflecting on the situation, but the apprehension of a rampaging grizzly bear tends to inspire the passion of fear, barring exceptional circumstances or an exceptional individual.

Aquinas next turns to the will:

> The sense appetite is subject to the will with respect to execution, which is accomplished by the motive power. For in other animals movement immediately follows the concupiscible and irascible appetites, as when a sheep flees immediately after becoming afraid of a wolf, because there is no superior appetite in them to resist. But man is not moved immediately by the irascible and concupiscible appetites: he waits for the command of the will, which is the superior appetite.[21]

The tendencies of the sense appetite present themselves to the will in order to be executed; they cannot force themselves on the subject without the will's consent. (Elsewhere he clarifies that this general rule does not always apply: in unusual circumstances, as when there is bodily indisposition, the passions can overwhelm the will.)[22] The will, however, cannot modify the passions in the way reason can. But though the will qua will does not shape the actual passions, the will is important to reason's modification of intentions, since it can command universal reason to saturate particular reason with its conclusions: "The sense appetite does not obey reason directly, but through the mediation of the will."[23]

21. *ST* I 81.3.

22. *ST* I-II 10.3. Aquinas discusses the capacity of the passions to move the will in various respects, sometimes in ways that diminish moral responsibility. See *ST* I-II 9.2 ad 3, 17.7 ad 2, 77.1, 77.3, 77.6–7.

23. *ST* I-II 46.4 ad 1.

Reason's Political Rule of the Passions

Aquinas frequently adverts to a favorite metaphor, borrowed from a brief but evocative sketch in Aristotle's *Politics*, to illustrate reason's control of the passions.[24] In an objection, he argues that our experience of internal conflict proves that the passions do not obey reason. Then he replies to this objection with a reflection on Aristotle's metaphor:

> Aristotle says in the *Politics* that both despotic and political rule can be observed in animals: for the soul governs the body with despotic rule, but the intellect governs the appetite with political and regal rule. Rule is despotic when someone rules slaves who cannot resist his mastery, because they have nothing of their own. Rule is political and regal, however, when someone rules the free: those who are subject to being governed by a ruler, but nonetheless have something of their own, on account of which they can resist his mastery.
>
> In this way, therefore, the soul is said to govern the body with despotic rule. For the members of the body cannot in any way resist the mastery of the soul: hand and foot are moved immediately by the appetite, as is any bodily member that can be moved by the will. But intellect or reason is said to govern the irascible and concupiscible powers with political rule, because the sense appetite has something of its own, and therefore can resist the mastery of reason. For it is natural to the sense appetite to be moved, not only by the estimative power in other animals, and for the cogitative power (directed by universal reason) in man, but also by imagination and sensation. So it is that we experience the irascible and concupiscible powers resisting reason when we sense or imagine something pleasurable that reason forbids, or something distressing that reason commands. And thus the fact that the irascible and concupiscible powers resist reason in something does not mean that they do not obey it.[25]

24. "At all events we may firstly observe in living creatures both a despotical and a constitutional rule; for the soul rules the body with a despotical rule, whereas the intellect rules the appetites with a constitutional and royal rule." Aristotle, *Politics* I.5, 1254b5, in *The Complete Works of Aristotle,* ed. Jonathan Barnes, 2 vols. (Princeton, N.J.: Princeton University Press, 1984). Aquinas refers to this same metaphor six times in various parts of the *Summa theologiae* (*ST* I 81.3 ad 2; *ST* I-II 9.2 ad 3, 17.7, 56.4 ad 3, 58.2, 74.1). Though his basic interpretation of it remains constant, his various references develop the metaphor in different ways. Note that Aquinas reverses Aristotle's use of the metaphor: instead of using the passions to understand politics, he uses politics to understand the passions.

For discussions of this metaphor and its centrality to Aquinas's theory of the passions, see G. J. McAleer, "The Politics of the Flesh: Rahner and Aquinas on *Concupiscentia,*" *Modern Theology* 15 (1999): 355–65; White, "The Passions of the Soul," 105–6; Gondreau, *Passions of Christ's Soul,* 273–76; Pasnau, *Aquinas on Human Nature,* 257–64; and Thomas Ryan, "Aquinas' Integrated View of Emotions, Morality, and the Person," *Pacifica* 14 (2001): 64–65.

25. *ST* I 81.3 ad 2.

It is not surprising that Aquinas appeals to Aristotle's metaphor so frequently. It beautifully captures some key points that are central to Aquinas's account of the passions: the passions operate independently of reason, but nonetheless are inclined to obey it, and yet if reason attempts to rule the passions like the soul rules the body, the passions will erupt in rebellion. Furthermore, the metaphor implies that the inclinations of the passions are basically legitimate, just in need of some guidance.[26] Elsewhere he echoes this view by distancing himself from some more extreme ideas about the soul's ideal mastery over passion. For instance, in response to Augustine's contention that genital arousal would have been subject to the will in the Garden of Eden, Aquinas instead maintains that the genitals have their own proper principles of motion that respond not to the rational powers, but to the apprehension of objects.[27] His assessment of the passions is notably optimistic. Despite the possibility of internal conflict, Aquinas trusts the fundamental orientation of the passions, as well as their capacity to be guided by reason.[28] On this point he departs from his contemporaries. In Bonaventure's view, the passions lack an instinctual drive toward conformity with reason and an intrinsic ordering to human flourishing. They can be forced to submit to reason (*obtemperat rationi*) by an exterior imposition, but their independent dynamism is an inherent threat to virtue.[29] Bonaventure does

26. McAleer brings out the legitimacy of the "wants" of the various passions in his interpretation of Aquinas on the political rule of reason: "Reason, he says, rules the flesh by a political or royal rule as when a governor rules over free men. Which is to say, rational appetite as the superior has the role of commanding the lower appetite but also the responsibility to ensure that the sense appetite is able to satisfy its legitimate wants. The model of political community is designed to alert the reader that the human is a composite of needs which must be brought into a well-ordered community of mutual satisfaction. Reason does not have an absolute authority over the senses so that it can command the senses in any manner it wishes" (McAleer, "Politics of the Flesh," 357).

McAleer revisits Aquinas's "politics of the flesh" in greater detail in *Ecstatic Morality and Sexual Politics*. One of the central claims of his book is that Aquinas's understanding of body and desire avoids the internal metaphysical violence implicit in many other accounts of sexual desire, sometimes in spite of their explicit goals.

27. *ST* I-II 17.9 ad 3; see also Augustine, *City of God*, 14.17, 14.20, 14.26. Aquinas's seeming affirmation of Augustine's position on this point in *ST* I 98.2 must be read in light of *ST* I-II 17.9 ad 3.

28. For a similar interpretation of Aquinas's understanding of the passions and their role in the moral life, and how this stems from his view that the passions can be guided by reason, see Gondreau, "The Passions and the Moral Life," esp. 431–42.

29. Bonaventure, *Commentaria in quatuor libros Sententiarum*, III 33.1.3 ad 1; Marie-Dominique Chenu, "Les passions vertueuses: L'anthropologie de saint Thomas," *Revue philosophique de Louvain* 72 (1974): 13–16; W. D. Hughes, Introduction, notes, and appendices to *Summa theologiae*,

not share Aquinas's metaphysics of appetite, and consequently he views the autonomy of the passions as a hindrance rather than a help to virtue. For Aquinas, the passions are not a threat to human virtue but an essential component, and the ideal relationship between the passions and reason is more fluid. Moreover, while the passions sometimes hinder the use of reason, sometimes they sharpen it, too, since "pleasure that follows the act of reason, strengthens the use of reason," and moderate fear concentrates the mind.[30] Virtue consists not in the forced submission of passion to reason, or the evisceration of passion into something manageable, but the rational ordering of the various faculties toward flourishing.[31] He builds his account of passion and virtue on this simple but controversial outlook.[32]

Passion and the Formation of Character

As individuals respond to particular events and establish patterns of interaction between passion and reason, character traits emerge. Through their past actions, individuals become disposed to act freely in certain determinate ways. The grumpy individual becomes habitually alert to opportunities for sarcastic remarks, and skilled in their delivery; the Boy Scout is quick to help an elderly woman cross the street, even after his daily good deed, and makes conversation with her easily. Aquinas addresses this topic under the category of *habitus*,[33] which he derives from Aristotle and defines as "determinations of powers toward specific actions."[34] Such determination is necessary be-

---

vol. 23: *Virtue* (New York: McGraw-Hill Book Co., 1969), 245–46; and Gondreau, *Passions of Christ's Soul*, 276–81.

30. Aquinas notes the salutary effects of pleasure in *ST* I-II 33.4 ad 1 and of fear in *ST* I-II 44.4. He discusses how the passions can hinder or sharpen reason in various places, including *ST* I-II 10.3, 33.3, 33.4 ad 1, 37.1, 44.2, 44.4, 46.4 ad 3, 48.3, 77.7. For a discussion of Aquinas's understanding of how passion influences reason, see Uffenheimer-Lippens, "Rationalized Passion and Passionate Rationality," 547–57.

31. Chenu gives a helpful overview of the importance of the passions to Aquinas and his disagreement with Bonaventure, and also of the neglect and disparagement Aquinas's theories received in his lifetime and afterwards. See Marie-Dominique Chenu, "Body and Body Politic in the Creation Spirituality of Thomas Aquinas," in *Western Spirituality: Historical Roots, Ecumenical Routes*, ed. Matthew Fox (Santa Fe, N.M.: Bear and Company, 1981), 193–214.

32. His outlook remains controversial. The tendency to regard the passions as *intrinsically* troublesome to rational behavior continues to pervade many ethical traditions, religious and nonreligious. For a similar assessment see Chenu, "Body and Body Politic."

33. In Latin the singular and plural of *habitus*, a fourth declension noun, are identical.

34. *ST* I-II 8.2 ad 3. He turns to the subject of *habitus* immediately after finishing his catalog

cause the rational powers "are not determined toward one particular action, but rather are indiscriminately oriented toward many; they are determined toward particular actions by *habitus*."[35] For instance, the human person is not equipped from birth to speak in a particular language: the capacity for communication must be specified and developed over time. Just as we learn languages over time, in a process that requires our rational engagement, so too are *habitus* in general formed by repeated rational and voluntary acts. Once formed, *habitus* incline the rational powers toward specific activities or operations without diminishing our freedom of action.[36] They are not "habits" of unthinking routine: the concept of *habitus* signifies the active engagement of the rational powers.[37]

Like the contemporary concept of character, *habitus* denotes a certain quality of stability. Multiple acts are required to establish *habitus*, and so multiple acts are required to change them, or at least an extended period of disuse.[38] *Habitus* vary in intensity, according to the stability and vigor with which

---

of the passions (questions 22–48), having spent the earlier portions of the *Prima secundae* framing moral action as the pursuit of happiness (questions 1–5), and discussing the will and its acts (questions 6–21). This structure accurately suggests that *habitus* naturally emerge from the interactions of the will and the sense appetite (that is, from the interactions of will's affections and the soul's passions), and their mutual shaping of each other. It also suggests the danger of viewing the *Treatise on the Passions* as an isolated tract without reference to the seamless connections Aquinas makes between the will, the passions, and their specification into character traits.

Much of Aquinas's detailed discussion of *habitus* in questions 49–54 is original to the *Summa theologiae* and lacks parallels in his other writings. Its placement within the *Prima secundae* provides a particularly apt context for Aquinas's reflection on this topic, presumably by deliberate design. See Anthony Kenny, Introduction, notes, and appendices to *Summa theologiae*, vol. 22: *Dispositions for Human Acts* (New York: McGraw-Hill Book Co., 1964), xix.

35. *ST* I-II 55.1. For an analysis of the relationship of *habitus* to nature, see Ryosuke Bernard Inagaki, "*Habitus* and *Natura* in Aquinas," in *Studies in Medieval Philosophy*, ed. John Wippel (Washington, D.C.: The Catholic University of America, 1987), 159–75.

36. Aquinas allows for purely intellectual *habitus* in some senses of the word, but qualifies them as not being *habitus* or virtues in the fullest sense since they do not involve the will (see *ST* I-II 56.3, 57.1). For example, Aquinas denies that animals have *habitus*, even though they can be trained to behave in certain ways, because these acquired behavioral dispositions do not involve the will: "animals do not have power to use or not to use, which seems to belong to the idea of *habitus*" (*ST* I-II 50.3 ad 2). In a footnote, Anthony Kenny argues that Aquinas would acknowledge that animals can refuse to, say, perform a trick, but for him this would not be the result of a willed decision, and therefore could not be a *habitus* (Kenny, notes to *Summa*, 34–35). For Aquinas, the intersection of estimative sense (i.e., natural instinct), bodily dispositions toward certain passions, and memory is sufficient to explain the behavior of animals.

37. This study has avoided the once popular translation of *habitus* as "habit" for precisely this reason. See *ST* I-II 51.2, and Servais Pinckaers, "Virtue Is Not a Habit," trans. Bernard Gilligan, *Cross Currents* 12 (1962): 65–81. "Disposition" or "active disposition" is favored by Kenny in his translation of questions 49–54 of the *Summa theologiae*.

38. *ST* I-II 51.2–3, 53.

they dispose toward a specific rational activity, and their intensity increases insofar as they become more deeply imbedded in the subject.[39] Growth in the intensity of a *habitus* occurs through repeated acts of an equal or greater intensity than its current intensity. Any such act may not necessarily deepen the intensity of the *habitus,* but always at least prepares for such growth; acts of diminished intensity may diminish the *habitus.*[40]

The concept of *habitus* does not simply express the strength of our resolve to behave in certain ways, much less some empirical estimation of our future actions. *Habitus* shape our entire psychological structure, not just the rational powers: they modify all faculties that have some capacity for being shaped by reason, and actually penetrate and subsist in them. Since the sense appetite is responsive to reason, and capable of being shaped by it, there are *habitus* in the sense appetite, that is, there are stable dispositions and inclinations of the passions to respond in certain determinate ways. He writes:

> It is not natural to the powers of the nutritive part to obey the command of reason, and so there are no *habitus* in them. But it is natural to the sense powers to obey the command of reason, and so there can be some *habitus* in them. For insofar as they obey reason, they can be said to be rational in a certain way, as Aristotle says in the *Ethics.*[41]

Since the passions are "rational by participation," reason can specify them, and, by repeated acts, shape them into *habitus* that resolve the various desires of the sense appetite and the will into stable dispositions. This formation of character in turn redounds back to our desires: it confirms them and propels us toward actions that will further deepen their embeddedness in us.

Virtue and Passion

By definition *habitus* are informed by reason, but they are not necessarily informed by right reason. Depending on the choices that formed a particular *habitus,* the rational powers may or may not tend to guide particular passions effectively toward virtue and happiness. For example, due to an accumulation of choices, someone may come to have either a short temper

39. *ST* I-II 52.1–2.
40. *ST* I-II 52.3.
41. *ST* I-II 50.3 ad 1; Aristotle, *Ethics* I.13, 1101b13–14.

or extraordinary patience. Similarly, someone habitually concerned with the well-being of others may experience great anger hearing about some injustice, while those less concerned about others do not. In each case, rational decisions penetrate and form the sense appetite. When they form it according to right reason, the passions are directed toward virtue. Disordered decisions, however, dispose the sense appetite toward vice and result in "irrational" passions.

When they are consonant with human nature and directed toward authentic human flourishing, that is, when they are perfective of human nature, *habitus* are virtues.[42] When they miss the mark, they are vices. The virtues, like *habitus* in general, are not simply patterns of behavior; they denote a creative dynamism toward a stable end.[43] Virtue perfects the powers of human nature by giving them the freedom to operate with new horizons. It does not perfect them in the sense of petrifying them according to established patterns of behavior, as though virtue were something rigid and limiting. It makes them more flexible, not less.

Virtuous *habitus* are perfective not just of reason and will, but of the passions as well: "Virtue in the irascible and concupiscible powers is nothing other than a certain habitual conformity of these powers to reason."[44] This view crystallizes in Aquinas's claim that the sense appetite can be the subject, that is, the seat or location, of virtue.[45] Although he is developing a position held by Aristotle, it was controversial in his time: many of his contemporaries, including Hugh of St. Cher, John of La Rochelle, and Bonaventure, disagreed and located virtue only in the reason and the will.[46] Their

42. *ST* I-II 55.3. "Virtue names a certain perfection of a power" (*ST* I-II 55.1).

43. Servais Pinckaers elaborates on this point elegantly. Virtue, he writes, "is not a habit, formed by the repetition of material acts. It is not some higher form of psychological automatism, which would actually have the effect of weakening and destroying the moral and spiritual value of the human act. Virtue gives man the capacity for invention. It gives him the ability to create the best possible human acts in the moral sphere. In contrast to the habit of tedious routine, it is a power for innovation and renewal" (Pinckaers, "Virtue Is Not a Habit," 81).

44. *ST* I-II 56.4. "Virtue begins in the reason and terminates in the appetite insofar as the appetite is moved by reason" (*ST* I-II 59.1). In these quotations, Aquinas does not specify that virtue is subject to right reason, as opposed to reason in general, but it is implied by the context.

45. *ST* I-II 56.4, 56.5 ad 1. Aquinas qualifies his claim by observing that virtue is in the passions only insofar as they participate in reason: "Virtue cannot be in the irrational part of the soul, except to the extent that it participates in reason." Therefore, he explains, "reason or mind (*ratio sive mens*) is the proper seat of virtue" (*ST* I-II 55.4 ad 3).

46. See Aristotle, *Ethics* III.10, 1117b23; Chenu, "Les passions vertueuses," 16–18; Hughes, appendices to *Summa*, 245–46; and Gondreau, *Passions of Christ's Soul*, 276–81.

position follows from their view of passion as fundamentally irrational, just as Aquinas's more optimistic outlook follows from his view of the passions as fundamentally desirous of reason's guidance. For them, the various moral virtues describe volitional dispositions to right behavior. For Aquinas, the various moral virtues are holistic character traits with passion and reason inclined (and mutually inclining) toward our *telos*. Accordingly, he classifies different virtues according to the passions they perfect: "temperance is concerned with the concupiscible passions; fortitude, with fear and daring; magnanimity, with hope and despair; meekness with anger."[47]

The significance of this controversy emerges more clearly when comparing the fulfillment of some moral precept with and without the assistance of the passions. For example, Aquinas distinguishes between continence and chastity. Chastity is a virtue and signifies right action with the cooperation of ordinate passion, whereas continence falls short of virtue and signifies right action despite unruly passion.[48] The continent man experiences tumult in his passions when tempted by something inappropriate, and yet nonetheless conquers the temptation. The chaste man, however, does not even experience internal upheaval, which implies not the absence of passion but rather ordinate passion.[49] Similarly, in equally infuriating circumstances, one man might restrain his anger only after much internal struggle, and may have to refrain from saying anything to avoid an explosion, and another man might restrain his anger with relative ease, and perhaps also express it judiciously without saying anything inappropriate. Aquinas is unequivocal that this ordering of the sense appetite is intrinsic to moral virtue. The rational powers may be directed toward the good, but unless the sense appetite is also rightly ordered, "the resulting action will not be perfect, and therefore the principle of that action will not be a virtue."[50]

Passion is not just tamed by virtue; ordinate passion "helps the execution of reason's command" and thus positively assists the performance of virtuous acts.[51] Among other things, a rightly ordered appetite is a precondi-

47. *ST* I-II 60.4. Aquinas's analysis of particular virtues in the *Secunda secundae* includes detailed discussion of their relationship to specific passions, as will be discussed in chap. 6.

48. *ST* I-II 58.3 ad 2.

49. *ST* I-II 70.3; *ST* II-II 151.1, 155.1, 155.3–4. Aquinas argues that Christ did not have continence, because continence implies internal disorder and something less than virtue (*ST* III 7.2 ad 3).

50. *ST* I-II 58.3 ad 2.

51. *ST* I-II 59.2 ad 3.

tion to the virtue of prudence.[52] There is a sense in which virtuous passions impart "affective knowledge" that assists moral decision making, so that the right choice is selected not just by the judgment of reason, but by the instinctual response of passion.[53] Aquinas does not employ the concept of "affective knowledge" frequently, but it is not foreign to his account: he explicitly speaks of *cognitio affectiva* when writing about kinds of knowledge of God.[54]

Aquinas rejects the idea that virtue eradicates passion.[55] Passion is an essential component of moral virtue:

> The moral virtues that are concerned with the passions as their proper matter cannot exist without them. The reason for this is that otherwise it would follow that moral virtue would make the sense appetite indifferent to everything. But virtue does not consist in the passions being subject to reason, apart from their own proper acts, but rather in the passions executing the command of reason through their own proper acts.[56]

If inordinate, the passions of the soul may incline to sin, "but insofar as they are ordered to reason, they pertain to virtue."[57] Even sorrow can be a mark of virtue when moderate and appropriate, contrary to Stoic philosophy.[58] The vehement expression of anger can also be virtuous, as in Aristotle's magnanimous man "who is open about what he loves and hates and in how he speaks and acts."[59] In sum, virtue does not eradicate passion but produces ordinate passions, that is, passions actively oriented toward human flourishing.[60] Besides shaping the passions according to right reason, virtue also generates passions, especially love and joy, via overflow from intense affections of the will.[61]

The more powerfully the will is directed toward some object, the more intensely the will's affections spill into the passions.[62] Consequently, when

52. *ST* I-II 57.4, 57.5 ad 3.

53. Daniel Maguire and Thomas Ryan give a lengthy treatment of "affective knowledge" and its role in Aquinas's moral theory, especially with regard to the virtues of prudence, fortitude, and temperance, and the gifts of the Holy Spirit. See Daniel C. Maguire, "*Ratio Practica* and the Intellectualistic Fallacy," *Journal of Religious Ethics* 10 (1982): 22–39 and Ryan, "Revisiting Affective Knowledge."

54. *ST* II-II 97.2 ad 2. See also *ST* II-II 60.1.

55. *ST* I-II 59.2.

56. *ST* I-II 59.5.

57. *ST* I-II 24.2 ad 3. See also *ST* I-II 24.3.

58. *ST* I-II 59.3.

59. *ST* I-II 48.3 ad 2; Aristotle, *Ethics* IV.3, 1124b26.

60. *ST* I-II 59.5 ad 1.

61. *ST* I-II 59.5.

62. *ST* I-II 24.3 ad 1. Aquinas adds that passion can also contribute to an action's moral good-

it is well-ordered, intense passion is a mark of intense virtue. It indicates that the will is powerfully inclined toward the good and that the sense appetite has been thoroughly suffused with right reason. "The more perfect the virtue," Aquinas writes, "the more it causes passion."[63] Virtue's most characteristic affections are joy and pleasure. Virtue generates joy because the will attains goods that it desires through virtue, and when the will attains some desired good, the volitional affection of joy necessarily results (hence the proverb: virtue is its own reward).[64] There is usually some sensible pleasure too as the joy spills over into the sense appetite. Aquinas acknowledges that virtue can coexist with some amount of sensible distress,[65] and also that virtue sometimes operates without pleasure (*non delectabiliter operatur*), but he argues that even in these cases virtue operates without sorrow (*sine tristitia*).[66] In his exclusion of *tristitia* from the operation of virtue, Aquinas seems to be thinking of an affection of the intellectual appetite, or at least a type of sorrow that is more interior and less sensible. Otherwise, it would be hard to see how moderate sensible distress, and not just physical pain, could be compatible with virtue.

Aquinas gives more attention to virtue than to vice in the *Summa theologiae*. In contrast to the *Summa de vitiis et virtutibus* of William Peraldus, one of Aquinas's principal models for the *Secunda secundae,* Aquinas does not discuss virtues and vices in separate sections.[67] Instead, in order to avoid prolixity and repetition, as he explains to his readers in the prologue to the *Secunda secundae,* he discusses vice within his treatment of the relevant virtue.[68] But brevity and pedagogical clarity are not his only objectives. The focus on virtue reflects Aquinas's desire to frame the moral life in terms of human flourishing, and not in terms of avoiding vice (which is the more difficult pedagogical enterprise, since ideal human functioning is often more open-ended and harder to imagine than colorful sins and vices). He spends the first seventy questions of the *Prima secundae* building a picture of the

ness when an agent makes a deliberate choice to be affected by passion in order to act more promptly.

63. *ST* I-II 59.5.

64. *ST* I-II 32.6, 34.4, 59.4 ad 1, 59.5, 60.2, 70.1 ad 2; *ST* II-II 28.1, 123.8; see also *ST* I-II 31.3–4, 33.4 For a virtue to cause joy it must truly be a virtue—that is, the subject's intellect, will, and passions must fully engage the *telos* of that particular virtue.

65. *ST* I-II 59.3. See also *ST* II-II 28.2.

66. *De virtutibus* 1.10 ad 15.

67. Boyle, "Setting of the *Summa*," 83–85.

68. Boyle notes that Aquinas probably has William Peraldus in mind when he speaks about the repetition he wants to avoid (ibid., 85).

virtuous life brick by brick, including its perfection in the beatitudes and the gifts and fruits of the Holy Spirit, before turning to vice.[69] Among other things, Aquinas's approach downplays the structural significance traditionally allocated to the seven deadly sins.[70]

Nonetheless, he does devote substantial attention to vice in the *Prima secundae,* and to particular vices in the *Secunda secundae.* As a type of *habitus,* vice, like virtue, resides in the sense appetite, and so much of his analysis of virtue applies to vice, only in reverse.[71] Vice also shapes the sense appetite but with negative consequences. It inclines the subject to take pleasure in disordered objects, and to lose sensitivity to spiritual goods; it also dulls the rational powers.[72] The spiritual sorrow that is the fruit of vice also spills over, engendering sensible sadness or pain, and tainting the sense appetite's enjoyment of even authentically desirable objects. Hence intense passion is a mark of intense vice, insofar as this intense passion is the consequence of evil acts.[73]

The passions and affections reveal moral character because they are essential to moral character. Aquinas claims, for example, that a man can be judged good or evil by what his will finds pleasurable.[74]

The Moral Quality of Passion

Passions are morally good or morally evil only to the extent that they reflect the influence of the will.[75] Bodily movements are morally good or morally evil only insofar as they are voluntary, he argues, and so too are the passions.[76] Citing Augustine, Aquinas affirms that passions are morally good when they spring from rightly ordered love and thus a rightly ordered will.[77] Similarly, passions are evil when their orientation is determined by a misdirected will. He distinguishes between generic passions and specific passions. The former have no moral quality; the latter are good or bad depend-

69. The number seventy signifies perfection in biblical and medieval numerology, and the fact that his overview of ideal human functioning spans exactly seventy questions is perhaps not an accident.

70. Jordan, "Invention of the *Summa theologiae,*" 94.

71. *ST* I-II 74.3.

72. For Aquinas's treatment of the psychological effects of specific vices, see chap. 6.

73. *ST* I-II 24.3 ad 3, 77.6.

74. *ST* I-II 34.4. See also *ST* I-II 24.1 ad 3.

75. *ST* I-II 24.1–2.

76. *ST* I-II 24.1.

77. *ST* I-II 24.2; Augustine, *City of God,* 9.4.

ing on their object. Moreover, because passions are movements of the sense appetite, not *habitus* like virtues and vices, no passion, considered in itself, is a vice.[78] For example, the word "envy" does not denote an elemental passion: it denotes either a specific passion, sorrow about the good of another, or a vicious *habitus* of the sense appetite disposed toward the same.[79]

With respect to the moral imputability of the passions, Aquinas differentiates between consequent and antecedent passions. Consequent passions follow acts of the will and flow from them as a natural consequence. They ratify the acts of the rational appetite on the level of the sense appetite. For example, a person prone to deliberate acts of violence might experience an excessive amount of anger. Consequent passions are the kind of passion most properly described as good or evil. By contrast, antecedent passions precede acts of the will, and oppose the preexisting dispositions of the will. In its most typical sense, antecedent passion is an involuntary movement that inclines the subject toward some disordered sensible object.[80] But it can also be an involuntary movement that is in accord with right reason but contrary to the subject's will.[81] In both cases, should the will follow the lead of antecedent passion, the resulting choice will be less voluntary, and therefore less imputable to the subject.[82] The person overcome by involuntary anger is less guilty of a crime, and the person who gives to the poor only out of an involuntary feeling of pity is less commendable.

There are two sources of antecedent passion in the human person: original sin, which affects the human race globally, and repented personal sin, that is, sinful actions chosen by the particular person in question and then disowned. Original sin causes antecedent passion in two ways. First, the interior disunity characteristic of original sin spawns passions that are in disharmony with each other and the will. These disordered passions are antecedent passions when they are not affirmed by the will. Second, because the entire human race is affected by original sin, we are frequently victims of the sins of others. Being sinned against can exacerbate the interior disunity characteristic of original sin, as when victims of violence develop involuntary violent

78. *ST* I-II 59.1 ad 2.

79. *ST* I-II 24.4, 45.1 ad 1, 59.1; *ST* II-II 35.1–2.

80. *ST* I-II 77.6.

81. Aquinas gives the example of doing something from pity rather than a rational decision: "It is more praiseworthy when someone does a charitable work from a judgment of reason than simply from a passion of mercy" (*ST* I-II 24.3 ad 1).

82. *ST* I-II 24.3 ad 1, 77.6.

tendencies, or when the neglected poor become more prone to envy. These sorts of passions would also be classified as antecedent by Aquinas.

The other source of antecedent passion is repented personal sin. Personal sin solidifies the disorder of original sin with respect to particular passions. In Aquinas's terminology, the passions generated by personal sin are consequent passions, as long as the sinner is impenitent. If personal sins are disowned, they might still cause disordered passions, but now such passions are antecedent passions. Our disordered choices permeate our passions through vice, so that even after we decide to change our behavior, our passions may still show their influence. For example, the reformed binge-eater is likely to struggle with strong temptations to gluttony, and these temptations, insofar as they are movements of the sense appetite, are antecedent passions. Antecedent passions manifest the material dimension of human affectivity: even after their objects have been abandoned by the will, reason's past penetration of the sense appetite remains to some extent, thus generating these antecedent passions.

The terminology of antecedent and consequent passion can be confusing. Aquinas's view of antecedent passions is often misinterpreted as implying that the moral value of a good action is diminished if it follows from some prompting of the passions.[83] This interpretation follows only if one reads "antecedent" to signify simply chronological precedence, and clearly this signification is not what he intended.[84] Antecedent passion primarily implies dissonance with the will's preexisting inclinations and affections.[85]

83. For example, see Mansfield, "Antecedent Passion," and Pasnau, *Aquinas on Human Nature*, 262–63. Knuuttila explicitly rejects this interpretation of Aquinas, citing Pasnau in particular (Knuuttila, *Emotions*, 253).

84. Aquinas's few scattered comments about antecedent passions mostly seek to explain why sins committed out of involuntary passion are less grievous than fully deliberate sins, not how passions relate to subsequent virtuous acts. When this context is overlooked, it is easy to misinterpret "antecedent" as signifying simply chronological precedence.

85. Aquinas's claim that neither Adam before the fall nor Christ experienced antecedent passion (*ST* I 95.2, *ST* III 15.4) clarifies the meaning of antecedent passion. He does not mean that neither was prompted by their passions before making a conscious decision, but that their passions always directed them in harmony with their wills' desire for the good. (See chap. 7 for a detailed discussion of how this plays out in Christ's affectivity.) Because each had a fully intact human nature and a will directed toward the good, antecedent passion was impossible: the integrity of their natures precluded disordered passions, and so all of their passions were good and in accord with their wills, and therefore not antecedent. Likewise, the virtuous experience less antecedent passion than others (*De veritate* 26.8; see also Mansfield, "Antecedent Passion," 229). Their passions are more in harmony with their wills, since reason has penetrated and shaped the sense appetite into virtue.

Knowing that pity prompted someone to be generous does not, of itself, tell us whether that pity diminishes or increases the moral value of the generosity. If one is moved by pity despite one's normal volitional disposition, then the passion is antecedent, and therefore diminishes the goodness of the moral act. If one is moved precisely because previous acts of kindness have formed an attentive disposition to the needs of others, then the passion is consequent, and therefore increases the virtuousness of the generosity.[86]

The Normative Quality of Generic Passion

The typical interpretation of Aquinas is that generic passion, that is, passion considered in itself apart from a specific object, is morally neutral or indifferent.[87] Many texts support this interpretation, and it is accurate as far as it goes.[88] Generic passion is a theoretical concept that does not exist in reality, and it cannot be morally good or morally bad, because passion must be specified by an object in order to take on a moral quality. It is not enough to know that someone is sad to judge the moral quality of the sadness. If someone is sad because a virtuous person suffers unjustly, the sadness has a positive moral quality; if someone is sad because a plan to rob a bank has been foiled by the police, the sadness has a negative moral quality.

However, the typical interpretation of generic passion as morally neutral can be misleading, if morally neutral is understood in the sense of having no intrinsic relation to the moral qualities of good and evil. For Aquinas, generic passion is neither morally good nor morally evil, because it does not have a specifying object; nonetheless, generic passion has an intrinsic relation to moral value, because it is normative for the moral value of specified passions. Therefore, rather than describing generic passion as morally *neutral*, it is better to describe generic passion as morally *normative*.

86. This account of things is complex, but, as Claudia Eisen Murphy argues, the complexity of Aquinas's account of our moral responsibility for our emotions is one of its great strengths, because it mirrors the complexity of human affectivity: "The great strength of Aquinas's complicated view of our responsibility for our emotions seems to me to rest in the fact that it distinguishes between cases in which responsibility for emotions depends on someone's control over these emotions and cases in which it does not" (Eisen Murphy, "Responsibility for Our Emotions," 202).

87. For example, see Judith A. Barad, "Aquinas on the Role of Emotion in Moral Judgment and Activity," *The Thomist* 55 (1991): 403; Leo Elders, *The Ethics of Aquinas: Happiness, Natural Law, and the Virtues* (Frankfurt am Main: Peter Lang, 2005), 98–99; and Gondreau, "The Passions of Christ's Soul," 392–393.

88. For example, see *ST* I-II 24.1–2, 24.4, 34.1, 39.1.

In order to clarify what it means to say that generic passion has a normative quality, it is necessary to consider again Aquinas's remarkably positive assessment of passion qua passion as something intrinsically ordered toward flourishing, and therefore virtue. Created by God, emanating from divine *appetitus*, and directing us toward our flourishing, the passions are ontologically good in their essential nature, and the proper functioning of the passions according to their own structure is integral to human flourishing. Consequently, the moral evaluation of specific instances of a particular passion turns on whether that passion is functioning according to its own inner structure. Since the passions in their inner structure are directed toward our flourishing, and since moral goodness consists precisely in that flourishing, moral goodness is the default orientation of generic passion, even though generic passion is not itself morally good.[89]

In his discussion of sadness, for example, Aquinas explains that it is good if someone becomes sad when confronted by something saddening:

> If something saddening or painful is present, it is good if someone becomes sad or feels pain because of it. For if someone does not become sad or feel pain in the presence of an evil, either he does not feel it or he does not count it as something repugnant, and, obviously, both possibilities are evils. Consequently, it is good that sadness or pain follows from the presence of an evil.[90]

The reason that it is good to be sad about an evil is not because there is a moral principle that any sentient creature with a body should feel sad in certain circumstances. The reason that it is good to be sad about an evil is because we have a passion of sadness that operates in certain ways, and it is good for the inclinations of our nature to reach their fulfillment. The measure against which the moral quality of a specific instance of sadness is measured is the internal structure of the passion of sadness itself, not some moral code derived from abstract principles that have nothing to do with

89. Aquinas seems to come close to saying this explicitly. In a passage from the *De malo*, Aquinas explains that the sense appetite's natural inclination is not toward sin, and that therefore God, as its creator, is not responsible for causing sin: "Sin does not come from the inclination of the irascible and concupiscible powers as instituted by God, but as the powers depart from the ordination that God himself instituted, for the powers were instituted in human beings to be subject to reason. And so it is not from God when they incline to sin contrary to the ordination of reason" (*De malo*, 3.1 ad 5, trans. Richard Regan). Since the passions become disordered, and therefore evil, only if they depart from the ordination instilled in them by God, it seems that, according to Aquinas, their default orientation is toward moral goodness.

90. *ST* I-II 39.1.

the fact of sadness. Generic sadness—that is, the conceptualization of the essential structure of sadness—plays an essential role in determining the moral quality of specific instances of sadness.

There is reason to think that the central purpose of the *Treatise on the Passions* is to characterize the varieties of generic passion, so that the moral quality of specific instances of passion can be evaluated against them. First, the *Treatise* is located in the middle of the *Prima secundae,* which Aquinas writes in order to clarify the moral evaluation of human action. Second, the *Treatise* focuses on nonmoral aspects of the passions, even though its context in the *Prima secundae* indicates that Aquinas is interested in the passions primarily insofar as they are relevant to his moral theory. Third, although Aquinas does not spend much time on the moral quality of the passions in the *Treatise,* he does discuss the issue occasionally, especially in questions 24, 34, and 39, thus indicating that the morality of the passions is on his mind as he is writing the *Treatise.* Fourth, Aquinas frequently refers back to the *Treatise* to explain his analysis of specific virtues and vices in the *Secunda secundae* (as will be discussed in chapter 6).

The most plausible explanation for these observations is that Aquinas wrote the *Treatise* primarily to provide norms for the moral evaluation of specified passion. The *Treatise* charts the inner structure of the passions because Aquinas intends to measure specific passions against their generic counterparts in subsequent sections of the *Summa.* But although the *Treatise* is oriented to the moral evaluation of human action, it does not focus on moral questions since its immediate purpose is to provide an account of generic passion. Nonetheless, as he writes the *Treatise,* Aquinas does discuss the moral quality of passions from time to time, because, even though such questions are not the immediate object of the *Treatise,* the moral analysis of the passions is in fact its ultimate aim.

The normative function of generic passion is not independent of reason, since passion is intrinsically oriented toward the guidance of reason. Passion does not respond only to its intentional object; it also responds to the guidance of reason, in the various ways discussed in this chapter. The passions have their own proper spontaneity, but this spontaneity is ordered to the service of reason, because "appetite tends toward conformity with reason."[91] Generic sadness is structurally oriented toward genuine evils: sadness is mor-

91. *ST* I-II 59.1.

ally good when it responds to a genuine evil, and it is morally bad when it responds to something that is not a genuine evil. Hence, it is morally good to feel sad after learning that a friend has died, and it is morally bad to feel sad after learning that an attempt to poison a friend did not work. In both cases, generic sadness is the norm against which the particular instance of sadness is measured. Generic sadness is naturally oriented to the guidance of reason, and when reason is functioning properly, it is evident that losing a friend is a genuine evil, but having murderous plans come to nothing is not. Feeling sad about failing to murder a friend implies a departure from reason's guidance, and therefore some amount of departure from the inner structure of the passion of sadness—hence the experience of such sadness is morally defective.

Aquinas's treatment of generic passion once again illustrates his positive evaluation of the passions, and his systematic integration of the passions into his moral theory.[92] Rather than comparing particular movements of the sense appetite to some apodictic system of morality, and then determining the proper ordering of the passions accordingly,[93] Aquinas roots natural law precisely in the appetites and tendencies of human nature.[94] Our natural inclinations in fact constitute the natural law.[95] "Everything op-

92. In a 1990 state-of-the-question overview of the passions in moral theology, William Spohn notes that "in recent years, ethics has become less suspicious of emotion's role in moral experience." In doing so, he suggests, it is beginning to catch up with Aquinas: "Moral theologians who inherited a rationalist natural-law tradition have not paid as much attention to [well-ordered affectivity] as did their supposed patron saint, Thomas Aquinas." See William Spohn, "Notes on Moral Theology 1990: Passions and Principles," *Theological Studies* 52 (1991): 69–87.

93. Robert Pasnau seems to interpret Aquinas in just this way, as though he constructs his account of the proper ordering of the passions by weighing them against standards that are independent of their inner structure and derived entirely from reason (Pasnau, *Aquinas on Human Nature*, 263–64). This interpretation does not do justice to Aquinas's explicit foundation of moral norms in the inclinations of human nature.

94. For an excellent overview and defense of how Aquinas roots ethics in the inclinations of the human person, see Robert Ashmore, "Aquinas and Ethical Naturalism," *New Scholasticism* 49 (1975): 76–86. It is interesting to compare Aquinas and Ashmore to George Terzis's critique of virtue ethics (though Terzis does not specifically criticize Aquinas). Terzi centers his critique on the alleged failure of virtue ethics to provide a foundation for normative ethical standards. See George N. Terzis, "Human Flourishings: A Psychological Critique of Virtue Ethics," *American Philosophical Quarterly* 31 (1994): 333–42.

For a discussion of how Aquinas derives morality from ontology, see Aertsen, "Thomas Aquinas of the Good," and Eleonore Stump and Norman Kretzmann, "Being and Goodness," in *Thomas Aquinas: Contemporary Philosophical Perspectives*, ed. Brian Davies (New York: Oxford University Press, 2002), 295–323.

95. See *ST* I-II 94.2. The relationship of natural law to natural inclinations is an area of considerable controversy in the interpretation of Aquinas. Many read Aquinas as equating the precepts of practical reason—and not the natural inclinations—with natural law. They point out that, accord-

posed to natural inclination is a sin," he writes, "because it opposes the law of nature."[96] In this understanding of natural law, the various command-

---

ing to Aquinas, law "is an ordinance of reason for the common good, given by the one who has care of the community, and promulgated" (*ST* I-II 90.4). Since natural inclinations do not pertain to cognition, it is argued, they cannot constitute an ordinance of reason. Therefore, natural inclinations may be closely related to natural law, but they cannot themselves constitute natural law.

However, certain texts indicate that Aquinas holds that the natural inclinations are indeed natural law, at least in some important sense, since through them creatures participate in the eternal law by which God directs the universe (*ST* I-II 91.2; see also parts of *ST* I-II 94.2, esp. ad 2). Moreover, since God is the legislator of natural law, natural inclinations can be still understood as an ordinance of reason—only of God's reason, not ours (see *ST* I-II 91.1). This interpretation of natural inclination as natural law finds particularly strong support in a text where Aquinas discusses how law exists in one way in God's intellect, and in another way in his creatures. He writes: "Law, being a rule and a measure, can exist in something in two ways. In one way, law is in the one who rules and measures. In another way, law is in what is ruled and measured, because something is ruled or measured to the extent that it participates in the rule or measure. Since all things under divine providence are ruled and measured by eternal law, as has been said [in *ST* I-II 91.1], it is evident that everything participates in eternal law to some extent, inasmuch as all things have their inclinations toward their own proper acts and ends precisely because they bear the impression of eternal law. . . . This participation in eternal law by rational creatures is called 'natural law' [*lex naturalis*]" (*ST* I-II 91.2).

The identification of natural inclinations with natural law need not deny the important connection between the precepts of practical reason and natural law: in this interpretation of Aquinas, the precepts are conceptualizations of our natural inclinations. It is through the precepts of practical reason—which all pertain to the fulfillment of the inclinations of human nature—that the natural inclinations become intelligible to our reason, and thus capable of directing our deliberations. In an important sense, then, the precepts also constitute the natural law: they make the normative character of a more basic ontological reality intelligible to reason, and in this way they provide moral guidance to rational agents.

Given these reflections about the close relationship between inclination and precept, and given that other texts seem to identify the precepts of practical reason with natural law (see esp. *ST* I-II 94.1; also parts of *ST* I-II 94.2), perhaps it is best to say that, for Aquinas, the natural inclinations and the precepts of practical reason can both be called natural law, albeit in different ways. The inclinations are natural law in its relationship to appetite, and the precepts are natural law in its relationship to reason. For a discussion of some of the competing interpretations of Aquinas presently on offer, see William E. May, "Contemporary Perspectives on Thomistic Natural Law," in *St. Thomas Aquinas and the Natural Law Tradition: Contemporary Perspectives*, ed. John Goyette, Mark S. Latkovic, and Richard S. Myers (Washington, D.C.: The Catholic University of America Press, 1994), 113–56. See also Matthew Levering, "Natural Law and Natural Inclinations: Rhonheimer, Pinckaers, McAleer," *The Thomist* 70 (2006): 155–201.

For an extended defense of an interpretation of Aquinas similar to the one given here, see Pamela M. Hall, *Narrative and the Natural Law: An Interpretation of Thomistic Ethics* (South Bend, Ind.: University of Notre Dame Press, 1994). She writes: "Aquinas holds that any knowledge of the natural law must be derived in part from desire for the goods to which men and women are directed by their natures; this form of directedness is in fact the primary sense of natural law for Aquinas. This means that people judge what is, or is not, in accordance with the natural law in part by deciding which actions are, or are not, conducive to those goods they so desire. . . . The core sense of natural law is, as I have argued, exactly this for Aquinas: a kind of teleology in human nature possessed within the *inclinationes*" (96–97, 99).

96. *ST* II-II 133.1.

ments contained in divine revelation are not in tension with either natural law or our natural inclinations. Rather, the divine law of the Old and New Testaments complements natural law by pointing our desires more explicitly toward their authentic fulfillment. Divine law does not thwart desire. Divine law educates desire.[97]

Aquinas's grounding of natural law in our natural inclinations manifests extraordinary trust in the passions, insofar as he holds that the generic structure of passion is a direct manifestation of our natural inclinations. The passions in their basic tendencies are not just oriented toward virtue and human flourishing; they constitute an indispensable norm and measure of natural law. Those choices that direct the passions toward their proper *telos* are morally good, and those choices that misdirect them are not. For Aquinas, natural inclination is law, and therefore so too is generic passion, that is, the passions themselves in their inner structure.[98]

97. This notion is drawn from the work of Livio Melina. He writes: "In the ethics of classical inspiration, and in particular in Thomistic ethics, the concept of *lex* is secondary and subordinate to that of *virtus*. The law, which maintains an irreducible character of exteriority, but which at the same time is recognized in its intrinsic rationality, has as its aim the guidance of men toward virtue. As such the law is reformulated and is understood to have as its finality the education of desire. In fact, we might say that virtue is desire educated to see the stars: appetite molded by reason, which maintains its intentional openness to the final end. Therefore the Commandments exist in function of an education of desire. So, on the one hand, they posit the external limits of its immediate satisfaction, in order to save its total openness; on the other hand, they forge its aspirations in conformity with their authentic ends. The Commandments deny our urges toward partial satisfaction so as to protect our secret and ultimate longing. Impeding the reduction of desire or its collapse into itself, the Commandments guide desire toward the stars." Livio Melina, "Desire for Happiness and the Commandments in the First Chapter of *Veritatis splendor*," trans. Margaret Harper McCarthy, in *Veritatis Splendor and the Renewal of Moral Theology*, ed. J. Augustine Di Noia and Romanus Cessario (Huntington, Ind.: Our Sunday Visitor, 1999), 148–49.

98. Aquinas and Hume share a certain amount of common ground about the normative role of the passions: neither of them thinks that reason alone is sufficient to undergird ethics. Judith Barad, for example, suggests that Aquinas's account of the passions vis-à-vis reason occupies a point midway between Hume and Kant (Barad, "Role of Emotion," 397–98). There are nonetheless very significant differences.

Reacting against an exaggerated emphasis on reason among his contemporaries, Hume famously writes: "Reason is, and ought to be, the slave of the passions, and can never pretend to any office than to serve and obey them" (Hume, *A Treatise of Human Nature*, 2.3.3). Aquinas would have rejected this formulation as it stands, but both Aquinas and Hume see the passions as morally normative. Aquinas, however, allows for more complexity in his conceptions of both passion and reason. Consequently, his understanding of how the passions relate to ethical norms is more nuanced.

For Aquinas, there is not just passion; there is generic passion and specified passion, and only generic passion is normative. Reason should respect the inner structure of passion, but not necessarily specific instances of it. Moreover, the relationship is reciprocal: passion should also respect the guidance of reason, because passion depends on reason and is oriented toward its guidance. First, passion does not arise apart from reason: passion is evoked by the apprehension of objects, and since such apprehension is influenced by rational judgment, so too is passion. Second, after being elicited, generic passion tends toward the guidance of reason, and depends on reason's judgments about what is truly of value. So, for Aquinas, passion has a normative role in ethics, but only generic passion, and only in conjunction with reason.

For Hume, however, there is not generic and specified passion; there is just passion. Moreover, the impulse of passion "arises not from reason, but is only directed by it" (2.3.3). Consequently, for Hume, passion is normative in an absolute sense, and reason should submit to its guidance without qualification. According to Hume, "'Tis not contrary to reason to prefer the destruction of the whole world to the scratching of my finger. 'Tis not contrary to reason for me to choose my total ruin, to prevent the least uneasiness of an *Indian* or person wholly unknown to me" (2.3.3). Hume goes on to explain that our "calm passions" incline us toward conventional moral behavior, thus rescuing his system from complete implausibility, but his account is nonetheless weighed down by these counter-intuitive claims about the non-irrationality of such strange preferences. Aquinas's account, however, can explain why such preferences are indeed contrary to reason, even while affirming that the passions have a normative role in ethics.

My appreciation for the similarities between Aquinas and Hume on the passions is indebted to the article by Judith Barad cited earlier.

CHAPTER 5

Original Sin, Grace, and Human Affectivity

The aphorism "grace perfects nature" is a central theme of Aquinas's anthropology.[1] It applies fully to his account of human affectivity, that is, of human affections and those *habitus* that constitute dispositions toward them. Just as grace does not alter or destroy nature but brings it to completion, so too grace perfects human affectivity while respecting its natural structure. The loss of grace in original sin leaves human nature wounded and incomplete but, according to Aquinas, still intact. Hope for restoration remains, including the restoration and rehabilitation of affectivity. This chapter will discuss Aquinas's view of original sin, grace, and human affectivity.

Human Nature, Grace, and Original Sin

For Aquinas the human condition cannot be understood apart from a narrative. In the beginning, God created man and woman in a condition of harmonious communion with God, each other, and all of creation.[2] Human nature was sound and free from suffering, death, and all internal or external conflict.

The greatest blessing of the state of original justice was sanctifying grace, which Aquinas describes as a certain kind of divine presence:

> In a general way, God is in everything by his essence, power, and presence, as the cause of effects participating in his goodness. Beyond this general way of God being in things, there is a special way particular to rational creatures, where God is said to be in them as the known is in the knower, and the loved

1. See *ST* I 1.8 ad 2.
2. *ST* I 94–102. See also Genesis 1–2.

in the lover. In these acts of knowing and loving, the rational creature touches [*attingit*] God himself. Therefore, in this special mode, God is not only said to be in the rational creature, but also to *dwell* in the rational creature as in his own temple.[3]

Sanctifying grace unites the rational creature to God, raises it up to participate in the divine nature, and gives it a share in God's own life.[4] Grace is an entitative *habitus,* meaning that it is not located in any particular power of the soul, but rather in its essence.[5] Sanctifying grace eventually bears fruit in the loving vision of God in the next life. For this reason he calls grace "the seed of God."[6]

Grace does more, though, than establish communion with God; the effects of sanctifying grace spill over into the various capacities of human nature. For the first man and woman, it caused "subjection of body to soul and the lower powers to reason," which Aquinas says was not something natural but a gift of supernatural grace.[7] Paradoxically, the first man and woman needed supernatural grace in order to bring the tendencies of their natural powers to proper fulfillment, and for these natural powers to function harmoniously under the direction of reason.[8]

This claim about life before the fall stems from Aquinas's view that human nature requires grace to fulfill its natural desires and potential.[9] As dis-

3. *ST* I 43.3.

4. *ST* I-II 110.4, 111.1. What exactly Aquinas means when he says that a created nature "participates" in the divine nature only fully emerges in the context of his larger Neoplatonic theme of metaphysical participation. For the purposes of this study, it suffices to say that sanctifying grace establishes a unique, mysterious union with God that could be known as a possibility only through divine revelation; it would not otherwise be imaginable. For a thorough exposition of the theme of participation in Aquinas's metaphysics, see Rudi A. Te Velde, *Participation and Substantiality in Thomas Aquinas* (New York: E. J. Brill, 1995).

5. *ST* I-II 110.4. Aquinas compares the loss of grace to the loss of bodily health in *ST* I-II 82.1.

6. *ST* I 62.3.

7. *ST* I 95.1.

8. There is some ambiguity about the necessity of grace for the proper functioning of natural powers in a state of original justice in the *Summa.* In *ST* I 95.1, it seems clear that the first man and woman required grace for the proper functioning of their natural faculties. However, in *ST* I-II 109.8, he suggests that it would have been possible for man in a hypothetical state of perfect nature to avoid even venial sin without habitual grace. It is difficult to reconcile these positions. Since the argument in *ST* I-II 109.8 depends on a hypothetical situation that Aquinas considers counter-factual (see *ST* I 62.3, 95.1; *ST* II-II 5.1), the position of *ST* I 95.1 is more relevant to interpreting him on this question. See also *Scriptum super libros Sententiarum* II 31.1.2 ad 3.

9. Since the publication of Henri de Lubac's *Surnaturel: études historiques* (Paris: F. Aubier, 1946), there has been controversy among interpreters of Aquinas about the destiny of human

cussed earlier, the rational appetite naturally has a desire for infinite good, and therefore it naturally desires God, who is the only infinite good that could possibly correspond to this infinite desire. At the same time, Aquinas is emphatic that human nature cannot completely satisfy its natural desires without sanctifying grace. Even with sanctifying grace, the happiness possible in this life is only partial and incomplete; perfect and true happiness is beyond our reach.[10] This is not just because of the statistical improbability of obtaining all that would lead to happiness. In this life, only finite goods are fully available to us, and since our desires are infinite, only the possession of God in the beatific vision can fully satisfy them.

The idyllic state of man and woman in paradise, then, was not just a result of coming fresh from the hand of God before sin could corrupt their natural perfection. It was also a function of the sanctifying grace that elevated their natural capacities and preserved their inner harmony. Without sanctifying grace, human nature would start to break apart.

For Aquinas, that is precisely what happened. Man and woman sinned and knowingly rejected God. Consequently, their privileged state of communion with God ended and sanctifying grace was lost. Immediately human nature, deprived of communion with God, began to unravel, and the first man and woman passed on their sad condition to their offspring, the entire human race. This is the narrative of human origins on which his theological anthropology rests.

---

nature. All agree that our ultimate destiny is supernatural. The controversy concerns the questions of whether human nature has a natural end independent of the supernatural end attained through grace, and whether grace is necessary for the human person to desire the beatific vision of the Trinity. The classical Thomist position staked out by Cajetan in the sixteenth century answers these questions in the affirmative, and de Lubac in the negative.

For brief overviews of the controversy, see Harm Goris, "Steering Clear of Charybdis: Some Directions for Avoiding 'Grace Extrinsicism' in Aquinas," *Nova et Vetera* 5 (2007): 67–79, and Brian Shanley, *The Thomist Tradition* (Dordrecht: Kluwer Academic Publishers, 2002), 162–66. For magisterial defenses of the classical Thomist position and the de Lubac position, respectively, see Lawrence Feingold, *The Natural Desire to See God according to St. Thomas Aquinas and His Interpreters* (Naples, Fla.: Sapientia Press, 2010), and Denis J. M. Bradley, *Aquinas on the Twofold Human Good: Reason and Human Happiness in Aquinas's Moral Science* (Washington, D.C.: The Catholic University of America Press, 1997). For a collection of articles on this topic, see Serge-Thomas Bonino, ed., *Surnaturel: A Controversy at the Heart of Twentieth-Century Thomistic Thought* (Naples, Fla.: Sapientia Press, 2009).

10. *ST* I-II 5.3.

Original Sin and Temptation

The precise nature of original sin, the extent of damage to human nature, and the prospects for recovery are topics of perennial controversy among theologians, and were such in the thirteenth century. Aquinas's views are original on many counts, and they have great influence on his account of the passions and human appetite in general.[11]

For Aquinas, the primeval fall of man resulted in the loss of sanctifying grace, but it did not change human nature in its most essential sense.[12] He writes: "By the sin of our first parent, nature was left to itself by the withdrawal of the supernatural gift that God had given to man."[13] The primary consequence of Adam's sin is not that something is added to human nature but that something is removed. For Aquinas, this privation of grace and this leaving of nature to itself, combined with the habitual disorder that this privation introduced into the different parts of the soul, is what constitutes original sin.[14] Human nature is wounded by original sin, but "the principles of nature from which nature is constituted and the properties that result from them, like the powers of the soul and other such things," remain intact after both original sin and personal sin.[15] According to Aquinas, before the fall of man, in the state of original justice, each human appetite instinctively moved toward goodness in harmony with the others, and there was complete freedom from internal temptation and antecedent passion. Sin destroyed the state of inner harmony called original justice, and sin impedes human nature from attaining its perfection, but "sin does not diminish nature itself."[16] The various principles of human nature lack the inner coordination and the subjection to God and reason that only grace can impart, but

11. For a discussion of Aquinas's sources on original sin, his originality, and his contemporaries, see T. C. O'Brien, Introduction, notes, and appendices to *Summa theologiae*, vol. 26: *Original Sin* (New York: McGraw-Hill Book Co., 1965), app. 1–9 passim.

12. For a discussion of how human nature is affected by original sin in Aquinas, and in what precise sense human nature remains intact after the fall, see Jean-Pierre Torrell, "Nature et grâce chez Thomas d'Aquin," *Revue thomiste* 101 (2001): 184–92, 199–201.

13. *ST* I-II 17.9 ad 3.

14. *ST* I-II 82.1 ad 1. Aquinas holds that original sin, in a qualified sense, is a corrupt *habitus*. Although original sin is not a *habitus* in the sense of inclining the powers of the soul to act in definitive ways, it does denote a generalized disharmony and disposition toward disordered actions, and in this sense it is a corrupt *habitus* (*ST* I-II 82.1).

15. *ST* I-II 85.1.

16. *ST* I-II 85.1–2.

in its essential structure, human nature—and therefore human appetite—remains what God created. Aquinas draws an analogy to physical illness to explain what happens to human nature after the fall.[17] Implicit in this analogy is the sense that just as a person remains substantially the same person after becoming sick, so too human nature remains substantially unchanged after the fall. "Sinners do not cease to be men, because sin does not destroy nature."[18]

The internal chaos common to the fallen human condition exists not because human appetites have become corrupted in their basic inclinations, but because in the absence of grace and original justice these appetites tend toward disintegration, pulling the human person in different directions. Original sin does not inject a positive inclination toward sin into human nature.[19] Instead, "once the harmony of original justice is shattered, the various powers of the soul strain toward conflicting objectives."[20] The sense appetite operates more independently of the rational powers—responding to objects according to its own criteria, even when opposed to the desires or aversions of the will and what might be the best interests of the human person taken as a whole—but its essential characteristics remain unaltered.

Consequently, because appetite survives the loss of grace, and because the natural inclination to virtue is nothing other than the natural appetite for the *telos* of human existence, the basic inclination to virtue also survives both original and actual sin, although lessened and weakened.[21] No matter how much internal chaos reigns, all human appetites retain their basic

17. "Just as sickness of body is a certain disordered disposition of the body, which breaks up the equilibrium essential to good health, so too original sin is called an infirmity of nature [*languor naturae*]" (*ST* I-II 82.1; cf. Augustine, *Commentary on Psalm 118,* Sermon 3). The analogy should not be pushed too far: bodily illness often involves the positive presence of something, e.g., a virus or bacteria, which would disrupt the analogy with the privation of original sin. But by drawing attention to the way bodily sickness "breaks up the equilibrium essential to good health," Aquinas indicates that he is drawing an analogy between the privation of original sin and the privation of bodily sickness, not the positive presence of something destructive.

18. *ST* II-II 25.6.

19. "From original sin follows some inclination toward disordered activity not directly, but indirectly, by removing the restraint of original justice, which had restrained disordered movements" (*ST* I-II 82.1 ad 3).

20. *ST* I-II 82.2 ad 2. Here I have used T. C. O'Brien's translation of the Latin in the Blackfriars *Summa* (with slight modification), as it vividly expresses a crucial point without departing from the meaning of Aquinas's plainer words: *soluta harmonia originalis iustitiae, diversae animae potentiae in diversa feruntur.*

21. *ST* I-II 85.1–2.

character and, according to the Creator's design, cannot help inclining fallen humanity toward the good, at least under some guise, and therefore to the perfection of the human person, which is virtue. The inclination to virtue remains "even in the damned."[22] For Aquinas, "human nature remains sound at its depths despite original sin, and its stream towards goodness, though partially choked up, is still to be relied on: he never thinks it is bad when it lacks grace, though tragic in its destiny, and impotent even within its own limits."[23] The inclination of fallen human nature toward sin is the sum total of our natural desires competing rather than cooperating with each other in the absence of the harmonizing influence of communion with God.

Aquinas also demystifies the activity of the devil. According to Aquinas, the devil can arouse desires and passions, but he does not have a monopoly on any particular passion or temptation. Angels and demons cannot directly influence the immaterial powers of intellect and will, but they can manipulate matter and thus influence sensible desires and passions, either by affecting the body or by stimulating the imagination.[24] Demonic temptation, then, does not constitute its own category of subjective human experience. It can only exaggerate the preexisting inclinations of nature. Demons manipulate matter; they do not occupy a permanent niche in our psyche.[25] "There is no sort of sin which does not sometimes result from the demons' suggestions," but neither is there any kind of temptation that does not sometimes result from the weakness of fallen human nature.[26] In a sense, there is nothing mysterious about diabolic temptation in Aquinas's account: preternatural agents are involved, but they act through natural causes. Consequently, even when temptation involves more than natural causes, its demonic origin is largely irrelevant to practical questions about virtue and vice, because human nature operates according to its own principles even when demonic activity is involved.

22. *ST* I-II 85.2 ad 3.

23. Thomas Gilby, Introduction, notes, and appendices to *Summa theologiae*, vol. 28: *Law and Political Theory* (New York: McGraw-Hill Book Co., 1966), 168.

24. Aquinas discusses the power of angels to affect the human psyche in *ST* I 111 and the power of demons in *ST* I 114.3–4 and *ST* I-II 80.2–4. Similarly, regarding the popular astrological belief that celestial bodies could affect the course of human lives, he denies that celestial bodies can influence the intellect or will, but he allows for them to affect the passions insofar as they affect the body (*ST* I 115.4; *ST* I-II 9.5).

25. *ST* I 114.3; *ST* I-II 80.4.

26. *ST* I 114.3 ad 3.

Aquinas's account of original sin and diabolic temptation opens the conceptual space to consider affectivity without suspicion. It provides a foundation to trust the basic inclinations of the passions and affections in spite of their partial unreliability.[27] In the face of sin and social disorder, Aquinas, prompted by his confidence in the ineradicable goodness of creation, and the conviction that "from the beginning it was not so" (Matthew 19:8), rejects pessimism, and looks beyond the problems of the present human condition for what lies beneath and above. In taking this approach, Aquinas makes a purely philosophical or scientific analysis of the passions possible from within the context of faith. Since the created order has its own integrity, it can be investigated without explicit reference to a divine being.

Grace and the Rehabilitation of Affectivity

Despite his positive evaluation of appetite and his optimistic interpretation of original sin, Aquinas is not sanguine about the possibility of virtue or the reliability of passion's guidance. Human nature, although retaining its basic capacities and properties, has been shattered by the privation of divine grace, and this wound permeates every faculty of the human person.[28] Reason, will, the irascible power, and the concupiscible power—the four principal powers perfected by virtue—are each wounded by original sin.[29]

27. In his comparison of Rahner and Aquinas on *concupiscentia,* G. J. McAleer maintains that Aquinas's account of desire is more positive and "sits better with today's mood respecting the flesh," despite Rahner's professed allegiance to Thomistic anthropology on this point, and his stated intention of rehabilitating the concept of concupiscence. McAleer concludes that "it is certainly surprising that the medieval Aquinas would be more 'with it' than the modern Rahner." See McAleer, "Politics of the Flesh," 355–56, 363, and also Karl Rahner, "The Theological Concept of Concupiscentia," in *Theological Investigations,* vol. 1 (Baltimore, Md.: Helicon Press, 1961).

28. He discusses the privation of original sin and its consequences in many places. See *ST* I 114.3, *ST* I-II 74.3 ad 2, 81–89 (esp. 85) passim, 109–14 (esp. 109) passim. For a discussion of Aquinas's understanding on the effects of original sin, see Mark Johnson, "St. Thomas and the «Law of Sin»," *Recherches de théologie et philosophie médiévales* 67 (2000): 80–95.

29. "Insofar as the reason lacks its ordering to the truth, there is the wound of ignorance; insofar as the will lacks its proper ordering to the good, there is the wound of malice; insofar as the irascible power lacks its proper ordering to the arduous, there is the wound of weakness; insofar as the concupiscible power lacks its proper ordering to pleasure through the moderation of reason, there is the wound of concupiscence. . . . By sin reason becomes dull in guiding what is to be done; the will is hardened to the good; acting well becomes more difficult; and concupiscence blazes up" (*ST* I-II 85.3). The list of the wounds of original sin derives from traditional formulae, but Aquinas makes the list his own. He defines each in terms of privation, especially the privation of guidance or direction.

Concerning the passions, Aquinas specifies that the irascible passions, since they depend more on reason, are less affected by original sin than the concupiscible passions.[30] Even with the wound of original sin, some virtue is possible, since the inclination to virtue remains inscribed in human nature, but completely authentic flourishing is impossible.[31] There is too much internal chaos for fallen man to keep everything properly ordered. "In human nature, if its integrity were intact, the inclination of reason would prevail," Aquinas writes, "but in corrupt nature what prevails is the inclination of concupiscence."[32]

Nonetheless, because the essential structure of nature remains intact after sin, restoration is possible. Since human nature remains oriented to virtue, assuming there is not some physical defect or incapacity, there is real hope for the rehabilitation of affectivity, no matter how wounded by original sin or personal sin. Like a Roman road buried by neglect, all the pieces are there; they just need to be uncovered and strengthened.

This work of renewal is made possible by the Incarnation of God's Son in Jesus Christ. For Aquinas, redemption is much more than the legal acquittal from the moral guilt of sin. Christ comes to restore and renew the Father's work of creation.[33] Through his life, death, and resurrection, Christ merits the re-infusion of sanctifying grace in fallen man, so that human nature in every aspect of its structure might be healed from the effects of sin, and we might share in God's life.[34] Sanctifying grace is infused directly by God into the soul, ordinarily (but not exclusively) through the sacrament of

30. *De veritate* 25.6; *ST* I-II 83.4. Aquinas holds that desire for pleasures of touch, and especially sexual pleasures, have become particularly unruly as a result of original sin.

31. On the possibility of virtue without sanctifying grace, see Brian Shanley, "Aquinas on Pagan Virtue," *Thomist* 63 (1999): 553–77. Thomas Osborne responds to aspects of Shanley's position in two subsequent articles. See Thomas M. Osborne, "The Augustinianism of Thomas Aquinas's Moral Theory," *Thomist* 67 (2003): 279–305, and "Perfect and Imperfect Virtues in Aquinas," *Thomist* 71 (2007): 39–64.

32. *ST* II-II 136.3 ad 1.

33. This understanding of redemption is indebted to Lawrence Donohoo.

34. Aquinas's understanding of grace and its transformation of the human person derives in part from the views on deification and divinization of the Eastern Church Fathers, to whom he is more attentive than many of his contemporaries (see Torrell, *Spiritual Master*, 36, 83, 126–28). A recent study compares Aquinas to Gregory Palamas, his near contemporary and an important representative of the Eastern Orthodox tradition, and concludes that their views on grace and deification are essentially compatible, even if couched within different theological vocabularies. See A. N. Williams, *The Ground of Union: Deification in Aquinas and Palamas* (Oxford: Oxford University Press, 1999).

baptism, or, for those already baptized who have lost grace through sin, the sacrament of penance.

The re-infusion of grace has two main effects: qua elevating grace (*gratia elevans*), it elevates human nature so that we can share in God's life, and qua healing grace (*gratia sanans*), it heals fallen human nature.[35] The elevating effect of grace is immediate, though the elevation can deepen and intensify over time, but grace does not immediately or completely repair the damage of original sin. It immediately restores a certain essential degree of inner harmony, and begins to assist growth in virtue, but complete restoration requires time and repeated human acts. Since character formation can occur only over time, and requires the exercise of human freedom, so too grace permeates character only over time, and requires the cooperation of human freedom. Whether grace's task is the infusion of virtuous *habitus* from scratch (such as in the case of a baptized infant), and thus the uninterrupted development of those virtues over time, or the more difficult task of eradicating the remnants of vicious *habitus,* and then transforming them into virtues, the gracing of human affectivity unfolds only over time.

Infused Virtue

The location or subject of sanctifying grace is the essence of the soul and not any specific power.[36] The infusion of sanctifying grace overflows in an organic way and permeates the powers of the soul and the affections of the will and the passions, thus establishing the infused virtues. "Just as from the essence of the soul flow its powers, which are the principles of works," Aquinas writes, "so again from grace flow the virtues into the powers of the soul, through which these powers are moved to act."[37] These virtues elevate the soul's operations in ways suited to a supernatural *telos*. These virtues are necessary for us to attain union with God, a destiny infinitely beyond our natural capacities, and they must be directly infused by God, because only God can expand our natural capacities sufficiently to attain to this union.[38] The infused virtues require human cooperation, and the human agent de-

35. *ST* I-II 109.2. For a detailed study of *gratia sanans* and *gratia elevans* in Aquinas, which also attends to the related issue of the potential of human nature to do good and avoid sin without grace, see Jean-Marc Laporte, *Les structures dynamiques de la grâce: grâce médicinale et grâce élevante selon Thomas d'Aquin* (Montreal: Bellarmin, 1973).

36. *ST* I-II 110.4.

37. *ST* I-II 110.4 ad 1.

38. *ST* I-II 51.4, 63.3, 113.2, 113.10. See also *De virtutibus* 1.10.

termines how they are exercised, but they have their origin in God.[39] Like other virtues, the infused virtues vary in intensity, with intensity measured by how deeply they are embedded in the subject.[40] Unlike purely natural virtues, however, they can be lost only by sinful actions that are serious and deliberate, that is, mortal or deadly, and as such constitute a rejection and repudiation of the gift of sanctifying grace.

The most important infused virtues are the theological virtues of faith, hope, and charity. Faith is a supernatural enlightenment of the intellect, while hope and charity orient the will toward God in a way beyond the unaided capacities of human nature.[41] Through them, we share in God's own knowledge of himself and love with God's own love. They thus broaden the horizons of human action, so that it is possible to act on a supernatural playing field, and eventually attain perfect union with God in the next life. But these virtues are not only oriented toward union with God: while they are unique in that they have God as their intentional object and ultimate end, they encompass other ends as well, such as loving one's neighbor, or hoping for the temporal and eternal salvation of the poor.[42]

Besides the infused theological virtues, Aquinas also maintains that there are infused moral virtues, that is, moral virtues ordered to actions that make sense only in the context of faith.[43] These virtues are oriented toward union with God, but they do not have God as their intentional object. Just as acquired virtues proceed from "certain natural principles pre-existing in us" (i.e., the natural inclinations of the various powers of the soul toward virtue), the infused natural virtues proceed from the theological virtues,[44] and they cannot exist without charity.[45] Each infused moral virtue parallels a corresponding virtue acquired purely through human action. Accordingly, they penetrate the sense appetite and all the other faculties of the soul just

39. See, for example, Aquinas's discussion of the infused virtue of charity in *ST* II-II 23.2. See also *De virtutibus* 1.11 ad 14.

40. See, for example, Aquinas's discussion of growth in charity in *ST* II-II 24.4.

41. *ST* I-II 62.3.

42. *ST* I-II 62.2.

43. For an overview of infused moral virtue and its relation to acquired virtue, see Romanus Cessario, *The Moral Virtues and Theological Ethics* (Notre Dame: University of Notre Dame Press, 1991), 94–125. See also Jeffrey Hause, "Aquinas on the Function of Moral Virtue," *American Catholic Philosophical Quarterly* 81 (2007): 1–20.

44. *ST* I-II 63.3.

45. *ST* I-II 65.2.

as the acquired virtues do, albeit in a different way. Whereas acquired virtue disposes the soul's powers according to the light of reason, infused moral virtue disposes the soul's powers according to the light of grace.[46] As such, infused moral virtue is not ancillary to the Christian life, but rather essential to its flourishing.[47] Furthermore, infused virtue is the only "perfect" virtue properly speaking, and acquired virtue, however well established, is intrinsically lacking and incomplete.[48]

The infused moral virtues typically coexist in the same subject alongside their acquired counterparts: for example, someone typically would have both acquired and infused kinds of prudence simultaneously. However, unlike the acquired moral virtues, the infused virtues cannot diminish, nor can they be lost except by mortal sin, because they flow from charity, which itself cannot diminish and can be lost only through mortal sin.[49]

Aquinas is exceptionally difficult to interpret on the infused moral virtues, and especially on the question of their relationship to their acquired counterparts, because he rarely addresses this topic explicitly, either in the *Summa theologiae* or anywhere else.[50] Consequently, controversy on this topic has occupied his interpreters for centuries.[51] Furthermore, while the reality of infused moral virtues was taken as a given in Aquinas's time, having been affirmed by authorities such as Augustine and Gregory,[52] many theologians since then, most notably Duns Scotus, have seen no reason to postulate infused moral virtues, and have argued instead that charity and the acquired moral virtues are sufficient to explain how acts of supernatural moral virtue are possible.[53] Even scholars and theologians otherwise com-

46. "For just as the acquired virtues perfect man to walk in accord with the natural light of reason, so the infused virtues perfect man to walk in accord with the light of grace" (*ST* I-II 110.3).

47. *ST* I-II 63.3.

48. *ST* I-II 65.1–2.

49. Aquinas discusses the loss of charity through sin in *ST* II-II 24.10.

50. For references to infused moral virtue in the *Summa*, see *ST* I-II 51.4, 55.4, 63.3–4, 65.2–3, 110.3–4; *ST* II-II 47.14, 53.1 ad 3, 104.3 ad 2, 133.1 ad 2, 136.3, 137.4, 161.5 ad 2; *ST* III 7.2, 89.1–2, 89.4. There are also some important references to infused moral virtue in *De virtutibus*, 1.10–11.

51. For a history and overview of traditional approaches to infused moral virtue, see John F. Harvey, "The Nature of the Infused Virtues," *Proceedings of the Tenth Annual Convention of the Catholic Theological Society of America* (1955): 172–221.

52. See Antonio Royo and Jordan Aumann, *The Theology of Christian Perfection* (Dubuque, Iowa: Priory Press, 1962), 63.

53. See Duns Scotus, *Questiones in III librum Sententiarum* 36.28, and Cessario, *The Moral Virtues and Theological Ethics*, 102–4. For an overview of Scotus on virtue, including infused vir-

mitted to his ethical system part company with Aquinas on this point, or at least avoid the topic. Consequently, as a result of the interpretative confusion and the questions about their existence, the infused moral virtues and their role in Aquinas's ethical system have been neglected and downplayed.[54] Nonetheless, despite Aquinas's incomplete treatment of the topic, and the controversies of interpretation it has generated, the notion of infused moral virtue has a central place in his anthropology and ethics. Since the infused moral virtues directly involve the passions and affections, it is necessary to wade into centuries-old controversies and attempt to clarify his position.

The first point of controversy is just how much Aquinas writes about the infused moral virtues. The answer to this question turns on whether the moral virtues discussed in the *Secunda secundae* are acquired or infused or both.[55] Aquinas does not offer any explicit clarification, and one standard presumption is that they are acquired moral virtues.[56] McKay, however, makes the case that the *Secunda secundae* is concerned with the infused moral virtues unless otherwise indicated.[57] Drawing on her work, many arguments can be marshaled in support of this interpretation. First, the *Secunda secundae* begins with a discussion of the theological virtues, and gives a methodical analysis of their various associated virtues (and opposed vices) and how they enable us to attain our supernatural destiny of union with God. Immediately afterward, Aquinas turns to the moral virtues. In this context, it would not make sense for Aquinas to be writing about

---

tue, see Bonnie Kent, "Rethinking Moral Dispositions: Scotus on the Virtues," in *The Cambridge Companion to Duns Scotus*, ed. Thomas Williams (Cambridge: Cambridge University Press, 2003), 352–76.

54. See Angela M. McKay, "The Infused and Acquired Virtues in Aquinas' Moral Philosophy" (Ph.D. diss., University of Notre Dame, 2004), 58. Bonnie Kent gives a similar assessment of the place of infused moral virtues in Thomist scholarship. See her "Habits and Virtues" in *The Ethics of Aquinas*, ed. Stephen J. Pope (Washington, D.C.: Georgetown University Press, 2002), 124.

55. Bonnie Kent gives an overview of this point of controversy. See Bonnie Kent, *Virtues of the Will: The Transformation of Ethics in Late Thirteenth Century* (Washington, D.C.: The Catholic University of America Press, 1995), 32–34.

56. See for instance Alasdair MacIntyre, *Whose Justice? Which Rationality?* (Notre Dame, Ind.: University of Notre Dame Press, 1988), 205, or Renée Mirkes, "Aquinas on the Unity of Perfect Moral Virtue," *American Catholic Philosophical Quarterly* 71 (1997): 589.

57. McKay, "Infused and Acquired Virtues," 1–5, 58–188. See also Réginald Garrigou-Lagrange, *Christian Perfection and Contemplation according to St. Thomas Aquinas and St. John of the Cross*, trans. M. T. Doyle (St. Louis: Herder, 1939), 61–62, and Etienne Gilson, *The Christian Philosophy of St. Thomas Aquinas*, trans. L. K. Shook (New York: Random House, 1956), 338–39.

acquired moral virtue while ignoring infused moral virtue, since, according to Aquinas, infused moral virtue proceeds directly from the theological virtues, and only infused virtue is of any help in attaining union with God. Second, his treatment of the moral virtues gives a prominent role to the gifts of the Holy Spirit, and the way they assist the moral virtues. Since the gifts imply sanctifying grace, it would not make sense for Aquinas to be writing about only acquired moral virtues. Third, his articles on specific vices often raise the question of whether their corresponding acts constitute mortal sins, and thus result in the loss of grace. This question is relevant only when possession of grace and infused moral virtue is presumed. It would be difficult to understand this interest in mortal sin if his primary interest were acquired virtue. Lastly, in discussions of a particular moral virtue, Aquinas sometimes explicitly indicates that he is talking about an infused virtue.[58]

In view of these observations, it cannot be maintained that the *Secunda secundae* is exclusively or even primarily concerned with acquired moral virtue. Nonetheless, it does not necessarily follow that the *Secunda secundae* is primarily concerned with infused moral virtue. It could also be the case that Aquinas is speaking about the moral virtues in general and that he means for his analysis to apply to both infused and acquired virtue, unless the context indicates otherwise. The interpretation of Aquinas's intentions depends in large part on the resolution of another controversial topic, namely, the relationship between infused and acquired virtue (which will be discussed below). If infused and acquired virtue are so closely connected that the operation of infused virtue subsumes within itself the operation of acquired virtue, to the point that most of the time it is redundant to talk about the operation of acquired virtue when someone possesses infused virtue, then McKay's interpretation may hold. Otherwise, the treatment of moral virtue in the *Secunda secundae* should be read as applying to both infused and acquired moral virtue, unless indicated otherwise.

The second point of controversy is how the infused virtues grow.[59] Acquired virtue increases in a straightforward manner. The acquired virtues

58. *ST* II-II 47.14, 53.1 ad 3, 104.3 ad 2, 133.1 ad 2, 136.3, 137.4, 161.5 ad 2.

59. For John Harvey's views, see Harvey, "Infused Moral Virtues," esp. 212–17. Taking the example of chastity, Harvey seems to suggest that infused chastity grows in conjunction with infused charity, and furthermore that such growth is entirely independent from growth in the acquired or natural virtue of chastity, which ideally happens in tandem.

and their growth are a function of the natural powers of the human person. Repeated virtuous actions, as long as they are of sufficient intensity, cause acquired virtue to grow and deepen.[60] The infused virtues are more complex. An increase in an infused virtue denotes the same thing as with acquired virtue, that is, an increase in how deeply the virtue is embedded in us,[61] but the infused virtues are infused by God and so depend primarily on God's activity, not ours. Consequently, their increase can only come directly from God.[62] Our actions can dispose us for an increase in the infused virtues, but it is God who grants the increase and determines the degree of growth.[63] Yet although he is emphatic that the infused virtues increase through God's infusion, Aquinas sometimes seems to affirm the opposite: that once received from God, an infused virtue can be increased by our actions.[64] John Arintero interprets Aquinas's ethics as implying that our actions are necessary for the growth of infused moral virtue, even though its actual increase comes from God.[65] Aquinas's few words on this subject make it difficult to discern whether he would agree, but Arintero's interpretation is plausible.

Aquinas gives the most attention to this topic in the special case of charity, where he states that acts of charity merit an increase of charity.[66] He claims that each and every act of charity merits an increase of charity, though the

60. *ST* I-II 52.3, 63.2; *De virtutibus* 1.9. Note that truly virtuous acts require personal involvement; they flow not just from habit but from *habitus*. See Pinckaers, "Virtue Is Not a Habit," 65–81.

61. *De virtutibus* 1.11.

62. *De virtutibus* 1.11, esp. 1.11 ad 12.

63. *De virtutibus* 1.11, esp. 1.11 ad 14; see also *ST* II-II 24.2, 24.6.

64. *ST* I-II 51.4 ad 3. See also Rebecca Konyndyk DeYoung, "Power Made Perfect in Weakness: Aquinas's Transformation of the Virtue of Courage," *Medieval Philosophy and Theology* 11 (2003): 175.

65. He writes: "These virtues, since they are infused, are not acquired by our own efforts; nor do we cooperate in their reception save by the acceptance of them. Yet, since they are planted in us as a seed or in a virtual state, it is our duty to cultivate and develop them by proper use and by means of the watering of divine grace. We also root them within ourselves more firmly by struggling against difficulties. Beginning as they do in an embryonic stage, although they are even more real than the other virtues, yet they do not exclude the opposite habits or the difficulty entailed in their use. Therefore it is necessary that they be organically formed through exercise and struggle; and this is effected as the spirit more and more subjects the flesh and builds up other virtuous habits which are incompatible with vicious tendencies." John Arintero, *The Mystical Evolution*, 2 vols., trans. Jordan Aumann (St. Louis: Herder, 1949), 1:212.

66. *ST* I-II 114.8; *ST* II-II 24.6 ad 1. For Aquinas's mature teaching on merit, see *ST* I-II 114. For a comprehensive study of the nature of merit in Aquinas and its relation to grace, see Joseph P. Wawrykow, *God's Grace and Human Action: "Merit" in the Theology of Thomas Aquinas* (Notre Dame, Ind.: University of Notre Dame Press, 1995).

increase does not always come immediately.[67] In explaining how this comes about, he draws a revealing comparison to the natural process of growth in animals and plants:

> The spiritual growth of charity is somewhat like bodily growth. Bodily growth is not a continuous movement in animals and plants, so that if something grew so much in so much time, there would necessarily be some proportionate growth during any given segment of that time period, as happens with physical movement. Instead, over a period of time, nature works by disposing for growth without actually causing anything to grow, and then afterwards nature brings about what it had prepared, and actually causes the animal or plant to grow. Similarly, charity does not actually grow in every act of charity, but every act of charity disposes for a growth of charity, because every act of charity makes a man more prompt to act according to charity in the future. Then, his aptitude for charitable acts increasing, a man breaks forth in an act of more fervent love as he strives toward the perfection of charity, and then charity grows in actual fact.[68]

The use of this analogy suggests that Aquinas sees human action and divine infusion as both involved in the increase of infused virtue. The associations of merit with extrinsic reward (e.g., "you did this, so I will give you that") can obscure what seems to be an intrinsic connection between human action and divine response. For Aquinas, acts of charity generate an increase in charity not by legal obligation but by organic cooperation. They seem to function in Aquinas's account like channels carved out near a body of water: though the workers removing earth do not actually pour water into the channels, the water naturally flows in to fill the vacuum.[69] We can infer that, for Aquinas, acts of the infused moral virtues function in a parallel fashion to acts of charity, since the infused moral virtues are always infused and lost along with charity.

The infused moral virtues are similar to acquired moral virtues in that voluntary virtuous acts lead to growth in virtue. Growth in infused moral virtue comes from God, but not in a way that makes human action irrelevant. However, the infused moral virtues grow in a sporadic fashion, depending on when God grants the increase, and cannot be lost or diminished

67. *ST* II-II 24.6 ad 1.

68. *ST* II-II 24.6.

69. This interpretation makes sense of Aquinas's puzzling comment in *ST* I-II 51.4 ad 3 that our actions can increase a previously existing infused *habitus*.

except by mortal sin. In contrast, the acquired moral virtues increase after any virtuous act of equal or greater intensity than our present degree of virtue, or at least are disposed toward such an increase, and may decrease after mildly vicious acts, or even virtuous acts of lesser intensity than our present degree of virtue.[70]

The third point of controversy is how infused virtue relates to acquired virtue.[71] This controversy centers on an important difference between infused and acquired moral virtue: infused moral virtue does not guarantee the ease normally associated with acquired moral virtue.[72] The classic example is someone struggling with addiction. A recovering alcoholic might be in a state of grace, and therefore possess the infused virtue of temperance, and yet still struggle with acts of temperance. While the infused virtue of temperance necessarily supplies enough grace to avoid mortal sins against temperance, it does not necessarily supply the characteristic ease of acquired virtue.[73] This aspect of infused moral virtue has been a particular source of perplexity for interpreters of Aquinas. If these infused *habitus* are truly virtues, how can they lack facility or ease, insofar as facility is a defining characteristic of virtue?[74] A common interpretation is that infused moral virtues simply do not confer facility, and facility only comes from the corresponding acquired virtue.

Many passages, however, demonstrate that Aquinas held that infused virtue conferred a certain kind of facility, even if, under certain circumstances, that facility is compromised or reduced.[75] In the following passage, Aquinas clearly affirms that infused moral virtue affects the passions and in doing so confers some assistance in acts of virtue:

70. *ST* I-II 52.3.

71. For an overview of this question, see Kent, *Virtues of the Will*, 32–33.

72. *ST* I-II 65.3 ad 2.

73. *ST* III 89.1 ad 3.

74. For a discussion of this controversy and an exposition of the standard Thomist interpretation, see Renée Mirkes, "Aquinas's Doctrine of Moral Virtue and Its Significance for Theories of Facility," *Thomist* 61 (1997): 189–218. For a history and overview of the concept of facility in infused moral virtue, see Harvey, "Infused Moral Virtues," 193–217.

75. McKay, "Infused and Acquired Virtues," 68–75. At least since Suarez, many scholastic theologians have affirmed a distinction between internal and external facility, such that infused virtues convey internal facility but not external facility. For a relatively recent account of the infused moral virtues that incorporates this distinction, see Réginald Garrigou-Lagrange, *The Three Ages of the Interior Life*, 2 vols., trans. Sr. M. Timothea Doyle (St. Louis: Herder, 1947), 1:57–66.

Those passions that incline us towards evil are not completely removed either through acquired or through infused virtue, except, maybe, by a miracle. . . . But passions of this sort are modified by both acquired and infused virtues, so that we are not stirred by them in an unrestrained way. However, (i) acquired virtue achieves this in one way and (ii) infused virtue in another. (i) For *acquired* virtue is effective to the extent that the struggle is felt less. This comes about from its own particular cause: when someone becomes accustomed to virtue through repeated actions, they then become unaccustomed to obey those passions, and accustomed to resist them. The consequence of this is that they feel less troubled by them. (ii) *Infused* virtue, by contrast, is effective to the extent that even if passions of this sort are felt, they do not take control. For infused virtue means that we refrain totally from obeying sinful desires, and as long as it remains in us, we do unfailingly. (Acquired virtue can fail in this way, but rarely, in the way that all natural inclinations occasionally let us down.)[76]

It is difficult to establish Aquinas's thought on this matter with as much clarity as would be desired, because he does not write much about the facility of infused moral virtues. He is not particularly concerned with this question, and typically addresses it only in his responses to objections. Nonetheless, given the weight of the textual evidence, McKay is clearly correct in her interpretation that Aquinas held that the infused moral virtues confer a certain kind of facility. Furthermore, the coherence of the opposite interpretation would be hard to maintain. It would imply, for example, that a recovering alcoholic would not find it subjectively any easier to avoid intemperance with grace than without grace—a conclusion that is completely implausible in any theological system that affirms that grace is ontologically transformative.

But do the infused virtues ever generate the more typical kind of facility, the kind that is associated with acquired virtue? Aquinas does not directly engage this question, but his treatment of *habitus* and virtue in the *Prima secundae* suggests that he would affirm that they do. Just like acquired virtues, through human acts, infused virtues gradually become more and more embedded in the cognitive powers and appetites, albeit in synergy with sanctifying grace. And so like acquired virtues, over time, the infused virtues penetrate more and more into the sense appetite, conferring facility not just on some vague supernatural level, but also on the level of the passions and

76. *De virtutibus* 1.10 ad 14, trans. E. M. Atkins (Cambridge: Cambridge University Press, 2005). I have slightly modified the translation.

affections. If this interpretation is correct, then it is easy to explain Aquinas's apparent silence on the topic of the facility of the infused moral virtues: he thinks it is obvious that most of what he says about virtue applies to infused as well as acquired moral virtue.

These considerations about facility suggest some tentative conclusions about the relationship between infused and acquired virtue. Since infused virtues and their acquired counterparts perfect the same power of the soul, infused virtue cannot operate without involving acquired virtue, and vice versa, to the extent that either exists in a particular person.[77] Acts of infused virtues can strengthen their acquired counterparts, or lead to the development of acquired virtues if they do not already exist. Similarly, when someone is in a state of grace, acts of acquired virtues always involve their infused counterparts, and thus, it seems, might lead to their growth.[78]

With these tentative conclusions about the relationship between infused and acquired virtue in mind, it is illuminating to consider in more detail the case of someone who receives sanctifying grace after having developed disordered tendencies in its absence.[79] For someone in this situation,

77. According to Renée Mirkes, Aquinas's account of infused virtue hinges on a profound unity of acquired and moral virtue, such that they are in a relationship analogous to the Aristotelian categories of matter and form. See Mirkes, "Perfect Moral Virtue," 590. G. P. Klubertanz argues for a similar interpretation that proposes a matter-form relationship between acquired and infused virtue. See G. P. Klubertanz, "Une théorie sur les vertus morales *naturelles* et *surnaturelles*," *Revue thomiste* 42 (1959): 569–75. Andrew Dell'Olio endorses the general approach of Klubertanz and Mirkes and develops it in his own way. See Andrew J. Dell'Olio, *Foundations of Moral Selfhood: Aquinas on Divine Goodness and the Connection of the Virtues* (New York: Peter Lang, 2003), 135–38.

Garrigou-Lagrange sees infused and acquired moral virtue as operating in tandem. He writes, "How are the virtues exercised? They are exercised simultaneously in such a way that the acquired virtue is subordinated to the infused virtue as a favorable disposition" (Garrigou-Lagrange, *Three Ages*, 63). However, based on the metaphors that he uses to explain his position further, he seems to portray acquired and infused virtues as two distinct realities that cooperate with each other, whereas Mirkes and Kluberantz argue for a more profound unity.

78. One particularly clear supporting text states that acquired virtue can merit eternal reward through the mediation of its infused counterpart, thus implying that the activity of acquired virtue always involves infused virtue when someone is in a state of grace. Aquinas writes, "Since we can merit nothing without charity, the actions of an acquired virtue cannot have merit without charity. However, the other virtues are infused in us together with charity; that is how the actions of an acquired virtue can be meritorious only by means of an infused virtue. For a virtue that is ordered towards a lower end can only bring about actions that are ordered to a higher end if this is done by means of a higher virtue. For example, the courage that is a virtue of a human being qua human being does not order its actions to the civic good except by means of that courage that is the virtue of a human being *qua* citizen" (*De virtutibus* 1.10 ad 4, trans. E. M. Atkins).

79. On this topic, see Michael Sherwin, "Infused Virtue and the Effects of Acquired Vice: A Test Case for the Thomistic Theory of Infused Cardinal Virtues," *The Thomist* 73 (2009): 29–52.

grace does not only infuse more and more virtue; grace must also work to overcome the effects of vices acquired in the absence of grace. In *De virtutibus,* Aquinas argues that acquired vices—acquired *habitus* oriented toward serious sin—cannot coexist with sanctifying grace. The moment grace is received, acquired vice ceases to exist: what remains is a certain tendency (*dispositio*) toward sin, but not a *habitus.*[80] At first this understanding of vice can seem puzzling, since it is obvious that an orientation toward sinful acts can remain after someone repents of past behavior. For example, addiction usually does not vanish after someone renounces a pattern of addictive behavior. However, Aquinas does not deny that strong tendencies toward sin remain; what he denies is that these strong tendencies constitute a *habitus.* All *habitus* are dispositions,[81] but only voluntary dispositions, that is, dispositions that are endorsed by the will, are *habitus.* So in Aquinas's system, the idea that acquired vice must cease to exist after the infusion of grace is entirely plausible and in fact constitutes a necessary conclusion. By the infused virtue of charity, the will acquires a stable orientation toward supernatural good.[82] And if the will is inclined toward supernatural good by the *habitus* of charity, it cannot be inclined toward serious sin by a different *habitus.* Serious sin by definition implies the abandonment of supernatural good, and so the will cannot be disposed toward supernatural good and serious sin at the same time: they are mutually exclusive. Therefore, at the moment of the infusion of grace, which always brings the infusion of charity, any vice inclined toward serious sin ceases to exist. The *habitus* of infused charity necessarily shatters the *habitus* of any such vice.

Nonetheless, while the presence of infused virtue gives a new facility in acts of virtue, strong tendencies toward sin may remain, and some disorder may still permeate the appetites. Virtue does not fully establish itself immediately. Over time, through the mediation of the infused virtues and repeated good actions, sanctifying grace overflows into the appetites, ordering them according to the rule of reason enlightened by faith. There may or may not be complete healing in a particular case, but there is a reordering of the appetites. In Aquinas's system, it is theoretically possible for those who break away from patterns of vice to experience eventually an interior

80. *De virtutibus* 1.10 ad 16.

81. *ST* I-II 49.1. See also Aristotle's *Metaphysics* V.20, 1022b10–12.

82. *De virtutibus* 1.10.

harmony comparable to that experienced by those who never needed to repent of such vice.

To what extent do the appetites remain shaped by the infused virtues after grace is lost? Aquinas unequivocally states that the infused virtues are lost immediately and completely when sanctifying grace is forfeited. He does not, however, directly engage the question of whether any effects of infused virtue might remain. The logic of his account, though, suggests that the infused virtues leave some remnants of their presence in the human psyche. Since the infused virtues require time and repeated actions to penetrate one's personality fully, even though the moment of their infusion marks a radical discontinuity in one's affectivity, it would seem that Aquinas would also hold that sin takes time to deform one's personality fully, even though the loss of infused virtue constitutes a dramatic psychological rupture. For example, those who possessed the infused virtue of temperance for many years might continue to benefit from its previous effects on their appetites, even after grace is lost.

The coherence of Aquinas's account of infused moral virtue is open to question, and it certainly demands greater clarification than he provides. Nonetheless, there is a definite logic to Aquinas's postulation of infused moral virtue. For Aquinas, virtue is the habituation of the powers of human nature toward determinate ends, and grace transforms the powers of the soul, so that we can perform whatever actions are necessary to attain the supernatural destiny of union with God. Consequently, by definition, there must be infused moral virtues. Furthermore, even in its sketchy form, Aquinas's account has many attractive features, and among them is the central place he gives to the transformation of affectivity.[83] For Aquinas, grace does not affect only the intellect and will; it permeates the passions and shapes every aspect of human personality. Moreover, this transformation is an organic process that dovetails with ordinary psychological development. It is not a violent, wrenching intervention that is once and for all. Rather, the perfection of human capacities continually deepens through every voluntary action that cooperates with God's grace. This understanding of graced human affectivity offers a balanced appraisal of the relationship between

83. For a contemporary account of how infused virtue influences the passions that draws on Aquinas, see Diana Fritz Cates, *Choosing to Feel: Virtue, Friendship, and Compassion* (Notre Dame: University of Notre Dame Press, 1997), 42–48.

nature and grace, and between human freedom and divine freedom. Aquinas's position suffers, however, from an inadequate account of the relationship between infused and acquired virtue, and from an inadequate explanation of why infused virtue does not necessarily involve the characteristic ease of acquired virtue.

The Gifts of the Holy Spirit

For Aquinas, the gifts of the Holy Spirit name a distinct anthropological category that denotes a particular way that grace elevates human nature, a category distinct from infused virtue but closely connected to it.[84] The gifts of the Holy Spirit had already been a theological topic for some centuries, but Aquinas drastically revises the tradition he inherits and integrates it with Aristotelian virtue ethics.[85] He is not content simply to reiterate the tradition; he presents the gifts as part of a comprehensive and coherent anthropology. The dilemma he faces is how to make the gifts of the Holy Spirit distinct from the infused virtues, while at the same time complementary to them. His solution is to define the gifts as a kind of *habitus* that follows neither the rule of reason alone (as with the acquired virtues), nor the rule of reason enlightened by faith (as with the infused virtues), but the rule of the Holy Spirit. Infused along with sanctifying grace, "the gifts are certain perfections of man which dispose him to follow well the instinct of the Holy Spirit."[86] Aquinas elaborates:

> The gifts are a sort of *habitus* that perfects man so that he promptly follows the instinct [*instinctus*] of the Holy Spirit, just as the moral virtues perfect the appetitive powers in their obedience to reason. . . . Just as there are virtues in every human power that has the capacity of being a principle of human acts (that is, reason and the appetitive power), so also are there gifts.[87]

The gifts are stable dispositions that enable the subject to respond promptly and easily to the inspirations of the Holy Spirit. Just as the virtues shape the

84. For an overview and contemporary exposition of Aquinas's understanding of the gifts of the Spirit, see Jean-Hervé Nicolas, "Les dons du Saint-Spirit," *Revue thomiste* 92 (1992): 141–52. Michael Sherwin gives a helpful analysis of how Aquinas's treatment of the gifts of the Spirit both manifests and clarifies his theology of knowing and loving. See Sherwin, *By Knowledge and By Love*, 163–70.

85. See Edward D. O'Connor, Introduction, notes, and appendices to *Summa theologiae*, vol. 24: *The Gifts of the Spirit* (New York: McGraw-Hill Book Co., 1973), app. 1–4.

86. *ST* I-II 68.2.

87. *ST* I-II 68.4. See also *ST* II-II 19.9.

cognitive powers and the appetites, so too the gifts shape the cognitive powers and appetites, albeit in order to conform them to a different principle.

Beyond the main elements of this overview, commentators have argued for centuries about Aquinas's precise understanding of the significance and nature of the gifts.[88] Perhaps due to this long-standing controversy, and the fact that his writings are difficult to interpret on this subject, the gifts have been neglected in treatments of Aquinas's ethics.[89] Nonetheless, in the prologue to the *Secunda secundae,* Aquinas lists the gifts of the Holy Spirit as integral to the treatment of the various virtues that will follow, thus indicating their significance to his project. In recent years, there has been a growing recognition that the gifts have a central place in Aquinas's ethics.[90] A complete account of Aquinas on the passions and affections must therefore include a treatment of the gifts, and thus enter into the attendant controversies.

One standard reading of Aquinas interprets the gifts as added-on dispositions that make it possible to respond promptly and easily to the inspirations of the Holy Spirit, when and if the Holy Spirit chooses to act.[91] The gifts are "activated" by the Holy Spirit relatively infrequently, usually in cases where the infused virtues fall short of what is needed to act according to God's will. But this reading makes it hard to understand why Aquinas defines the gifts as *habitus*: the gifts simply seem to name ways that from time to time the Holy Spirit might choose to inspire someone living in a state of grace, not infused dispositions.

Since the gifts are *habitus,* and *habitus* are present even when not involved in any act, the gifts must somehow stamp our personality, even when we are not moved by any particular inspiration of the Holy Spirit. Although Aquinas does not explain in detail how the gifts function, because he defines them as *habitus,* it is clear that they do not add another dimension to our psyche: they influence and shape our cognitive powers and our appetites. Even when the gifts are dormant, our personality still bears their stamp, just as our personality remains stamped by the virtue of justice even when there

88. Complicating matters further, Aquinas's views on the gifts of the Holy Spirit evolve significantly over his lifetime, and even in the course of writing the *Summa* (see O'Connor, appendices to *Summa,* app. 4–5).

89. Even Stephen Pope's excellent *The Ethics of Aquinas* almost completely overlooks the gifts of the Spirit.

90. See Charles Bouchard, "Recovering the Gifts of the Holy Spirit in Moral Theology," *Theological Studies* 63 (2002): 539–58. See also Pinckaers, *Sources of Christian Ethics,* esp. 151–67.

91. Royo and Aumann, *Theology of Christian Perfection,* 79–103.

is no need to exercise it. Moreover, just as the virtue of justice inclines toward acts of justice, even when there is no immediate opportunity for such acts, so too the gifts of the Holy Spirit incline toward acts inspired by the Holy Spirit, even in the absence of such inspiration. Over time, the rule of the Holy Spirit becomes more and more embedded in our personality, so that we anticipate the Holy Spirit's movements.[92] Furthermore, just as the infused virtues admit of growth and degrees, so too do the gifts.[93] The more one's faculties are shaped by the gifts, the more promptly and easily one can follow the inspirations of the Holy Spirit.

The gifts complement the infused virtues by making it possible to be guided by the Holy Spirit more directly.[94] While the infused virtues operate under the guidance of reason, the gifts do not. Through the gift of counsel, for example, the Holy Spirit directs us toward a concrete course of action without necessarily providing rational justification.[95] Similarly, through the gift of fortitude, the Holy Spirit inspires a supernatural serenity and a firmness of resolution in the face of difficulties that exceed what could be attained by rational considerations, even rational considerations enlightened by faith.[96] The operations of the gifts cannot be collapsed into the category of infused virtue, because they go beyond reason, although without contradicting it, in a way that infused virtue does not.

Since the gifts affect the natural capacities of the human person, and the gifts are infused and lost with sanctifying grace, what, according to Aquinas, remains of the effects of the gifts once they are lost through serious sin? Aquinas does not address this question. Nonetheless, if the infused

92. Angela McKay seems to have a similar interpretation of how the gifts anticipate the Holy Spirit. She writes that, according to Aquinas, they are not merely a mechanism to receive motion from the Holy Spirit, but also "real affective yearnings, so to speak, for that motion." McKay, "Infused and Acquired Virtues," 38. See also Francis L. B. Cunningham, *The Indwelling of the Trinity: A Historico-Doctrinal Study of the Theory of St. Thomas Aquinas* (Dubuque, Iowa: Priory Press, 1955), 201.

93. Aquinas maintains that the filial fear associated with the gift of fear increases as charity increases (*ST* II-II 19.10). However, Aquinas does not discuss how the gifts grow in degree. Since *habitus* grow in proportion to the intensity of corresponding acts, it would seem that the gifts grow in proportion to the intensity of the Holy Spirit's inspirations.

94. "What is perfect according to the order of its nature still needs help from a higher nature, just as man, however perfect, needs help from God. And in this way virtues need help from the gifts, which perfect the powers of the soul so that they are moved more perfectly by the Holy Spirit" (*ST* III 7.5 ad 1).

95. *ST* II-II 52.1 ad 1.

96. *ST* II-II 139.1.

virtues have consequences that perdure even after they are lost, insofar as they shape the soul's powers, it would make sense for the gifts to likewise leave traces in our personality. The gifts do not carve a new section in the human psyche that only the Holy Spirit can enter; they shape the affections and appetites to work more naturally with the Holy Spirit's inspirations. Consequently, even after grace is lost, some shaping of affections and appetites should remain. For example, Aquinas would surely claim that the gifts of the Holy Spirit were present to a high degree in Mother Teresa of Calcutta. If she were to lose sanctifying grace through serious sin (as might be difficult to imagine), Aquinas might expect her affective disposition to retain many of its former qualities, such as a high degree of empathy and compassion, even though that same disposition came into being only through the activity of the gifts.

A related question is how often Aquinas thinks that the gifts are activated by the Holy Spirit. Many interpretations minimize the frequency of these inspirations and see them as extraordinary interventions. Servais Pinckaers, however, argues that the Holy Spirit plays a much more active role in Aquinas's ethics than is commonly recognized. Pinckaers notes that Aquinas uses the Latin word *instinctus* when describing the inspirations of the Holy Spirit, and argues that the choice of this word reflects a sense that the Holy Spirit plays a continuous, subtle role in guiding and strengthening us, and that the significance of this word choice has been minimized by Aquinas's commentators for fear of correlating the gifts too closely with animal instinct.[97] This interpretation makes better sense of Aquinas's assertion that the gifts are *habitus*—that is, stable dispositions—than the contrary position that the gifts are only infrequently and sporadically activated by the Holy Spirit.[98]

Aquinas enumerates seven gifts of the Holy Spirit: understanding, counsel, wisdom, knowledge, piety, fortitude, and fear.[99] This list of seven gifts derives from an ancient exegetical tradition regarding Isaiah 11:2–3, a passage that describes the spiritual attributes of the Messiah. This exegetical tradition grounded discussion about the Holy Spirit's role in the Christian

97. See "L'Instinct et L'Esprit au couer de l'éthique chrétienne," in *Novitas et veritas vitae: Aux sources du renouveau de la morale chrétienne,* ed. C.-J. Pinto de Oliveira (Fribourg: Éditions universitaires, 1991), 213–23, esp. 220.

98. McKay, "Infused and Acquired Virtues," 39n57.

99. *ST* I-II 68.4.

life in a common vocabulary, but there was little consensus in the tradition about the exact nature of each gift. Given the ambiguity of the tradition, it is not surprising that Aquinas sometimes vacillates in his definition of individual gifts[100] and that his rationale for correlating particular gifts with particular realms of human experience can be vulnerable to accusations of arbitrariness. However, because Aquinas's account of the gifts shifts the focus from the phenomenology of individual gifts to a systematic reflection on their common internal structure and anthropological grounding, it does not stand or fall on his treatment of particular gifts. His account easily accommodates additional gifts or alternative understandings of the gifts he already includes. For Aquinas, what is most important about the gifts is that they mark out an important category of graced human affectivity.

For Aquinas, the gifts clearly affect the passions and affections.[101] He writes, "The appetitive power, in that which pertains to others, is perfected by piety; in that which pertains to self, is perfected by fortitude against the fear of dangers; against inordinate desire for pleasures, by fear."[102] Elsewhere he notes that the gifts lead us to fulfill our obligations to our neighbors "with fervent desire" and "with more abundant affection" than would virtue alone.[103] Nonetheless, the significance of Aquinas's account of the gifts to his understanding of human affectivity and his ethics is often overlooked. In a recent article, Charles Bouchard describes how he gradually realized that he had not given adequate attention to the role of grace and affectivity in Aquinas's moral theory. He argues that interpretations of Aquinas that neglect his treatment of the gifts and their transformation of affectivity risk serious distortion of his understanding of the Christian life.[104] He is clearly correct: for Aquinas, the gifts are integral to graced human affectivity.

The Beatitudes

After discussing the gifts of the Holy Spirit, Aquinas turns to the beatitudes. As with the gifts, the beatitudes were a traditional locus of theological speculation about the spiritual life, and since Aquinas devotes only one

100. See O'Connor, appendices to *Summa*, app. 4–5.

101. For more textual evidence of this interpretation, see *ST* I-II 68.3–6, 69.3, 79.3 and also *ST* II-II 19, 121, 139.

102. *ST* I-II 68.4.

103. *ST* I-II 69.3.

104. Bouchard, "Gifts of the Spirit," 541–49.

question to the beatitudes and then does not talk about them much elsewhere, it might seem as though Aquinas gives them due treatment because it is expected, but he does not truly integrate them into his theology. The scholarly consensus seems to have settled on this interpretation, if only by default, as the secondary literature on Aquinas's treatment of the beatitudes is even more sparse than the secondary literature on his treatment of the gifts.[105]

A closer look at Aquinas's account of the beatitudes, however, suggests the opposite conclusion. First, in the rhetorical structure of Latin works, the beginning and the end of a work are most important, and so by treating the beatitudes in question 69, almost at the pinnacle of the account of human flourishing's essential structure that he gives in questions 1–70 of the *Prima secundae*, Aquinas has placed his exposition of the beatitudes in a conspicuous and prominent position.[106] Second, Aquinas's interpretation of the beatitudes is highly original.[107] Theologians had long correlated individual gifts with individual beatitudes, and Augustine's schema was especially widely known in the thirteenth century. But while Aquinas notes and incorporates Augustine's schema, he also departs from it. His originality, and especially his break from Augustine, is hard to reconcile with an interpretation of Aquinas that sees him as not particularly interested in how the beatitudes relate to his larger theological agenda.

Third, and most importantly, Aquinas's account of the beatitudes is seamlessly integrated with his account of the virtues, and especially his account of the gifts of the Holy Spirit.[108] He writes: "The beatitudes are distin-

105. Pinckaers is an especially notable exception. In *The Source of Christian Ethics*, Pinckaers writes at some length about the beatitudes, and especially Aquinas's treatment of them. He has also written an excellent meditation on the beatitudes which draws especially on Aquinas. See Servais Pinckaers, *The Pursuit of Happiness—God's Way: Living the Beatitudes*, trans. Mary Thomas Noble (New York: Alba House, 1998).

106. This point was suggested to me by Michael Sherwin.

107. Pinckaers, *The Pursuit of Happiness*, 195–99.

108. In *ST* I-II 69.1–2, Aquinas describes the beatitudes as the consequence of both the virtues and the gifts, seemingly in deference to Ambrose, who correlates the beatitudes with the cardinal virtues (see *ST* I-II 69.1 ad 1). However, he explicitly says that the beatitudes are attributed more to the gifts than to the virtues in *ST* I-II 70.2. Moreover, in *ST* I-II 69.3, he connects the beatitudes to the gifts, and makes a point of explaining why individual beatitudes are related to the gifts rather than the virtues. It seems evident, therefore, that while the beatitudes bear some relation to the virtues—at the very least, the gifts presuppose and complement the activity of the virtues, and so the beatitudes must be related to the virtues as well—Aquinas defines the beatitudes primarily in terms of their relation to the gifts.

guished from the virtues and the gifts, not in the way that *habitus* are distinguished from each other, but in the way that acts are distinguished from *habitus*."[109] In this passage, Aquinas relates the beatitudes to the acts of the virtues and the gifts. In the following article, he further explains that they are related especially to the acts of the gifts. They are "preparations or dispositions" for eternal happiness, and also "rewards," in the sense of being an inchoate taste of what will be brought to completion in the next life, obtained as the direct result of the activity of the virtues and gifts.[110] And just as Aquinas correlates gifts with virtues in the *Secunda secundae,* since the gifts complement the virtues, he also correlates beatitudes with gifts, since the beatitudes are effects of the gifts.[111] Aquinas is clearly more interested in systematically integrating the beatitudes with the rest of his theology than accommodating established tradition. For example, in his discussion of the gift of piety, he notes that Augustine pairs this gift to the beatitude "Blessed are the meek," but apparently prefers to match piety with the beatitudes "Blessed are those who hunger and thirst for justice" and "Blessed are the merciful," because, as he explains, "one ought to fit the beatitudes to the gifts according to their objects and acts."[112]

In his exposition of how the beatitudes relate to the gifts, Aquinas subdivides the beatitudes into three categories.[113] The first category includes those beatitudes that facilitate the attainment of beatitude, by removing the impediments that would ensue from a life centered on pleasure. Through the gifts, we moderate our attachment to riches and honors, and so attain the first beatitude, "Blessed are the poor in spirit." We also moderate the passions through the gifts, in ways that go beyond the moderation of the virtues. The beatitude "Blessed are the meek" involves the moderation of the irascible passions, and the beatitude "Blessed are those who weep" involves the moderation of the concupiscible passions. The second category includes those beatitudes that perfect the active life, that is, those actions

109. *ST* I-II 69.1. His view of the beatitudes as more linked to the gifts than virtues is evident in the following passage: "Someone approaches the end of beatitude by the operations of the virtues, but chiefly by the operations of the gifts. Because when we speak of eternal beatitude, reason is not sufficient: it is the Holy Spirit who leads us to eternal beatitude, and it is the gifts that perfect us to obey and follow the Holy Spirit" (*ST* I-II 69.1).

110. *ST* I-II 69.2.

111. See *ST* II-II 8.7, 9.4, 19.12, 45.6, 52.4, 121.2, 139.2.

112. *ST* II-II 121.2.

113. *ST* I-II 69.3. See also Matthew 5:3–12 and Luke 6:20–26.

that we perform out of either justice or mercy, and so includes "Blessed are those who hunger and thirst for justice" and "Blessed are the merciful." It also includes "Blessed are the peacemakers," insofar as the gifts perfect the active life by perfecting our relations with our neighbors. The third and final category concerns the perfection of the contemplative life, and includes only one beatitude, "Blessed are the clean of heart."

Aquinas also pairs individual beatitudes with individual gifts. However, he seems less interested in resolving exactly which gift matches which beatitude; he is more interested in the relationship of individual beatitudes to the gifts considered as a whole. In the longest and most substantial of his articles on the beatitudes, Aquinas dedicates the body of the article to showing how the beatitudes perfect the human person through the gifts, and relegates the pairing of beatitudes with gifts to the responses to the objections. Moreover, his pairing of specific beatitudes with specific gifts is not nearly as systematic as his account of how the category of the beatitudes relates to the category of the gifts. Some of the proposals, moreover, seem somewhat tentative.

Aquinas's account of the beatitudes once again manifests his interest in human flourishing, and in how the virtues and gifts perfect the powers and dispositions of the human person. It also manifests his attention to human affectivity. He defines two of the beatitudes in reference to the passions, and he makes comments about the passions and affections throughout his treatment of the beatitudes.

The Fruits of the Holy Spirit

In question 70 of the *Prima secundae,* at the culmination of his account of human flourishing's essential structure, Aquinas turns finally to the fruits of the Holy Spirit, another topic neglected in the secondary literature. This category of psychological phenomena derives from Paul's list of certain "fruits of the Holy Spirit" in Galatians 5:22.[114] Like the gifts and

114. Paul enumerates nine fruits, namely, love, joy, peace, patience, kindness, goodness, faith, gentleness, and self-control. However, Latin copyists added three fruits in a common manuscript tradition, in order to clarify certain fruits with close synonyms. So in Aquinas's list of the fruits, there is longanimity and patience (*longanimatas* and *patientia*) instead of just longanimity (*longanimitas*); modesty and gentleness (*modestia* and *mansuetudo*) instead of just modesty (*modestia*); and continence and chastity (*continentia* and *castitas*) instead of just continence. See O'Connor, appendices to *Summa,* app. 7, 148–50.

the beatitudes, the fruits had been a traditional locus of theological speculation for centuries, and also like the gifts and beatitudes, the fruits had been only vaguely defined in the theological imagination. Aquinas offers a creative reinterpretation of the fruits as the final product of the Holy Spirit's activity in the human person. Fruit signifies something final and pleasant, Aquinas explains, and in this way our actions are fruits, because they are the actuation of human powers, and the final end of those powers.[115] If a fruit proceeds from the rational faculty, it is a fruit of reason, but if a fruit proceeds from the Holy Spirit, then it is a fruit of the Holy Spirit, as though arising from a "divine seed."[116] In this way, "the fruits of the Holy Spirit are certain final and pleasant products that grow in us by the power of the Holy Spirit."[117] Therefore, in his discussion of the various gifts of the Holy Spirit in the *Secunda secundae,* Aquinas correlates gifts with fruits, just as he correlates gifts with beatitudes.[118]

The fruits describe all sorts of affections and affective qualities: the joy and peace that flow from charity; patience and long-suffering in the face of difficulties; more fervent service of others through "the good fire of love"; restraint of anger; and the moderation of "interior desire" by continence and chastity.[119] Of the various fruits of the Holy Spirit, Aquinas gives special attention to charity, since it constitutes the most important of the theological virtues. He also gives great attention to the two fruits of joy and peace, which Aquinas sees as the direct result of charity, and he devotes a question to each immediately after his discussion of charity in the *Secunda secundae,* as will be discussed in the next chapter.[120]

Aquinas devotes an article to the question of the relationship between the beatitudes and the fruits. He states that the beatitudes are classified as fruits, but not vice versa: the beatitudes are a subset of the fruits. According

115. *ST* I-II 70.1.

116. *ST* I-II 70.1.

117. *ST* II-II 8.8.

118. See *ST* II-II 8.8, 19.12 ad 4, 52.4 ad 3, 121.2 ad 3, 139.2 ad 3. Aquinas also talks about peace as an effect—and seemingly a fruit—of the gift of wisdom in *ST* II-II 45.6 ad 3. Aquinas gives much less attention to specific fruits than to specific beatitudes, and typically discusses how they correlate with specific gifts and virtues only in a response to an objection. But since the beatitudes are a kind of fruit, the lack of explicit attention to specific fruits is easy to explain: he seems to think that his extended treatment of the beatitudes suffices.

119. *ST* I-II 70.3.

120. Aquinas's interest in joy and peace, and his discussion of them immediately after his questions on charity, suggest that his reflection on the fruits of the Holy Spirit may have had a crucial role in the development of his understanding of how joy and peace are related to charity.

to Aquinas, fruits can be effects of any virtue or gift (and here he must mean infused virtue, since otherwise the Holy Spirit would not be involved), but beatitudes are effects only of gifts, and therefore are a more perfect kind of fruit.[121]

Aquinas affirms, following Augustine, that the traditional list of fruits is not definitive; other fruits can be attributed to the Holy Spirit.[122] Nonetheless, he thinks that all other fruits can be reduced to one of the traditional fruits. He writes: "The acts of all the gifts and virtues can be reduced to one of these fruits by a certain sort of fittingness, since all the virtues and gifts must necessarily order the mind in one of the ways characteristic of these fruits."[123] His reasoning in this passage is telling: Aquinas implicitly discloses that what he sees as most essential to the fruits is that they order, and thereby perfect, the mind and the interior affections of the human person. For Aquinas, the fruits are not phenomena haphazardly associated with the activity of the Holy Spirit; they correlate to the determinate ways in which the Holy Spirit perfects the various faculties of the human person.

121. *ST* I-II 70.2.
122. *ST* I-II 70.3 ad 4; see also Augustine, *Commentary on Galatians*, 5:22–23.
123. *ST* I-II 70.3 ad 4.

CHAPTER 6

The Flourishing of Human Affectivity

In the *Prima secundae,* Aquinas presents an overview of human psychology and its development through virtue and its deformation by sin. In the *Secunda secundae,* he builds on this foundation, and offers a detailed description of how specific virtues bring the human person to full flourishing. Along the way, he also discusses specific vices, but vice is a secondary focus, as indicated by the structural priority given to the virtues, and the disproportionate attention they receive. For Aquinas, the life of virtue is defined by what it is, not by what it is not, and the same applies to virtuous affectivity. It is telling that it is even possible—which it is—to give a satisfactory account of what virtuous affectivity looks like for Aquinas without alluding to his description of the vices.

There is no need to strain to see how Aquinas's discussion of virtue and vice relates to human affectivity. Quite the opposite: affectivity is a central concern of the *Secunda secundae.* Throughout Aquinas seems intent to show how the passions and affections are brought to perfection through virtue and grace and how they are put into disarray by vice. By contrast, he hardly ever discusses the role of precept or commandment in shaping human affectivity (or indeed in ethics more generally).[1] He frequently refers back to the *Prima secundae* and specifically the *Treatise on the Passions* as background for his analysis of specific virtues and vices, an indication that affectivity is very much on his mind.[2] In fact, there is reason to think that

1. Aquinas structures some of the questions on justice (*ST* II-II 64–76, 81–108) around certain commandments of the Decalogue, but he does not announce that he is doing so. See Dalmazio Mongillo, "La struttura del 'De iustitia': Summa theologiae II-II qq. 58–122," *Angelicum* 48 (1971): 355–77; P. Markus Christoph, "Justice as an Infused Virtue in the *Summa Theologiae* II-II and Its Implications for Our Understanding of the Moral Life" (Ph.D. diss., University of Fribourg, 2010).

2. See *ST* II-II 2.10, 7.1, 17.1, 17.4, 17.8, 19.2, 23.3 ad 2, 23.4, 28.1, 28.3, 34.1, 34.3, 34.5 obj 2, 36.1

his attention to the concept of affection vis-à-vis passion actually deepens in the course of writing the *Secunda secundae.* The word *affectus* appears more than twice as often in the *Secunda secundae* than it does in the *Prima secundae.*[3] Moreover, Aquinas defines many of the virtues in terms of appetite and affectivity, but in such a way that the passions are not necessarily involved. It is possible that Aquinas began to use the word *affectus* more frequently because he had come to recognize more clearly that virtues can involve affection without involving passion, and in consequence he came to a greater appreciation of the usefulness of the category of affection.

Following the order of the virtues given in the *Secunda secundae,* this chapter will discuss Aquinas's account of how specific virtues perfect human affectivity and how specific vices deform it.

The Theological Virtues

The organization of Aquinas's discussion of virtues and vices is marked by precision and pedagogical elegance.[4] He begins with the theological virtues, ascending from faith, the gateway to the life of grace, and culminating in charity, the highest and most important virtue, theological or otherwise.[5]

obj 3–4, 41.2, 47.1 ad 1, 47.9 ad 3, 54.2 ad 3, 58.9 obj 1, 123.3, 123.8, 123.10, 123.11 ad 1, 125.1 obj 1, 125.2, 127.1, 128.1 ad 6, 129.6 ad 2, 129.7, 141.3, 141.4 obj 4, 141.7 obj 3, 144.1–2, 147.8 obj 2, 158.1–2, 158.5, 161.1, 168.2, 171.2 obj 1, 180.1, 180.7.

These references include only places where Aquinas *explicitly* refers back to the *Treatise on the Passions.* There are many other places where he reiterates its analysis without explicitly referring back to the *Treatise.*

3. The *Index Thomisticus* available on the Corpus Thomisticum website (www.corpusthomisticum.org) indicates that there are 193 instances of *affectus* and 42 instances of the close synonym *affectio* in the *Secunda secundae,* compared with 67 instances of *affectus* and 43 instances of *affectio* in the *Prima secundae.* This increase is significant, even taking into account the greater length of the *Secunda secundae.*

By way of comparison, *passio* occurs in 1131 instances in the *Prima secundae,* but it occurs in only 403 instances in the *Secunda secundae.* This statistic is somewhat misleading, because *passio* has many meanings unrelated to *passiones animae.* Nonetheless, the sharp drop in its use seems to indicate that, compared to the *Prima secundae,* Aquinas is less concerned with the *passiones animae* and more interested in *affectus* in the *Secunda secundae.*

4. The best single volume overview of the various aspects of Aquinas's ethics is *The Ethics of Aquinas,* ed. Stephen J. Pope (Washington, D.C.: Georgetown University Press, 2002). It provides a helpful discussion of many of the topics covered in this chapter. For a contemporary Thomistic exposition of the seven virtues, see Romanus Cessario, *The Virtues, Or the Examined Life* (New York: Continuum, 2002).

5. For a contemporary account of the theological virtues that draws on Aquinas, see Josef Pieper, *Faith, Hope, Love* (San Francisco: Ignatius Press, 1997).

From charity he descends to the moral virtues in order of importance: from prudence and justice to fortitude and temperance. The questions on charity thus constitute the centerpiece of the rhetorical structure of the *Secunda secundae*. Faith and hope widen natural horizons and make room for the possibility of supernatural charity, and then charity overflows and permeates all the powers of the soul, ordering and elevating the moral virtues.

Faith

The questions on faith that open the *Secunda secundae* provide the foundation for all that follows. It is through faith that God is known, and so it is through faith that God becomes the intentional object of hope and charity. Together these three theological virtues provide the context and grounding for the other virtues of the Christian life. Aquinas's choice to begin the *Secunda secundae* with the theological virtue of faith, however, does not only reflect the dependence of the other virtues on faith; it also underscores his intention to situate his ethics within the context of Christian faith.[6]

For Aquinas, faith is primarily a virtue of the intellect, though it also involves the will. The virtue of faith is established when, by consent of the will, the intellect receives supernatural knowledge of God that is dark and obscure but also certain.[7] This certainty is not naturally explicable. Although faith depends on rational grounds, such as the persuasiveness and beauty of Christ's ethical teachings or the evidence of miracles, it is beyond reason. Therefore the certainty of faith cannot be attributed to any natural source of knowledge; it comes from God's grace. Faith makes charity possible, since knowledge is a necessary precondition for love, but it also depends on charity to be most fully itself.[8] Without charity, faith is "unformed" and imperfect because it is not fully directed toward its final end, that is, God.

Aquinas's views on the virtue of faith evolve in some significant ways over the course of his life. Attention to these developments sheds light on

6. It also strengthens the case for interpreting his discussion of moral virtues as primarily concerned with infused moral virtues.

7. *ST* II-II 2.1, 2.9, 4.1, 4.8. See also Avery Dulles, *The Assurance of Things Hoped For: A Theology of Christian Faith* (New York: Oxford University Press, 1994), 33–36, and Romanus Cessario, *Christian Faith and the Theological Life* (Washington, D.C.: Catholic University Press, 1996). For a careful textual study of Aquinas's psychology of faith, see Benoit Duroux, *La psychologie de la foi chez s. Thomas d'Aquin* (Tournai, Belgium: Declée, 1963).

8. *ST* II-II 4.3–4. On the relationship between faith and charity in Aquinas, see Sherwin, *By Knowledge and By Love*, 119–203.

his mature thought, and especially the role of affectivity in his account of faith.[9] In his commentary on the *Sentences*, Aquinas holds that the intellect is given to understand that it is God who speaks in the proclamation of the Gospel, and then this supernatural knowledge of itself moves the will to assent to God's self-revelation.[10] After discovering the decrees of the Council of Orange, and their affirmation of the necessity of God's grace for even the beginnings of faith, Aquinas modifies his theology accordingly. He seems to have concluded that his earlier account downplayed the role of grace, since in his earlier account the will seems to assent to God's revelation on its own natural power, and not by any prompting of God's grace. In the *Summa*, therefore, Aquinas emphasizes the activity of God in the will as well as in the intellect. He affirms that the assent of faith "is from God who interiorly moves us through grace" and that while faith depends on the will, it must be "prepared by God through grace" to make an act of faith.[11] Aquinas describes this divine influence on the will as inspiring a certain kind of affection. He writes, "Faith is a gift of grace that inclines man to believe through a certain affection for the good."[12] According to Aquinas, the divine gift of faith does not involve just the infusion of supernatural knowledge; it also involves the infusion of affection for the good made known by this knowledge.

The importance of affection in Aquinas's account of faith is highlighted by his discussion of the faith of demons. Aquinas denies that the demons have the infused virtue of faith precisely because their knowledge of God does not involve affection. Since the infused virtue of faith implies an affective inclination toward the divine good, and since the demons lack any such affection, Aquinas argues, their faith is not a gift of grace. Rather, "they are compelled to believe from the sharpness of their natural intellect."[13] This understanding of demonic faith clearly demonstrates that, for Aquinas, faith implies an affective appreciation for divine good, and not just sheer knowledge of supernatural realities.[14]

9. Michael Sherwin provides a thorough exposition of the evolution of Aquinas's theology of faith, and especially his growing sensitivity to its affective dimensions. See Sherwin, *By Knowledge and By Love*, 131–46. The discussion that follows is indebted to his analysis.

10. *Scriptum super libros Sententiarum* III 23.3.2 ad 2.

11. *ST* II-II 6.1; 6.1 ad 3. See also *ST* II-II 2.9 ad 3, which affirms that God infuses an interior *instinctus* that impels the will's assent.

12. *ST* II-II 5.2 ad 2.

13. *ST* II-II 5.2 ad 2.

14. For a discussion of this divinely inspired affection and its relationship to faith, see Cessario, *Christian Faith*, 137–40.

Aquinas's attention to the affective dimension of faith emerges further in his description of faith's effects on the human psyche. The virtue of faith does not only influence the human person in the very specific ways in which it is directly infused by God; it also overflows into other realms of affectivity. The appetites respond to objects known by faith in similar ways to objects known by natural means. Since the affections respond to knowledge, and faith imparts knowledge, faith influences the affections.[15] And since the knowledge of faith gives access to the true nature of things and their true value, faith orders the affections according to the true value of things, and thus purifies the heart.[16]

Aquinas gives special attention to the connection between faith and the passions of hope and fear. He writes: "Faith generates hope insofar as it makes us consider the rewards that God will give to the just, while it is the cause of fear insofar as it makes us consider the punishments that God will inflict on sinners."[17] The appetites respond to intentional objects, not material objects, and the same applies to those objects known through faith. The same material object—God—inspires different responses depending on the lens through which he is perceived. For a believer lacking charity, the supernatural knowledge of God inspires servile fear, whereas the believer whose faith is informed by charity experiences filial fear.[18] These two different believers perceive God through different lenses, and in consequence the supernatural knowledge of faith elicits different affective responses.

Aquinas holds that faith is supported and deepened by the Holy Spirit's gifts of understanding and knowledge.[19] These gifts perfect the knowledge of God given through faith, as well as the knowledge of creation as it relates to God and the content of God's revelation.[20] They influence affectivity as

15. Aquinas explicitly affirms that faith influences the affections while discussing the purification of the heart by faith. He first objects: "It seems that the purification of the heart is not an effect of faith. For purity of heart principally consists in affection. But faith is in the intellect. Therefore faith does not cause the purification of the heart." Then he responds: "What is in the intellect is the principle of what is in affection, insofar as a known good moves affection" (*ST* II-II 7.2 obj, ad 1).

16. *ST* II-II 7.2.

17. *ST* II-II 7.1 ad 2.

18. *ST* II-II 7.1–2.

19. For a discussion of the gifts of understanding and knowledge and how they related to the virtue of faith, see Cessario, *Christian Faith*, 169–80. For a discussion of the gift of understanding, see Joseph Ignatius McGuiness, "The Distinctive Nature of the Gift of Understanding," *The Thomist* 3 (1941): 217–78.

20. *ST* II-II 8–9, esp. 8.6. The precise kind of knowing that corresponds to each gift is not

well as cognition, just as theological faith involves both will and intellect. The gift of knowledge enhances both the sorrow for sin and the consolation that flows from faith, and leads to well-ordered affection for created things.[21] It corresponds to the beatitude, "Blessed are those who mourn," since it leads to sorrow for sin and sin's harmful consequences.[22] Similarly, the gift of understanding leads to joy as the appetite rejoices in the intellect's being enlightened by the gift of understanding, and it assists the contemplation of divine realities and thus the attainment of beatitude.[23] It also corresponds to the beatitude "Blessed are the clean of heart," which involves "the purification of affection from inordinate affections."[24] Aquinas's attention to how these gifts and beatitudes complement theological faith further underscores his view that God influences human affectivity through the virtue of faith.

Aquinas's very precise definition of faith allows him to specify more exactly its relation to the various powers of the human person. It also allows him considerable ease in distinguishing between the individual who believes but lacks charity and the individual who has both faith and charity. His attention to infused affectivity can accommodate, for instance, the classic literary figure of the tortured believer who is torn between faith and a decadent lifestyle. In Aquinas's system, this inner torment can be described as the tension between affection for the truths proposed by divine revelation (infused with theological faith) and affection for sin and the pleasure of sin.

Aquinas's interest in faith's influence on affectivity is striking, as is his application of psychological principles originally established in reference to natural phenomena. His attention to the affective dimension of faith is not accidental, as though he just happens to cover it in the course of a meandering exposition. It is the direct result of his understanding of the vir-

---

entirely clear. The gift of understanding primarily signifies a contemplative, intuitive grasp of God, while the gift of knowledge primarily signifies practical knowledge about created things. Nonetheless, it seems that, according to Aquinas, the contemplative intuition of the gift of understanding also influences practical decisions, and the gift of knowledge is also directed toward God himself, especially insofar as God is revealed in creation. The blurriness of Aquinas's distinctions between these two gifts suggests that, because Aquinas is making use of a traditional vocabulary that he did not invent, the traditional nomenclature of the gifts may not fully capture the nuances of his actual working system. Aquinas himself notes the difficulty of distinguishing between the gifts that involve cognition in *ST* II-II 8.6.

21. *ST* II-II 9.4 ad 1, ad 3.

22. *ST* II-II 9.4.

23. *ST* II-II 8.8, 9.4 ad 3.

24. *ST* II-II 8.8.

tues as perfections of our natural faculties, and his stronger emphasis on the effect of grace on the will after his discovery of the decrees of the Council of Orange.

Hope

Aquinas uses the same word, *spes,* for both the passion of hope and the theological virtue of hope.[25] His view of theological hope, moreover, is deeply informed by his understanding of the passion of hope, and vice versa.[26] Historical circumstance is a factor: Aquinas first treats of the passion of hope in his commentary on Peter Lombard's treatment of theological hope, as there is no separate discussion of the passion of hope in Lombard's *Sentences.*[27] Nonetheless, although this close pedagogical connection between the passion and the virtue may have had its origins in circumstances beyond his control, Aquinas seems content with it. When he writes the *Summa,* he can arrange his materials in any way he prefers, but he continues to link the virtue with the passion. In fact, he seems to have structured the *Summa*'s account of each to parallel the other.[28] Certainly, in his view the passion and the virtue share many similarities, and in the course of his questions on theological hope, Aquinas often refers back to the *Treatise on the Passions.*[29] Both involve appetite. The passion of hope is a movement of the sense appetite, and the theological virtue of hope is located in the intellectual appetite. Both also depend on cognition, and more specifically, some expectation of a future good, or at least the possibility of its attainment. Each requires a cognitive appraisal of the desired good as attainable, and without such a judgment, the passion of hope would not be elicited, and theological hope could not be sustained. Aquinas draws on his account of the passion of hope to explain how theological hope relates to its intentional object. Like the passion of hope, he explains, theological hope is a tending toward a future good that

25. For a close study of Aquinas's understanding of theological hope, with special attention to cross-textual comparison of his different writings, see Servais Pinckaers, "La nature verteuse de l'espérance," *Revue thomiste* 58 (1958): 422–32, 623–44.

26. Aquinas draws on his understanding of the passion of hope to make sense of theological hope from his earliest writings. For some texts outside the *Summa* that connect theological hope to the passion of hope, see *Scriptum super libros Sententiarum* III 26; *De veritate* 25.3 ad 5; *De virtutibus* 4.1, 4.3.

27. Peter Lombard, *Sententiae* III 26.

28. I am indebted to Lawrence Donohoo for this observation.

29. See *ST* II-II 17.1, 17.4, 17.8, and 19.2.

is difficult to attain, namely, God, insofar as God satisfies the human desire for happiness.[30] But there are differences as well. Unlike the passion of hope, theological hope is a *habitus* and not a discrete movement of an appetite.[31] It is an affective disposition toward particular appetitive movements, but it is not itself an affection, that is, a movement of appetite. Nonetheless, an *act* of theological hope directly parallels the passion of hope.

Theological hope is a kind of love of God, namely, love of God not in himself but for the happiness God gives. However, unlike the love of charity, theological hope is not oriented toward God purely as God, but "intends to obtain something for the one hoping."[32] Hope leads to charity, and hope also inspires joy as the intellectual appetite rests in anticipatory possession of the good toward which it is directed.[33] By defining hope in this way, Aquinas provides a solution to a prominent medieval controversy: the question of whether or not charity involves any concern for personal interest.[34] Some rejected the idea that charity permitted any self-interest, others the idea

30. *ST* II-II 17.1–2.

31. *ST* II-II 17.1.

32. *ST* II-II 17.8. There are differences of opinion on whether the "tending toward" of hope can be understood as a kind of desire. De Letter rejects such an interpretation and argues that Aquinas's notion of hope should be characterized not as desire but as trust or expectation. See Prudentius De Letter, "Hope and Charity in St. Thomas," *The Thomist* 13 (1950): 218–31; 342–52. His argument, however, fails to recognize that any movement of appetite toward a non-possessed good is by definition a movement of desire, at least in some sense. Since hope is a *habitus* located in the appetite, acts of hope must be acts of appetite, and therefore, in an important sense, of desire. Mary Michael Glenn recognizes hope as involving desire, but nonetheless agrees with De Letter that its defining characteristic is confident expectation. Consequently, like De Letter, she seems to conflate the cognition to which hope responds with hope itself. Mary Michael Glenn, "A Comparison of the Thomistic and Scotistic Concept of Hope," *The Thomist* 20 (1957): 27–74.

The view of hope as a love of desire is defended by William Hill in an appendix to his translation of the relevant questions of the *Summa*. Romanus Cessario also interprets hope as a love of desire. See William J. Hill, Introduction, notes, and appendices to *Summa Theologiae*, vol. 33: *Hope* (New York: McGraw-Hill Book Co.; London: Eyre and Spottiswoode, 1966), appendix 3, 142–43; and Romanus Cessario, "The Theological Virtue of Hope (IIa IIae, qq. 17–22)," in *The Ethics of Aquinas*, ed. Stephen J. Pope (Washington, D.C.: Georgetown University Press, 2002), 236–38.

33. *ST* II-II 17.8, 20.4 ad 2.

34. Michael Sherwin gives an overview of this medieval controversy over the theology of charity, which has its roots in the interpretation of Augustine, and argues that Aquinas's innovative account, and especially his account of hope's relation to charity, successfully reconciles the primary intuitions of various opposed positions. Michael Sherwin, "Aquinas, Augustine, and the Medieval Scholastic Crisis concerning Charity," in *Aquinas the Augustinian*, ed. Michael Dauphinais, Barry David, and Matthew Levering (Washington, D.C.: Catholic University of America Press, 2007), 181–204, esp. 201–04.

that charity could exclude it. By defining hope in these terms, Aquinas affirms the goodness and virtuousness of seeking one's personal fulfillment, while also distinguishing it from the selflessness of charity (which nonetheless remains a virtue of the appetite and therefore of desire, although of God-centered rather than self-centered desire).

Aquinas's understanding of the precise object of hope, that is, to what exactly it tends, is complex, and it undergoes some evolution over the course of his writings.[35] In his mature teaching, hope's object is twofold: God as he is desirable for personal fulfillment and happiness, and the earthly goods and divine assistance necessary to attain God.[36] This account of the object of theological hope strengthens the link with the passion of hope: it means that, in Aquinas's system, theological hope is bound to generate the passion of hope, insofar as any natural good that is helpful for salvation can simultaneously be the object of both virtue and passion, with a consequent mutual strengthening of each.[37]

By presenting theological hope as a virtue of appetite, Aquinas deemphasizes the cognitive dimension of hope. Even though hope necessarily responds to some cognitive appraisal of the future, this cognitive appraisal is placed within the sphere of faith, and distinguished from the actual content of theological hope. For Aquinas, hope involves certain expectation, but this certain expectation is an affective tending toward God, not a judgment about the future.[38] Knowledge of what to expect in the future, which

35. See Hill, *Hope*, Appendix 4, 144–48, and Wawrykow, *God's Grace and Human Action*, 129–37, 247–59. In his commentary on the *Sentences*, Aquinas holds there is one object of hope, namely God (*Scriptum super libros Sententiarum* III 26.2.2). In the *Summa*, Aquinas holds that there are two goods or objects to which hope tends: God and the assistance necessary to reach our final end. For this reason, Aquinas explains, it is possible to hope not only for heavenly beatitude, but also for whatever lesser goods may be instrumental in attaining God (*ST* II-II 17.4, 17.7, 19.1).

36. *ST* II-II 17.2, 17.4.

37. These observations are inspired by Josef Pieper's Thomistic treatment of theological hope, where he notes that theological hope can inspire natural hope, and thus lead to a kind of rejuvenation and eternal youthfulness. He writes: "The supernatural vitality of hope overflows, moreover, and sheds it light also upon the rejuvenated powers of natural hope. The lives of countless saints attest to this truly astonishing fact . . . nothing more eminently preserves and founds 'eternal youth' than the theological virtue of hope. It alone can bestow on man the certain possession of that aspiration that is at once relaxed and disciplined, that adaptability and readiness, that strong-hearted freshness, that resilient joy, that steady perseverance in trust that so distinguish the young and make them lovable" (Pieper, *Faith, Hope, Love*, 110–11). For a study of Peiper's account of hope, see Bernard Schumacher, *A Philosophy of Hope: Josef Pieper and the Contemporary Debate on Hope*, trans. D. C. Schindler (New York: Fordham University Press, 2003).

38. *ST* II-II 18.4.

includes certain knowledge of God's unchanging good will toward us, forms part of the cognitive content not of hope, but of faith. Hope presupposes faith's knowledge, but acts of theological hope are not acts of knowing.[39] The certainty of hope derives in a way from the certainty of faith: "hope tends to its end with certainty, in a way participating in faith's certainty, which is in the cognitive power."[40] Furthermore, the cognitive judgment that supplies the certainty of hope is not an absolute expectation of salvation, but rather faith's certain knowledge that God infinitely desires our salvation and actively assists us to obtain it.[41] This account of theological hope's dependence on faith's knowledge corresponds neatly with its parallel passion, since the passions depend upon cognition but are distinct from it.

Aquinas matches theological hope with the gift of fear. Because the gift of fear encourages filial fear of God, it also corresponds to the beatitude "Blessed are the poor in spirit," since reverent submission to God implies an attitude of trust in God and a simultaneous acknowledgement of dependence.[42] He explains that filial fear and hope complement and strengthen each other.[43] There is an internal coherence to this position, since both affections pertain to the future: hope is a desire for a future good, and filial fear is a desire to avoid a future evil. But since other plausible matching between virtue and gift could be made (and in fact he links the gift of fear to temperance elsewhere),[44] the structure of the passions outlined in the *Prima secundae* seems partly responsible for the connection Aquinas makes between hope and fear. In the *Treatise on the Passions* he opposes the passions of hope and fear,[45] and his placement of the two passions in opposition to each other makes it more natural for him to draw a connection between the virtue of hope and the gift of fear.

The parallels between the passion of hope and the virtue of hope, and the reliance on the *Treatise on the Passions* to explain theological hope, are

39. Aquinas describes hope's dependence on faith as follows: "In one way, the object of hope is eternal beatitude, and in another way, divine help. Both of these are proposed to us by faith, through which it becomes known to us that we can attain eternal life, and that divine help is provided to us for this purpose" (*ST* II-II 17.7).

40. *ST* II-II 18.4.

41. William Hill captures this precision about hope's certainty succinctly: "The certainty that the Christian experiences in his hope is precisely his untroubled assurance that the power and mercy of God orders him (though fallibly) to salvation" (Hill, *Hope*, Appendix 7, 164).

42. *ST* II-II 19.12.

43. *ST* II-II 19.9 ad 1.

44. *ST* II-II 141.1 ad 3.

45. *ST* I-II 23.2.

further indications that Aquinas's theory of the passions plays a central role in his theological anthropology. Furthermore, by locating hope in the will, Aquinas unequivocally defines the virtue of hope as a perfection of human affectivity, and not as a perfection of human cognition.

Charity

Charity is the summit of the theological virtues and the font of the infused moral virtues, and the questions on charity are the pivot on which the *Secunda secundae* turns: they complete the section on the theological virtues, and then transition the discussion to the execution of charity's commands through the cardinal virtues. The questions on charity are also among the most elegant and tightly structured of any of the seven virtues considered in the *Secunda secundae,* with each question leading naturally to the next. Discussion flows seamlessly from the nature of charity in itself to its necessary fruits in the human psyche. Aquinas gives particular attention to the affective dimension of charity, explaining how charity orders all of the passions and affections, generating joy and peace in the highest part of the soul. It is noteworthy that his lengthiest discussion of joy and peace in the *Summa* immediately follow his questions on charity.

The relevance of the questions on charity to Aquinas's account of human affectivity is often overlooked, and his subsequent questions on joy and peace are infrequently examined in the secondary literature. The connection between charity and affectivity is easy to overlook because Aquinas provides the metaphysical framework required to grasp what is going on much earlier in the *Prima secundae,* and so he does not feel the need to make the connection more explicit for the reader. Nonetheless, when the questions on charity are read in light of his *Treatise on the Passions,* a striking symmetry emerges. Just as the passion of hope provides a metaphysical backdrop for theological hope, so too the passion of love serves as a natural analogue for the supernatural love of charity, though the analogy is not as pointed as it is with hope.[46] Like the passion of love, charity is oriented

46. Aquinas explicitly draws on an analogy between the passion of love and the theological virtue of charity in *ST* I-II 70.3 and *ST* II-II 28.1. In both of these instances, he refers back to the *Treatise on the Passions.* Aquinas makes this connection between charity and the passion of love from his earliest writings, just as he also makes a connection between theological hope and the passion of hope from the beginning of his career. Besides these texts in the *Summa,* see *Scriptum super libros Sententiarum* III 27; *De veritate* 25.3 ad 5; and *De virtutibus* 4.1 ad 6, 4.3.

toward a good, in this case God, the supreme good. Charity loves God for his own sake and thus "attains God himself in order to rest in him, not in order that we might get something from him."[47] And just as the passion of love leads to the passion of pleasure in the presence of its intentional object, theological charity, by attaining God and resting in him, causes joy and peace. The sense appetite reaches its fulfillment in the passion of pleasure, and the intellectual appetite reaches its fulfillment in the virtue of charity and its attendant joy and peace.

Charity is a virtue of appetite and is located in the will.[48] As a movement of the intellectual appetite, charity responds to cognition, and so every act of charity requires cognition. Consequently, love of God presupposes knowledge of God.[49] Although a virtue of appetite, charity is dependent on the intellect and particularly the knowledge that comes through faith.[50]

The object of charity is complex. God is the primary object of charity, but he is not the only object of charity. The theological virtue of charity is also directed toward others and oneself, insofar as they are loved in God and for God.[51] Similarly, although God is the primary source of happiness, he is not the only source of happiness, nor will he be such even in heaven.[52] Aquinas makes space for the full range of human desires within his vision

For a discussion of the relationship between various kinds of natural love and the supernatural virtue of charity, see Jordan Aumann, "Thomistic Evaluation of Love and Charity," *Angelicum* 55 (1978): 534–56.

47. *ST* II-II 23.6.

48. *ST* II-II 24.1.

49. *ST* II-II 27.4 ad 2.

50. *ST* II-II 24.1. For a discussion of charity's relationship to faith, see Sherwin, *By Knowledge and By Love*, 152–63.

51. *ST* II-II 25.1. Gerald J. Beyer discusses the relationship and unity between love of God and love of neighbor in Aquinas. See Gerald J. Beyer, "The Love of God and Neighbour according to Aquinas: An Interpretation," *New Blackfriars* 84 (2003): 116–32.

52. Bonnie Kent expresses this point well: "Those with the virtue of charity might nonetheless develop the natural virtues and exercise them both for their intrinsic worth and for the sake of God. . . . Thus a Christian's daily conduct in selling cars, caring for patients, or teaching philosophy, and likewise, her routine behavior with family and friends, can express both her love for strictly human goods *and* her love for God. To put it crudely, Thomas does not regard God as some jealous lover who insists that people care for no one but Him and for no happiness other than the happiness they could have in His presence. God Himself gave human beings bodies and emotions; God Himself made human beings social (political) animals, inclined by their very nature to seek happiness in the company of others of their kind. Heaven itself should not be regarded as some eternal tête-à-tête with God. Like Augustine, Thomas describes heaven as a community (or city), where Christians enjoy not only the community of God but also the company of the saints" (Bonnie Kent, "Habits and Virtues," 125–26).

of charity and authentic human happiness. Some theologies minimize desires not directly concerned with God to the point of irrelevance, with finite goods relativized to nothing compared to the infinite good of God; Aquinas has a place for everything.

Charity logically proceeds from faith and hope, but orders and enlivens the other two theological virtues.[53] Aquinas specifies that "charity is not in the will (*voluntas*) considered in the sense of free choice (*liberum arbitrium*)."[54] It is seated in the will and not in the capacity to make free choices. With this specification, Aquinas makes clear that charity does not affect human action only in moments of decision, like a *deus ex machina* that appears out of nowhere only when it is needed. Charity is a habitual affective disposition that provides a stable shape to a person's character and affectivity. It influences concrete acts organically. Over time, charity ordinarily becomes more rooted in the soul, and it is in this way, by permeating the soul more deeply, that charity is said to grow or increase in intensity.[55]

Aquinas holds that charity, as a *habitus,* is a created reality in the soul.[56] This understanding of charity explicitly responds to the opinion of Peter Lombard, who holds that acts of charity are the direct effect of the Holy Spirit dwelling in us, and as such are unmediated by any *habitus.*[57] According to Aquinas, Lombard's view of charity does not leave room for the voluntariness and creative dynamism essential to virtue, because it reduces the human agent to a conduit for the Holy Spirit. Aquinas's critique of Lombard has a rhetorical and persuasive force that is not easily overcome. It is also presented with more bluntness and passion than is typical for Aquinas.[58] He apparently sees this question as a critical issue. In the context of his system, he seems correct to judge it as such: the entire notion of *habitus* as a disposition actuated by our free choice would be called into question

53. *ST* II-II 17.8, 23.6–8.

54. *ST* II-II 24.1 ad 3.

55. *ST* II-II 24.5.

56. *ST* II-II 23.2.

57. Peter Lombard, *Sententiae* I 17. For a careful analysis of Aquinas's response to Peter Lombard, see Eberhard Schockenhoff, "The Theological Virtue of Charity (IIa IIae, qq. 23–46)," in *The Ethics of Aquinas,* ed. Stephen J. Pope (Washington, D.C.: Georgetown University Press, 2002), 248–50.

58. Furthermore, when Aquinas tackles the same issue in *De virtitubus* 2.1, he uses even stronger language: he describes a certain related opinion as ridiculous (*ridiculum*), a word he uses very rarely according to the *Index Thomisticus.* See R. J. Batten, Introduction, notes, and appendices to *Summa Theologiae,* Vol. 34: *Charity* (New York: McGraw-Hill Book Co.; London: Eyre and Spottiswoode, 1966), 11 note d.

if the most perfect movement of the will, that is, the act of charity, was not actuated by us, but only by the direct intervention of God. Aquinas's notion of charity as a created *habitus* at our disposal does more than preserve the voluntariness of acts of charity. It carves out space not just for authentic human freedom, but also for authentic human creativity, because it is the human person, and not God, who determines the concrete manifestations of God's gift of infused charity. At the same time, because charity is infused directly by God, Aquinas is in a strong position to defend traditional Christian belief in the necessity of grace and our complete incapacity for charitable action without divine assistance.

Aquinas defines charity as friendship (*amicitia*) with God.[59] As such, it implies mutual love and "a certain union of affection."[60] He is among the first to describe charity in such terms and the most articulate of its early exponents.[61] Aquinas's analogous use of human friendship to define charity has many sources, the most notable being Aristotle's *Nicomachean Ethics* and John's Gospel (where Jesus tells his apostles that he no longer calls them servants but friends), both of which Aquinas cites in his first article on charity.[62] Nonetheless, whatever his reliance on previous sources and theo-

59. *ST* II-II 23.1. Aquinas describes charity from multiple perspectives, but he gives priority to his definition of charity as friendship, insofar as it is offered in the first article in the first question on charity. Louis Hughes comments: "We can be left in no doubt that for St. Thomas the thesis: 'charity is a kind of friendship of man for God' is the most significant thing that can be said about this divine form of love, from the fact that he gives us a fully scientific demonstration of it in the opening article of the section on charity in the *Summa Theologiae*." Louis M. Hughes, "Charity as Friendship in the Theology of Saint Thomas," *Angelicum* 52 (1975): 165. For a study of Aquinas's philosophy of friendship, see Daniel Schwartz, *Aquinas on Friendship* (Oxford: Clarendon Press, 2007).

60. *ST* II-II 27.2.

61. Hugh of St. Victor seems to be the first to connect the theological virtue of charity as such to friendship (in *De sacramentis* 2.13.11). However, Aquinas may be the first to integrate the Aristotelian concept of friendship into a systematic portrayal of charity. See M.-Joseph Keller and M.-Benoît Lavaud, "La charité comme amitié d'apres saint Thomas," *Revue thomiste* 34 (1929): 445–46; A. Stévaux, "La doctrine de la charité dans les Commentaires des *Sentences* de Saint Albert, de Saint Bonaventure et de Saint Thomas," *Ephemerides Theologiae Louvaniensis* 24 (1948): 85–87; Anthony Keaty, "Thomas's Authority for Identifying Charity as Friendship: Aristotle or John 15?" *The Thomist* 62 (1998): 585n14; Guy Mansini, "*Similitudo, Communicatio,* and the Friendship of Charity in Aquinas," in *Thomistica*, ed. E. Manning (Leuven: Peeters, 1995), 1; and Schokenhoff, "Theological Virtue of Charity," 246.

62. See *ST* II-II 23.1; *John* 15:15; Aristotle, *Ethics* VIII.2–3, 1155b–1156b. Scholars debate the relative significance of Aquinas's sources to his account of charity. See Keaty, "Charity as Friendship," 581–601 and L. Gregory Jones, "The Theological Transformation of Aristotelian Friendship in the Thought of St. Thomas Aquinas," *The New Scholasticism* 61 (1987): 373–99. For a discus-

logians, given his departure from theological tradition, Aquinas's decision to interpret charity as friendship is evidently part of a deliberate strategy. Because friendship implies a strong sense of affectivity, it is reasonable to suppose that Aquinas's interest in how the virtues perfect human affectivity led him to find the image of friendship particularly apt for charity. This supposition becomes all the more plausible when considering how Aquinas describes human friendship. Aquinas holds that friendship involves a union of affection, and he describes friendship in terms of love (*amor*).[63] The love of desire (*concupiscientia*) loves something or someone for the sake of personal well-being, but the love of friendship loves someone as another self, and wants good for the other in the same way as for oneself.[64] Moreover, Aquinas maintains that friendship constitutes a *habitus*,[65] thus implying that it is an appetitive and affective disposition. All of these descriptions of human friendship in terms of affectivity apply to Aquinas's account of the divine friendship of charity.

Friendship with God implies some kind of *communicatio*, that is, some kind of sharing and benevolent affect.[66] This *communicatio* is primarily God's sharing of his own happiness with us,[67] and so is radically disproportionate. Still, it is not entirely one-sided, because friendship, even divine friendship, is necessarily reciprocal and mutual. Unless we accept it and cooperate with it, God's offer of grace cannot establish this sharing of God's life and happiness in us, precisely because this life and happiness involves communion. In the *communicatio* of divine friendship, God's life and love flows through us back to himself. We are fully involved in God's inner life of Trinitarian communion, and our reciprocity is necessary to this *communica-*

---

sion of the analogy between human and divine friendship, see Leo Bond, "A Comparison between Human and Divine Friendship," *The Thomist* 3 (1941): 54–94.

63. *ST* II-II 23.1, 27.2. For a discussion of the difference between the love of friendship and the love of concupiscence, see Guy Mansini, "*Duplex amor* and the Structure of Love in Aquinas," in *Thomistica*, ed. E. Manning (Leuven: Peeters, 1995): 137–96.

64. *ST* I-II 28.1. Aquinas takes the idea of the friend as another self from Aristotle. See *Ethics* IX.4, 1166a31, IX.9, 1169b6.

65. *Sententia libri Ethicorum* VIII.5; see also Aristotle, *Ethics* VIII.5, 1157b.

66. For discussion of the meaning and significance of *communicatio* in Aquinas's account of charity, see Mansini, "Charity in Aquinas," 1–26, Sherwin, *By Knowledge and By Love*, 149n11; Joseph Bobik, "Aquinas on *Communicatio*, the Foundation of Friendship and *Caritas*," *The Modern Schoolman* 64 (1988): 1–18; and Joseph Bobik, "Aquinas on Friendship with God," *The New Scholasticism* 60 (1986): 257–71.

67. *ST* II-II 23.1.

tio, even though our reciprocity is simply the return to God of what God has given to us.

There is an obvious affirmation of the value of human friendship implicit in Aquinas's formulation of charity, perhaps consciously set against the sort of individualist asceticism that would be suspicious of friendship.[68] A positive view of friendship is also evident in Aquinas's argument that our family and friends have more of a claim on our charity than those we do not know or our enemies,[69] and, perhaps even more strikingly, in his argument that it is more meritorious to love our friends than our enemies.[70] His prioritization of charity for family and friends over charity for enemies evinces a strong appreciation for the positive moral value of friendship. It also suggests that Aquinas sees charity primarily as the fulfillment of desire (albeit non-egocentric desire), and only secondarily as an obligation, rather than as a species of moral obligation that is occasionally pleasant.

Of the theological virtues, charity has the most pervasive effects on the appetites and the affections, and Aquinas frequently discusses them. Significantly, and probably deliberately, his remarks focus on charity's influence on the affections, not the passions, thus including movements of both appetites. He cites approvingly Augustine's description of charity as our most completely ordered affection.[71] Aquinas discusses whether one's "affection of charity" should be greater toward some persons than others and concludes in the affirmative.[72] Charity makes our affections accord with God's.[73] It unites all other virtues, gathering them together and ordering them to the love of God. "The love of God is unitive," he writes, "since it leads man's affection from the many to the one."[74] To describe this integration, Aquinas

68. Fergus Kerr, "Charity as Friendship," in *Language, Meaning, and God,* ed. Brian Davies (London: Geoffrey Chapman, 1987), 1–23, and Keaty, "Charity as Friendship," 592n26.

69. *ST* II-II 26.6–13. For a discussion of the order of obligation in charity, see Jean Porter, "*De ordine caritatis:* Charity, Friendship, and Justice in Thomas Aquinas' *Summa theologiae," The Thomist* 53 (1989): 197–213.

70. *ST* II-II 27.7. Aquinas qualifies his judgment, noting a sense in which it might be more meritorious to love one's enemy, but after making this caveat he again affirms the general moral superiority of loving a friend over loving an enemy.

71. *ST* II-II 23.3. It is unlikely that Aquinas would have used the word "affection" in this way were he not quoting Augustine, since Augustine seems to conflate the virtue of charity with the affection of charity, whereas Aquinas would likely distinguish between the virtue of charity and the operation of charity, that is, the affection of charity.

72. *ST* II-II 26.6.

73. *ST* II-II 26.9 obj. 3.

74. *ST* I-II 73.1 ad 3.

calls charity "the form of the virtues," because "all the other virtues in some way depend on charity,"[75] and because charity enlivens the other virtues and shapes their orientations toward the specific goods desired by charity and consistent with it.[76] Charity affects how the intellect judges particular objects as desirable or repugnant, and in this way influences how the affections will respond.[77] Grace "softens affection by the fire of charity."[78] These examples illustrate Aquinas's interest in the influence of charity on human affectivity.

After discussing charity, Aquinas turns to joy and peace, two of the fruits of Holy Spirit that Paul identifies in Galatians 5:22. The placement of the questions on joy and peace immediately after the questions on charity emphasizes the connection of joy and peace to charity and Aquinas's interest in the affective consequences of charity. Joy is the affection Aquinas associates most closely with charity. "The spiritual joy that is about God," he writes, "is the effect of charity."[79] Furthermore, no other virtue "operates with more pleasure" than charity.[80] The intensity of the joy varies according to the intensity of charity, and, if intense enough, it may overflow from the will to the sense appetite. The joy of charity manifests the essential structure of any sort of joy, insofar as it results from the will resting in the possession of a desired good. The difference is that in this case the desired good is God:

> Joy is caused by love, either because what is loved is present, or simply because what is loved is in possession of its own goodness. This second way especially pertains to the love of benevolence, through which someone rejoices that his friend is doing well, even if the friend is absent. In contrast, sadness follows from love, either because what is loved is absent, or because what we wish well is deprived of its goodness, or suffers some evil. Now charity is love of God, whose goodness is immutable since God himself is his own goodness. And from the fact that he is loved, God is in the lover, on account of his most noble effect, which is that, as John says, "he who remains in charity, remains in God and God in him" (1 John 4:16). Therefore spiritual joy, which comes from God, is caused by charity.[81]

75. *ST* I-II 62.2 ad 3.
76. *ST* II-II 23.8. Aquinas also calls charity the mother of the other virtues in *ST* II-II 23.8 ad 3.
77. *ST* II-II 24.11.
78. *ST* I-II 79.3.
79. *ST* II-II 28.1. See also *ST* I-II 70.3.
80. *ST* II-II 23.2.
81. *ST* II-II 28.1.

God is not the only source of this spiritual joy; created goods can also cause spiritual joy when they are appreciated in relation to their Creator.[82] Furthermore, it is not only the love of charity that causes spiritual joy. A less perfect form of spiritual joy also results from hope, that is, from loving God for what he gives.[83] As with the joy that comes from charity, the intensity of the joy varies according to the intensity of theological hope.

The connection between charitable action and joy mirrors the connection between the passions of love and pleasure. As discussed in chapter 3, the structure of the intellectual appetite parallels the structure of the sense appetite, and Aquinas alludes to this parallel in his treatment of charity's relationship to joy.[84] The first movement of the intellectual appetite is love, and this love leads to joy when the loved object is present, just as the passion of love leads to pleasure when its object is present. Building on this understanding of the intellectual appetite, Aquinas holds that acts of charity, which are acts of the will, terminate in joy as the will comes to rest through them in the divine good. "Joy," he writes, "is not another virtue distinct from charity but rather a certain act or effect of charity."[85] This joy is twofold: joy in God for being God, and joy in the divine good as shared by us.[86]

Acts of the will result in joy only when they attain their desired object. Acts of charity, however, always attain their desired object, because the virtue of charity implies the presence of God in the soul through sanctifying grace, and thus acts of charity always attain their proper end of God. Consequently, Aquinas reasons, acts of charity always produce joy, even if imperfectly so in our present earthly condition. This claim follows necessarily from his accounts of intellectual appetite and the virtue of charity. He writes: "The love of charity is necessarily followed by joy. For every lover rejoices at being united with what is loved. But charity always has present God, whom it loves, for as John says, 'he who abides in charity, abides in God and God in him' (1 John 4:16). Hence charity leads to joy."[87] Acts of charity always cause joy because acts of charity presuppose the theological virtue of charity, which in turn presupposes God's indwelling in the soul. Consequently, acts of char-

82. "Created goods only excite spiritual joy to the extent that they are referred to the divine good, from which spiritual joy properly arises" (*ST* II-II 9.4 ad 1).

83. *ST* II-II 28.1 ad 3.

84. *ST* II-II 23.3 ad 2, 28.1, 28.4.

85. *ST* II-II 28.4. See also *ST* II-II 28.1.

86. *ST* II-II 28.2.

87. *ST* I-II 70.3.

ity always attain their proper end, that is, God, and therefore, as with any act of the will that attains its proper end, acts of charity always result in joy.

Aquinas notes, however, that the joy of charity can be mingled with sadness. He devotes an article to the question of how his claim that acts of charity always cause joy can be reconciled with the seeming contradictions presented by concrete human experience. His answer is that the charitable act of itself produces joy, but our experience of this joy can be hindered by anything that stands in the way of our neighbor's or our own "participation in the divine good."[88] He does not elaborate, but his idea seems clear: Aquinas wants to maintain that acts of charity in themselves cause joy, but that accompanying affections or sensations can drown out the joy. Elsewhere, for example, he affirms that bodily pain can make us insensible to the soul's delight in virtue.[89] But even in those cases when the joy of charity is drowned out, the virtue of charity itself operates without sadness (*sine tristitia*).[90]

The other principal effect of charity is peace.[91] Aquinas describes peace as "a union of the inclinations of the appetites"[92] and also, following Augustine, as "the tranquility of order."[93] This peace is desired by everyone but can be attained only through charity.[94] Without grace there can be no true peace, only the illusion of peace.[95] Charity, by centering the various appetites in the love of God, directs each appetite in harmony with the others and thus generates peace. Nothing but charity can do this, because we have been created in such a way that our disparate desires can operate in harmony only if they are ordered by charity. Charity is assisted in this task by the Holy Spirit's gift of wisdom. The gift of wisdom supernaturally enlightens the intellect, and thus helps to create peace by putting things in proper order.[96] It thus correlates with the beatitude "Blessed are the peacemakers."

88. *ST* II-II 28.2.

89. *ST* II-II 123.8.

90. *De virtutibus* 1.10 ad 15.

91. For an exposition of Aquinas's account of interior peace, with particular attention to his appropriation of Augustine and Dionysius, see Heather McAdam Erb, "Interior peace: *Inchoatio vitae aeternae*," in *Wisdom's Apprentice: Thomistic Essays in Honor of Lawrence Dewan, O.P.* (Washington, D.C.: The Catholic University of America Press, 2007), 260–81. Erb contrasts Aquinas's understanding of peace as the coordination of various elements, notably contemplation and action, with a certain monastic ideal that emphasizes separation from the world and the quieting of one's heart.

92. *ST* II-II 29.3 ad 3.

93. *ST* II-II 29.1 ad 1, 29.2; Augustine, *City of God*, 19.13.

94. *ST* II-II 29.2–3.

95. *ST* II-II 29.3 ad 1.

96. *ST* II-II 45.6. Even though the gift of wisdom is primarily about the contemplation of

Charity is like a combination that puts all the tumblers of a lock to precisely the right setting: "the end of all human actions and affections is the love of God, by which we attain our ultimate end," and so when the love of God orders our actions and affections, everything falls into place.[97] Only charity can unite the appetites in the calm and union of peace, because only charity directs us toward true and infinite goodness.

> Peace consists in the calm and union of the appetite. Just as appetite can tend toward what is authentically good, or what is only apparently good, so peace can be either true or only apparent. There cannot be true peace unless the appetite is directed toward what is truly good, since every evil, even if it appears good in some way, and thus calms the appetite to some extent, nevertheless has many defects, so that the appetite remains restless and perturbed. Hence true peace can be only in good persons and about good things. The peace of the wicked is only apparent peace; it is not true peace.[98]

Aquinas clarifies that perfect peace can be enjoyed only in heaven. Such peace "consists in the perfect enjoyment of the highest good, where all appetites are united by resting in that one object."[99] In this life, imperfect peace is the most we can hope to attain. Such imperfect peace consists in a certain harmony of our inclinations and tendencies. Because our fallen world is full of suffering, this internal harmony cannot satisfy every desire, but it puts us in the best position to thrive when external circumstances cooperate, and the best position to endure when they do not. In the state of innocence, charity's ordering of the various affections not only would have generated this internal harmony, but also would have satisfied all of our desires, because everything needful was available in paradise and because we would not have experienced any disordered antecedent passions. Original sin and its consequences place the possibility of such perfect peace beyond our reach. In our fallen world, charity can generate a certain kind of internal harmony, but it cannot entirely eliminate the possibility of disordered desire, nor can it satisfy every well-ordered desire.

---

divine realities, it also influences affectivity, so that "by wisdom bitterness is turned into sweetness, and labor into rest" (*ST* II-II 45.3 ad 3). The gift of wisdom orders the affections through the mediation of the gift of fear, insofar as the gift of fear flows from wisdom's consideration of divine excellence (*ST* I-II 68.4 ad 5).

97. *ST* II-II 27.6.

98. *ST* II-II 29.2 ad 3.

99. *ST* II-II 29.2 ad 4.

Just as charity integrates the affections and generates peace, disordered love of self leads to dissipation and restlessness. Aquinas writes:

> The love of God is unitive, since it leads man's affection from the many to the one, and in this way the virtues that are caused by the love of God are connected together. But self love scatters man's affection to diverse things, for the temporal goods that man desires for himself out of self love are various and diverse. Consequently, the vices and sins that are caused by self love are not connected together.[100]

Centering ourselves on something other than God can never entirely satisfy, because anything other than God is necessarily finite and therefore less than what the intellectual appetite craves with its desire for infinite good. And if the will is unsatisfied and restless, our other desires, in order to fill the vacuum, inevitably become dislocated from their proper objectives, and end up restless and disordered among themselves. Centering ourselves on finite goods may generate some partial harmony among our passions and affections, and thus provide some amount of interior peace. Nonetheless, any such interior peace cannot last, because the will cannot rest in any finite good for long before it starts to desire something else. Unless our will turns to God, we are condemned to a futile search for something more than we have, with each newly acquired good always failing to satisfy, and our desires and passions becoming increasingly restless and misdirected.

Charity also leads to mercy, which Aquinas defines in terms of appetitive movement. Following John Damascene, Aquinas describes mercy as "a kind of sorrow" evoked by the misery of others, and he concurs with Augustine's description of mercy as "compassion in our heart for another's misery that impels us, if we can, to offer relief."[101] Mercy implies that we regard our neighbor's good as our own, that in some sense we love our neighbor as another self, and so we are saddened over our neighbor's loss as though it were our own.[102] Consequently, mercy prompts us to come to the aid of our neighbors.[103] Mercy can refer to movements of either the sense appetite or the intellectual appetite, and it can also refer to a virtue insofar as it denotes a stable, moderated disposition toward feeling sympathy and compassion

100. *ST* I-II 73.1 ad 3.
101. *ST* II-II 30.1, John Damascene, *De fide orthodoxa* 2.2, Augustine, *City of God*, 9.5.
102. *ST* II-II 30.2.
103. *ST* II-II 30.4.

at the distress of others.[104] Because it involves both sorts of appetites, while mercy implies affective response to the distress of others, it does not necessarily involve a dramatic or sensible response: it could involve the intellectual appetite, but not the sense appetite.

Charity also leads to virtues of beneficence, almsgiving, and fraternal correction—all virtues that, like mercy, are directed toward the well-being of others and the alleviation of their suffering.[105] In this way, charity plays an integral role in fostering the good of the entire community above and beyond the requirements of justice, insofar as charity goes beyond claims of what individuals are strictly owed. Charity does not only direct us toward works of mercy, so that we perform them out of graced willpower. It transforms our affectivity, and the affectivity of societies, so that individuals and societies find themselves interiorly impelled toward concrete acts of beneficence, almsgiving, and fraternal correction.

Charity, Sacrifice, and Asceticism

In a fallen world, charity can sometimes allow for the sacrifice of certain desires in favor of more important desires, and on some occasions charity can even demand such sacrifice. In the state of original justice, there would have been no need to choose between the desire for life and the desire for other goods, but in our fallen world, the hero sometimes must sacrifice life for the well-being of others, and the martyr sometimes must sacrifice life for higher ideals or commitments. In our fallen condition, moreover, fasting from food and drink for spiritual reasons can be virtuous, but otherwise fasting for spiritual reasons would not be virtuous. As a consequence of original sin, we experience disordered passions, and fasting helps us to overcome the negative effects of these disordered passions.[106] Similarly, after the fall, celibacy becomes a virtuous option as a way to foster the goods

104. *ST* II-II 30.3.

105. *ST* II-II 31–33.

106. In *ST* I-II 63.4, Aquinas notes that according to human reason, the health of the body is the only important consideration when regulating the consumption of food and drink, but according to divine revelation, "chastising the body" in the interests of attaining better self-control is also important, following Paul's exhortation in 1 Corinthians 9:27. Similarly, in *ST* I-II 69.3, Aquinas discusses how the beatitudes encourage us to regulate the concupiscible passions in a way that goes beyond natural reason, to the point that radical detachment may become appropriate and necessary. In these passages, Aquinas does not explicitly reject the notion that fasting could be virtuous before the fall, but such a conclusion can be inferred.

It cannot be inferred, however, that Aquinas would claim that the only justified spiritual

of the spirit and the contemplation of God, but in the state of innocence it would not have been praiseworthy.[107] For Aquinas, properly ordered sacrifice and asceticism do not thwart desire, nor do they constitute an end in themselves: they are means to the fulfillment of desire in a fallen world.

The Moral Virtues

Employing traditional categories, Aquinas divides moral virtue into the four cardinal virtues of prudence, justice, fortitude, and temperance.[108] He is not content, however, to simply restate the tradition: he takes these traditional categories and reinterprets them according to his anthropology. His lengthy exposition of the cardinal virtues consistently centers on how each perfects a particular power of the soul. Each virtue is connected with other virtues and other powers, but they are primarily associated with one specific power of the soul. Prudence perfects the intellect; justice perfects the will; fortitude perfects the irascible passions; and temperance perfects the concupiscible passions. For Aquinas, the virtues are not categories of external behavior; they are convenient ways to talk about the perfection of particular aspects of the human person.

Prudence

Among the moral virtues Aquinas ranks prudence first.[109] Quoting Augustine, Aquinas defines prudence as "knowing what things to desire and

motive for asceticism is the overcoming or remedying of internal disorder. Moreover, it is unlikely that he would, since, as Aquinas is well aware, Christ did not suffer from any internal disorder, and yet he often fasts in the Gospels. Nonetheless, in Aquinas's system, all fasting is directed toward overcoming or remedying the disorder introduced by sin. For example, Aquinas affirms that Christ fasted in order to teach us the necessity of fasting in *ST* III 41.3, thus connecting Christ's fasting to remedying the effects of sin, albeit in us rather than in himself.

For a discussion of the value of fasting in Aquinas, see Stephen Loughlin, "Thomas Aquinas and the Importance of Fasting to the Christian Life," *Pro Ecclesia* 17 (2008): 343–61.

107. *ST* I 98.2 ad 3.

108. For a Thomistic overview of moral virtue, see Cessario, *Moral Virtues and Theological Ethics.* For a contemporary account of the cardinal virtues that draws on Aquinas, see Josef Pieper, *The Four Cardinal Virtues: Prudence, Justice, Fortitude, and Temperance* (Notre Dame: University of Notre Dame Press, 1966).

109. See *ST* I-II 61.2–4, 66.1, 66.3; *ST* II-II 47.6. For an overview of Aquinas's treatment of prudence, see James F. Keenan, "The Virtue of Prudence (IIa IIae, qq. 47–56)," in *The Ethics of Aquinas,* ed. Stephen J. Pope (Washington, D.C.: Georgetown University Press, 2002), 116–30. For a discussion of prudence with a view toward Aquinas's relevance to contemporary moral theology, see Cessario, *Moral Virtues and Theological Ethics,* 72–93.

what things to avoid."[110] Prudence, however, does not determine the ultimate end of human striving, which is implicit in the structure of human nature, but rather determines the proper means to that end.[111] Prudence is not only concerned with knowledge. It also involves the execution of an intellectual judgment about what is to be done. In fact, the implementation of a prudential decision is the chief act of prudence, and someone who executes a poor decision is less imprudent than someone else who fails to execute a good decision.[112] Consequently, although prudence is primarily a virtue of the intellect, it also involves the will and the sense appetite.[113] It consists not only in knowing, but also in desiring, since "its principal act is to guide and thus to apply one's knowledge to one's desiring and functioning."[114] It fixes the virtuous mean for the passions to strive toward, and gives order and direction to the motion that springs from our appetites.[115] Prudence penetrates even deeper than appetite: Aquinas writes that "prudence by a certain application extends to the interior sense," especially insofar as it involves memory and the processing of past experiences.[116]

Furthermore, Aquinas claims that prudence involves virtuous, rightly ordered appetite.[117] Prudence requires the appetitive powers to be rightly ordered in order to execute good decisions and, through the added sensitivity provided by appetitive inclinations, to discern a good decision in the first place. "Prudence implies right appetite," he writes, because "prudence commands right actions, which cannot happen without right appetite."[118] There is a circular, symbiotic relationship between prudence and affectivity in Aquinas's account. Prudence both depends on virtuous appetite and guides appetite toward virtue.

Memory is an integral element of Aquinas's account of prudence. Pru-

110. *ST* II-II 47.1; see also Augustine, *lxxxiii Questiones*, 61.

111. *ST* II-II 47.6. The end of the moral virtues is known through *synderesis*, a *habitus* of practical reason (see *ST* I 79.12 and *ST* II-II 47.6 ad 1).

112. *ST* II-II 47.8.

113. *ST* II-II 47.1 ad 3, 47.5, 47.8. Regarding the relationship of prudence to the sense appetite, see *ST* II-II 47.4, 47.7 ad 2, 47.9 ad 3, 47.13 ad 2.

114. *ST* II-II 47.16.

115. *ST* II-II 47.7 ad 2, 47.9 ad 1.

116. *ST* II-II 47.3 ad 3.

117. *ST* II-II 47.4, 47.13 ad 2. For an exposition of Aquinas's account of prudence with particular attention to its affective dimension, see Livio Melina, "La prudenza secondo Tommaso d'Aquino," *Aquinas* 49 (2006): 381–393. For a reflection on the relationship between prudence and affectivity, with frequent reference to Aquinas, see Charles J. O'Neil, "Is Prudence Love?" *The Monist* 58 (1974): 119–139.

118. *ST* II-II 47.13 ad 2.

dence "comes to know the future from the past and present," and consequently it depends on memory in a special way.[119] However, prudence is not forgotten when memories are forgotten, because prudence involves not only knowledge, but also appetite, and so the effects of prudence remain even after specific relevant memories are forgotten.[120] Aquinas notes that "the experience that prudence relies upon does not only come from memory, but also from the practice of making upright decisions."[121] This distinction seems to indicate that Aquinas has a rather narrow understanding of memory: for Aquinas, memory pertains to knowledge on the level of facts and data, but not to ingrained patterns of behavior that are the enduring residue of past experiences and choices.[122]

Because prudence depends on memory and the gradual ordering of appetite, it requires time to develop. Older people tend to be more prudent because their age sobers the passions and gives them long years of experience to draw upon.[123] This natural development of prudence, however, is supplemented by the power of grace. Infused prudence is communicated to all who have grace, giving them the capacity to direct the virtues toward their supernatural destiny. Baptized children without the use of reason possess the *habitus* of prudence even though they cannot perform acts of prudence.[124] At first glance, this claim seems implausible and forced, but its actual meaning is reasonable. Since grace provides whatever is necessary to retain possession of grace, and since infused prudence is necessary to avoid mortal sin, baptized children must have a preexisting infused disposition toward prudent acts by the time they reach the age of reason, at which point, according to Aquinas, the loss of grace through mortal sin becomes possible. It is reasonable, therefore, to presume they have some kind of inchoate infused prudence from baptism. The alternative is to argue that they receive infused prudence right as they reach the age of reason, which is doubly problematic: it implies a nonorganic relationship between nature and grace, and it assumes a simplistic notion of the age of reason, as though children attain the use of reason in a single instant.

119. *ST* II-II 47.1.

120. *ST* II-II 45.16.

121. *ST* II-II 45.16 ad 2.

122. *ST* II-II 49.1 seems to confirm this interpretation of Aquinas.

123. *ST* II-II 47.14 ad 3, 47.15 ad 2.

124. *ST* II-II 47.14 ad 3.

Infused prudence is complemented by the gift of counsel, through which the Holy Spirit guides us toward particular decisions. This guidance is experienced subjectively as a quieting of anxiety and a sense of inner certainty regarding a course of action.[125] The gift of counsel corresponds to the beatitude "Blessed are the merciful," since it directs our works of mercy.[126] This description of the gift of counsel, with its attention to the calming of anxiety, once again shows Aquinas's interest in the affective dimension of prudence, as well as his organic understanding of how God's grace perfects the natural operations of the soul. For Aquinas, prudence is more than technical knowledge and the volitional readiness to execute decisions; it also involves the shaping of affective dispositions by reason and grace.

Justice

After prudence Aquinas turns to the virtue of justice, which he regards as the highest of the three remaining cardinal virtues.[127] Contemporary discussion of justice is preoccupied with the adjudication of rights and legal obligation. It focuses on what the individual is owed by society and other free agents, and occasionally with what the individual is obligated to render in return.[128] In contrast, following Aristotle, Aquinas describes justice as a quality of soul, defining the virtue of justice as "the *habitus* by which someone renders to each his due (*jus*) with a constant and perpetual will."[129] Although his questions on justice address issues of debt and obligation, his

125. By the gift of counsel, Aquinas writes, our minds are moved by God so that "the anxiety of doubt is calmed" (*ST* II-II 52.3).

126. *ST* II-II 52.4.

127. *ST* II-II 58.12. Justice ranks higher than fortitude and temperance because it has its seat in the rational appetite, whereas the latter are located in the sense appetite, and, according to Aquinas, the rational appetite is metaphysically prior to the sense appetite.

128. These observations about the contrast between Aquinas and modern thought are largely inspired by Servais Pinckaers. He describes the default modern understanding of justice and its origins as follows: "The modern era is characterized by its subjective conception of rights, as formulated by fourteenth-century nominalism. From that time on, rights refer not to what I owe others, but to what others, and society, owe me. Rights have changed hands: I think now in terms of my won rights, not those of others. The fundamental orientation of justice has been reversed: the burden of the debt falls on others, not on me. Justice no longer implies a quality of soul, a movement outward toward others; it concentrates on the defense of external rights. In this sense it is a matter of taking rather than giving" (Pinckaers, *Sources of Christian Ethics*, 38–39). See also "The Role of Virtue in Moral Theology," trans. Mary Thomas Noble, in *The Pinckaers Reader: Renewing Thomistic Moral Theology*, ed. John Berkman and Craig Steven Titus (Washington, D.C.: The Catholic University of America Press, 2005), 294–97.

129. *ST* II-II 58.1. See also Aristotle, *Ethics* V.5, 1129a–1138b.

focus is on how the virtue of justice regulates relationships and shapes human affectivity.[130] Justice is not an abstract ideal against which we measure ourselves; it denotes an affective disposition toward others, and a constant inclination to give them what they are owed. It is oriented not just to individuals, but also to communities and the common good.[131]

Throughout the questions on justice, Aquinas's primary interests are the nature of just human relationships and the affective dimensions of various virtues and vices, not the resolution of complex cases of conscience. In fact, in the questions on justice, Aquinas uses the terms "affection" and "interior passions" with some frequency. It seems plausible that his sustained reflection on justice generated a deeper sensitivity to the category of *affectus,* since the virtue of justice involves, in Aquinas's account, precisely those appetitive movements that are not passions and yet are still constitutive of character and personality.

Justice is seated in the will and not the sense appetite.[132] Nonetheless, it concerns many aspects of affectivity. To give unworthy people the benefit of the doubt implies "good affection."[133] He praises the midwives who saved Hebrew infants from Pharaoh for "their affection of benevolence toward the Jews," which in context means something more than warm feelings toward those they were assisting, something seemingly on the level of the will.[134] Aquinas's account of justice is warm and humane, emphatically not cold and legalistic. Aquinas includes friendship, concord, gratitude, affection, humanity, and benevolence among the potential parts of justice (that is, virtues closely connected to justice and thus classified under it).[135] The virtue of friendliness or affability, which pertains to being agreeable toward others in ordinary dealings, is placed under the cardinal virtue of justice.[136] He specifies that the virtue of friendliness is principally a matter of "affection" and not outward words or actions.[137] This sort of friendliness is different from the friendship of charity. Aquinas places the virtue of friendliness

130. Pinckaers characterizes Aquinas's account of justice as being concerned with relationships between persons within society (Pinckaers, *Sources of Christian Ethics,* 37–38).

131. *ST* II-II 58.5.

132. *ST* II-II 58.4, 58.9.

133. *ST* II-II 60.4 ad 2.

134. *ST* II-II 110.4 ad 4.

135. *ST* II-II 80.1. While this particular article is more an attempt to show continuity with ancient authors like Cicero and Aristotle than an articulation of Aquinas's own views, nonetheless it is fully consonant with his understanding of justice.

136. *ST* II-II 114.1.

137. *ST* II-II 114.1 ad 1.

under justice because it pertains to an affective orientation to give others what they are owed, since, in order to live in society, we require a certain amount of civility and pleasant social interaction.[138] The friendship of charity, however, is an affective orientation toward others that wills their good out of love for God, and not only the rendering of what they are owed.[139] The difference between the friendship of charity and the friendliness of justice is evident in Aquinas's account of mercy and beneficence, each of which falls under the virtue of charity. Neither mercy nor beneficence is concerned with what we owe. Mercy involves sorrow at another's distress because the other is seen as another self, even when the other is morally depraved or an enemy,[140] and beneficence pertains to doing good for others simply out of love for them.[141] The difference between charity and justice in the realm of human relationships is especially evident in his discussion of fraternal correction, where he states that correcting a sinner for the sinner's well-being pertains to the virtue of charity, but correcting a sinner for the sake of the common good pertains to the virtue of justice.[142]

Aquinas defines religion and its associated virtues as dispositions to render God what he is owed, and so he discusses them in his questions on justice. His treatment of these virtues dovetails with his treatment of charity and contains many references to affectivity. The virtue of religion "implies an ordering to God," whom "we must assiduously choose as our last end," and therefore, seemingly, implies a certain affective disposition toward God.[143] The act that flows from religion is devotion, "an act of the will by which man gives himself promptly to God's service."[144] Devotion causes spiritual joy, but also godly sorrow in those who have not yet attained God perfectly, or in those who are reflecting on their weakness.[145] Continual prayer consists of "continuing in affection for the one thing to be desired,"

138. "Because man by nature is a social animal, he owes to his fellows, as a requirement of personal integrity, the manifestation of truth, without which human society could not last. Now just as man could not live in society without truth, neither can he live in society without pleasure, because, as Aristotle says, no one can stay long with the sad or joyless. And so, as a sort of natural requirement of personal integrity, man is obliged to live with others in a pleasant way, unless for some reason it is necessary and helpful to sadden them" (*ST* II-II 114.2 ad 1; see also Aristotle, *Ethics* VIII.5, 1157b15). See also *ST* II-II 23.3 ad 1, where Aquinas distinguishes between justice, friendship, and the specific friendship of charity.

139. *ST* II-II 23.1, 25.1–2.

140. *ST* II-II 30.2. See also *ST* II-II 25.6, 25.8.

141. *ST* II-II 31.1.

142. *ST* II-II 33.1.

143. *ST* II-II 81.1.

144. *ST* II-II 82.3.

145. *ST* II-II 82.4.

an allusion to Christ's praise of Mary for choosing the one thing needful (Luke 10:42).[146] Bodily signs of humility "arouse our affection to surrender ourselves to God."[147] We have a "natural inclination" (*naturalis inclinatio*) to honor God.[148] Vocal praise of God inclines our affection toward God, and through such praise our affection ascends to God.[149] Knowledge of God is not only theoretical but also "affective or experimental," and by this knowledge of God "a person experiences in himself a taste of divine sweetness, and complacency in the divine will."[150] Spiritual merit, he writes, "does not consist principally in an exterior gift or act or passion, but in an interior affection."[151] The virtue of penitence concerns the will's sorrow over past sins and is classified under justice.[152]

These various examples demonstrate that Aquinas's account of the virtue of religion is concerned with affectivity, and not just our legal obligations toward God. One of the clearest manifestations of this attention to affectivity comes in his account of the gift of piety, the gift of the Holy Spirit that supplements the virtue of justice. Aquinas writes that through the gift of piety, the Holy Spirit disposes us to reverence God with "filial affection."[153] The definition of piety in terms of affection and Aquinas's claim that the gift of piety complements the virtue of justice again underline the status of justice as an affective disposition.

Because Aquinas classifies justice as a virtue of the will, and not as a virtue of the passions, Jean Porter concludes that justice "should be understood as a settled policy or a standing commitment to act in certain ways, rather than as a tendency to feel in certain ways and then to act accordingly."[154] Her conclusion is misleading, however, because it distracts from the affective dimension of Aquinas's account of justice. While it is true that justice is not a virtue of the passions, justice is a virtue of appetite, and therefore it involves affectivity. Understanding justice as "a settled policy or a standing commitment" does not adequately capture the affective element

146. *ST* II-II 83.14 ad 2.
147. *ST* II-II 84.2.
148. *ST* II-II 85.1.
149. *ST* II-II 91.1.
150. *ST* II-II 97.2 ad 2. See also *ST* II-II 180.1 where Aquinas explains that the contemplative life pertains to the affections as well as the intellect.
151. *ST* II-II 100.1 ad 3.
152. *ST* III 85.1, 85.3.
153. *ST* II-II 121.1. Aquinas correlates piety primarily with the beatitudes of justice and mercy, due to the correspondence in their "objects and acts" (*ST* II-II 121.2).
154. Jean Porter, "The Virtue of Justice (IIa IIae, qq. 58–122)," in *The Ethics of Aquinas*, ed. Stephen J. Pope (Washington, D.C.: Georgetown University Press, 2002), 275.

of justice. Porter herself seems to recognize that her image of justice can be misleading, because she is careful to nuance her interpretation by noting that justice "also implies that the just individual is motivated by a desire to preserve and promote justice," although "this rational love of justice is not a passion."[155] Attention to the category of *affectus* allows for more precision in describing how the virtue of justice shapes personality: justice may not concern passion, but it always concerns affection, and therefore it is a virtue of human affectivity and not just a settled policy.

Furthermore, Aquinas holds that justice and its associated virtues are sometimes involved in guiding and directing the passions, albeit as a secondary priority. It belongs to justice, he explains, to direct our inner passions toward others and what we owe them, even if, properly speaking, the passions do not fall under justice.[156] The virtue of liberality is a notable example. He defines liberality as concerned with the generous and proper use of riches.[157] Its object is riches, but the "inner passions" are its matter, and liberality is judged not by the amount of money given but by the giver's affection.[158] The liberal man manifests an affection that is free from attachment to riches.[159]

Since liberality is concerned with the passions and particularly the concupiscible passions, Aquinas feels a need to defend his placement of liberality under justice rather than temperance.[160] In a response to an objection, he explains that temperance is concerned with the desires and pleasures of the body, but liberality is concerned with the desires and pleasures of the soul, and so therefore belongs under justice.[161] This response is one of the few places in the *Summa* where he employs the distinction between *passio corporalis* and *passio animalis*. Its invocation here may indicate that he is straining to find some way to distinguish between the love of riches and the love of sensible goods, as when he speaks of "inner passions" without defining what they are. He seems to display some ambivalence about classifying liberality under justice. On the one hand, liberality pertains to money and therefore, seemingly, to justice, but on the other hand, it pertains to the concupiscible passions and therefore temperance. In any case, his account

155. Porter, "Virtue of Justice," 275.
156. *ST* II-II 58.8 ad 3, 58.9 ad 3.
157. *ST* II-II 117.1–2.
158. *ST* II-II 117.2 ad 1, 117.3 ad 3. See also *ST* II-II 31.1 ad 2.
159. *ST* II-II 117.2.
160. *ST* II-II 117.5 ad 2, 134.4 ad 1, 157.1.
161. *ST* II-II 117.5 ad 2.

of liberality is another indication of the prominence of affectivity within his concept of justice.

The affective dimension of justice in Aquinas should not be exaggerated. Many of the questions on justice do not directly engage the question of affectivity, but instead are concerned with almost mathematically precise clarifications of obligation. Still, the context in which Aquinas conducts such clarification is crucial: his purpose is not simply to deduce specific obligations from more general obligations, but rather to investigate what is materially required to bring an affective disposition toward fair play to fruition. Even though, for Aquinas, justice is a habitual affective disposition toward others, and not simply a matter of fulfilling external obligations, it is not always obvious how to express such a disposition in the concrete order of things. Consider the case of someone who steals a neighbor's cow and then, five years later, has a change of heart and wants to restore what he has stolen. But since cows typically produce more cows every year, along with milk, what should he give his neighbor after five years?[162] There is no way around such questions in any theory of justice, as tedious as they may be, but by framing justice in terms of affective disposition, Aquinas offers a refreshing alternative to many early modern and contemporary accounts of justice.

Fortitude

After prudence and justice, Aquinas turns to fortitude (*fortitudo*).[163] He defines fortitude in two different but complementary ways. Considered according to its formal principle, fortitude is the virtue that puts the rule of reason into passion that otherwise might "draw away from what reason dictates through fear of dangers or hardships."[164] Considered according to the power of the soul that it perfects, fortitude is the virtue located in the irascible passions.[165] From this perspective, fortitude is about ordering the irascible passions to correspond with our *telos*.

162. For Aquinas's discussion of restitution, see *ST* II-II 62.

163. *Fortitudo* can also be translated as courage. I have chosen to translate it as fortitude because fortitude has connotations of endurance, while courage has connotations of attacking, and Aquinas makes it clear that endurance is more central to the virtue of *fortitudo*. For a study of Aquinas on fortitude that engages contemporary psychology, see Craig Titus, *Resilience and the Virtue of Fortitude* (Washington, D.C.: The Catholic University of Ameria Press, 2006).

164. *ST* I-II 61.2. See also *ST* II-II 123.1–3.

165. *ST* I-II 56.4, 61.2.

There is a certain tension between these two perspectives on the virtue of fortitude. While they are complementary, they do not always overlap. A non-irascible passion might incline us to draw away from what reason dictates, as when sadness must be moderated by the virtue of patience so that it does not prevent us from acting courageously. But the irascible passions sometimes require virtue in matters that do not involve shirking a difficult course of action, as when immoderate anger must be restrained by the virtue of gentleness. The moderation of sadness and the restraint of immoderate anger each concern the virtue of fortitude according to one perspective, but not the other. The moderation of sadness falls under fortitude considered according to its formal principle of overcoming obstacles to what reason dictates, and the restraint of immoderate anger falls under fortitude according to its material principle of perfecting the irascible passions. Aquinas, however, places the moderation of sadness under fortitude, under the virtue of patience, and he places the restraint of immoderate anger under temperance, under the virtue of gentleness.

Aquinas is aware of the tension between his two definitions of fortitude, and his account is marked by an attempt to balance these competing perspectives. His account generally incorporates both definitions, but when there is some conflict between them, he favors fortitude considered under its formal principle, as the overcoming of fears and obstacles. He explains his method of classification as follows:

> The annexation of secondary virtues to a principal virtue is determined not only by their matter, but even more by their mode of operation, because in each form is more important than matter. So, although perseverance, due to its matter, seems to belong with temperance, not fortitude, perseverance belongs with fortitude due to its mode of operation, inasmuch as interior firmness helps us to face difficulties of long duration.[166]

Consequently, for Aquinas, fortitude is mainly concerned with the passions of fear and daring, and to some extent the passion of hope, since the moderation of these passions is essential to the overcoming of obstacles and dangers, and since these virtues belong with fortitude according to both their formal and material principles.[167] But fortitude extends beyond the

166. *ST* II-II 137.2 ad 1.
167. *ST* II-II 123.3.

sphere of the irascible passions and includes some concupiscible passions. Certain secondary virtues of fortitude, such as patience, are directed to the endurance of suffering and sadness, in order to assist the overcoming of obstacles, and thus belong to fortitude according to their mode of operation.[168] Throughout, Aquinas often demonstrates particular interest in how the virtue of fortitude orders the irascible passions according to reason. In this way, he integrates his original anthropological commitments with the traditional formulation of fortitude.

Fortitude is more about the restraint of fear than the moderation of daring, since it is more difficult to overcome fear than to moderate daring.[169] He explains, "The virtue of fortitude, whose purpose is to keep us steadfast, principally concerns the passion that impels us to flee from bodily evils, namely fear, and in consequence it also concerns daring, which attacks fearful things in the hope of something good."[170] Even though it is properly concerned with fear and daring, he argues, fortitude can also encompass hope, insofar as hope is linked to daring.[171] Anger also falls under the direction of fortitude when anger performs a function similar to daring, that is, when it seeks to overcome some difficulty.[172]

Aquinas emphasizes that fortitude is a quality that permeates a person's character. It therefore manifests itself especially in sudden emergencies, when there is little time for deliberation, and innate dispositions suddenly come to the fore. He writes: "Fortitude is especially concerned with sudden unexpected events, because according to Aristotle, sudden unexpected dangers especially manifest the *habitus* of fortitude, for *habitus* act in a natural way. Hence when someone does something virtuous without premeditation as required by some sudden unexpected danger, this especially manifests that fortitude is habitually and firmly present in the soul."[173] This observation underlines the importance Aquinas attaches to his claim that the irascible passions are the seat of fortitude, and thus truly permeated by virtue. For Aquinas, the virtue of fortitude is not about a standing commitment to

168. *ST* II-II 136.4.

169. *ST* II-II 123.3, 123.6, 123.11 ad 1. For a careful and sympathetic analysis of Aquinas's claim that endurance is more difficult than courageous aggression, see DeYoung, "Power Made Perfect," 156, 159–69.

170. *ST* II-II 141.3.

171. *ST* II-II 123.3 ad 3.

172. *ST* II-II 123.10, 123.11 ad 1.

173. *ST* II-II 123.9. See also Aristotle, *Ethics* III.8, 1116a3.

courageous acts; it is a stable disposition in the passions themselves. Aquinas hints that fortitude has implications beyond an orientation to courageous acts when, as an aside, he mentions that fortitude "implies a certain steadfastness in the passions."[174] Aquinas seems to be suggesting that fortitude generates a habitual self-possession that responds to fears with equanimity, and that manifests itself in one's entire affective disposition.

For Aquinas, "the principal act of fortitude is more enduring, standing unmovable in the midst of dangers, than attacking," a view that echoes Aristotle's understanding.[175] He also agrees with Aristotle that fortitude is most properly concerned with the dangers of death in warfare.[176] Nonetheless, Aquinas presents the warfare of martyrdom, rather than physical combat, as the paradigm of fortitude.[177] In the question on martyrdom, which immediately follows his introductory question on fortitude, he argues that, considered under the aspect of the love that motivates it, "martyrdom is the most perfect in kind among human acts, since it is a sign of the greatest charity."[178] This presentation of martyrdom as the paradigm of fortitude is a vivid example of how Aquinas does not simply tack on Christian elements to Aristotle's account of fortitude; instead, he undertakes a decisive transformation.[179] For Aristotle, the virtue of fortitude is a matter of strength and aggressive valor, and conquering internal and external obstacles.[180] For Aquinas, fortitude might include these elements, but it is more concerned with "the strength of the soul in enduring or resisting evil."[181] While Aris-

174. *ST* II-II 129.7 ad 1.

175. *ST* II-II 123.6. See also *ST* II-II 123.3, 123.11 ad 1, and Aristotle, *Ethics* III.9, 1117a33.

176. *ST* II-II 123.5. See also Aristotle, *Ethics* III.6, 1115a35.

177. *ST* II-II 123.5 ad 1, 124.2–3.

178. *ST* II-II 124.3.

179. See DeYoung, "Power Made Perfect," 147–50.

180. See DeYoung, "Power Made Perfect," 152, and Aristotle, *Ethics* III.6, 1115b5. In her article, DeYoung argues that Aristotle's view of fortitude places primacy on aggression over endurance, although she acknowledges that there is some ambiguity about the matter (DeYoung, 159–60n58). Aquinas seems to interpret Aristotle differently: Aquinas cites Aristotle as an authority for his position that courage is concerned more with enduring than attacking (*ST* II-II 123.6). Still, DeYoung's essential point stands: for Aristotle, the context of endurance is the valiant attempt to overcome some difficulty, whereas for Aquinas, the context of endurance in its highest instance is the passive acceptance of evil for the sake of some higher good.

181. DeYoung, "Power Made Perfect," 152. She summarizes the difference in outlook as follows: "The main point of making martyrdom the paradigm is to show that courage can be expressed as much or more in suffering as it can in striking out against a threat. The military paradigm has, until very recently, been restricted to males and even further restricted to males

totle pays tribute to the importance and value of endurance, his focus is on aggressively seeking to accomplish some objective, come what may, and it is therefore especially the province of the strong and powerful. Aquinas's focus, however, is on the internal ordering of the irascible passions, an ordering that is compatible with some amount of sorrow,[182] so that they do not interfere with the decision to lay down one's life for the truth. While relatively few face either the dangers of physical combat or the threat of martyrdom, the selection of the latter as the paradigm of fortitude represents a shift away from a view of fortitude as concerned with the performance of external acts to a view more focused on the internal ordering of the passions.

Another virtue associated with fortitude is magnanimity, which Aquinas defines as "a certain straining of the soul to great things."[183] He classifies it as a perfection of the passion of hope, and "magnanimity is concerned particularly with the hope of something difficult."[184] In consequence, magnanimity is characterized by confidence (*fiducia*), since "confidence implies a certain firmness of hope, coming from some consideration that forms a vehement opinion that the good in question is attainable."[185] The strong hope associated with magnanimity also implies a certain inner security (*securitas*), which banishes the passion of despair.[186] This approach to the virtue of magnanimity, with its focus on the passion of hope, represents a radical transformation of Aristotle's account.[187] Aristotle gives a character sketch of the behavior and general manner of the magnanimous man.

---

who meet certain requirements for ability and physical strength. To make martyrdom the model to follow allows anyone who is able to suffer to echo this supreme example of courage in their own lives, and leaves physical power, with its attendant gender and age limitations, out of the picture. Anyone who is weak, vulnerable, or unable or unwilling to use force is a candidate for practicing this virtue—including women, children, the elderly, the economically and socially disempowered, and even the disabled. In this way, the implications for Aquinas's transformation of this Aristotelian virtue are radical in ways Aristotle would neither have dreamed of nor approved" (DeYoung, "Power Made Perfect," 170).

182. *ST* I-II 59.3, *ST* II-II 123.8.

183. *ST* II-II 129.1.

184. *ST* II-II 129.6. Elsewhere he writes: "Magnanimity directly concerns the passion of hope, and indirectly concerns honor, insofar as honor is the object of hope" (*ST* II-II 129.1 ad 2).

185. *ST* II-II 129.6. For a discussion of Aquinas on magnanimity, see Gauthier, *Magnanimité*, 281–371.

186. *ST* II-II 129.7.

187. R. E. Houser also notes that Aquinas's account of magnanimity breaks with Aristotle, but he focuses on how Aquinas describes humility as a complementary virtue to magnanimity, rather than his attention to the passion of hope (Houser, "Virtue of Courage," 310–312).

He does not attempt to single out a thematic perfection that integrates the magnanimous man's personality beyond that of self-conscious greatness. Aquinas, however, roots magnanimity in the passions of hope and despair, something completely foreign to Aristotle's approach, even while reiterating much of Aristotle's description of the magnanimous man.[188] In doing so, Aquinas again manifests his interest in connecting the moral virtues to the elemental passions of the sense appetite that he painstakingly identified in the *Prima secundae*.

Aquinas undertakes a similar transformation of the virtue of magnificence, which pertains to spending lavish amounts of money in order to make something great.[189] He reiterates much of Aristotle's account, but then defines magnificence with respect to the passion of hope. He writes: "Magnificence concerns expenditure in relation to hope, and the attaining of something difficult—not something difficult in a general sense, as with magnanimity, but in a determinate matter, namely expenditure. Hence magnificence seems to be in the irascible passions, just like magnanimity."[190] He notes that the poor man can be magnificent in a certain sense, since "the principal act of virtue is the interior choice," thus again placing the emphasis on the human psyche rather than exterior works.[191] Nonetheless, in terms of its internal coherence, his account of magnificence is somewhat less successful than his account of magnanimity. In one article, he remarks that the love of money, along with the actual expenditure of money, constitutes the matter of the virtue of magnificence, but later he says that the moderation of the love of money falls under the virtue of liberality and not magnificence.[192] In general, the question on magnificence is more derivative than the question on magnanimity, and Aquinas gives less attention to the passions involved. Still, the fact that he links magnificence to the irascible passions, even though this connection sits uneasily with Aristotle's schema, manifests Aquinas's overarching vision of fortitude as the ordering of the irascible passions.

188. Throughout his question on magnanimity, Aquinas echoes and affirms Aristotle's description of the magnanimous man, even down to physical comportment. However, he does sometimes qualify or nuance his account (see *ST* II-II 129.3 ad 3, ad 5 and Aristotle, *Ethics*, IV.5, 1123a–1125a). Moreover, the connections he makes with the passions of hope and despair are entirely his own innovations.

189. *ST* II-II 134.1–3.

190. *ST* II-II 134.4 ad 1.

191. *ST* II-II 134.3 ad 4.

192. Compare *ST* II-II 134.3 and 134.4 ad 1.

Patience is unique among the virtues associated with fortitude because it governs a concupiscible passion: it "preserves the good of reason in the face of sadness, so that the reason does not succumb to sadness."[193] As such it presents some difficulties for Aquinas.[194] Is fortitude about attacking and enduring obstacles, or is it about the ordering of the irascible passions? By including patience in his discussion of fortitude, Aquinas shows that he ultimately ranks the first quality over the second. Nonetheless, he recognizes the difficulties associated with classifying patience under fortitude and goes to some length to defend it. He explains that since patience pertains to the overcoming of evil, it falls under fortitude and not temperance, even though temperance is the virtue more properly associated with the concupiscible passions.[195] He also makes a point of linking patience to longanimity, the virtue that pertains to the calm endurance of suffering over a long period of time in the hope of attaining some good, and that is therefore related to the passion of hope.[196] It is as though Aquinas wants to strengthen the irascible pedigree of patience by connecting it to a virtue that is explicitly related to an irascible passion.

As with any virtue, the exercise of fortitude causes pleasure. Sometimes, however, "sensible bodily pain makes the soul unable to feel the pleasure of virtue."[197] Aquinas argues that this does not jeopardize fortitude's status as a virtue for two principal reasons. One he takes from Aristotle: "It is not necessary for bravery that a brave man delights with sensible pleasure; it suffices that he is not sad."[198] The other and more original explanation, which draws explicitly on his metaphysics of affectivity, is that there are different kinds of pleasure and pain, some physical and some spiritual, and it is possible to experience them simultaneously because they are located in different human faculties.[199] In some circumstances, even though pleasure occurs in one part of the soul, it is not experienced subjectively as pleasurable because pain or sorrow elsewhere overwhelms it.

193. *ST* II-II 136.1. See also his discussion of perseverance vis-à-vis the moderation of the passions in *ST* II-II 137.1 ad 1.

194. Houser gives a good exposition of the difficulties that the virtue of patience presents to Aquinas's treatment of fortitude (Houser, "Virtue of Courage," 315).

195. *ST* II-II 136.4 ad 2.

196. *ST* II-II 136.5.

197. *ST* II-II 123.8.

198. *ST* II-II 123.8. See also Aristotle, *Ethics*, III.9, 1117b8–15.

199. *ST* II-II 123.8. Aquinas explicitly refers back to *ST* I-II 31.3 to explain the various kinds of pleasures and pains. For a detailed discussion of fortitude and its attendant pleasure, pain, and sorrow, as well as the role of divine grace, see DeYoung, "Power Made Perfect," 171–79.

Aquinas states that, in special circumstances, divine grace can enhance the natural pleasure that accompanies fortitude. When it does, God's grace "more strongly elevates the soul to the divine, in which it delights, than it is afflicted by bodily pains. Thus blessed Tiburtius, while walking barefoot over burning coals, said that it seemed like he was walking on rose petals."[200] Furthermore, the Holy Spirit's gift of fortitude strengthens the mind in such a way that fear is banished, and so it becomes easier to act courageously.[201] The gift of fortitude corresponds to the beatitude "Blessed are those who hunger and thirst for justice," because fortitude is concerned with what is difficult, and it is very difficult to perform works of virtue with an "insatiable desire" for justice.[202]

Temperance

The last of the cardinal virtues is temperance.[203] Desire for sensible goods is good in its essential nature, but it requires the direction and guidance of reason and will. The virtue of temperance is nothing other than the quality of having the desires of the sense appetite permeated with reason. As such it is located in the concupiscible passions. "Temperance," he writes, "implies a kind of moderation, and principally concerns the passions that tend toward sensible goods, namely desire and pleasure, and in consequence it also concerns the sadness that comes about from the absence of such pleasures."[204] It is especially concerned with pleasures of touch and the desire for them, since these passions especially require moderation, both because they are closely connected to our natural inclinations toward food and reproduction, and therefore involve great pleasure, and because their objects are more necessary for our survival.[205] Aquinas writes that "the passions more vehemently impel us to seek something the more they follow natural inclination."[206] As in the case of fortitude, Aquinas synthesizes two views of temperance. From one perspective, he sees temperance under the formal principle of moderating those passions that "urge us toward something against reason," and from another perspective he sees

200. *ST* II-II 123.8.

201. *ST* II-II 139.1.

202. *ST* II-II 139.2.

203. For a study of Aquinas on temperance from an analytic perspective, see Shawn D. Floyd, "Aquinas on Temperance," *Modern Schoolman* 77 (1999): 35–48.

204. *ST* II-II 141.3.

205. *ST* II-II 141.4, 141.7.

206. *ST* II-II 155.2.

temperance as the harmonious ordering of the concupiscible passions.[207] Sometimes he favors one view, sometimes the other.

By this point in the *Secunda secundae,* the overarching theme of Aquinas's exposition of temperance is very familiar to the reader of the *Summa:* the passions are good of their nature, and the goal of virtue is not their eradication but their guidance, so that they spontaneously incline toward our ultimate *telos.*[208] This is a constant refrain in his consideration of various specific virtues, including abstinence, sobriety, chastity, clemency, and gentleness.[209] In each of these virtues, Aquinas affirms the goodness of the desire under consideration, whether it is the desire for food, drink, sex, or vindication. Then he frames temperance not as quashing desire, but as permeating it with reason, so that it instinctively inclines toward what will bring the human person to the greatest flourishing. The integral role of virtuous passion in temperance is demonstrated by the distinction he makes between continence and chastity. Continence denotes a *habitus* of avoiding sexual sin despite intense inner conflict, whereas chastity not only avoids sexual sin but enjoys cooperation and inner harmony among the passions.[210] Aquinas concedes that continence is a virtue in one sense, but denies that it is a virtue in the fullest and most proper sense.

Sometimes Aquinas is read as though temperance is only about restraint of indulgence. This is a serious misinterpretation. Among other things, it overlooks Aquinas's claim that a finely honed desire for the honorable and beautiful, and a correspondingly sophisticated palate in discerning what is truly exceptional, are integral parts of temperance.[211] Aquinas's view that

207. *ST* I-II 61.2.

208. In a carefully argued article, Giuseppe Butera objects to the sort of interpretation of Aquinas that sees virtuous passions contributing spontaneously toward acts of virtue, even before being directed explicitly by reason. He acknowledges that his interpretation departs from the mainstream, but nonetheless thinks that the texts of Aquinas warrant this reading. Much of his position turns on his understanding of antecedent passion, which he seems to interpret as meaning chronologically antecedent, rather antecedent in the technical sense that is discussed in chap. 4. It is beyond the scope of this study to respond to his argument in detail, but this monograph is committed to a different reading of Aquinas, and in its entirety provides a response to his reading. In particular, Butera does not seem to give sufficient attention to the metaphysical category of appetite, and how the passions, as expressions of appetite, draw us toward our final end. See Giuseppe Butera, "On Reason's Control of the Passions in Aquinas's Theory of Temperance," *Medieval Studies* 68 (2006): 133–60.

209. See *ST* II-II 146, 147, 149, 151, and 157 passim.

210. *ST* II-II 155.1.

211. See *ST* II-II 145.2–4. After discussing a typical misreading of Aquinas's account of temperance as restraint, Diana Fritz Cates offers this evocate description of his understanding of temper-

temperance concerns more than restraint becomes particularly clear when the questions on temperance are read alongside his earlier discussions of the metaphysics of appetite and passion, to which he frequently refers in them. Since both desire and pleasure are not simply tolerable but in fact ontologically good, it follows logically that Aquinas would have a positive understanding of their role in the moral life.

His positive and holistic interpretation of temperance includes attention to its beneficial consequences in other aspects of human psychology and to the ways its associated virtues reinforce each other. Virtuous dispositions toward food, for instance, calm excessive carnal desire.[212] Gentleness (*mansuetudo*) "especially makes a man self-possessed."[213] Temperance preserves against the harm caused by excessive desire.[214]

Aquinas places some virtues under temperance even though they order irascible passions, because they involve the moderation that constitutes the principal end of temperance. Following Seneca and Cicero, Aquinas places the moderation of excessive anger under temperance, since anger involves desire for revenge, and as such sometimes requires restraint.[215] There are two virtues that moderate anger, clemency and gentleness: "clemency moderates exterior punishment, while gentleness diminishes the passion of anger."[216] He explains that even though they concern irascible and not concupiscible passions, these virtues are about restraint, and therefore they share the "form" of temperance. They are assisted by the gift of piety, "by means of which the saints are free from irrational anger."[217] Aquinas's placement of the virtues that moderate anger under temperance rather than fortitude

ance: "Thomas indicates that temperance is a habit of responding to sense impressions of food, drink, and sexual relations with desires and pleasures that are beautiful. The desires and pleasures of the temperate person exhibit 'a certain moderate and fitting proportion' (IIa IIae, q. 141, a. 2, ad 3). They are internally well-balanced and coordinated relative to the end of excellent human functioning. The desires and pleasures of the temperate person also reflect the dignity of rational animality. One displays the honor peculiar to a human being when that person experiences desire and pleasure, not in a brutish or slavish way, but in the mode of reflective awareness and rational governance (IIa IIae, q. 141, a. 1, ad 1; Ia IIae, q. 31, a. 5)." Cates, "The Virtue of Temperance (IIa IIae, qq 141–170)" in *The Ethics of Aquinas*, ed. Stephen J. Pope (Washington, D.C.: Georgetown University Press, 2002), 323.

212. *ST* II-II 146.2 ad 2, 147.1, 147.8.

213. *ST* II-II 157.4.

214. *ST* II-II 141.8 ad 1. For his description of the harm that temperance prevents, see *ST* II-II 142.4, 144.2.

215. *ST* II-II 157.3. See also Seneca, *De clementia* II.4, and Cicero, *De inventione* II.54.

216. *ST* II-II 157.1.

217. *ST* III 39.6 ad 4.

emphasizes the importance of restraining anger over and above the importance of channeling anger toward a positive goal. However, this placement should not be misconstrued as implying exaggerated suspicion about anger, or pessimism about the possibility of virtuous anger. Although Aquinas maintains that we are more prone to excessive anger than insufficient anger,[218] he emphatically affirms throughout the *Summa* that anger can be virtuous, and specifically names the lack of sufficient anger as a vice opposed to the proper moderation of anger.[219]

Aquinas has a particularly creative and original account of the virtue of humility, which he also places under temperance. Instead of defining humility as an intellectual virtue of appropriate self-regard, or a pattern of lowly behavior, he defines humility in terms of the passion of hope. He acknowledges that awareness of one's deficiency is a condition of humility, but he claims that humility is a virtue of appetite, and specifically of hope.[220] The function of humility, he writes, is "to temper and restrain the soul so that it does not tend immoderately to elevated things."[221] Perhaps to prevent the reader from misinterpreting this definition as an implicit condemnation of the striving for great things, he emphasizes that humility and magnanimity order the passion of hope in complementary ways. Each is concerned with desire for an arduous good, with humility restraining from excess, and magnanimity fortifying against despair.

This unusual treatment of humility, with its focus on how humility moderates the passion of hope, manifests once again Aquinas's interest in the passions and how the virtues perfect the passions. Having this interest firmly in mind seems to have led Aquinas to his new perspective on humility. It also seems to make Aquinas aware that placing humility under temperance raises questions, insofar as humility does not pertain to a concupiscible passion, and so he makes a point of defending his placement of humility under temperance, just as he made a point of defending his placement of clemency

218. *ST* II-II 157.2 ad 2.

219. *ST* II-II 158.8. For recent discussions of Aquinas on the possibility of virtuous anger, particularly in comparison with other Christian understandings of anger, see Michael Rota, "The Moral Status of Anger: Thomas Aquinas and John Cassian," *American Catholic Philosophical Quarterly* 81 (2007): 395–418; and William C. Mattison III, "Interpretation of Jesus' Prohibition on Anger (Mt 5:22): The Person/Sin Distinction from Augustine to Aquinas," *Theological Studies* 68 (2007): 839–64.

220. *ST* II-II 161.1–2.

221. *ST* II-II 161.1.

and gentleness under temperance. He explains that "humility is seated in the irascible power, but it is a part of modesty and temperance because it operates in the same way."[222]

Aquinas does not make many explicit references to the assistance of grace in the questions on temperance, but it is evident that he assumes the possession of sanctifying grace, since he frequently asks whether a particular vice involves mortal sin and thus the loss of grace. Furthermore, he assigns the gift of fear to temperance. Like temperance, the gift of fear is an affective disposition, and, according to Aquinas, it helps the individual to avoid intemperance by disposing the individual toward affective reverence for God.[223]

The Taxonomy of Fortitude and Temperance

Aquinas frequently explains that he categorizes a particular virtue under fortitude because it modifies the irascible passions, or under temperance because it modifies the concupiscible passions.[224] He also makes a point of justifying his categorization when a virtue does not modify the typical passions of its cardinal virtue.[225] His attention to these issues is perhaps the clearest indication that Aquinas is attempting to synthesize the traditional paradigm of fortitude as overcoming obstacles, and temperance as restraining desire, with his more original paradigm of fortitude as the ordering of the irascible passions, and temperance as the ordering of the concupiscible passions. His synthesis ultimately favors traditional formulations, but he emphasizes that there is something unusual about virtues being assigned to fortitude when they modify concupiscible passions, or virtues being assigned to temperance when they modify irascible passions. In this way, he affirms the importance of the rule even when he goes against it. He makes it clear that the problematic virtues of patience, clemency, meekness, and humility are not the most characteristic examples of their respective cardinal virtues, and he underlines this point by discussing them toward the end of the questions on fortitude and temperance.

222. *ST* II-II 161.4 ad 2.

223. "For just as it is through the virtue of temperance that someone draws back from depraved pleasures for the sake of the good of reason, so it is through the gift of fear that someone draws back from depraved pleasures out of fear of God" (*ST* I-II 68.4 ad 1). See also *ST* II-II 19.12 ad 4, 141.1 ad 3. He also matches the gift of fear with theological hope, as discussed above.

224. *ST* II-II 129.5, 134.4, 160.1.

225. *ST* II-II 136.4 ad 2, 137.2, 157.3, 161.4, 166.2.

In general, Aquinas's synthesis is successful. He manages to affirm traditional definitions of fortitude and temperance while infusing them with his own anthropology.

Vice and Psychological Pathology

According to Aquinas, "sins are located mainly in affection [*in affectu*],"[226] and his treatment of vice is primarily concerned with its psychology. His main interest is to analyze the structure of vice, especially as it relates to affectivity, not to offer judgments on innumerable moral decisions. He prefers to describe vices in terms of affections and affective dispositions, rather than external actions and behavior patterns, although he discusses the latter as well. He also attends to the psychological implications of vice, such as how specific vices influence specific passions and affections and how one vice spawns another. In many ways, his descriptions of individual vices read like clinical descriptions of psychological pathologies. This anthropological focus makes his analysis of specific vices particularly engaging. Leaving aside the merits of his analysis, his approach is a refreshing contrast to those ethical systems that focus almost exclusively on the moral value of particular decisions, and in the process neglect the psychological context and consequences of those decisions.

A notable characteristic of Aquinas's analysis of vice is his attention to deficient as well as excessive passion and affection. This attention partly stems from Aristotle's principle of locating virtue in the mean, but it also derives from Aquinas's theological conviction that human appetites in their elemental ontology are created by God and therefore good. So Aquinas lays out the vice of excessive fear, but also fearlessness;[227] of intemperance, but also insensibility;[228] of excessive anger, but also insufficient anger;[229] of excessive striving for great things, but also insufficient striving.[230] Even vices of deficiency that are much less common than their opposites receive careful consideration. For example, the vices of insensibility and fearlessness receive due attention from Aquinas, even though they are less common than the opposed vices of indulgence and cowardice. When he does not name a

226. *ST* II-II 118.6.

227. *ST* II-II 125, 126.

228. *ST* II-II 142.

229. *ST* II-II 158.

230. *ST* II-II 130–32, 133.

vice of deficiency for a particular virtue, he goes out of his way to emphasize that virtue is about the proper fulfillment of appetite, not just its restraint. For example, although Aquinas devotes a question to the vice of drunkenness without formally considering some opposing vice of excessive sobriety, he does explain that abstinence from alcohol for unreasonable motives is vicious.[231] Except in specific cases, Aquinas gives no indication that he regards excessive passion as intrinsically more vicious than deficient passion. Time and again he reiterates the principle that the passions are not intrinsically disordered, and in fact are essential to virtue, often referring back to the *Prima secundae.*

The anthropological foundation established in the *Treatise on the Passions* gives Aquinas a platform to present vice as the corruption of something good, and not something unremittingly evil. It also gives him the tools to isolate exactly where each vice takes a wrong turn and corrupts something otherwise good. Consequently, he is not limited to phenomenological descriptions of vicious affectivity; he can also say something about the metaphysics of vice and, therefore, what causes it and what corrects it.

Aquinas's attention to affectivity leads him to creative interpretations of traditional vices, as is evident, for example, in his accounts of envy and pride. Citing John Damascene, Aquinas defines envy as a species of sadness, and specifically sadness over another's goods, which are seen by the envious man as diminishing his happiness.[232] Throughout his analysis of envy, Aquinas draws on the account of human affectivity given earlier in the *Prima secundae.* For instance, when defining envy, he focuses on the intentional object of envy—a diagnostic approach that follows from his classification of passions according to their intentional objects.[233] Aquinas places envy within an ontological context, and classifies it as a specific instance of a generic passion. In doing so, he implicitly rejects the notion that envy is some elemental force in human nature. Instead, he presents envy as the corruption of something basically good, that is, sadness. This move allows for a robust affirmation of the goodness of human nature despite the potential for vicious passions such as envy. Aquinas never specifies whether the sadness of envy is only sensible or sometimes also spiritual. He seems to

231. *ST* II-II 150.1 ad 1.
232. *ST* II-II 36.1. See also John Damascene, *De fide orthodoxa* 2.14.
233. *ST* II-II 36.1.

think that envy can refer to movements of either appetite.[234] For example, he affirms that demons experience envy, and demons do not have sense appetites, so he must think that it is possible to experience envy in the will, at least in some analogous sense.[235]

Aquinas's analysis of pride reveals a similar dependence on his metaphysics of affectivity. He rejects the idea that pride is a vice of the intellect, even though he acknowledges that pride is linked to an inflated sense of self.[236] Instead, he defines pride as a vice of appetite that involves "a desire for immoderate excellence, a desire which is not in accord with right reason."[237] Since such striving relates to attaining a difficult good, Aquinas locates pride in the irascible power. He explains, however, that in this case the irascible power should be taken in a wider sense, and that pride involves not only the passions but also the intellectual appetite. Pride implies that the will desires immoderate greatness, and thus concerns spiritual as well as sensible objects. In this way pride is attributed to the demons, since the demons have a will but not a sense appetite.[238] He opposes pride to the virtues of magnanimity and humility, since these virtues moderate the striving for difficult things.[239] Pride can also be understood as a kind of aversion (*aversio*) to God, insofar as the desire for immoderate greatness leads to an aversion to being subject to God and his rule.[240]

As with envy, Aquinas's anthropology and his attention to affectivity leads him to an innovative interpretation of pride. Aquinas offers a very precise definition, unlike many other accounts of pride that only gesture vaguely toward an exaggerated sense of personal greatness. Moreover, as with envy, Aquinas's approach allows him to affirm the basic goodness of the appetite that pride corrupts: pride is not the expression of an elemental force within

234. The first objection and response in *ST* II-II 36.3 is particularly suggestive of this interpretation of envy.

235. *ST* I 64.3.

236. *ST* II-II 162.3 ad 1, 2.

237. *ST* II-II 162.4.

238. "If the difficult good which is the object of pride were only something sensible, something that the sense appetite tends toward, it follows that pride would be in the irascible part of the sense appetite. But because pride concerns a difficult good that can be either sensible or spiritual, it follows that pride can be found in the irascible power, not only in the sense of being in a part of the sense appetite, but also in the wider sense of being in the intellectual appetite. In this way pride is attributed to the demons" (*ST* II-II 162.3). Elsewhere he also refers to pride as an *affectus* in a way that could refer to either appetite. See *ST* II-II 162.2 ad 2.

239. *ST* II-II 162.1 ad 3.

240. *ST* II-II 162.6.

human nature, but the corruption of our striving for goods that are difficult to attain.

Aquinas's treatments of envy and pride exhibit another characteristic feature of his system: vicious affectivity encompasses affections of the will as well as passions of the soul. In many places, Aquinas notes that a particular vice involves inappropriate affection (though he does not always use the word "affection"), as in his treatments of despair, hatred, *acedia*, envy, idolatry, avarice, prodigality, ambition, vainglory, pusillanimity, pride, and *curiositas*.[241] He usually does not specify in which appetite this affection is located. Sometimes, in discussing an aspect of some vice, he talks only about affection, without mentioning passion; other times, he refers to the passions or to the sense appetite, but in a context that does not exclude movements of the intellectual appetite. This ambiguity seems deliberate. It seems Aquinas wants to invoke the general category of affectivity without committing himself to a particular appetite, either because he wants to imply that the vice involves both appetites, or because he is hesitant to decide which sort of appetitive movements are more characteristic of a particular vice. In any case, the category of affection allows for the possibility of vicious affectivity that is not intrinsically bound to our animal nature, and thus enables Aquinas to discuss the affective dimension of specific vices without being committed to locating them in the passions.

Aquinas's view that vicious affectivity encompasses affections of the will as well as the passions allows for new perspectives on traditional vices. The case of *acedia* (often translated as "sloth") is particularly interesting. Today *acedia* is generally associated with laziness. For the early Christians, however, it refers to a kind of spiritual weariness, something that afflicts those committed to a disciplined religious life, and the associated temptation to flee.[242] Aquinas inherits this understanding of *acedia*, and then develops it in a way that is generally considered to mark a unique and original mo-

241. For despair, see *ST* II-II 20 (esp. 20.4); hatred, *ST* II-II 34 (esp. 34.2, 34.6); *acedia*, *ST* II-II 35; envy, *ST* II-II 36; idolatry, *ST* II-II 94 (esp. 94.4); avarice, *ST* II-II 118 (esp. 118.2, 118.6, 118.8); prodigality, *ST* II-II 119 (esp. 119.1); ambition, *ST* II-II 131 (esp. 131.1); vainglory, *ST* II-II 132 (esp. 132.1); pusillanimity, *ST* II-II 133 (esp. 133.2); pride, *ST* II-II 162 (esp. 162.3, 162.6); and *curiositas*, *ST* II-II 167 (esp. 167.1). DeYoung argues that avarice's love of money is seated in the intellectual appetite. See DeYoung, "Aquinas on *Acedia*," 201n80.

242. For a systematic exposition of the concept of *acedia* in various key thinkers of the patristic era, and the appropriation of this tradition in the middle ages, see Jean-Charles Nault, *La saveur de Dieu: l'acédie dans le dynamisme de l'agir* (Paris: Les Éditions du Cerf, 2006), 27–169.

ment in the history of the concept. He classifies *acedia* as a vice opposed to charity, and especially the joy that is the fruit of charity, thereby expanding its applicability to all Christians and not just hermits and monks.[243] Charity loves the divine good for its own sake, and leads to joy in it, while *acedia* is saddened by the consideration of the divine good, and inclines away from it. His conceptualization of *acedia* again displays his predilection for interpreting vices vis-à-vis the anthropological structure of human affectivity, rather than external patterns of behavior or legal obligations.[244]

The precise interpretation of Aquinas's account of *acedia* is a matter of some difficulty and controversy. Aquinas defines *acedia* as involving "sorrow over spiritual good on account of the accompanying bodily toil," and particularly sorrow over the divine good to which charity is directed.[245] But is this sorrow carnal or spiritual? In some passages, Aquinas implies that *acedia* can refer to a movement of the sense appetite.[246] However, he uses only the word *tristitia* in conjunction with *acedia,* never *dolor,* which is significant because, for Aquinas, *tristitia* can refer to sadness of either appetite, but *dolor* refers only to a movement of the sense appetite.[247] Furthermore, he emphasizes that *acedia* is not just a movement of the sense appetite, and

243. The summary given here of the history of interpretation of *acedia* and Aquinas's place within it is drawn from DeYoung. She describes Aquinas's originality as follows: "Aquinas's account deserves special attention because it stands at a key point in the history of *acedia,* a point at which previous strands of the Christian virtue tradition converge and after which the heuristic force of the traditional schema of virtues and vices is considerably dissipated. . . . His characterization of *acedia* as the kind of sorrow opposed to the joy of charity diverges from the tradition (both before and after him) in subtle but interesting ways" (DeYoung, "Aquinas on *Acedia,*" 174). For a discussion of *acedia*'s opposition to joy, see Jean-Charles Nault, "Acedia: Enemy of Spiritual Joy," *Communio* 31 (2004): 236–58.

244. In his detailed study of the notion of *acedia* in medieval thought, Siegfried Wenzel also remarks on the anthropological emphasis of Aquinas (though he seems to blur the distinction between passion and affection), as well as his originality. He writes: "We have seen how Thomas Aquinas, with the help of Aristotelian psychology, was able to connect *acedia* with one of the main passions and consequently show very clearly the place and function *acedia* has in man's affective and volitive life. No similar analysis had been even attempted in Christian theology before the thirteenth century. . . . At the root of *acedia* lies, not physical exhaustion or a weakening of man's will or intellectual darkness, but a disorientation of his affect, or as we would say today, his emotional life." Siegfried Wenzel, *The Sin of Sloth: Acedia in Medieval Thought and Literature* (Chapel Hill: University of North Carolina Press, 1967), 64.

245. *ST* I-II 84.4. See also *ST* II-II 35.2.

246. See *ST* II-II 35.1 ad 1–2, 35.3. DeYoung gives a good presentation of the textual support for this interpretation of Aquinas, even though she ultimately rejects it (DeYoung, "Aquinas on *Acedia,*" esp. 182–91).

247. DeYoung, "Aquinas on *Acedia,*" 182n30.

reason's consent is integral to *acedia* in its most proper sense.[248] He also lists *acedia* as a vice against charity, which clearly involves the will, and contrasts it with joy, which is an affection of the will.[249] Most importantly, in *De malo,* Aquinas explicitly locates *acedia* in the intellectual appetite.[250] In consequence, although there is some ambiguity, it seems that while the sadness of *acedia* involves the passion of sadness, it is first and foremost a movement of the intellectual appetite.

From time to time, Aquinas offers phenomenological descriptions of *acedia,* often by quoting some authority. Perhaps his most striking claim is that *acedia* implies "a certain disgust of working" (*quoddam taedium operandi*), a description that is notably focused on its affective aspects.[251] However, his phenomenological descriptions are sometimes hard to reconcile with his metaphysical claims. For example, Aquinas connects *acedia* to an inclination to avoid physical exertion.[252] However, he defines *acedia* as a vice that has a spiritual object, the divine good, and he explicitly rejects the idea that *acedia* is a vice that shrinks from the divine good insofar as it involves physical labor or the sacrifice of pleasure, because, he argues, that would make *acedia* a carnal vice, not a spiritual vice.[253] It is therefore hard to say exactly what within the sphere of human experience Aquinas is pointing toward in his account of *acedia.* It is sadness about the divine good, and it involves a disgust of working, but not a disgust of physical labor as such. How might these different characterizations be integrated into a coherent conceptual-

248. *ST* II-II 35.3. See DeYoung, "Power Made Perfect," 185.

249. Regarding *acedia,* see *ST* II-II 35.1–2; regarding joy being an affection of the will, see *ST* I-II 31.3.

250. See *De malo* 11.1 and DeYoung, "Aquinas on *Acedia,*" 193.

251. *ST* II-II 35.1. Although *taedium* can be translated as "weariness" as well as "disgust," the latter makes its affective connotations much more clear. The translation is inspired by Nault, who translates *taedium operandi* as "dégoût de l'action," and who draws attention to this phrase as an important element of Aquinas's account of *acedia.* He argues that it constitutes a second definition of *acedia* (Nault, *Le saveur de Dieu,* 280–89).

A secondary meaning of *operor* is "to perform religious rites, worship." See *Oxford Latin Dictionary,* ed. P. G. W. Glare (Oxford: Oxford University Press, 1985), 1252. Aquinas may intend to evoke this meaning in his choice of the word *operandi,* although he primarily seems to mean "working."

252. *ST* I 63.2 ad 2; *ST* I-II 84.4; *ST* II-II 35.1, 35.4 ad 2–3. See also De Young, "Aquinas on *Acedia,*" esp. 189–91

253. "It cannot be said that *acedia* is a special vice because it shrinks from spiritual good as being laborious or burdensome to the body, or as impeding the body's pleasure, since this would not distinguish *acedia* from carnal vices, in which someone seeks bodily rest and pleasure" (*ST* II-II 35.2). See also DeYoung, "Aquinas on *Acedia,*" 194–95.

ization of *acedia*? One plausible interpretation is that, for Aquinas, *acedia* is a sadness about the divine good because it has been falsely apprehended as something unworthy of effort, so that someone is disinclined to doing what is necessary to attain it.

Aquinas links *acedia* to the violation of the commandment to keep holy the Sabbath. This precept "commands us to rest our mind in God, which is contrary to mental sadness (*tristitia mentis*) about the divine good," and so it follows that *acedia* inclines us violate it.[254] Aquinas's linking of *acedia* to the Sabbath gives us a clue about its phenomenology. It is a sort of sadness that inclines us to avoid spiritual activity such as Sunday worship—that is, activity that is directed toward a spiritual good, but that does not involve physical labor in any obvious sense. In a derivative way, *acedia* might incline us to avoid physical work, such as the exertion of getting out of bed on Sunday morning, but its primary effect is to make it difficult for us either to apprehend spiritual goods as good or to act to attain them. Hence Aquinas's proposed remedy to *acedia:* namely, to think more about spiritual goods, "since the more we think about spiritual goods, the more pleasing they become to us."[255] Aquinas does not seem to be advocating that we chain ourselves to church pews until we are free from *acedia*. Rather, he is suggesting that when spiritual goods cease to interest us, we should seek a fresh perspective on them: since *acedia* requires the apprehension of the divine good as unworthy of effort, correction of this erroneous appraisal should cause *acedia* to evaporate. Easier said than done perhaps, but for Aquinas, it is nonetheless a necessary element of the cure for *acedia*.

Many have argued that Aquinas's concept of *acedia* corresponds to the modern concept of boredom.[256] Some editions of the Gilby *Summa* in fact translate *acedia* as "spiritual boredom" or "spiritual apathy."[257] While

254. *ST* II-II 35.3 ad 1.

255. *ST* II-II 35.1 ad 4.

256. Michael Risposa explicitly links boredom with Aquinas's account of *acedia* in his extended essay about boredom within religious contexts. See Michael Risposa, *Boredom and the Religious Imagination* (Charlottesville: University of Virginia, 1999), esp. 11–40. John Casey offers a similar interpretation, connecting Aquinas's account of *acedia* with boredom and especially Baudelaire's *ennui*. See John Casey, "Sloth," *New Blackfriars* 81 (2000): 82–83. See also Bruce Williams, "The Capital Vices in Contemporary Discourse," *Angelicum* 84 (2007): 44–46. Medieval notions of *acedia* are sometimes globally correlated with the modern notion of boredom, as in Lars Svendsen, *A Philosophy of Boredom*, trans. John Irons (Bath: Reaktion Books, 2005), 49–52.

257. In explaining his translation of *acedia* as spiritual apathy, Thomas Heath explains:

a strong case can be made for some correspondence between *acedia* and boredom, especially insofar as Aquinas's description of *acedia* involves *taedium*—a word that is itself sometimes translated as "boredom"—there is enough dissimilarity to caution against any claim of wholesale equivalence. Perhaps the most obvious dissimilarity is that, in popular understanding, boredom denotes a psychological state that does not *by definition* imply moral defect, while *acedia* is a vice and does imply moral defect (although it should be noted that Aquinas seems to acknowledge the possibility of being "attacked" by *acedia* in a way that does not imply sin).[258] Consequently, it seems more accurate to say that *acedia* is a cause of boredom, and perhaps the preeminent cause, but that it is neither identical with boredom nor its only possible cause.

Another feature of Aquinas's analysis of specific vices is his attention to their psychological consequences, especially in his exposition of the capital vices. He explains that the capital vices are so named not necessarily due to the degree of their sinfulness but because "a capital vice is one from which other vices more frequently arise."[259] The spiritual sorrow of *acedia* leads to restlessness and the seeking after illicit pleasure to alleviate its sadness.[260] It also leads to despair.[261] Hatred can be caused by anger, but especially by

"'Spiritual apathy' seems best to catch the phenomenon Thomas is describing, i.e., a bored indifference towards religious and spiritual matters." Thomas Heath, Introduction, notes, and appendices to *Summa Theologiae*, Vol. 35: *Consequences of Charity* (New York: McGraw-Hill Book Co.; London: Eyre and Spottiswoode, 1972), 21.

258. *ST* II-II 35.1 ad 2. In his Thomistic analysis of the vice of *acedia*, Urban Voll cautions against interpreting symptoms associated with *acedia* with the vice itself: "The word [*acedia*] as used by the desert Fathers, scholastic theologians, and later writers apparently signifies some depressing, constricting tedium or ennui. The dullness, listnessness and apathetic 'I don't care' attitude could, of course, manifest itself on every level: physical lassitude, intellectual boredom, moral and religious tepidity. And just as obviously, there could be a number of causes for such moods." Urban Voll, "The Vice of Acedia," S.T.D. Diss., Dominican House of Studies, Washington, D.C., 1964, 70.

259. *ST* II-II 34.5. Elsewhere he explains in more detail: "A sin is called 'capital' from a metaphorical sense of the word 'head' (*capis*), meaning that a sin is a principle or director of other sins. In the same way, a capital vice is that from which other vices originate. . . . A capital vice is not only a principle of other vices, but also their director and in a certain sense their leader" (*ST* I-II 84.3). Aquinas develops his presentation of the capital vices more in the subsequent article and in the process he gives an overview of the various capital sins and how they relate to each other (*ST* I-II 84.4). For an application of Aquinas's thought on the capital vices to contemporary discussion, with particular attention to his analysis of their affective consequences, see Williams, "Capital Vices," 29–47.

260. *ST* II-II 35.4 ad 2–3.

261. *ST* II-II 20.4.

acedia,[262] and pride leads to envy.[263] The experience of sadness leads to the desire to remove the cause of the sadness, and since envy is caused by the envied and what they possess, envy leads to hating those envied and to taking pleasure in their misfortune.[264] The self-absorption of avarice involves disorder in one's "interior affections," leads to callousness about the needs of others, and gives rise to "disquiet" and "anxiety about superfluous concerns."[265] Excessive fear of failure leads to pusillanimity.[266] Gluttony leads to dullness of wit, a corrupt taste for unseemly joys, and an inclination toward buffoonery.[267] Through the vice of lust, the concupiscible passions move so vehemently toward sexual pleasure that they subordinate the higher powers of reason and will to themselves.[268] On the level of reason, lust leads to blindness of mind and inconstancy. On the level of appetite, inordinate love of pleasure develops, along with hatred of the God who forbids immoderate pleasure. It also leads to "affection for this present world" and "despair of the future world," because "a person bound by carnal pleasures finds spiritual pleasures distasteful and does not seek them."[269] These examples all exhibit Aquinas's interest in developing a holistic understanding of vice (and also his characteristic curiosity).

Virtue, Vice, and Affectivity

From the brief overview given in this chapter, it is overwhelmingly evident that Aquinas's account of the virtues and vices is deeply informed by his metaphysics of affectivity, and that a major theme throughout the *Summa*, and especially the *Secunda secundae*, is the perfection of human affectivity by virtue and its deformation by vice. A strong case can also be made for a more wide-ranging claim: that the theme of human affectivity and its perfection by virtue is one of the major organizing principles of the *Summa*—that it is not just one of many themes, but a theme of central structural importance to his project.

262. *ST* II-II 158.7 ad 2.

263. *ST* II-II 162.8 ad 3.

264. *ST* II-II 36.4 ad 3.

265. *ST* II-II 118.1 ad 2, 118.7, 118.8 ad 4.

266. *ST* II-II 133.2 ad 3.

267. *ST* II-II 148.5–6.

268. *ST* II-II 153.5. Elsewhere he advances the principle that the more sexual pleasures are sought, "the more the power of concupiscence increases and the more the power of the mind is weakened" (*ST* II-II 151.3 ad 2). See also *ST* II-II 55.8 ad 1.

269. *ST* II-II 153.5. Aquinas also identifies imprudence and folly as a consequence of lust (*ST* II-II 46.3, 53.6, 55.8 ad 1).

It is true that Aquinas relies on the traditional categories of the three theological virtues and the four cardinal virtues to provide the basic structure of the *Secunda secundae*. It is also true that he leaves some amount of ambiguity about the affectivity of particular virtues and vices, especially on the question of whether they involve the sense appetite or the intellectual appetite or both, and more clarity might be expected if the theme of affectivity were indeed a major organizing principle. Nonetheless, given the unusual attention that Aquinas gives to the metaphysics of affectivity in the *Prima secundae*, and the frequency with which he explicitly refers back to the *Treatise on the Passions* in the *Secunda secundae*, and recognizing that Aquinas is pioneering a radically new approach and so a certain degree of roughness is to be expected, it is highly plausible that Aquinas did indeed consciously intend to construct the *Secunda secundae* partly around the theme of affectivity.

The sheer originality of the *Secunda secundae* supports this interpretation. Mark Jordan suggests that the *Secunda secundae* manifests a structural innovation that is not found in Aristotle or any other of Aquinas's predecessors or contemporaries: the organization of its contents according to the three theological virtues and the four cardinal virtues, with all other virtues and vices placed under one of these seven virtues.[270] "The innovation is bold for being so simple," he writes.[271] Although there are countless catalogs of virtues and vices by both pagan and Christian authors, there was no fixed order. The *Secunda secundae*, on the other hand, "applies the conclusions of a philosophically astute moral analysis to what had been taught in the unruly theological forms of *sententiae*, exhortations, *exempla*, cases, and other *pastoralia*."[272] One of the best-calculated effects of this new organization "is to push the seven capital vices to the margin."[273]

Aquinas states in the prologue of the *Secunda secundae* that he intends to discuss vices and sin "according to their matter and object," rather than according to other categories, such as whether the sins are from thought, word, or deed, or whether the sins stem from weakness, ignorance, or malice.[274] Because "virtues operate rightly about the same matter in which their

270. Jordan, "Invention of the *Summa theologiae*," 91–95.

271. Ibid., 91.

272. Ibid., 95.

273. Ibid., 94.

274. *ST* II-II prologue. Jordan discusses how Aquinas is rejecting the taxonomy of sin given by Peter Lombard. Lombard distinguishes according to whether the sins are of thought, word, or

opposite vices fail," vice by definition concerns the same thing as virtue, and so, Aquinas explains, he has organized his consideration of "the entire matter of morals" around his discussion of the virtues.[275] The "matter of morals" is nothing other than the cognitive powers and the appetites and their operations—which therefore includes human affectivity. Consequently, there is reason to think that the newness of the *Secunda secundae*'s structure reflects the newness of Aquinas's idea of making affectivity, and especially its flourishing, a major organizing principle of theological ethics.

deed (see *Sententiae* II 42.4) and whether from weakness, ignorance, or malice (see *Sententiae* II 22.4). These distinctions have their origins in Jerome, *Super Ezechielem* 43.23–35 and Isidore, *Sententiae* II 17:3–4, respectively. See Jordan, "Invention of the *Summa theologiae*," 94.

275. *ST* II-II prologue.

CHAPTER 7

The Affectivity of Christ

In the thirteenth century, the passions of Christ were a common topic of theological speculation. Among Aquinas's contemporaries, Alexander of Hales gives the most attention to Christ's passions, and in fact his work influences Aquinas, but none give the topic as much sustained attention as Aquinas.[1] Moreover, Aquinas's account of Christ's affectivity is not confined to his discussion of Christ's passions, as becomes evident when his writings on Christ are examined with the category of affectivity in mind. As well as constituting an important element of his Christology, Aquinas's exposition of Christ's affectivity also constitutes an important element of his account of human affectivity: for Aquinas, Christ's affectivity is a fully human affectivity, and in fact the exemplar of human affectivity. This chapter will discuss Aquinas's account of the passions and affections of Christ, with particular attention to its relevance to his account of human affectivity more generally.[2]

Historical Context

Aquinas's account of Christ's affectivity, and especially of Christ's passions, cannot be properly understood without reference to his theological predecessors, because they set the terms of the debate. Aquinas is working within a framework that is not his own, and it requires extra effort to discern whether he truly endorses his inherited framework, or whether he is only paying lip service in order to subvert it.

1. Gondreau, *Passions of Christ's Soul,* 88–100, 375–76.

2. Paul Gondreau provides the principal point of reference for scholarship on Aquinas's account of Christ's affectivity with his *Passions of Christ's Soul,* to which this chapter is particularly indebted. For a brief but excellent overview of Aquinas's account, with particular attention to its relevance to contemporary ethics and theological anthropology, see Craig Steven Titus, "Passions in Christ: Spontaneity, Development, and Virtue," *The Thomist* 73 (2009): 53–87.

Hilary of Poitiers is the most significant of Aquinas's theological predecessors on the topic of Christ's passions. In the fourth century, Hilary maintained that Christ somehow suffered the crucifixion without feeling his body's pain in his soul. He adopts this position in part to safeguard the divinity of Christ against Arian beliefs: although Hilary fully affirms that Christ suffered, he disputes the idea that Christ suffered in a way that fully penetrated his person, which according to Hilary would be unworthy of Christ's divinity.[3] In one representative text, Hilary affirms that Christ suffered in his body without experiencing pain (*dolor*): "He had a body that could suffer, and it did suffer, but he did not have a nature that could experience pain."[4] Because of his historic defense of orthodox beliefs about Christ in a critical period of upheaval, and because he was the first of the Church Fathers to take a strong position of any kind on the psychology of Christ's suffering, Hilary's authority on the topic of Christ's passions was immense during the Middle Ages. In their accounts of Christ's affectivity, the major theological figures of the thirteenth century struggle to make sense of Hilary's writings, because they want to affirm the reality of Christ's sufferings and to reject anything that seems to diminish Christ's humanity. However, they cannot simply ignore Hilary, because he is too important. Consequently, medieval theologians are often on the defensive when they assert a realistic account of Christ's passions. They are clearly trying to harmonize their affirmation of the full humanity of Christ's suffering with Hilary's less realistic account. In the end, the tensions involved often lead to very convoluted explanations of Christ's passions. For the most part, medieval theologians propose benign interpretations of Hilary's problematic texts, and try to maintain that there is an essential continuity between his position and their own.[5] Still, they do not stop there: while deferring to Hilary in some ways, they also advance more boldly realistic interpretations of Christ's sufferings, and introduce their own innovations.

3. For a discussion of Hilary's historical context, his theological motives, and his enduring influence on medieval theology, see Gondreau, *Passions of Christ's Soul*, 48–51, 388–402, and Kevin Madigan, *The Passions of Christ in High-Medieval Thought: An Essay on Christological Development* (New York: Oxford University Press, 2007), 3–22, 51–71.

4. Hilary of Poitiers, *De Trinitate* 10.23.

5. Scholars are divided about whether or not medieval interpretations of Hilary are at all plausible. Madigan takes a very critical view (see Madigan, *Passions of Christ*, esp. 58–62). Trent Pomplun is of the opposite opinion. He argues that medieval interpretations of Hilary can be plausible. See Trent Pomplun, "Impassibility in St. Hilary of Poitiers's *De Trinitate*," in *Divine Impassibility and the Mystery of Human Suffering*, ed. James F. Keating and Thomas Joseph White (Grand Rapids, Mich.: Eerdmans Press, 2009), 187–213.

After Hilary, the next most important figure is Peter Lombard. His *Sentences* provide a lengthy discussion of Christ's passions that relies heavily on Scripture and various patristic authorities.[6] By bringing attention to the subject, and collating the most significant Scripture texts and theological opinions, Peter Lombard significantly advances theological reflection on the passions in Christ. He also sets the stage for the ensuing discussion of the thirteenth century, insofar as his *Sentences* becomes the standard textbook for teaching in universities. In consequence, it becomes almost required for theologians to have an opinion on Christ's passions. Moreover, when they discuss the topic, they tend to follow the way Peter Lombard frames the issues, insofar as his treatment of the subject had no competitors in either its thoroughness or the extent of its dissemination.

Besides Hilary and Peter Lombard, Alexander of Hales, Albert, and Bonaventure are also importance sources for Aquinas, especially their commentaries on the *Sentences*.[7]

Aquinas's historical context explains some otherwise puzzling aspects of his presentation of Christ's passions. Despite his decisively optimistic account of the passions, Aquinas discusses Christ's passions only in the context of discussing the "the defects of soul" that Christ took upon himself in assuming his human nature.[8] Furthermore, there is a defensive tone to his account, as though Aquinas attributes passions to Christ only because it is strictly necessary to do so. This seemingly suspicious attitude toward Christ's passions reflects the theological framework that he has inherited and must work within, not anything intrinsic to his own system. Hilary's authority in the field of medieval Christology binds Aquinas to work with Hilary's vocabulary. In consequence, Aquinas seems more hesitant to affirm a realistic account of Christ's passions than he actually is. Aquinas's approach also reflects the influence of Peter Lombard. For example, the placement of his analysis of Christ's passions under the heading "defects of soul" follows the lead of Peter Lombard, as does his attention to only some of Christ's passions (pain, sadness, fear, wonder, and anger), even though

6. Peter Lombard, *Sententiae* III 15–17.

7. See Alexander of Hales, *Glossa in quatuor libros Sententiarum* III 15, and *Summa theologiae* III 1.1.4.3.1–2; Albert, *Commentaria in quatuor libros Sententiarum* III 15–17; and Bonaventure, *Commentaria in quatuor libros Sententiarum* III 15. For a discussion of the influence of Lombard and Aquinas's contemporaries on Aquinas's account of Christ's passions, see Gondreau, *Passions of Christ's Soul*, 76–100.

8. *ST* III 15.

he would clearly attribute other passions to Christ as well.[9] It is important to keep in mind the historical origins of Aquinas's treatment of Christ's passions: otherwise, features that actually testify to a positive evaluation of them can seem to indicate the opposite.

Methodology and Christological Foundation

The person of Christ figures prominently in the organization and structure of the entire *Summa,* and not just the *Tertia Pars.* In the prologue before the second question of the *Summa,* Aquinas explains its scheme as follows: "We will treat first, of God; second, of the rational creature's movement toward God; and third, of Christ, who, as man, is our way to God."[10] Aquinas deliberately places his Christology after his accounts of God and the human person. His theology and anthropology thus provide an ontological foundation for his discussion of Christ, who is both God and man and the necessary way to the Father. This placement is highly significant: it reveals Aquinas's desire to situate his Christology within a metaphysical context, and indicates that Aquinas's Christology cannot be properly understood apart from either his theology of God or his anthropology.

The content of his Christology is rooted first and foremost in Scripture. "We ought not to say anything about God," he writes, "that is not found in sacred scripture either explicitly or implicitly."[11] Aquinas turns to Scripture, and particularly the Gospels, as his primary source on the nature of Christ's humanity. While Christian theologians necessarily turn to the Gospels for information about Christ, Aquinas reads Scripture in a way that distinguishes him from his contemporaries. He stands apart in his emphasis on the literal sense of scriptural texts, and his relative neglect of the sort of mystical and allegorical exegesis that is dominant among his contemporaries.[12] Furthermore, in his interpretation of scriptural texts, Aquinas often turns to the ecumenical councils. He incorporates council documents into his Christology as soon as he discovers them, as is evident from certain doctrinal developments between his major theological works, and his attention to council documents significantly exceeds that of his contemporaries and immediate

9. Compare *ST* III 15 with Peter Lombard, *Sententiae* III 15–17.
10. *ST* I 2, prologue.
11. *ST* I 36.2 ad 1.
12. See Torrell, *The Person and His Work,* 58–59.

successors.[13] He also relies heavily on the writings of patristic authorities, and Aquinas stands out for his exceptional familiarity with Greek Fathers, whose writings were only beginning to be read in the West.[14] In his lifetime, he was known to have a particular interest in acquiring new sources, and he would sometimes travel from place to place to consult documents.[15]

Aquinas divides his discussion of Christ in the *Tertia pars* into two sections. He first lays out the metaphysics of the Incarnation, and then applies this metaphysics to a close reading of the Gospels. The first section (q 1–26) considers "the mystery of the Incarnation, by which God was made man for our salvation" and the second section (q 27–59) considers "those things that our savior, God incarnate, did and suffered."[16] The first section is closely argued, and builds gradually, whereas the second section is more topical. His discussion of Christ's passions falls midway through the first section, and explicitly builds on the principles and conclusions of the earlier questions.

Aquinas offers the foundational principles of the first section in the context of a reiteration and elaboration of Chalcedonian Christology. Jesus Christ is true God and true man, the Word made flesh, whose divine nature is joined to his human nature inseparably and without mingling.[17] Having assumed a human nature through the Incarnation, the Second Person of the Trinity employs it as an instrument of his divinity.[18] Since Christ is fully human, he reasons, everything that can be attributed to our nature must also be attributed to Christ's human nature. He writes: "Nothing that God has planted in our nature was lacking to the human nature assumed by the Word of God."[19] From this principle, it follows that Christ's affectivity is fully human, that "Christ had assumed a true human nature, with all its natural affections."[20]

13. Joseph Wawrykow, "Hypostatic Union," in *The Theology of Thomas Aquinas*, ed. Rik Van Nieuwenhove and Joseph Wawrykow (Notre Dame, Ind.: University of Notre Dame Press, 2005), 236–37, 245–46. For examples of Aquinas's use of the councils in the *Summa*, see *ST* III 2.1–3, 2.6.

14. For information about the patristic authorities that Aquinas draws on for his account of Christ's passions, see Gondreau, *Passions of Christ's Soul*, 47–71. Hilary, Augustine, and John Damascene are foremost among them.

15. Torrell, *The Person and His Work*, 140.

16. *ST* III, prologue.

17. *ST* III 2.1.

18. *ST* III 2.2, 2.6. For Aquinas's views on Christ's humanity, see Paul Gondreau, "The Humanity of Christ, the Incarnate Word," in *The Theology of Thomas Aquinas*, ed. Rik Van Nieuwenhove and Joseph Wawrykow (Notre Dame, Ind.: University of Notre Dame Press, 2005), 252–76.

19. *ST* III 9.4.

20. *ST* III 21.2.

In fact, Christ's affectivity is more human than ours, not less. He is entirely without sin, "because sin does not belong to human nature, of which God is the cause; but rather sin is contrary to nature, having been introduced by the instigation of the devil."[21] Christ's soul is imbued with sanctifying grace,[22] and from this *habitus* flows the perfection of his various faculties. Aquinas writes: "Since the grace of Christ was utterly perfect, it flowed into virtues that perfected every single power of the soul and all of the soul's actions. And thus Christ had all the virtues."[23] In addition, Christ possessed the gifts of the Holy Spirit.[24] Christ's affectivity, then, through sanctifying grace, the virtues and the gifts, and his utter lack of sin, is, according to Aquinas, more truly human than ours, which is marked by the wounds of original sin. This conclusion runs seamlessly from his anthropology; it is not strained or forced. This tight coherence is a notable achievement, since many other theologies struggle to account for how Christ could be without sin, and yet still remain fully human. For Aquinas, Christ's affectivity is perfect not because he is somehow immune to the inclinations of human nature, but because in him they are in complete harmony with each other.

Nonetheless, although Aquinas holds that Christ's affectivity is fully human, he also affirms that there are certain aspects of his affectivity that even a graced and sinless human person would not have in common with him. There are some dissimilarities between Christ's affectivity and the affectivity of the rest of humanity that are ontologically unbridgeable. Aquinas's affirmation of these affective dissimilarities in Christ does not stem from any suspicion of human nature, as though he wants to distance Christ from ordinary affective phenomena that he thinks would be undignified for Christ to experience. Rather, Aquinas affirms these affective dissimilarities almost reluctantly, because he thinks they are necessary consequences of Christ's divinity, and specifically the peculiar knowledge he possesses as a divine person. To understand Aquinas's understanding of Christ's affectivity, therefore, it is necessary to turn to his understanding of Christ's knowledge.

According to Aquinas, then, Christ experienced three kinds of knowledge in his human soul: "acquired" empirical knowledge of the sort proper

21. *ST* III 15.1. See also John Damascene, *De fide orthodoxa,* III.20.

22. *ST* III 7.1, 7.9–13.

23. *ST* III 7.2. Aquinas elsewhere specifies that Christ did not, however, have the virtues of faith and hope, as will be discussed later in this chapter.

24. *ST* III 7.5.

to human modes of cognition;[25] infused supernatural knowledge of created reality and of divine revelation;[26] and immediate beatific knowledge of God and all things in God.[27] The first two kinds of knowledge have no appreciable effect on Aquinas's account of Christ's affectivity vis-à-vis ordinary human affectivity. The first kind is simply ordinary human knowledge, and the second kind, Christ's supernatural knowledge of created reality, amounts to a collection of "facts" that do not influence Christ's affectivity. The third kind of knowledge, however, presents a serious challenge for Aquinas. The immediate beatific knowledge of God necessarily causes supernatural joy, and the constant experience of this joy sets Christ apart from the rest of humanity. The consequent tension informs his account of Christ's affectivity in very significant ways, as will be discussed later.

The attribution of supernatural knowledge to Christ's humanity was the norm in Aquinas's theological milieu. Moreover, although it is often thought that the ascription of beatific knowledge to Christ derives from his metaphysics, recent scholarship suggests that Aquinas did not deduce this doctrine, but instead assumed that it was part of the deposit of faith; he tries to show that it is a fitting truth, but he does not try to prove its metaphysical necessity on the basis of other Christological principles.[28] Compared to

25. *ST* III 9.4.

26. Through this infused knowledge, Christ was granted two sorts of knowledge. "First, Christ knew whatever can be known by man through the illuminating power of the active intellect, such as whatever belongs to the human sciences. Second, through this infused knowledge, Christ knew everything that has become known to men through divine revelation" (*ST* III 11.1).

27. "Through some light coming from the divine nature, the soul of Christ, which is a part of his human nature, was perfected with the beatific knowledge of seeing God in his essence" (*ST* III 9.2 ad 1). Because of this beatific knowledge of God, Christ knows everything that exists at whatever point in the entire course of time. "The soul of Christ," he writes, "knows in the Word everything that exists in any time whatsoever, and also the thoughts of men, of whom he is the judge" (*ST* III 10.2). Aquinas explains that Christ's beatific vision of the divine essence begins from the first moment of Christ's conception (*ST* III 34.4). For a discussion of Aquinas's account of the vision of God through the divine essence, see Jean-Pierre Torrell, "La vision de Dieu «per essentiam» selon saint Thomas d'Aquin," *Recherches Thomasiennes: Études Revues et Augmentées* (Paris: Librairie Philosophique J. Vrin, 2000), 177–97.

28. According to Torrell, Aquinas does not try to prove that Christ had the beatific vision: "for him it is a given of faith," and he simply tries to show how it is fitting. See Jean-Pierre Torrell, "Saint Thomas d'Aquin et la science du Christ: une relecture des Questions 9–12 de la Tertia Pars de la «Somme de théologie»," *Recherches Thomasiennes: Études Revues et Augmentées* (Paris: Librairie Philosophique J. Vrin, 2000), 200. Guy Mansini comes to a similar conclusion. He writes, "The reason St. Thomas affirms Christ's immediate vision of God, we are sometimes told, is that he thinks this follows as a metaphysical necessity from the fact of the hypostatic union." To the contrary, Mansini goes on to argue, the texts cited in defense of this position ultimately amount

his contemporaries, what is unusual about Aquinas's Christology is not his affirmation that Christ possessed this supernatural knowledge, but rather his affirmation that Christ acquired knowledge over the course of his life through ordinary human means.[29] This departure from conventional theological opinion seems to have been a hard-fought conclusion: in the *Tertia pars* he admits changing his mind about Christ's human knowledge and acknowledges that he now attributes a certain kind of acquired knowledge to Christ that he had not before.[30]

The Passions of Christ

The philosophy and theology of affectivity developed in the *Prima pars* and the *Secunda pars* serves as the basis for Aquinas's study of Christ's affectivity in the *Tertia pars*. The application of anthropology to Christology is justified by a strong affirmation of Christ's solidarity with humanity. Aquinas explicitly validates the import of his anthropology into his Christology by adverting to the principle that nothing in our human nature is lacking in Christ's. Consequently, unless something peculiar to Christ's divinity presents special considerations, everything that Aquinas asserts about human nature applies also to Christ. As he explains, "Christ permitted all the powers of his soul to act in their own normal ways."[31]

Consequently, Aquinas affirms that Christ experienced the passions of the soul as something implied by his assumption of human nature:

> The soul is said to experience passion in operations that are characteristic of the soul, or at least more proper to the soul than to the body. Although the soul is said to experience passion in this way on the level of the intellect as well as

to arguments from fittingness. Aquinas affirms that Christ has the beatific vision in the first place only because he takes it as a datum of faith. See Guy Mansini, "Understanding St. Thomas on Christ's Immediate Knowledge of God," *Thomist* 59 (1995): 93, 101. The interpretations of Mansini and Torrell seem plausible.

29. *ST* III 9.4, 12.2.

30. In *ST* III 9.4, Aquinas acknowledges that his attribution of acquired knowledge to Christ represents an evolution in his thought, as is evident in comparison with *Scriptum super libros Sententiarum* III 14.3 and III 18.3.

31. *ST* III 18.5. One reason that Aquinas does not give a fuller treatment of Christ's passions may be that he assumes that the reader understands that everything affirmed about human affectivity applies to Christ, unless otherwise specified, and so he thinks it is necessary to discuss Christ's affectivity only in those matters where there might be controversy.

on the level of sensation, as was said in the *Secunda pars*, it is the affections of the sense appetite that are most properly called passions of the soul. Christ had these passions, along with everything else that belongs to human nature.[32]

In various ways, Aquinas affirms that each of Christ's passions operates according to its own nature, and according to the normal mode of human passion. In the *Compendium theologiae*, he states that Christ "permitted each of his lower powers to be moved by its own impulse."[33] Elsewhere he asserts that Christ desired the basic necessities of life, and the pleasure associated with them:

> The flesh naturally desires what is pleasurable to it, through the desire of the sense appetite. But since man is a rational animal, the flesh of man desires such things according to the manner and order of reason. And in this way, the flesh of Christ, through the desire of the sense appetite, naturally desired food and drink and sleep, and other such things that are desired in accordance with right reason.[34]

Aquinas has no difficulty in affirming Christ's experience of human desire and passion, because he has no difficulty in affirming the ontological goodness of appetite, and therefore doing so presents no threat to the dignity or reality of Christ's divinity. Christ's perfect humanity is not in tension with his experience of passion: in fact, it causes Christ to experience passion more intensely than we do. For example, Aquinas affirms that Christ's suffering on the cross was greater than any other human suffering, because his humanity was more perfectly human, and therefore his body and soul were more sensitive.[35] Aquinas's anthropology provides the basis for a markedly positive evaluation of Christ's passions, and gives Aquinas the resources to mount a strong rejoinder to those suspicious of the idea that Christ experienced the same passions we do.

32. *ST* III 15.4. As discussed in chap. 3, this text has some important interpretative consequences in making sense of the category of affection. By using the phrase "affections of the sense appetite" to contrast Christ's passions with the movements of his intellectual appetite, Aquinas strongly implies that "passion" and "affection" are not coextensive terms. As such, this passage constitutes one of the clearest indications of what Aquinas means by *affectus*. In consequence, it is plausible to infer that reflecting on Christ's affectivity leads Aquinas to refine both his analysis of human affectivity and the language he uses to speak about it.

33. *Compendium theologiae* 232, trans. Cyril Vollert, modified (St. Louis: Herder, 1947).

34. *ST* III 15.2 ad 2. See also John Damascene, *De fide orthodoxa*, 3.14

35. *ST* III 46.6.

Nonetheless, in union with his predecessors and contemporaries, Aquinas claims that Christ's experience of the passions differed from ours in significant ways. The differences especially concern the relationship between reason and passion. On account of these differences, Aquinas sometimes calls Christ's passions "propassions," a term coined by Jerome in the fourth century and widely used among Aquinas's contemporaries.[36] He also states that Christ did not experience "perfect passion," in the technical sense of a passion that has become overwhelming and immoderate.[37] He summarizes the differences between Christ's passions and our passions in the following passage:

> The passions were in Christ in a way other than in us, in three ways. First, as regards their object, because in us these passions are commonly drawn toward illicit things, which was not the case in Christ. Second, as regards their origin, because in us these passions frequently forestall the judgment of reason, but in Christ all movements of the sense appetite arose in accordance with the guidance of reason. . . . Third, as regards their effect, because in us sometimes these movements are not settled firmly in the sense appetite, but also drag along reason. But this was not the case in Christ, because the movements that naturally belong to human flesh, through his supervision, so remained in the sense appetite that reason was in no way impeded from doing what was appropriate.[38]

What exactly Aquinas means here is open to a variety of interpretations. The key hermeneutical question is what it means for the passions to be "in accordance with the guidance of reason." Does Aquinas mean that passions occurred in Christ only after reason's explicit command? Or does Aquinas mean to affirm something less dictatorial about reason's guidance of passion?

It is not possible to give a confident answer based on this text alone. But when this question is considered in the context of Aquinas's anthropology

36. Jerome uses the term "propassion" in his *Commentariorum in Matheum* 4.26.37. During his career, Aquinas does not use the term often, even while commenting on the *Sentences*, which uses the expression frequently. He begins to make significant use of it only in the *Summa theologiae*, and even there he uses it sparingly. For a discussion of Aquinas's use of the term "propassion," see Gondreau, *Passions of Christ's Soul*, 368–71. Aquinas's departure from theological convention may reflect a reluctance to use language that could be misconstrued as implying that Christ's passions were somehow essentially different from ours.

37. *ST* III 15.6 ad 1.

38. *ST* III 15.4. For an extended discussion of this passage, see Gondreau, *Passions of Christ's Soul*, 333–74.

and his repeated affirmations that Christ's human nature is in complete solidarity with ours, the answer is clear. Aquinas must mean to apply to Christ his preferred metaphor of reason ruling the passions politically, implying that Christ's passions enjoyed their own proper autonomy and spontaneity, while also instinctively following the guidance of reason. In other words, Aquinas does not mean that Christ became angry only after he commanded himself to become angry, but rather that Christ spontaneously became angry in ways that complemented his reason and cooperated with its implicit judgments. As discussed in chapter 4, Aquinas holds that the passions can be the seat of virtue and that reason can permeate the passions, in contrast to Bonaventure, so that the passions cooperate spontaneously with reason. So Aquinas has no difficulty affirming that Christ's passions may chronologically precede the conscious judgment of Christ's reason. He does, however, exclude from Christ those spontaneous movements of disordered passion that Aquinas calls antecedent passion.

Aquinas also gets at the question of what distinguishes Christ's passions from ours under the topic of the *fomes peccati,* "the tinder of sin," a technical term used by Peter Lombard to designate the sinful inclinations endemic to wounded human nature.[39] Aquinas excludes any sinful inclinations from Christ's person, explaining that since Christ's passions were virtuous and ordered by reason, his passions were never immoderate or inclined toward sin. Consequently, the temptations that Christ experienced were always "exterior"; Christ never experienced "interior" temptation.[40] He writes: "The *fomes peccati* implies an inclination of the sense appetite toward what is contrary to reason. It is evident, therefore, that as virtue becomes more perfect in someone, the *fomes peccati* also becomes weaker in him. Since Christ's virtue was utterly perfect, it follows that there was no *fomes peccati* in him."[41] The relationship between reason and passion in Christ, then, is not something unique to a God-man, but rather the full flourishing of human nature. The virtuous experience the same thing—albeit imperfectly and without complete constancy, since the *fomes peccati*

39. See Peter Lombard, *Sententiae* III 30.8.

40. *ST* III 15.2 ad 3. See also Gondreau, *Passions of Christ's Soul,* 350–64. As Gondreau suggests, given what Aquinas holds about the power of demons to influence human imagination (*ST* I-II 80.2), Aquinas would seem to classify such temptation as exterior, and therefore something Christ could experience (Gondreau, *Passions of Christ's Soul,* 356–57).

41. *ST* III 15.2.

can never be completely eradicated from wounded human nature.[42] "Christ had absolutely no disordered desires," not because he was less human, but because he was more human.[43]

Christ's Natural Affections and God's Will

After the clarification that Christ's passions were ruled by reason in a way that did not destroy their spontaneity, another question remains. Is there any way in which Christ's passions were drawn to objects that were not fully endorsed by reason's judgment? For instance, did Jesus ever desire something he knew he should not choose?

Aquinas answers with an emphatic affirmative. This emerges especially when he considers episodes from the life of Christ, particularly when the devil tempts Christ to change stones into bread and when Christ prays in the Garden of Gethsemane.[44] While discussing Christ's prayer for the preservation of his life in Gethsemane, Aquinas writes, "He wanted to show that it is permissible for a man to want on the level of natural affection something that God does not will."[45] Reason's penetration of Christ's passions did not prevent his passions from desiring something that would have been inappropriate for him to seek. Still, it did prevent his passions from tugging so forcefully toward inappropriate objects that it became difficult for him to resist: "In Christ, neither the divine will, nor the will of reason, was hindered or impeded by the natural will, or the appetite of sensuality."[46] He makes an even stronger claim in the *Compendium theologiae:* "Christ's soul could desire something in its higher part that it shrank from in its lower part, and yet there was no conflict of appetites in him or rebellion of the flesh against the spirit, such as occurs in us owing to the fact that the lower appetite exceeds the judgment and measure of reason."[47] Aquinas asserts there was never any conflict between Christ's appetites, despite the apparent evidence to the contrary in the tension implicit in Christ as he prays in the garden.

There are two objections to the internal coherence of Aquinas's position. The first objection is that it does not make sense for passions supposedly informed by reason to desire an inappropriate object, that is, something ir-

42. *ST* I-II 74.3 ad 2.
43. *ST* III 7.2 ad 3.
44. See *ST* III 18.1, 18.5–6, 21.2, 21.4 ad 1, 41.
45. *ST* III 21.2.
46. *ST* III 18.6.
47. *Compendium theologiae,* trans. Cyril Vollert, modified, 232.

rational. It would be a contradiction in terms. On one level, this objection stands: if the passions desire something irrational, they cannot be said to be guided by reason. However, it is important to distinguish the sense in which the object of Christ's passions could be something inappropriate or irrational. While it would be contrary to reason to have a large meal before some medical tests, instead of observing the required fast, it would not be contrary to reason to desire food while keeping the fast. In fact, it might seem odd if someone kept the medical fast without desiring to eat. Similarly, while it might be contrary to reason to criticize publicly a powerful tyrant after he imprisons an innocent family member, it would not be contrary to reason to feel anger and to desire justice. The criterion for the rationality of a passion is not some calculus of utility with respect to some ultimate objective determined by reason, such that a passion may be deemed rational only if it directly assists the attainment of this ultimate objective. *The criterion for the rationality of a passion is the passion itself.* Every appetitive movement expresses a natural inclination toward some *telos*, and this inclination, which has its origin in God, is the measure against which it is judged.[48] The extent to which a passion is in accord with the sense appetite's *telos* is the extent to which that passion can be said to be in accord with reason. For example, when someone takes pleasure in something bad or when someone is sad about something good, we conclude that there is something irrational at work, because the sense appetite is not functioning according to its God-given nature.[49] We do not, however, judge that there is something

48. The normativity of natural inclination does not obviate the need for reason's assistance in sorting out what exactly constitutes the *telos* of some innate instinct. Aquinas acknowledges that our inclinations and desires have been distorted by original sin. So reason can be necessary to discern which appetitive movements express our authentic inclinations and which do not, in a way that would never have been necessary for Adam or Christ. Nonetheless, this sorting of authentic and inauthentic desires remains a question of epistemology, not metaphysics. The question is not how do we determine what is morally good or morally bad, but rather how do we come to know with certainty the nature of our desires. We can come to an incorrect conclusion about the status of a particular desire without undermining the principle that our natural inclinations are morally normative. Furthermore, even in our fallen condition, the experience of desire and passion itself has something to contribute to the process of discerning our authentic desires. It is not something that the fallen human person should or even could conduct from deductive logic alone.

49. "If something saddening or painful is present, it is good if someone becomes sad or feels pain because of it. For if someone does not become sad or feel pain in the presence of an evil, either he does not feel it, or he is not count it as something repugnant, and, obviously, both possibilities are evils. Consequently, it is good that sadness or pain follows from the presence of an evil" (*ST* I-II 39.1).

wrong when a passion is directed toward an appropriate object—say, anger at an injustice—even if, for whatever reason, it would be completely inappropriate to act on it.

This argument might seem to undermine the need for reason to regulate passion. If passion is its own measure of rationality, why bother with reason? Why check the passions against any external standard? The answer is that part of any passion's *telos* is the service of reason. Sometimes a passion moves toward a goal that reason approves, so that the passion attains its immediate objective and serves reason at the same time. Other times, however, the lower appetite must give way to the higher appetite. Even though this seems to involve a rejection of the lower appetite's *telos,* such deference is not counter to its nature, since the lower appetite naturally inclines to serve the higher one. The passions are "born to obey reason," as discussed earlier in chapter 4, and in consequence a certain resignation about not reaching their own proper ends when trumped by reason is integral to the nature and *telos* of the passions.

This first objection to the internal coherence of Aquinas's account of Christ's passions forces an important clarification: when we say that a passion is evoked by an inappropriate object, it is important to distinguish between different senses of the word "appropriate." On the most obvious level, we judge an object inappropriate if it does not serve the goals of the human person taken as a whole. Nonetheless, a passion that is evoked by an object that is inappropriate on this level might be deeply appropriate on a more basic level, even though this passion should not supplant the judgment of reason in determining what is to be done.

The second objection to the coherence of Aquinas's position relates to his claim that there is an absence of conflict between Christ's appetites. The objection is straightforward: if Aquinas acknowledges that Christ's appetites incline toward different things—that in the Garden of Gethsemane he desires both to preserve his life and to accomplish the Father's will—then it is patently obvious that there is conflict between his appetites.

It seems possible, however, to muster an answer to this objection from within Aquinas's system, even though it is true that Aquinas does not do so himself.[50] Clearly Aquinas does not claim that Christ was absolutely free

50. After examining this sort of objection, Paul Gondreau does not seem as optimistic about the resources of Aquinas's position: he concludes that Aquinas does not adequately justify his

from inner conflict; he readily acknowledges that Christ desired contradictory things simultaneously. His point seems to be that Christ's divergent desires did not rupture Christ's interior harmony, and it was in this sense that there was no conflict between his appetites. He writes: "For if a man wants one thing on the level of the intellectual appetite, and another thing on the level of the sense appetite, there is not any contradiction in this—unless the sense appetite is so strong that it prevails and alters, or at least impedes, the rational appetite, for in that case something of the contrary motion of the sense appetite reaches the rational will."[51] As discussed above, the *telos* of the sense appetite includes the service of reason. Even though Christ's love of his own life is in conflict with his mission, there remains an even deeper harmony between his lower and higher appetites, insofar as his sense appetite accepts the priority of his rational appetite.

Ultimately, Aquinas's position hangs on there being a difference between desiring something and being tempted by it, or, as J.-H. Nicolas puts it, between experiencing a good as desirable and actually desiring it.[52] The internal coherence of his account of Christ's affectivity stands or falls on whether this distinction is granted. If we acknowledge that there is a difference between desiring some good and being actively drawn to act according to that desire against our better judgment, then the coherence of Aquinas's account of Christ's passions stands. And while it might be debatable, this distinction does seem reasonable: for example, a married man might find a woman attractive without being tempted to commit adultery.

Beatific Knowledge and Christ's Affectivity

Christ's beatific knowledge of God presents a challenge to Aquinas's attempts to maintain Christ's solidarity with humanity, since this beatific knowledge causes constant supernatural joy to an extent far beyond any ordinary affective phenomena. Aquinas attempts to solve this problem by isolating the experience of beatific joy to Christ's intellectual appetite. He acknowledges that it might seem that such joy would make it impossible

claim that there is no conflict between Christ's appetites. See Gondreau, *Passions of Christ's Soul,* 309–17.

51. *ST* III 18.6.

52. Jean-Hervé Nicolas, *Synthèse domatique: De la Trinité à la Trinité* (Fribourg: Éditions Universitaires, 1985), 407–8.

for Christ to suffer, since the soul's joy normally overflows to the body, and since this beatific joy is immense.[53] But by a special exercise of divine power, Aquinas claims, Christ prevented the normal process of overflow: "By a dispensation of divine power, the pleasure of divine contemplation remained in the mind of Christ, and did not flow into the sense powers, which would have prevented the experience of any sensible pain."[54] Aquinas goes on to explain that this divine dispensation made it possible for Christ to experience sorrow as well. Presumably it is also what made it possible for Christ to experience finite joys, or even to do anything at all, rather than just being completely absorbed in his beatific knowledge, though Aquinas does not directly address this question.

Another consequence of Christ's beatific vision is that Christ did not have the theological virtues of faith and hope. He did not have faith, because "from the first instance of his conception, Christ had the full vision of God in his essence."[55] Moreover, except in a limited sense of hoping for what he had not yet obtained, like the immortality and glory of his body, Christ did not have theological hope either, since through hope "someone waits with longing for what one does not yet have," and he was already in possession of the vision of God's essence.[56]

Aquinas's affirmation that the earthly Christ possessed beatific knowledge of God introduces substantial discontinuity between Christ's affectivity and ours. Beyond the experience of beatific joy itself, which far exceeds any ordinary human experience, certain problems are introduced along with the special divine dispensation that Aquinas claims must exist to keep the beatific joy shut up in Christ's intellectual appetite. The affirmation of this divine dispensation implies that Christ's affections do not operate according to their nature, insofar as the affections of the will do not fully engage the passions of the sense appetite. This disengagement is foreign to human experience. It is also of questionable coherency with the rest of Aquinas's account. Throughout the *Treatise on the Passions* and elsewhere, Aquinas describes a kind of interpenetration of sense appetite and intellectual ap-

53. Torrell discusses Aquinas's account of the crucified Christ experiencing some kind of joy even in the midst of his agony. See Jean-Pierre Torrell, *Le Christ en ses mysteres: La vie et l'oeuvre de Jésus selon saint Thomas d'Aquin*, vol. 2 (Paris: Desclée, 1999), 330–39.

54. *ST* III 15.6. See also *ST* III 14.1 ad 2, 15.5 ad 3, 15.10, 46.7–8.

55. *ST* III 7.3.

56. *ST* III 7.4.

petite. Although they are different faculties, they do not operate independently. In his discussion of Christ's passions, however, Aquinas isolates the operation of the different appetites, something he does nowhere else in his account of human affectivity, in order to resolve the difficulties presented by Christ's beatific knowledge.

The implications of Christ's beatific knowledge, and the contrasts between Christ's affectivity and ours, become clearer in his discussion of selected passions. Whereas Aquinas indicates that sorrow in us sometimes involves the intellectual appetite,[57] he maintains that Christ's sorrow was only in the sense appetite.[58] Similarly, since fear normally involves an element of uncertainty, Aquinas argues that Christ's knowledge of the future prevented him from experiencing fear in the same way we do,[59] so he experienced fear in only a qualified sense. Although Aquinas does not discuss Christ's joy, it seems that, by the logic of his system, Christ had even less room to experience human joy than he did to experience human suffering. Since joy is movement of the intellectual appetite, and since any finite joy of his earthly life would be swallowed up and overwhelmed by his beatific joy, it does not seem that it would be possible for Christ to experience ordinary human joy. Even if movements of pleasure in his sense appetite registered in his consciousness, such pleasure, by definition, would not be joy.

Aquinas's strategy for making sense of Christ's beatific knowledge introduces significant discontinuities between Christ's affectivity and ours. His approach does not just jeopardize his affirmation of the authenticity Christ's humanity. It also creates problems for his account of ordinary human affectivity, because it isolates the movements of the different appetites from each other. His discussion of the differences between appetites in Christ reifies them in a way that his discussions of general human affectivity do not. By claiming that it is conceivable that the appetites could function without affecting the movements of the other, even if only in the case of Christ, Aquinas atomizes the faculties of the human person in a way that belies the com-

57. *ST* I-II 35.7; *ST* II-II 84.9 ad 2. See also DeYoung, "Aquinas on *Acedia*," 182n30.

58. *ST* III 15.6. Boyd Taylor Coolman argues that this position is a deficiency of Aquinas's Christology, and he contrasts Aquinas with Alexander of Hales on this point. For example, in contrast to Aquinas, in *Quaestiones disputatae "antequam esset frater"* 16.2.3.48, Alexander of Hales affirms that Christ suffered in the superior part of his reason. See Coolman, "The Salvific Affectivity of Christ According to Alexander of Hales," *Thomist* 71 (2007): 19–21, 29–31.

59. *ST* III 15.7.

plexity of human affectivity and undermines his general theory of affectivity.

It is telling that in his earlier writings Aquinas holds that Christ experienced physical pain only in his body and denies that he felt it in his soul. Later, after more reflection, Aquinas argues that it would have been impossible for Christ to experience pain in his body without also feeling it in the soul, thus arriving at a more plausible account of Christ's humanity.[60] Similarly, his account of Christ's fear also undergoes some development: at first he claims that Christ's fear could originate only in bodily pain, but later he expands his understanding of fear to accommodate other possible triggers.[61] Aquinas's initial reluctance to attribute suffering to Christ's soul suggests that he has a strong theological instinct against the idea that suffering could enter into the depths of Christ's being. He seems more willing to err on the side of diminishing Christ's solidarity with humanity than to risk betraying what he sees as the necessary implications of his divinity.

The affirmation of Christ's beatific knowledge raises significant challenges to Aquinas's attempt to offer a fully realistic account of Christ's humanity. But regardless of the merits of Aquinas's position on Christ's beatific knowledge,[62] the elements of discontinuity between Christ's affectivity and ours derive from his understanding of the metaphysical implications of Christ's divinity, and not from any uneasiness about attributing ordinary human experiences to Christ.

Christ's Prayer in the Garden

Historically, Christ's prayer in the Garden of Gethsemane has been an important locus of Christological speculation.[63] Aquinas's analysis of the event

60. Compare *Scriptum super libros Sententiarum* III 15.2.3 sol 1–2 with *Compendium theologiae* 232 and *ST* III 15.6. See Gondreau, *Passions of Christ's Soul*, 380–88.

61. Compare *Scriptum super libros Sententiarum* III 15.2.2 sol 3 with *ST* III 15.7. See Gondreau, *Passions of Christ's Soul*, 409–10.

62. For an illuminating exchange about whether the earthly Christ possessed the beatific vision and a basic summary of what is at stake, see Thomas Joseph White, "The Voluntary Action of the Earthly Christ and the Necessity of the Beatific Vision," *Thomist* 69 (2005): 497–534, and Thomas G. Weinandy, "The Beatific Vision and the Incarnate Son: Furthering the Discussion," *Thomist* 70 (2006): 605–15. For sympathetic discussion of Aquinas's affirmation of Christ's beatific knowledge, see Mansini, "Christ's Immediate Knowledge of God." For critical discussion of Aquinas's position, see Gondreau, *Passions of Christ's Soul*, 441–52, and Torrell, "La science du Christ," 198–213.

63. See Matthew 26:36–44, Mark 14:32–39, and Luke 22:40–46.

prompts some important clarifications about Christ's affectivity.[64] In order to make sense of Christ's desire to be spared his crucifixion, Aquinas employs a threefold distinction in Christ's willing, partly derived from John Damascene and others: the will of sensuality (*voluntas sensualitatis*), the will-as-nature (*voluntas ut natura*), and the will-as-reason (*voluntas ut ratio*).[65] The will of sensuality is another expression for sense appetite. The latter two kinds of willing relate to the intellectual appetite. The will-as-nature refers to the intellectual appetite in its natural inclination toward unspecified good. The will-as-reason refers to the intellectual appetite insofar as it has been specified by choice toward a determinate end. Aquinas uses this threefold distinction to describe the psychological dynamics underlying Christ's prayer in Gethsemane:

> Christ permitted all the powers of his soul to act in their own normal ways. Now it is evident that the will of sensuality naturally shrinks from sensible pain and bodily wounding. Similarly, the will-as-nature rejects what is contrary to nature, and what is evil in itself, like death and other such things. However, the will-as-reason can choose such things in order to attain some end. For example, on the level of the will-as-reason, some ordinary man might choose to be cauterized for health reasons, even while his sensuality and his will-as-nature shrink from being burned.[66]

On the basis of this threefold distinction, Aquinas argues that Christ's prayer in Gethsemane expresses his will of sensuality and his will-as-nature, but not his will-as-reason.[67] This has important consequences for Aquinas's account of human affectivity more generally. In analyzing Christ's prayer in this way, Aquinas explicitly affirms that some of our desires are unchosen movements of the intellectual appetite. In other words, it is possible for an affection of the will to be independent of the exercise of free choice. This point is implicit in his anthropology, but nowhere else does he elaborate on

64. For a discussion of Christ's affectivity in the Garden of Gethsemane, see Paul Gondreau, "St. Thomas Aquinas, the Communication of Idioms, and the Suffering of Christ in the Garden of Gethsemane," in *Divine Impassibility and the Mystery of Human Suffering*, ed. James F. Keating and Thomas Joseph White (Grand Rapids, Mich.: Eerdmans Press, 2009), 214–45.

65. *ST* III 18.2–3. See also John Damascene, *De fide orthodoxa* 2.22–23. Damascene himself relies on Maximus and Nemesius. For a discussion of Aquinas's sources for this threefold distinction in kinds of Christ's willing, see Gondreau, *Passions of Christ's Soul*, 309–17.

66. *ST* III 18.5.

67. *ST* III 21.3.

it with such clarity. In any case, Aquinas's consideration of the agony in the garden shows that Aquinas does not limit his account of Christ's affectivity to consideration of his passions; it also includes consideration of the affections of his will.

Aquinas's analysis of Christ's prayer is difficult to reconcile with his claim that Christ experienced the beatific vision in his soul. Aquinas explicitly affirms that the will-as-nature and the will-as-reason are not separate faculties: they are rather the same psychological faculty considered under its propensity to different sorts of appetitive movements.[68] Since Christ had beatific knowledge in his human soul, and since his intellectual appetite was moved to beatific joy in consequence, it is difficult to see how there is room on the level of Christ's will for anything not in complete harmony with the will-as-reason. One solution to this difficulty might be to designate different levels of the will, with different sorts of movements of the will correlating with each different level, and then to locate the beatific joy at the highest level of the will. Such a solution is not unworkable within his system, but it does present some drawbacks. Aquinas's understanding of rational appetite would have to be revised in order to accommodate a hierarchical ordering of the will's movements, where each different sort of movement is generically different from the others, and such revision would undermine his understanding of the will as a single, non-reducible power of the soul. Another solution is to reconsider the claim that Christ experienced the beatific vision of God in his human soul during his earthly life.

Christ as the Salvific Exemplar of Human Affectivity

Aquinas's primary reason for affirming the authenticity of Christ's humanity is his belief that it has been revealed by God, and taught by the Gospels and the Church. But he also offers reasons why it was fitting, in view of his salvific mission, for Christ to be fully human in every respect. Aquinas lists three soteriological reasons that explain why Christ assumed the weaknesses of our present condition. He writes, "Christ took our defects upon himself to make amends for us, to prove the truth of his human nature, and to become an example of virtue for us."[69] He frequently invokes these three

68. *ST* III 18.3.
69. *ST* III 15.1. See also *ST* III 14.4 ad 2.

reasons to explain the fittingness of various aspects of Christ's affectivity.

The first set of reasons concerns Christ's satisfaction for sin. In discussing why Christ needed to assume a human intellect, Aquinas cites the patristic axiom that "what is not assumed is not able to be healed."[70] The same applies to other aspects of Christ's human nature, including the passions: they are assumed in order that Christ might heal them. Furthermore, since satisfaction requires suffering, and suffering requires weakness and vulnerability, it is necessary that Christ experience human weakness, and thus that Christ assume a human nature in which he can experience pain, sorrow, and fear.[71] At the same time, there are some weaknesses that are not helpful to the work of redemption, and these are not assumed.[72] For this reason, for instance, Christ is sinless, and does not even experience the *fomes peccati*, since the weakness and imperfection of sin and interior temptation would only obstruct the work of redemption. Furthermore, it is not just the assumption of weakness that makes reparation possible, but also Christ's fullness of grace and virtue.[73] Aquinas summarizes the synergy between Christ's perfections and weaknesses in the following passage:

> Satisfaction for another's sin has for its quasi-matter the punishments that one sustains for the sin. But the principle of such satisfaction is the *habitus* of the soul that leads one to want to make satisfaction for another. It is from this principle that satisfaction has its efficacy, for satisfaction is efficacious only because it flows from charity, as it will be explained later. And therefore it was necessary for Christ's soul to be perfect regarding the *habitus* of knowledge and virtue, so that he would have the inner capacity to make satisfaction, and for Christ's body to be subject to infirmities, so that he would not lack the matter of satisfaction.[74]

In this passage, Aquinas draws attention to the importance of Christ's charitable affect in the work of redemption. While emphasizing the salvific importance of Christ's charity during his passion may seem like an obvious

70. *ST* III 5.4. In the text Aquinas cites this axiom as part of a longer quotation from John Damascene, *De fide orthodoxa* 3.6.

71. *ST* III 14.1.

72. Aquinas writes: "He took upon himself our defects for salvific reasons, so that he could make satisfaction for our sin, not because such defects were due to him. And therefore it was not necessary that he take upon himself all of our defects, but only those which sufficed to make satisfaction for the sin of the entirety of human nature" (*ST* III 14.4 ad 2).

73. *ST* III 14.4, 15.1–2.

74. *ST* III 14.1 ad 1.

move, it represents a significant shift in focus from Anselm's theory of salvation.[75]

The second set of reasons concerns the credibility of Christ's humanity. Aquinas argues that it was important for Christ to share in the weakness of the human condition in order to make his humanity credible, an argument originally made by Peter Lombard.[76] Aquinas frames the principle as follows: "Since human nature is known to us only as subject to these bodily defects, if the Son of God had assumed human nature without them, he would not seem to be truly human, nor to have true flesh, but only imaginary flesh."[77] This sort of argument carries with it some questionable suppositions about the sheer possibility of assuming human nature without being subject to the ordinary range of passions, but this should not be seen as implying that Aquinas thinks it is possible to be human without being susceptible to passions. It is evident from the rest of his anthropology and Christology that he sees the passions as integral to human nature, and the argument from credibility was a standard argument in Aquinas's time (which indicates once again how much Aquinas's theological milieu was suspicious of making Christ's affectivity seem too much like ours). He is simply making use of whatever arguments he can to strengthen his affirmation of a strong similarity between Christ's passions and our passions.

The third set of reasons concerns the salvific example given by Christ. Aquinas holds that Christ assumed ordinary human affectivity for our instruction. This emerges especially in his threefold explanation of why Christ prayed in Gethsemane in the way that he did: "First, he wanted to show that he had assumed a true human nature, with all its natural affections. Second, he wanted to show that it is permissible for a man to want something on the level of natural affection that God does not will. Third, he wanted to show that man should submit his own affection to the divine will."[78] Christ shows us what virtuous affectivity looks like, and therefore what it looks like to be truly human, so that we can imitate him, both by striving for vir-

75. On this point and for a study of satisfaction in Aquinas's soteriology, see Romanus Cessario, *The Godly Image: Christ and Salvation in Catholic Thought from Anselm to Aquinas* (Petersham, Mass.: St. Bede's Publications, 1990). For an overview of satisfaction in medieval theology, see J. Patout Burns, "The Concept of Satisfaction in Medieval Redemption Theory," *Theological Studies* 36 (1975): 285–304.

76. See Peter Lombard, *Sententiae* III 15.1.

77. *ST* III 14.1.

78. *ST* III 21.2.

tue and by accepting as fully compatible with virtue—and even necessary for virtue—those aspects of human affectivity that otherwise might seem like moral imperfections. In this way, Christ's human affectivity helps bring about our salvation. Aquinas maintains that his passion provides a particularly salvific example of virtuous affectivity.[79]

Aquinas takes the instructive role of Christ's affectivity seriously, and often adverts to it in his evaluation of the passions. For instance, in the *Prima secundae,* he argues that sorrow must be compatible with virtue, because Christ experienced sorrow in the Garden of Gethsemane.[80] In the *De malo,* he argues that anger is not always sinful, because Christ was angry.[81] The influence is not unidirectional: as discussed above, his evaluation of Christ's affectivity relies on his theory of the passions. At one point, for example, he argues that Christ could experience anger, because anger is praiseworthy when reasonably ordered.[82] Furthermore, as discussed above, wrestling with Christ's passions and affections seems to have forced Aquinas to clarify his account of human affectivity in certain respects. In particular, his reflection on Christ seems to have led him to a deeper appreciation of the need for a distinction between affections of the sense appetite and affections of the intellectual appetite; a more precise articulation of the goodness of the passions even when it would be inappropriate to act upon them; and a distinction between will-as-nature and will-as-reason, which he finds necessary to understand Christ's prayer in the garden.

Aquinas's account of human affectivity cannot be separated from his theology of Christ's affectivity. They are in dialogue with each other, and each reinforces the other's positive evaluation of affectivity. For Aquinas, Christ is the model and exemplar of graced human affectivity, and therefore of human affectivity in general, and yet, in order to understand Christ, it is necessary to reflect on human experience, not just sacred Scripture.

79. Aquinas discusses the salvific quality of the example of virtue given by Christ's passion in *ST* III 46.3–4.

80. *ST* I-II 59.3.

81. *De malo* 12.1 sc 4.

82. *ST* III 15.9.

CHAPTER 8

A Preliminary Evaluation of Aquinas on Emotion

The previous chapters have sought to present and analyze Aquinas's account of the emotions and probe its internal coherence. This chapter will discuss how it might be deployed in contemporary conversation about the philosophy and theology of emotion. It will propose that Aquinas's category of affection corresponds to the category of emotion, and therefore Aquinas's account of affection should be seen as Aquinas's account of emotion. Then it will offer a preliminary evaluation of Aquinas's account of emotion.

Affection and Emotion

Aquinas classifies psychological phenomena such as desire, joy, sadness, fear, anger, and hope as affections, and, when he is more specific, as either passions of the soul or intellectual affections. Since these psychological phenomena are today classified as emotions, it seems at first glance that there is a clear correspondence between Aquinas's category of affection and the contemporary category of emotion.

However, those who hold that emotion includes cognition or perception might object to this interpretation. They might argue that, for Aquinas, only affection together with cognition constitutes emotion.[1] Although Aqui-

1. For precisely this reason, Claudia Eisen Murphy does not identify passions with emotions. She holds that, in the light of contemporary discussion of emotion, passion combined with its proximate cognitive together constitute emotion. She writes: "Now most contemporary philosophers interested in the emotions have argued, and I tend to agree, that 'emotions,' whatever else they involve, involve at least cognitive states. So Aquinas's passions, don't, on their own, constitute emotions. But because it is a necessary condition for the occurrence of a passion that there be evaluative cognition of an object, it turns out that Aquinas's passions, taken together with their proximate cognitive cause, make up a complex that could match our understanding of 'emotions'" (Eisen Murphy, "Responsibility for Our Emotions," 168).

nas excludes any cognitive element from the passions and affections themselves, because he holds that movements of the sense appetite and rational appetite necessarily depend on cognition (cognition being taken as including perception), particular passions and affections cannot be considered as fully describing the psychological phenomena now identified as emotions.

This alternative interpretation of Aquinas cannot be sustained. It implies that what we call joy and what Aquinas calls joy are two different things: that when we talk about joy, we are talking about a mental and physiological state that includes both a feeling dimension and a cognitive dimension, but when Aquinas talks about joy, he is talking about only the feeling dimension of joy. However, Aquinas does not think he is talking about only part of the phenomenon of joy: he thinks he has fully described joy in classifying it as an affection and a movement of appetite. So to say that for Aquinas affection does not constitute emotion on its own does not take him seriously enough on his own terms. Aquinas thinks he is talking about anger when he describes it as a passion, and he thinks he distinguishes anger from the apprehension of the intentional object that causes the anger. What grounds do we have on which to claim that, on Aquinas's account, the passion of anger is not really the emotion of anger but only half of it? It is much more reasonable to conclude that Aquinas excludes any element of cognition or perception from the internal structure of emotion.

It is a distortion to claim that Aquinas's account of emotion should be understood to include affection's cognitive cause as well as affection itself. In fact, careful consideration of his writings should lead to the exact opposite conclusion. It is fair to say that Aquinas's account of emotion is wrong, but it is not fair to say that when he talks about joy, he really means to talk about only the feeling aspect of joy. There are many strands of his account that are amenable to cognitivist theories, but he cannot be cited as an early advocate of either cognitive or perceptual theories without extensive eisegesis.

Moreover, there are some advantages in making a sharp distinction between cognition and appetite while maintaining their essential unity of operation. First, the distinction between cognition and appetite allows more precision in the way we talk about emotion and its relation to knowledge. For example, we often make a conceptual distinction between the feelings associated with anger and the perceptions and rational judgments involved in that anger, even when they are experienced simultaneously. If emotion is defined as encompassing cognition as well as affectivity, then another term is needed to describe the affective or feeling dimension of emotion, and yet another term is needed to describe the cognitive dimension of emotion. So that means we now have three categories: emotion, emotional feeling, and emotional cognition. While there are certain advantages to defining emotion in this way, especially insofar as it emphasizes the importance of cognition for emotion, it seems like a needless multiplication of categories. Having only two essential categories, emotion and cognition, allows for more clarity and precision in the discussion of emotional phenomena.

Second, it is more natural for us to speak about emotion as a response to some kind of cognitive appraisal, rather than as something that includes both cognitive appraisal and its associated response. It fits better with ordinary conversation about emotion. When someone says, "I feel angry" or "I am afraid" or "I am sad," we understand what is meant, even when we do not know why the person feels this way. We presume that there are reasons, conscious or otherwise, and we may immediately ask what they might be, but inquiring about the reasons is another question and a different question. "How are you feeling?" and "Why do you feel that way?" are getting at two different realities.

Third, when a sharp distinction is drawn between emotion and cognition, it is easy to account for the common experience of seemingly identical cognitive appraisals resulting in very different emotional responses. For example, when we are tired or hungry, we are more likely to respond with irritation to ordinary stimuli. Aquinas can account for this possibility easily: he can say that the physiological dimension of the sense appetite has been affected by fatigue, and so its response to stimuli is exaggerated. A strict cognitivist account must claim that somehow the cognitive powers themselves have been affected by fatigue and are actually making a different cognitive appraisal of the stimuli. While this sort of explanation is defensible, it requires cognition to work in a certain way. Aquinas's account does not require anything about how cognition works: for Aquinas, any given cognitive appraisal may or may not be affected by physiology, and either way his account stands. But a strict cognitivist account cannot stand if it turns out that some cognitive appraisals, however few, are not affected by physiology and yet are still associated with different emotional responses.

The tendency of contemporary philosophers to refer to emotions as mental states contributes to the tendency to see Aquinas's account of emotion as including his account of cognition as well as his account of affection. The idea of a mental state can seem like a mental snapshot, as though it refers to the entirety of an individual's interior dispositions and activity at some particular instant of time (at least those that concern the mental phenomenon in question). So, for those who categorize emotions as mental states, it is natural to conclude that, in order to reconstruct Aquinas's account of emotion, it is necessary to synthesize his account of both affection and cognition. And Aquinas would certainly affirm that the mental state of an angry person—in this sense of a mental snapshot—involves both affection and cognition. However, he would also affirm that the anger itself does not involve the operation of a cognitive power, even though it responds to cognition.[2]

Emotions, Affective Dispositions, and Passions of the Body

Two important questions remain about the category of emotion in Aquinas's account. First, what is the status of affective *habitus*? These dispositions are intrinsically related to appetitive movements and yet are not appetitive movements themselves. They do not need to be activated to exist. For example, affective dispositions clearly perdure even in those who are comatose—when they wake up, they retain the same character traits, unless there is significant brain damage—and yet we would not want to say that the comatose experience emotions, at least in any normal sense. Moreover, for Aquinas, affective dispositions and affections are not just different realities: affective dispositions are defined in terms of their relationship to affec-

2. The possibility of such confusion in interpreting Aquinas suggests that there might be something inadequate with the conception of emotion as a mental state. In ordinary conversation, we do not speak about particular emotions as though they describe the entirety of an individual's relevant dispositions and activity. We speak about emotions as phenomena that subjects experience without being fully defined by them. "I am angry" implies that there is a subject of the anger who in some sense "possesses" the anger and that is "other" to the anger. The fact that our way of speaking about emotion implies some distance from subject and emotion, and that the subject's "possessing" of the emotion is distinct from the emotion itself, suggests that viewing emotions as mental states is problematic. If a mental state is understood to refer to the entirety of an individual's relevant interior dispositions and activities at some moment in time, and our way of speaking about an emotion excludes the "possessing" of the emotion, then to say that emotions are mental states is to claim more for emotions than ordinary conversation can justify. It seems preferable to distinguish between emotions and emotional states, and to say that emotions are components of mental states, while emotional states are kinds of mental states.

tions. So if affections are emotions, then to say that affective dispositions are also emotions would imply that affections are affective dispositions, which is absurd. For this reason, while it is not possible to understand Aquinas's account of emotion without reference to affective dispositions, the categories of *habitus*, virtue, and vice should not be correlated with the contemporary category of emotion. They can be called emotional dispositions, but not emotions.

However, the line between affective disposition and emotion can be blurry when considering, say, people prone to excessive fear. Such persons can seem not only disposed to react fearfully but also to be in a constant state of fear. In extreme cases, it seems as though their entire experience of the world is shaped by fear. So it does not seem adequate to describe their psychological state as simply being disposed toward excessively fearful reactions. But this seeming difficulty stems from a notion of *habitus* as static and frozen, as opposed to an understanding that sees a more dynamic interplay between the potency of *habitus* and the actuality of individual appetitive movements. In Aquinas's account, habitually anxious persons are not simply disposed to react toward stimuli with excessive fear: they are constantly reacting, perhaps in very subtle ways, to intentional objects that they see as threats to their well-being. This continuous stream of emotion is distinct from its corresponding *habitus* but still depends on it and, at the same time, constantly affirms and even deepens it. So the case of persons prone to excessive fear does not call into question the nonidentity of affective dispositions with emotions.

Second, if we conclude, as seems reasonable, that in his mature thought Aquinas still distinguishes between *passiones corporalis* and *passiones animalis,* what is the status of the passions of the body vis-à-vis the category of emotion? Ordinary conversation unambiguously distinguishes between physical sensations and emotions. Physical sensations are not considered emotions. Emotions are intentional, but physical sensations are not: we are angry "at" someone, but we have physical pain "in" a part of our body. Since we do not consider nonintentional physical sensations to be emotions, and since such physical sensations are considered *passiones corporalis* by Aquinas, the passions of the body should not be considered emotions either. Nonetheless, physical sensations are often closely connected to emotions in ways that are difficult to untangle. For example, an itch is a physical sensation, but it quickly gives rise to the desire to scratch it. For Aquinas, an itch is a passion of the body, but the desire to scratch the itch is a passion of the soul.

In summary, when Aquinas's account of emotion is put into conversation with contemporary theories, Aquinas should be seen as advocating a theory of emotion that equates emotion with intentional feeling, views emotion as intrinsically dependent on cognition (including perception) and usually but not necessarily involving the body, and limits emotion's extension to discrete psychological events, thus excluding long-term affective dispositions from being considered emotions (but not moods, as long as a mood is understood as a more or less continuous series of similar emotions). Does this make Aquinas a cognitivist or a noncognitivist? The conceptual markers of feeling and cognition are not very helpful when it comes to classifying Aquinas, as seems to be increasingly the case when it comes to classifying contemporary philosophers of emotion as well.

With this understanding of the shape of Aquinas's concept of emotion, it is now possible to turn to a discussion of its merits. While a comprehensive evaluation of Aquinas's account of emotion is beyond the scope of this study, the following overview should suffice to sketch its enduring relevance to the philosophy and theology of emotion, as well as some of its most significant lacunae.

The Nature of Desire

The prominence that Aquinas gives to the theme of appetite from beginning to end of the *Summa theologiae* is one of the most outstanding features of his metaphysics and his anthropology. His concept of appetite, anchored in his understanding of the nature of being itself, gives a metaphysical foundation to the psychology of human emotion that is absent from many other accounts. He takes seriously the simple notion that all created being tends toward its *telos* by the appetite implanted in it by God (a notion, incidentally, that is fully compatible with evolutionary theory)[3] and then ap-

3. The affirmation of teleology does not imply the rejection of evolution. In fact, evolution presupposes teleology, insofar as evolution is a mechanism oriented toward a *telos*, that is, the survival of the species. Moreover, Aquinas's account of teleology does not require any particular evolutionary theory to affirm evolution in a logically coherent way. Nonetheless, some theories of

plies it to human psychology. In all matters that concern human action, including ethics, the nature of appetite is an indispensable reference point for Aquinas. Since desire and all other forms of emotion are manifestations of appetite, emotion in all its elemental forms is not just tolerable: it is essential to human flourishing.

The essential logic of his position is unassailable from within the Judeo-Christian understanding of creation ex nihilo. In the first chapter of Genesis, God creates the world and calls it good, and then creates man and woman and calls them very good. Consequently, everything constitutive of our nature must be good.

However, human experience seems to contradict this otherwise airtight theological conclusion. We are subject to birth defects, physical infirmities, inner disorder, and various kinds of seemingly pointless suffering, all of which defy classification as good in any obvious sense, and yet seem part and parcel of human nature, or at least the human condition. Since so many human desires lead to destruction and moral evil, appetite seems especially untrustworthy. Furthermore, the doctrine of original sin gives a theological basis for mistrusting the inclinations of human nature after the fall. In the beginning, our nature may have been entirely good, and our desires trustworthy. But since then, human sin has corrupted human nature, and our nature and our inclinations are neither good nor trustworthy any longer. These two factors—the ubiquity of physical suffering and internal disorder and a certain understanding of original sin—are often enough for Christian theologians to conclude that appetite cannot be a reliable measure of ethics or human destiny in a fallen world.

---

evolution, especially those that emphasize convergence, are more complementary. For example, Simon Conway Morris, professor of evolutionary paleobiology at Cambridge University, has argued that, contrary to certain interpretations of evolution, evolutionary outcomes are not necessarily random, in the sense of being entirely dependent on chance circumstances. He musters an array of evidence to show that evolutionary processes often converge at similar outcomes through very different histories. See Conway Morris, *Life's Solution: Inevitable Humans in a Lonely Universe* (Cambridge: Cambridge University Press, 2003).

The convergence interpretation of evolution is especially compatible with Aquinas's account of appetite, since it sees the endpoints of evolution as significantly shaped by biology, and therefore ontology, and not just environment and chance. Consequently, it becomes easier to affirm that evolution is the natural unfolding of the various *appetitus* already present in creation, according to their own inner logic, even while simultaneously affirming that creation is directed toward its various *teloi* by the Author of creation. Evolution is a testable claim about a certain kind of teleology present in the world; Aquinas's account of *appetitus* is a philosophical claim about its metaphysical structure and the origin of this teleology in God.

Aquinas, however, is not ready to give up on the intrinsic goodness of human nature and human appetite in the face of these two concerns. Instead, he applies himself to a careful analysis of original sin that, in keeping with his metaphysics, refuses to give evil any positive existence. His account of original sin can be read as the solution to a puzzle: Aquinas is trying to explain how our experience of appetite can involve distortion and inclination toward evil, without positing anything intrinsically evil within human nature's constitutive elements. As a result, where others see a mysterious inclination toward sin as such, Aquinas sees a mass of desires competing with each other as a "natural" consequence of the loss of divine grace and the internal harmony it coordinated. With this understanding of original sin, Aquinas can defend, on theological grounds, why human appetite remains fundamentally oriented toward the authentic *telos* of the human person even after the fall.

However, the more fundamental challenge to his positive evaluation of human appetite remains: the fact that the experience of disordered desire is inextricably part of our fallen experience of desire. It is possible to accept his account of original sin, but also to see it as useless in any practical sense. In theory, our most basic inclinations may be trustworthy guides to human destiny, but since, according to Aquinas, our subjective experience of desire takes place within a fallen context, the identification of our most basic inclinations is not obvious. How can we abstract the essential structure of desire from an inherently corrupt experience of desire?

The challenge of this difficulty presents a serious epistemological problem for Aquinas's account. However, the gravity of the problem should not lead us to conclude that it is intractable. Aquinas's approach is instructive. Aquinas affirms that the human condition is rife with proclivities toward all kinds of evil, but at the same time he grounds his ethics in our natural inclinations, without any misgivings about the possibility of arriving at the truth about our natural inclinations in our fallen condition. Aquinas does not think that the truth about our natural inclinations is self-evident: he explicitly recognizes that knowledge of the precepts of the natural law, which is intimately connected to knowledge of our natural inclinations, can become lost or obscured.[4] Nevertheless, while he recognizes that knowledge of our natural inclinations cannot be taken for granted, his calm assurance about what they are indicates that he thinks that, with the proper method,

4. *ST* I-II 94.4.

we can indeed arrive at the truth about our natural inclinations without getting caught up in an intractable epistemological quandary.

Aquinas's method of identifying natural inclinations is to analyze the constitutive elements of a given nature, and then see what brings that nature to fulfillment. Since everything that exists, insofar as it exists, is good, and since all being is intrinsically linked to appetite, the task of identifying natural inclinations amounts to observing what something is, and then, on the basis of that observation, coming to a conclusion about what its *telos* must be. A revealing example of his methodology emerges in his argument that animals would have eaten each other even before the fall. Observing that the bodies of some animals are oriented toward the killing and eating of other animals, he argues that, since their predatory qualities are authentic aspects of their nature, they must be good, and cannot have come into existence only as a result of sin.[5] Therefore, he concludes, some animals must have been carnivorous even before the fall. He does not begin with abstract speculation about whether it would be appropriate for animals to kill each other in paradise. He begins with a close examination of what actually exists, trusting that whatever exists comes from God, and therefore, in its essential ontological structure, contains within itself its own measure of goodness.

He brings to bear the same kind of analysis on human nature. He looks at the structural elements of human physiology—for example, the orientations toward food and drink—and concludes that since these material features are intrinsic to human nature, they must be good and correspond to natural inclinations. He also looks at the human intellect, with its structural orientation toward making sense of the world, and concludes that there is a natural inclination toward knowing the truth.[6] Aquinas's philosophical analysis of our natural inclinations is complemented by his theological reflection on Christ's human affectivity. For Aquinas, Christ is a reference point for what human affectivity should look like, and he takes Christ's hu-

5. *ST* I 96.1 ad 2.

6. Aquinas seems to attach particular significance to the animal dimension of the human person when determining what is "natural" to the human person, as when he distinguishes between natural and nonnatural desires (*ST* I-II 30.3). Elsewhere, however, he clarifies that this distinction corresponds to only one meaning of "natural," and that in another sense that which flows from rationality should also be considered natural to the human person (*ST* I-II 31.7; see also *ST* I-II 94.2).

man affectivity as a measure for our own. His meditation on Christ's life as narrated in the Gospels seems to have confirmed his confidence in the trustworthiness of human appetite with all its attendant inclinations.

Although Aquinas does not engage skeptical concerns about the possibility of knowing our natural inclinations, his pre-Cartesian confidence is not easily dismissed. He does not ask much from the skeptic. He maintains that our natural inclinations can be divided into a handful of inclinations, such as the inclinations toward food, reproduction, knowledge of truth, and human society, all of which are difficult to deny as integral characteristics of human nature.[7]

Aquinas does not engage many of the subjective implications of his account, but some interesting conclusions can be drawn. First, because our inclinations are oriented toward the perfection of the human person, they are fundamentally trustworthy. We can discover something about human flourishing by reflecting on our subjective experience of desire. Our experience of desire cannot be taken entirely at face value, due to the possibility of disordered desire and self-deception, but it does provide a legitimate, if incomplete, basis for determining how we should live. Many systems of mo-

7. *ST* I-II 94.2. For a discussion of the various kinds of natural inclinations that Aquinas identifies and their relationship to his ethics, see Pinckaers, *Sources of Christian Ethics*, 408–56.

Skeptics might deny that there are any inclinations constitutive of human nature, or indeed that there is such a thing as human nature. There have been many philosophical movements in the twentieth century that deny the existence of any common human nature. However, their actual claims often fall short of their rhetoric. No one seriously denies that we need food or that we are bound to time and space. Very few would deny that we universally desire friendship and human affection, or that we share other such universal inclinations. They may want to claim that these inclinations can be shaped in different ways—and to an extent Aquinas would agree—or they may want to claim that we should live without reference to these basic inclinations, but that is different from denying the fact of their existence.

Furthermore, all ideologies that run roughshod over human nature sooner or later are shattered by it. For instance, the honest hedonist who lives long enough eventually becomes jaded and finds that his philosophy of life does not satisfy, and often as not destroys his body in the process, because human nature does not thrive on decadence no matter how much someone might wish that it would. Likewise, political or social ideologies that deny some aspect of human nature may thrive for some period of time on the strength of their positive aspects, but eventually the truth about human nature asserts itself and such ideologies fall apart (as happened with the former Soviet Union). Later generations not personally invested in implementing an ideology often find its failures so obviously incompatible with their experience of life that they wonder why it was ever attractive (and so often fail to grasp the real problems that the earlier generations had been reacting against). As Lawrence Donohoo put it in a lecture at the Dominican House of Studies, ideology can lay down pavement over human nature, but sooner or later vegetation starts to come up through the cracks.

rality present a vision of what the virtuous person looks like, and it is left to the individual to figure out how to get there. For example, a certain vision of patience might be presented, with close attention to its various characteristics and requirements. Meanwhile, the practical question of how to become patient is seen as an entirely different question, perhaps belonging to the field of psychology or spirituality. In Aquinas's system, it is not absolutely necessary to know what the finished product looks like in order to flourish; our inclinations provide sufficient guidance of themselves.

Aquinas makes the goodness of appetite the cornerstone of his account of emotion, and he thinks through very carefully all of the implications of doing so. The result is a persuasive and attractive theology of emotion that reconciles a firm affirmation of the goodness of creation with the empirical fact of inner disorder and the theological doctrine of original sin.[8] His understanding of the nature of desire is both realistic and liberating. It adequately accounts for the ubiquitous reality of psychological and moral disorder, while nonetheless affirming that our authentic desires are seconded by God, or rather, that we are seconding what God has first established. He also offers reasons for a qualified optimism, because, for Aquinas, all of our authentic desires contain within themselves God's promise of their fulfillment. The shape of Aquinas's argument is hard to reject within the context of Christian faith. He makes a strong case that such an interpretation of desire is the necessary consequence of affirming the goodness of creation.

Categories of Appetitive Movements

Aquinas's account of emotion includes a variety of categories of appetitive movements. He distinguishes psychological phenomena by their location in the sense appetite or the intellectual appetite. He separates concupiscible passions from irascible passions. He also creates a category of generic affections that have not been specified according to an object and thus have no moral quality. These different categories of appetitive movements give Aquinas the tools to speak about emotion with more precision.

8. The "theology of the body" proposed by Pope John Paul II in a series of papal audiences on the body, sexual desire, and erotic love, seems to have a similar focus: the recovery of the goodness of desire. The attractiveness of this project seems to be a significant factor in the great popularity of these very dense technical lectures. See John Paul II, *Theology of the Body* (Boston: Pauline Books and Media, 1997).

Aquinas's distinction between passions and intellectual affections offers a promising avenue for differentiating between emotional phenomena, especially those that seem to vary in psychic depth.[9] For example, Aquinas argues that joy is different from pleasure, and involves a movement of the intellectual appetite. Within the realm of human experience, it does seem possible to experience something pleasant, perhaps even intensely so, that still lacks some amount of psychic depth. It also seems possible to experience something pleasant that satisfies in a deeper way, even in the midst of something painful. His distinction between passion and intellectual affection offers a promising way to interpret these phenomena: the first case describes pleasure without joy, and the second case describes joy, which may or may not be accompanied by pleasure. Similarly, the possibility of affection without a bodily component makes sense of the common ascription of affections such as love and joy to God and the angels. It also points the way toward imagining what in our experiences might, for instance, correspond to angelic joy.

The faculty psychology that undergirds Aquinas's distinction between passion and intellectual affection is not as popular now as it was in antiquity and the Middle Ages. However, its declining fortunes may stem from subsequent distortions and not any fatal flaw in its essential features. Whatever the ultimate verdict on faculty psychology, its intellectual pedigree goes back to Aristotle, and it has a fair claim to be taken seriously. At its best, faculty psychology provides a way to talk about psychological phenomena while avoiding the messy task of charting exactly how the mechanisms of the human psyche function. It works within our subjective experience of being human, and thematizes different aspects of human psychology from the inside. For example, we have the capacity to think abstractly, and this capacity is named the intellect; we have the capacity to make choices, and this capacity is ascribed to the will. Faculty psychology makes it possible to talk about different psychological phenomena without being committed to any particular explanation of them, beyond some general claims about how

9. There are some interesting parallels in contemporary philosophy of emotion. Nussbaum defends the coherence of imagining emotions without any bodily component; Stocker offers a consideration of the place of what he calls "intellectual desire" and "intellectual emotion" in human experience. See Nussbaum, 59–60, and Michael L. Stocker, "Some Considerations about Intellectual Desire and Emotions," in *Thinking about Feeling: Contemporary Philosophers on Emotion*, ed. Robert C. Solomon (New York: Oxford University Press, 2004), 135–48.

they relate to the basic elements of human nature (e.g., that humans are composed of material and immaterial components, that the sense appetite involves both the body and the soul, etc.). Aquinas identifies the powers of the soul as distinct realities because it makes it easier to talk about various aspects of human experience with precision, not because he thinks that the different powers in their actual operation are ontologically separable from each other.

The danger is that faculty psychology can be taken too literally. A wedge gets driven between the different faculties, so that, for instance, the will is seen to operate independently of the intellect. There is the particular danger of making the distinction between passion and intellectual affection too radical. Human experience is much more fluid than such models would suggest. Aquinas avoids these pitfalls with his frequent attention to the interaction between the different faculties, but other advocates of faculty psychology are not always so scrupulous.

The division of the passions into the concupiscible and the irascible is one of the most important structural features of Aquinas's account of emotion. At first glance, differentiating emotions according to the ease or difficulty of achieving their objective can seem arbitrary. Nonetheless, it holds up when reflecting on human experience. There are first-order emotions that often have objectives beyond their own resources to achieve, and there are also second-order emotions that serve first-order emotions by tackling obstacles that get in the way of their interests. In their inner structure, some emotions seem concerned with basic goods and basic evils, while other emotions seem concerned with difficult objects and the service of more elemental emotions. Anger, for example, does seem to be "the armor-bearer of desire."[10] Furthermore, Aquinas seems right to claim that the passions he identifies as irascible are more influenced by rational consideration than those he identifies as concupiscible. Desire and aversion, pleasure and sadness, are difficult to summon or disperse by rational argument, but persuasion can elicit or dissipate fear, courage, and anger, typically by "showing" these passions that the concerns of the concupiscible passions are either safe or in danger. This hierarchy of the passions—with the irascible passions serving the concupiscible passions, and not the other way around—

10. *ST* I-II 46.2 obj 1; see also Nemesius, *De natura hominis*, 21.

has significant implications when it comes to discerning authentic human flourishing from its counterfeits and various other ethical questions, as will be discussed below.

Aquinas's bracketing of moral considerations from metaphysical analysis of the passions in the *Treatise on the Passions* is an original maneuver without obvious precedent. This bracketing allows Aquinas to look at the passions with a kind of equanimity, focusing on how they work and what purpose they serve, without worrying about the moral implications of his analysis. In the *Treatise on the Passions,* he discusses their metaphysics, and then he addresses their relationship to *habitus* (both virtuous and vicious) in the later parts of the *Prima secundae.* Later, in the *Secunda secundae,* he discusses the moral quality of specific passions, insofar as they are the acts of the various virtues and vices and have specific sorts of objects. His methodological separation between anthropology and morality depends on an ontological premise: it is possible only because Aquinas regards every passion as good unless corrupted. Envy, for example, is not an elemental component of human affectivity; it is the corruption of something good, that is, the passion of sadness. Without his trust in the ontological goodness of the passions, he could not presume that envy shared the same essential structure as virtuous sadness, nor could he draw on his analysis of generic affectivity when evaluating the passions associated with other virtues and vices, as he does throughout the *Secunda secundae.*

There are many advantages to Aquinas's method of analyzing the structure of affectivity in the abstract before engaging questions of morality. It avoids confusing questions of anthropology with questions of ethics, and at the same time grounds ethics in anthropology. However, Aquinas's method presupposes that human desire is fundamentally oriented toward the good. It does not work without this presupposition. Consequently, it is incompatible with many understandings of the human person—materialist and secular as well as religious—because they lack Aquinas's confidence in the fundamental orientation of human desire.

Passion's Natural Obedience to Reason

The relationship of emotion to cognition is perhaps the preeminent question of contemporary philosophy of emotion. Aquinas's account of this relationship has much to recommend it. His complex philosophical anthropology allows him a great deal of precision in his analysis of how emotion relates to different kinds of cognition.

One of the most crucial elements of Aquinas's account of emotion is the premise that the passions naturally obey reason and naturally tend toward conformity with reason.[11] Everything hangs on whether he is right on this premise. If he is not, the passions cannot be the seat of virtue. Furthermore, the spontaneity of the passions could not be anything but a threat to the mastery of reason and will, even if they happen to align with the guidance of reason from time to time, since the passions would be completely untrustworthy.

Before evaluating the merits of his position, it is important to clarify exactly what Aquinas claims about the passions and reason. First, the natural tendency of the passions toward conformity with reason is not complete subjection to reason. Moreover, Aquinas does not hold that reason commands the passions absolutely. Citing Aristotle, he maintains that its rule is political, not despotic. He does not fully explain what it means for reason to rule the passions politically. Nonetheless, what he wants to claim is clear: that the passions naturally tend to follow reason, and actually seek out reason's guidance, as long as reason does not command the passions to do something contrary to their nature. Reason guides the passions, but it does not supplant them, and the passions do not just accept reason's guidance, they incline toward it, albeit imperfectly.

Does Aquinas's claim about passion's natural obedience to reason hold up? Experimental psychology may help here, since Aquinas's claim is partially testable, and might be proven or disproven by experiment. Experimental observation, however, is not strictly necessary; this question can also be approached by reflection on personal experience and general observations about human psychology.[12] When his claim is unpacked, it is less radical than it might seem at first. It simply thematizes ordinary experience in a way that is wide-ranging in theoretical implications.

11. See chap. 4. The analysis given in this section is greatly indebted to the work of Conrad Baars and Anna Terruwe.

12. Aquinas himself alludes to personal experience in making his case for the tendency of the passions to follow reason. He writes, "Anyone can experience this in himself: by applying certain universal considerations, anger, fear, and other such things can be mitigated or instigated" (*ST* I 81.3).

For example, the phenomenon of anger presents itself to our consciousness and motivates us toward some kind of retaliatory action. Anger, however, stops short of making a decision: it presents itself, but then waits for us to make a judgment about the situation and decide upon a course of action. Once we have evaluated the situation and decided upon a course of action, anger responds accordingly. If we decide on some retaliatory action, the anger becomes directed toward that end. If we decide not to act on the anger, over time, the anger begins to fade, unless the cause of the anger continues to provoke us, by either continual experience of some injustice or a recurring memory. In other words, reason rules the passions politically: reason can guide anger to some extent, but if it tries to extinguish anger inappropriately, the passions rebel and anger continues to assert itself.

The passions also obey reason when reason helps shape the intentional objects to which the passions respond. The irascible passions are especially responsive to reason in this way because, as Aquinas maintains, their objects are more shaped by reason than those of the concupiscible passions. When we realize that the cause of our anger is not a genuine injustice—for example, when we realize that we deserved some criticism after all, or that our friend was not in fact the source of a calumnious rumor—our anger might dissipate immediately. The passions obey reason insofar as reason reshapes the intentional object of our anger so that it is no longer perceived as an injustice, and consequently our apprehension of that intentional object no longer elicits anger.

The natural obedience of passion to reason is the foundation of Aquinas's account of how virtue and grace perfect human affectivity. Since the passions naturally incline toward reason's guidance, virtue does not imply any internal violence. Furthermore, grace does not transform affectivity by the imposition of something foreign to human nature, nor is grace a *deus ex machina* that magically solves the problem of internal disorder. Virtue and grace bring natural inclinations to fruition; they do not beat them into submission or eradicate them and replace them with something else. This account of virtuous and graced affectivity is nonviolent and humane, especially in contrast to those accounts that see virtue and grace in constant tension with our natural inclinations. Passion's tendency toward conformity with reason also explains the possibility of habitually vicious passions. Because the sense appetite tends toward conformity with reason, the will's defective choices, through the mediation of reason, can corrupt the sense appetite beyond the disorder characteristic of original sin.

For Aquinas, the spontaneity of the passions is a positive feature of human affectivity. The movements of the sense appetite in their inner structure are complementary to the movements of the intellectual appetite. Unless the passions become corrupted and disordered, their independence is not a threat to interior freedom, but a support to it. The passions have their own source of energy, and when guided by reason, their resources assist the will in its striving toward its chosen objectives. But the spontaneity of the passions can be considered a support to virtue only if Aquinas is correct that the passions tend toward conformity with reason. Otherwise, Aquinas's account of virtuous affectivity comes crashing down: the spontaneity of the passions becomes a wild card that must be held in perpetual suspicion.

The idea that the passions tend toward reason's guidance allows for an interesting rapprochement of faculty psychology with certain features of the psychology of Sigmund Freud. While Aquinas does not have concepts of repression or the unconscious, his system has room to account for them. Aquinas's distinction between different kinds of cognition and affection parallels Freud's division of the human psyche into different centers of knowing and desiring.[13] Furthermore, according to Aquinas, the passions have an intrinsic relationship to reason, and yet are beyond its absolute control—two necessary premises of any adequate explanation of the phenomenon of repression. Two clinical psychologists, Anna Terruwe and Conrad Baars, have used Aquinas's anthropology to propose a theory of repression.[14] They argue that it is possible for a passion to become the intentional object of another passion—a possibility that Aquinas explicitly discusses when he argues that fear itself can be feared[15]—and that the phenomenon of repression results when an irascible passion becomes trained on another passion that is seen as a threat to personal well-being.

13. It could be argued that particular reason and the sense appetite—which are both corporeal—roughly correspond to the sphere of the unconscious, and that the intellect and the intellectual appetite—which are both incorporeal—roughly correspond to the sphere of the conscious. In this interpretation, the cognitions of the particular reason and the movements of the sense appetite become conscious only when they are apprehended by the intellect; otherwise they remain unconscious.

14. See Terruwe and Baars, *Loving and Curing the Neurotic*. This line of thought is first developed in Terruwe's *The Neurosis in the Light of Rational Psychology*.

15. *ST* I-II 42.4.

For example, someone might come to regard anger as an inherently negative experience, through either some traumatic experience or a moralistic upbringing. Perhaps someone grows up with an abusive alcoholic relative, and then consciously or unconsciously decides to avoid being angry at all cost. Or perhaps someone is taught from an early age that anger is almost always a sin, or at least a sign of moral inferiority. According to Terruwe and Baars, in these circumstances, anger might become an object of fear, because anger is seen as a negative experience that must be avoided at all costs. When an anger-inducing situation arises, fear might overwhelm the anger and hide it from conscious awareness. Nonetheless, because reason does not have despotic rule of the passions, only political rule, the fear that reason has directed against anger cannot extinguish the anger. Anger does not evaporate simply because it is unwanted; it dissipates when the anger-inducing injustice is overcome or accepted. Consequently, anger continues to move toward its proper *telos,* which is the elimination of some present evil, and so in mutilated form anger continues to operate within the individual's psyche, perhaps bursting out into consciousness in unexpected ways from time to time. In this way, Terruwe and Baars maintain, Aquinas's account has the resources to account for the phenomena of repression and unconscious emotion identified by Freud.

From their analysis of repression, Terruwe and Baars propose a solution. This repression will continue, they argue, until the anger receives guidance from reason. Therefore, reason must either direct the anger toward some plan of action, or, after acknowledging the anger as directed toward a legitimate injustice, decide that the injustice is not worth addressing. Whatever the merits of their explanation of repression, Terruwe and Baars show that Aquinas's account of emotion is not intrinsically incompatible with some of the central concepts of Freudian psychology.

Emotion and Ethics

For Aquinas, the relationship between emotion and ethics is simple and elegant: optimal psychological functioning and moral goodness are identical. An action is morally good if it involves the voluntary choice to act in ways consonant with our natural inclinations and our psychological constitution. If an action involves something in disharmony with our inclinations and the structure of human emotion, then it is morally defective to intend to act in such a way. Our sins against God are also and always sins against our deepest desires.[16] Or, as Aquinas puts it in the *Summa contra gentiles*, "God is not offended by us except when we are acting against our own good."[17]

For Aquinas, ethics involves more than the analysis of discrete choices: it is concerned with persons more than their actions. The virtuous life is not about the accumulation of praiseworthy accomplishments; it is about the cultivation of a fully human personality. Consequently, while Aquinas is concerned with discrete choices, he is also interested in how those choices form personality and character. The category of virtue is a way to describe what happens when choices become embedded in our personality, so that we become actively disposed toward future acts of goodness, that is, toward acts consonant with authentic human flourishing and psychological health. For Aquinas, virtue is not a burden; it is not an external pattern of ideal behavior that we must squeeze ourselves inside. To the contrary: virtue is the expansion of the self to its full potential for greatness, happiness, and creativity. The parameters of virtue are determined by the teleology of human nature, not by rules or conventions. Aquinas's account of emotion makes it vividly clear why virtue is its own reward. It also affirms our sense that there is something wrong with an ethical system that is more about rule-following than happiness.

Furthermore, actions directed toward virtuous ends are morally defective if they are achieved by drawing on inappropriate interior resources. Even if the rational powers are directed toward the good, unless the sense appetite is rightly ordered, "the action that follows will not be perfect, and therefore the principle of that action will not be a virtue."[18] When properly understood, this analysis resonates with our intuitions about moral character. It can be disturbing, for example, to observe someone perform a "morally correct" action with exaggerated fear, or without any joy, as though acting from sheer willpower. We sense that something is not right. Aquinas has a place for these intuitions. According to Aquinas's understanding of virtue, for an action to be virtuous, the concupiscible passions and the desires of

16. This point was made by Joseph Guido during a liturgy of the 2001 General Chapter of the Dominican Order.

17. *Summa contra gentiles* III 122.2.

18. *ST* I-II 58.3 ad 2.

the intellectual appetite must have priority over the irascible passions. For example, when a man avoids adultery more from fear of public scandal than love of his wife, something is disordered about his moral character, even if he is faithful and his love for his wife is genuine. Fear might have an appropriate place in a virtuous disposition, but the irascible passions should not become the principal motivations for "morally correct" actions. The irascible passions are ordered to the concupiscible passions, and when the irascible usurp the priority of the concupiscible passions, there is a violation of this structure, and therefore moral defect. Similarly, it is not enough for someone to do good and avoid evil from sheer willpower. Sometimes it might be necessary to run roughshod over the passions, but if someone's intellectual affections habitually fail to enlist the cooperation of the passions, there is something wrong.[19]

Aquinas's account of emotion and ethics resonates with our intuitions about moral character. In our day-to-day interactions, we routinely make judgments about character based on affective dispositions. For example, when considering whether someone can be trusted, perhaps during a job interview, we look for emotional cues, and not just the record of their past behavior. We can certainly be fooled, but the reason we can be fooled is that we see affective dispositions as revealing something about moral character. It is possible to discern someone's ethnic heritage from facial characteristics with a reasonable degree of accuracy, because facial characteristics are inextricably bound up with ethnic heritage. In the same way, it is possible to discern aspects of someone's character from emotional cues, because affectivity is inextricably bound up with virtue and vice.

Moreover, the affective qualities we consider when evaluating someone's character are not only on the level of more obvious affective dispositions. For example, over time we might discern that someone is sensitive to issues of justice, and particularly quick to defend the interests of others. This judgment identifies more than a pattern of behavior; it identifies an affective disposition toward justice that we sense is stable. A just disposition does not always manifest many tangible signs of emotion, but it has recognizable affective qualities that transcend differences in personality type.

19. Such a defective moral strategy becomes particularly endemic among those who define their moral lives solely in terms of obedience to divine commandments, which of their nature emphasize the role of the will in choosing to obey or disobey.

Aquinas's view of justice as a disposition of the intellectual appetite, and not a pattern of behavior and his more general view that some virtues are affective dispositions of the intellectual appetite offer a compelling account of these intuitions about justice. Affective dispositions do not involve only obvious emotional phenomena; they also involve subtle emotions that do not have as many tangible features—emotions that, in Aquinas's account, are affections of the intellectual appetite.

Anthropology and ethics are tightly linked for Aquinas, and it is impossible to understand his ethics while neglecting his anthropology. His ethics stands or falls on the validity of his anthropology. If he is wrong about the nature of desire and the structure of emotion, then he is wrong, at least substantially, about ethics. Consequently, any adequate evaluation of Aquinas's ethics must also evaluate his account of emotion.

Virtue and Freedom

Servais Pinckaers has shown that Aquinas's understanding of freedom is radically different from the view that has come to dominate Western culture since the late Middle Ages.[20] For Aquinas, freedom is primarily about freedom for excellence, the capacity to achieve human excellence. However, for William of Ockham and much of Western culture after him, freedom is primarily about freedom of indifference, the capacity to choose good or evil. While freedom for excellence includes freedom of indifference—since the capacity to achieve human excellence implies the capacity to reject it, insofar as human excellence involves creativity and the ownership of personal actions—freedom of indifference does not entail freedom for excellence. For example, someone afflicted with the vice of gluttony can choose not to eat a fifth doughnut and start down the path of moderation and nutrition from that moment on. However, the virtue of temperance cannot be acquired immediately any more than someone can instantaneously drop ten pounds simply by deciding to lose weight. The capacity to embrace and embody human excellence takes time, and repeated virtuous choices, to acquire.

Freedom is commonly understood as being able to do what we desire. It is conceived in almost legal terms, as though the parameters of freedom are determined by balancing the widest possible range of personal action with

20. See Pinckaers, *Sources of Christian Ethics*, esp. 327–99.

the legal rights of others, and as though the task of philosophical analysis is simply to determine the appropriate balance. Aquinas's account of emotion is compatible with this definition of freedom, with this crucial twist: freedom is being able to do what we *truly* desire.[21] Freedom is about the capacity to fulfill those desires that are in harmony with our natural inclinations, and thus bring lasting happiness. Freedom is only about the capacity to make bad choices—and about being able to do whatever we desire, no matter how frivolous or self-destructive—in a derivative way. The freedom to make bad choices is important, not because there is any intrinsic value in being free to make bad decisions, but because if we are not free to make bad decisions, we cannot be free to make *good* decisions. We cannot have freedom for excellence without freedom for sin, because the ability to love implies the ability to refuse to love.

Consequently, virtuous *habitus* play a crucial role in authentic freedom. The desire to compete in the Olympics cannot come to fruition without dedication, self-discipline, and years of practice. Competition on that level requires certain acquired dispositions and abilities that take a long time to develop. Similarly, in order to attain the happiness we cannot help but desire, we need the virtues, that is, the perfection of our natural capacities according to our *telos*. In this way, virtue is necessary for freedom in the fullest sense of the word, because only virtue—and particularly virtue informed by God's grace—enables to us to do what we *truly* desire. Furthermore, since virtue denotes the capacity to act according to our natural inclinations with ease and pleasure, virtue *is* freedom.

Desire as a Basis for Ethical Discourse

In *After Virtue*, Alasdair MacIntyre argues that contemporary discourse about ethics has become hopelessly muddled because there are so many

21. Here "what we truly desire" refers to those desires that correspond to our natural inclinations and therefore who we truly are. It is also possible to interpret "what we truly desire" as a tautology: anything we desire we truly desire by the fact that we desire it. Although this phrasing is therefore liable to misinterpretation, it has the advantage of being in verbal continuity with the common definition of freedom as being able to do what one wants (a definition that has deep roots in Western culture, and goes back at least to the ancient Greeks). It also relates the nature of freedom with the truth about man and Christ's teaching about freedom: "If you continue in my word, you are truly my disciples, and you will know the truth, and the truth will make you free" (John 8:31–32).

vastly different ethical systems using similar language. The claim that a certain action is right or wrong, ethical or unethical, is now unhooked from a common point of reference.

By grounding ethics in anthropology, Aquinas suggests a way out of this impasse: namely, by anchoring ethical discourse in questions of desire. Instead of asking whether a certain action is right or wrong, taking a hint from Aquinas, we can instead ask whether that action corresponds to our natural inclinations, and therefore leads to authentic flourishing and—to eliminate any possible ambiguity in the term "flourishing"—the most profound happiness. If we accept Aquinas's claim that there is a common human nature, and that our natural inclinations are the measure of moral value, then anchoring ethics in questions of desire opens up many possibilities for fruitful conversation between ethical systems. The universal experience of desire, when deployed as a common point of reference, can bridge vastly different perspectives. Regardless of their ethical system or vocabulary, all participants in ethical discourse have personal experience of desire and direct observations about human tendencies and the structure of the human person. In consequence, they can all appeal to the same points of reference and have intelligible discussions about ethics.

Without doubt, this method of ethical discourse would surface profound disagreements about which desires express our natural inclinations and which desires corrupt or distort our natural inclinations. It would also surface disagreements about joy, happiness, and what constitutes the most profound fulfillment of human potential. These sorts of disagreement, however, promise to be more productive than disagreements about moral obligations and their respective priority (though without jettisoning the concept of obligation or consigning this latter class of disagreements to irrelevance). When our arguments are rooted in desire, there is always something concrete that we can reference: our experience and our observations (scientific or otherwise). Furthermore, arguing about what we truly desire and the nature of happiness is much more interesting than reciting reasons why we are, or are not, morally obligated to perform or avoid a certain action. Discussions based on questions of desire also tend to be more friendly, since they presume a common project—that is, the clarification of the inner workings of the human psyche and what leads to happiness—and do not require any participant to adopt another's ethical vocabulary in order for the conversation to be meaningful.

One danger of this method of ethical discourse, however, is the possibility of losing sight of the gravity of the moral issues involved. We do not intuitively connect questions of desire to questions of morality, and so this method runs the risk of treating the inquiry into our desires and natural inclinations like an interesting academic project. But this inquiry is much more than an exercise in philosophical clarification, because it has enormous practical implications for the ordering of personal lives and societies. Centering ethical discourse in questions of desire does not replace the moral categories of good and evil, right and wrong; it gives them an ontological foundation. There is no substitute for the moral categories of good and evil. Theft of another's livelihood is not just contrary to our deepest inclinations: it is evil and it is wrong.

Due to the possibility of self-deception and rationalization, ethical discourse centered on inquiry into questions of desire requires a heightened amount of self-scrutiny and a recognition that others may be unwilling or unable to operate on the highest level of intellectual honesty. This healthy awareness of human weakness should not prejudice a presumption of good faith, but neither must participants entirely refrain from strong challenges to the moral integrity of others, given what is at stake. For example, if William Wilberforce had only challenged the English to reconsider whether the enslavement of other human persons is compatible with our natural inclinations, rather than forcefully condemning slavery and calling for a change of heart, it is unlikely that he would have been successful in abolishing the slave trade. Sometimes shifting the focus of a conversation from disinterested inquiry to existential choice is inappropriate and unhelpful, even (and perhaps especially) in the realm of political discourse, but other circumstances might in fact demand it.

Omissions and Lacunae

Although the internal logic of Aquinas's system is fundamentally sound, there are some notable omissions and lacunae. The most striking is that he does not describe the subjective experience of emotion: his primary interest is the *metaphysics* of affectivity, and not the *experience* of affectivity.[22] This

22. One promising way to develop Aquinas's theology of emotion would be to compare Aquinas with the sixteenth-century Spanish mystic John of the Cross and supplement Aquinas's ap-

omission can make his account difficult to penetrate, and it leaves unresolved many questions about how it relates to concrete experience. He also neglects psychological pathology apart from his consideration of vice. Unlike many modern psychologies, Aquinas offers a comprehensive vision of what the psychologically healthy human person looks like. However, he does not engage the reality of mental illness, nor is he is aware of many pathologies that have been identified by modern psychological research.

Aquinas's account of emotion gives little attention to the place of memory in human psychology, and rarely even mentions it. On this point he has less excuse, especially since memory plays a major role in Augustine's anthropology, with which he was very familiar. Nonetheless, he avoids serious problems because he connects memory to intentions, calling memory a "treasury" of intentions.[23] Consequently, because the apprehension of intentions involves memory, and because intentions elicit emotional response, memory is firmly integrated into his account of emotion. Furthermore, memory plays a crucial if hidden role in his concept of *habitus*, insofar as memory is implicitly involved in his claim that voluntary actions can dispose us toward similar voluntary actions in the future. Still, Aquinas's concept of memory needs to be developed, especially with regard to psychological pathologies, which often involve memory in some fashion.

Another notable problem with Aquinas's account of emotion is his deficient attention to interpersonal relationships. The role of interpersonal relationships in the development of virtuous affectivity is seriously overlooked, as is the especially formative influence of parents on the affectivity of their children.[24] Nonetheless, this deficiency should not lead to the hasty judg-

proach accordingly. In the *Ascent of Mount Carmel* and *The Dark Night,* John gives a detailed description of how the passions are transformed by God's grace and the life of virtue, with particular attention to how this evolution is experienced by the individual subject. Among the classics of spiritual theology, they are virtually unparalleled for their combination of theological rigor and phenomenological description. Although their anthropologies are different, they are similar enough that John's work might suggest some helpful ways to flesh out Aquinas's theology of emotion with regard to its subjective dimension. See John of the Cross, *Collected Works of John of the Cross,* trans. Kieran Kavanaugh and Otilio Rodriguez (Washington, D.C.: Institute of Carmelite Studies, 1964).

23. *ST* I 78.4.

24. The role of interpersonal relationships in affective flourishing is a particular concern of Terruwe and Baars, and in their work they seek to develop a Thomistic account of emotion that can encompass these sorts of issues. Their research and clinical work is especially concerned with the problem of inadequate affective affirmation and its therapeutic treatment. On this topic, see especially their book *Healing the Unaffirmed.*

ment that Aquinas is uninterested in interpersonal relationships. In fact, Aquinas gives an extraordinary amount of attention to friendship, and his understanding of charity as friendship with God, although now a theological commonplace, was not typical of his theological milieu.

These lacunae are the most pressing and notable deficiencies of his account of emotion. There are many other aspects of emotion that demand closer attention than he gives, and his account requires revision in the light of modern advances. However, with its many positive and sometimes prescient features, the fundamental structure of his account does not have to be jettisoned in order to address these weaknesses.

CHAPTER 9

Toward a Contemporary Theology of Emotion

Aquinas's theology of emotion is fundamentally open-ended. Although it is committed to a number of foundational principles, it also provides a platform from which to engage topics that he does not. This chapter will discuss some of its applications to various topics, in order to give a sense of the horizons that his work opens up, and the ways that it can be used to construct a contemporary theology of emotion.

Emotion and Discernment

A perennial topic of Christian spirituality is discernment, that is, the task of determining through reflection and prayer where God might be leading. One of the classic models of discernment was developed by Ignatius of Loyola, the founder of the Jesuits. In the *Spiritual Exercises,* Ignatius identifies peace and consolation as indicators that a particular option is in harmony with God's will, and anxiety and discontent as indicators of the opposite.[1] Although Aquinas does not explicitly write about discernment, his anthropology provides theological principles that complement Ignatius's practical guidelines. For Aquinas, God's will is manifested in our desires, and so the discernment of God's will coincides with the discernment of our deepest desires. Furthermore, his anthropology suggests an important clue for uncovering what our deepest desires might be: the experience of interior peace. According to Aquinas, peace results when our various desires are in a state of harmony. Consequently, when peace follows from the consideration of a particular option, this peace is a positive indicator (although not

1. Ignatius of Loyola, *The Spiritual Exercises,* trans. David Fleming (St. Louis: Institute of Jesuit Studies, 1978). See especially his "Guidelines for the Discernment of Spirits," nos. 313–36.

a certain one) that the option under consideration is in harmony with our desires, and therefore with God's will. Joy is another indicator: since God's will for us is our deepest happiness, thinking about some option in harmony with it tends to cause joy. But, as Aquinas notes, joy can be drowned out by other interior experiences. Therefore, interior peace is a more reliable indicator: since interior peace consists in the harmony of our desires, rather than the conscious experience of any particular emotion, it is less likely to be drowned out. In this way, approaching Ignatius with Aquinas's anthropology enhances appreciation for his practical wisdom.

Theology of Asceticism

Aquinas's account of emotion also provides a humane grounding for religious asceticism. For Aquinas, the ascetic restraint of desire and pleasure is appropriate only to the extent that it serves other desires. He assigns no positive value to the pursuit of deprivation for the sake of deprivation, as though pain and suffering had positive value in themselves. In fact, he judges such behavior to be vicious, as in his treatment of the vice of insensibility. For Aquinas, asceticism is always in the service of a greater good; sacrifice for its own sake is pointless and unethical. The value of fasting, for instance, derives from its relation to other goods. Fasting trains the body and passions to respond more easily to reason, as when runners jog with weights on their legs as a training exercise. Fasting also fosters prayer and a spirit of recollection, which serves our desire for communion with God. And since prayer benefits our neighbors, it also serves our desire to advance the well-being of others and to alleviate suffering.

Aquinas's theology of emotion also points beyond some aspects of traditional asceticism to a broader understanding of penitential practice. For example, the Christian tradition has always placed emphasis on the value of fasting and the restraint of anger. Aquinas also places great value on fasting—his life as a Dominican friar in the early days of the order was especially marked by fasting—and the moderation of excessive anger, but his account of emotion strongly implies that the ascetic training of other passions, and especially fear, is also necessary.[2] In the Gospels, Christ tells his disciples

2. I am indebted to Conrad Baars for this idea. See his *Feeling and Healing Your Emotions*, esp. 265–67. The ascetic denial of excessive fear could possibly be integrated by Christian com-

not to be anxious about their daily needs, and repeatedly encourages them not to fear, but Christian tradition has not been as emphatic about this aspect of Christ's teaching as it has been about the need for fasting and the need for the restraint of excessive anger. Aquinas's theology calls for an asceticism that seeks to redress every kind of psychological imbalance, and not just the tendency to indulge disordered desires and excessive anger. This approach affirms the value of penitential practices while also connecting them more closely to our desire for happiness and drawing attention to the need for the ascetic training of all our emotions.

Forgiveness and Anger

Ironically, Aquinas writes a great deal about the goodness of anger in the *Summa,* but he does not give much attention to forgiveness, except in the sense of God's forgiveness of sins.[3] The reverse might have been expected from a Christian theologian, given the prominent place of forgiveness in Christian ethics. Nonetheless, he comes close to discussing human forgiveness in his treatment of gentleness, which moderates anger, and clemency, which moderates punishment.[4] Furthermore, by affirming the possibility and even necessity of virtuous anger, Aquinas excludes many naïve interpretations of Christ's command to forgive, some of which call for the complete renunciation of anger and of the desire to fight injustice. Consequently, although he does not explicitly discuss human forgiveness in the *Summa,* Aquinas nonetheless lays the groundwork for a refreshing approach to the subject.

Drawing on Aquinas's account of the passions, Conrad Baars proposes that forgiveness is about dispersing anger after it has ceased to be useful.[5] In

munities into the liturgical year. Just as Lent is recognized as a time particularly dedicated to self-denial, perhaps Easter could be seen as a time particularly dedicated to courage and fearlessness and heightened trust in God's providence. The theme of Resurrection and the Scripture readings of the Easter season already emphasize divine power and casting aside fear.

3. I have identified only one place in the entire *Summa* where forgiveness of a fellow sinner is discussed: *ST* I-II 113.2. Even here the topic is broached mainly in order to speak about God's forgiveness.

4. ST II-II 157; Montague Brown, "St. Thomas Aquinas on Human and Divine Forgiveness," *Saint Anselm Journal* 6 (2009): 1–8. As Brown notes, Aquinas explicitly addresses the topic of human forgiveness in *Expositio in orationem dominicam* 5.

5. Conrad W. Baars, "Anger and Forgiveness," in his *I Will Give Them a New Heart: Reflec-*

this interpretation, the first step toward understanding forgiveness is, paradoxically, to understand the positive value of anger and its drive toward the elimination of an injustice. In an ideal situation, anger successfully assists in the elimination of the injustice, and then the anger dissipates. But when it is beyond someone's power to rectify the injustice and the transgressor is unrepentant, or when the injustice is not worth rectifying, the situation is more complicated. As long as someone apprehends the injustice as something that requires redress, the anger does not dissipate and it cannot dissipate. It continues to drive toward its *telos* of eliminating injustice, even though that *telos* is either unattainable or not worth attaining, and the ensuing frustration only compounds the problem. Forgiveness provides the way out of this vicious cycle. Because the passions respond to the direction of reason, useless anger can be redirected through forgiveness and dispersed.

The process of dispersing anger is complex, however, because reason's rule of the passions is political, not despotic. First, the angry person must decide to forgive, that is, the angry person must stop seeking redress for the injustice that the anger drives toward. But it is not enough to decide to forgive; forgiveness begins in the will but ideally extends to the passions. The angry person must also start to apprehend the injustice in such a way that it ceases to provoke anger. In other words, the intentional object of the passion must be reshaped, so that the sense appetite no longer sees it as a present evil that must be eliminated. This reshaping of the intentional object requires a rational reevaluation of the situation. Otherwise, unless the angry person reevaluates the situation, anger will continue to smolder whenever the injustice comes to mind, even if a decision has been made to forgive.

Forgiveness is a process, and the initial decision to forgive only begins it. The angry person would not have decided to forgive without having come to the conviction that, at least on some level, redress is not necessary for the injustice. However, the decision to forgive does not require that the angry person come to this conviction about every conceivable aspect of the injustice. For example, when the angry person calls to mind a particularly infuriating aspect of the injustice, the supposedly dispersed anger may come back in full force. In order to disperse the anger entirely, these infuriating aspects must be reevaluated, so that the angry person comes to conclude

tions on the Priesthood and the Renewal of the Church (Staten Island, N.Y.: Alba House, 2008), 215–46.

that even these aspects do not require redress. Then the anger will again fade of its own accord—in some cases more easily than in others, depending on the emotional provocation of the injustice and its complexity.

When the injustice is minor, it is relatively easy to reframe an injustice so that it can be forgiven. For example, after a friend annoys us in some way, we might consider the good our friend has done for us, or the fact that no malice was intended, and conclude that this small injustice does not require redress. When the injustice is serious—when the harm done is permanent and especially destructive—the conviction that the injustice does not need to be redressed usually requires faith in God. Grave harm is difficult to forget, and only God has sufficient power to set things right, even if only in the next life. Therefore, the dispersion of anger toward someone who has done us grave and irreparable harm usually requires the theological virtues: faith in God's power and providence; hope that he will act to overcome the injustice; and charity to choose forgiveness.[6] It is possible to forgive grave and irreparable harm without explicit faith in God, but it is much more difficult.

Forgiveness and the dispersion of anger are not incompatible with desire for earthly justice. For example, a woman might forgive her husband's killer, and her anger might dissipate completely over time, but she might still desire that the killer serve a prison sentence. Her attitude toward the killer is entirely compatible with genuine forgiveness. She has accepted and forgiven the grave, irreparable harm of her husband's murder, and while she wants the killer to be punished, her desire for punishment is not a desire for revenge: it is a desire for other goods, such as the protection of society and the killer's rehabilitation, and perhaps also the honoring of her husband's memory.

Emotion and the Theology of Preaching

Aristotle initiates sustained metaphysical analysis of the passions, and it is striking that he writes more about the passions in the *Rhetoric* than in any of his works on human nature or ethics. For Aristotle, rhetoric must engage the passions, and this engagement requires detailed knowledge of the pas-

6. Trust in God's power to overcome harm also opens up the possibility of self-forgiveness. When the harm done to self is very grave and beyond any hope of repair by natural means, faith in God is usually necessary for authentic self-forgiveness as well.

sions and their structure. In an interesting parallel to Aristotle's discussion of the passions in the *Rhetoric,* Aquinas discusses the relevance of affectivity to preaching, although he does not spend much time on the topic. Toward the end of the *Secunda secundae,* Aquinas turns his attention to the particular charisms, or gifts, that God gives to certain individuals for the benefit of the community. One such charism relates to speech and communication. He identifies three aspects of effective communication, one of which concerns the intellect, and two of which relate to emotion:

> The knowledge that someone receives from God cannot be turned to the benefit of others except by means of speech. And because the Holy Spirit does not fall short in anything that is useful to the Church, it provides members of the Church not only with the gift of tongues, by which someone speaks so that different people can understand, but also with the grace of speech, by which someone speaks effectively.
>
> ✧
>
> This happens in three ways. First, in order to instruct the intellect, as when someone speaks in order to teach. Second, in order to move the affection, so that people listen to the word of God willingly, as when someone speaks in order to delight his hearers—though in doing so, the speaker must not seek applause for himself; rather he must seek that others are drawn to hear the word of God. Third, in order that others come to love what the words signify, and desire to fulfill them, as when someone speaks to influence his hearers. In order to bring this effect about, the Holy Spirit uses man's tongue as a sort of instrument, and then the same Spirit brings the interior work to completion.[7]

The importance that he attributes to affectivity in the matter of preaching can seem surprising coming from Aquinas, in that his theological writings do not seem interested in evoking an emotional response. If anything, Aquinas seems dedicated to removing any trace of emotion from his theology, as if to preserve the objectivity of his investigations. But his works of theology are a very specific form of communication: when we speak "in order to instruct the intellect, as when someone speaks in order to teach," we are doing something different from either speaking "to move the affection" or speaking so that "others come to love what the words signify." It is very clear from what he says above that, for Aquinas, one of the primary objectives of

7. *ST* II-II 177.1.

preaching is to move the emotions of those listening, and in particular to inspire delight in both the manner of communication and the Word of God.

It is unfortunate that Aquinas does not develop this dimension of his thought in more detail, but the shape of his anthropology suggests how he would expand it. First of all, in terms of its ethical content, sound preaching directs hearers to approach moral demands with all of the resources of the human person, emotions included, and not just willpower. Preaching that only calls for a rational commitment to the Christian life without connecting this rational commitment to emotion is deficient. When a preacher habitually fails to connect the moral life to desire and emotion, the preacher is implicitly suggesting that morality is about the detached decisions of a disembodied will. Moral exhortation that only appeals to the will, especially the kind of exhortation that simply encourages people to "try harder,"[8] reinforces the psychological pathology of those who are falling short of certain moral norms precisely because they have been trying to fulfill them without the assistance of their emotional resources and God's grace.[9] Each time they are told (implicitly or explicitly) that the solution to their moral failures is to try harder, the preacher confirms them in a strategy that is bound to fail: namely, to seek to fulfill Christ's commands without integrating their emotions or relying on God's grace.

Furthermore, good preaching appeals to the right kinds of emotion, and the right balance of emotion. For instance, a preacher who presents fear as the primary motive for avoiding sin implicitly conveys a warped understanding of morality, as well as a warped understanding of Christ's teaching. In fact, such preaching not only fails to convey a correct understanding of virtue, it actually encourages vice, insofar as it encourages exaggerated and disproportionate fear. Good preaching might appeal to fear, but not in a way that gives fear, implicitly or explicitly, a disproportionate place in the moral life. Just as virtue is first about the concupiscible passions, and only second about the irascible passions, so too is good preaching. Good preaching primarily inspires desire and delight or aversion and sadness (depending on what is being discussed). It only secondarily inspires irascible passions such as daring, fear, and anger, and only insofar as these passions

8. Criticism of the "try harder" message was a favorite theme of John Burke in his lectures on preaching at the Dominican House of Studies.

9. This point is indebted to an observation by Frank Sutman.

help achieve desirable ends and help avoid what causes pain or sadness. Moreover, good preaching is not just oriented toward the passions: it is also oriented toward intellectual affections. So good preaching might not evoke what would be described in ordinary conversation as an "emotional" response, and yet might still delight and move the hearer, albeit on a different level.

Sensitivity to the affective dimension of preaching does not require that its cognitive dimension be downplayed. To the contrary, a sound understanding of human affectivity leads to an appreciation for the importance of its intellectual content, since the passions and affections respond to cognition. Sometimes the most effective way to influence a congregation positively is simply to inspire and strengthen faith. Even without directly engaging moral issues, such preaching will "move the affection" and help the hearers "come to love what the words signify, and desire to fulfill them," because faith consoles and sustains, encourages theological hope, and organically inspires love of God and neighbor and concrete acts of charity.

It is one thing to desire to preach in a way that appropriately engages and summons the emotions of those listening; it is another thing to actually succeed in doing so. A preacher cannot simply command those listening to feel a certain emotion. Preaching is an art, and there are no mathematical principles that guarantee success. Nonetheless, Aquinas's account of the structure of emotion provides some helpful guidelines. According to Aquinas, appetitive movements naturally result when prompted by their corresponding intentional objects. It follows that good preaching presents objects for consideration that naturally evoke the intended passions or affections. To inspire desire for some virtue, a preacher shows how that virtue makes it possible to attain something desirable; to inspire aversion for some vice, a preacher shows how it deforms human affectivity and leads to unhappiness; to inspire daring, a preacher describes something good that can be attained only by overcoming some difficulty, emphasizing both the goodness of the final goal and the possibility of overcoming the difficulty; to inspire anger, a preacher shows how the hearers have suffered some kind of injustice that needs redress, even if only vicariously in those who have been exploited.

But how does the preacher know which intentional objects will inspire what? First, it must be acknowledged that there is too much diversity among individuals and cultures to expect that the same intentional object will inspire the same emotional reaction in all hearers. At the same time, because we all share a common human nature, we also share the same emotional structure, and some objects can be expected to evoke certain responses with great reliability.[10] Furthermore, different sociological groups have different emotional predispositions, and if these are known, intentional objects can be chosen accordingly. For instance, when preaching in Columbus, Ohio, positive references to Ohio State Football are likely to elicit a positive emotional response; in other places, especially Ann Arbor, the opposite is the case. So in order to appropriately engage the audience on an affective level, the task of the preacher is twofold: to know well the structure of human emotion, and to know well the audience and its psychic terrain. This knowledge leads to an intuitive grasp of how the truths of faith can be conveyed in a way that connects on an emotional level.

This kind of knowledge cannot be taught; it can only come from reflection, the lived experience of faith, and getting to know the audience who will hear the preaching, so that the preaching can be directed toward its particular situation. In other words, the primary requirement for effective preaching is honest listening: to oneself, to others, and above all to the Word of God. Study of sociology, psychology, philosophy, theology, and Scripture are helpful, but connecting the truths learned in this kind of study to preaching requires an intuitive grasp of which intentional objects will inspire which emotions. This intuitive knowledge flows from self-knowledge and the psychological transformation worked by God's grace; a sound grasp of Christian doctrine is crucial and necessary, but it is not enough. It is partly for this reason that Christian tradition has always emphasized the importance of silence, prayer, and contemplation for those engaged in preaching the Gospel, as well as a sincere commitment to the Christian life, since these things foster this intuitive knowledge.[11] Contemplation and union with God

10. There is a great deal of common ground even in the case of mental illness or extreme emotional imbalance. What Polonius says of Hamlet often applies: "though this be madness, there be a method in't" (*Hamlet* Act II, Scene 2).

11. Pinckaers describes the paradox of the personal being the most universal and the necessity of turning inward in order to reach outward: "The more authentically personal an experience is, the greater its resonance in the human audience. St. Augustine's Confessions bears this out; so do the works of Rousseau. By the same token, the more deeply we enter into our own solitude, the more clearly we will be able to perceive what is in the heart of others and the more we will

in prayer help to overcome self-deception and superficial approaches to faith, so that the preacher knows instinctively what is deepest and most essential.

Ultimately, then, what makes preaching most effective is not rhetorical skill, and not even detailed knowledge of religious doctrine or Scripture, but an intuitive knowledge of God and Christ's teaching that resonates with the lived experiences of the hearers. Natural gifts in communication can enhance preaching, but even in their absence—and sometimes because of their absence, when it testifies to the sincerity of the preacher's faith—preachers can be effective if they have this intuitive knowledge. If what they say connects with the truth about God and the truth about the human person, even if it is poorly expressed, preachers delight their hearers and move them to put their faith in God and live accordingly.

Boredom, Desire, and God

Aquinas's account of emotion, and particularly his distinction between passion and affection and his analysis of the vice of *acedia*, provides a fruitful anthropological foundation from which to thematize the phenomenology of boredom, an emotional state of peculiarly modern interest. Consequently, turning now to boredom provides an opportunity to illustrate Aquinas's enduring relevance, and so serves as a fitting conclusion to this study.

Boredom is an elusive concept. Its origins are relatively recent, even when extending consideration to the older French idea of *ennui*.[12] Nonethe-

---

be able to relate to them in depth. Thus solitude opens us to the truest, vastest communication" (Pinckaers, *Sources of Christian Ethics*, 69).

12. The modern concept of boredom traces back to the French word *ennui*, which itself derives from the Latin phrase *mihi in odio est*. This phrase gradually morphed into the vulgar Latin word *inodiare* and then the old French word *ennuyer* ("to annoy"). Eventually *ennui* came to indicate something similar to what we now call boredom.

The first appearance of *ennui* in an English text is in 1667, when John Evelyn observes that there is no parallel in English to the French *ennui*. Its first attested use in English syntax is by George Berkeley in 1732 in *Alciphron* (II.17). The word "bore" in the sense of dull is first attested in a letter by the Earl of March in 1766, and the word "boredom" first appears in 1852 in Charles Dickens's novel *Bleak House* (II.28). See *The Oxford English Dictionary*, 2nd rev. ed. (Oxford: Clarendon Press, 1989).

Walker Percy reports that the word "boredom" may come from the French word *bourrer*, to stuff, although without giving any sources. He uses this etymology to suggest that boredom "is the self being stuffed with itself." See Walker Percy, *Lost in the Cosmos: The Last Self-Help Book* (New York: Farrar, Strauss, Giroux, 1983), 70–71.

less, references to boredom, being bored, and finding something or someone boring are now ubiquitous. People assume that other people know what they are talking about when they speak of being bored. Many observers have noted an increase of boredom in Western society, and some even argue that it is uniquely characteristic of modern times.[13] Boredom has been a common theme in modern literature and drama.[14] In the popular press, many social problems and various self-destructive behaviors are routinely attributed to boredom. Yet for all that, from its incorporation into our cultural imagination and our emotional lexicon until the present, boredom has rarely been the subject of sustained philosophical or theological investigation, although since Schopenhauer it has been mentioned frequently in continental philosophy.[15] Until recently it was neglected in psychological stud-

13. According to Elizabeth Goodstein, "boredom is an experience of modernity, of modern temporality" and "a form of subjective malaise proper to modernity." It "epitomizes the dilemma of the autonomous moral subject." Elizabeth S. Goodstein, *Experience without Qualities: Boredom and Modernity* (Stanford, Calif.: Stanford University Press, 2005), 6, 18, 3.

According to Lars Svendsen, "Boredom is the 'privilege' of modern man. While there are reasons for believing that joy and anger have remained fairly constant throughout history, the amount of boredom seems to have increased dramatically. The world has apparently become more boring" (Svendsen, *A Philosophy of Boredom*, 21).

14. For example, Chekhov's *Uncle Vanya*, Baudelaire's *Fleurs de Mal*, and Flaubert's *Madame Bovary* are all concerned with boredom and might each be considered a study of boredom or *ennui*. Huysmans's *À Rebours* deserves special note as a study of decadent boredom perhaps unparalleled in extravagance. In the twentieth century, the number of well-known artistic works (whether of literature, film, or music) especially concerned with boredom expands exponentially.

For a vast survey of the theme of boredom in Western literature from antiquity to the twentieth century, see Reinhard Kuhn, *The Demon of Noontide: Ennui in Western Literature* (Princeton, N.J.: Princeton University Press, 1976).

For a literary history of boredom over the past couple centuries, focusing on the close study of certain representative texts, see Patricia Meyer Spacks, *Boredom: The Literary History of a State of Mind* (Chicago: University of Chicago Press, 1995).

15. A notable exception is Heidegger's lengthy analysis of boredom in a series of lectures in 1929–30, first published in German in 1983. See Martin Heidegger, *The Fundamental Concepts of Metaphysics: World, Finitude, Solitude*, trans. William McNeill and Nicholas Walker (Bloomington: Indiana University Press, 1995), 59–167. Pascal discusses *ennui* in his *Pensées*, which makes him one of the earliest philosophers to write at length about boredom. Some of the other continental philosophers for whom boredom is an important theme (and arguably a central category in their anthropology) include Schopenhauer, Kierkegaard, Nietzsche, and Sartre. Kierkegaard's *Sickness unto Death* and Sartre's *Nausea* can be interpreted as wrestling with the problem of boredom. For an illuminating discussion of boredom in Schopenhauer and Nietzsche, see Bernard Reginster, "Nietzche's 'New Happiness': Longing, Boredom, and the Elusiveness of Fulfillment," *Philosophic Exchange: Annual Proceedings* 37 (2007): 16–40. For an overview of the history of boredom in philosophy, see Svendsen, *A Philosophy of Boredom*, 49–106. Kuhn's survey of Western literature also gives attention to philosophers in various places. For a philosophical and

ies as well.[16] Boredom is one of those concepts that is used so prodigiously that it escapes critical scrutiny (as once was the case with the concept of emotion) because people assume its meaning is transparent. The modern experience of boredom calls out for more critical analysis—and response—than it has yet received.

The Phenomenology of Boredom

The first step in making sense of boredom is to describe its phenomenology. What, then, are the characteristic features of boredom, judging from the way people talk about it? Those who are bored find their situation uninteresting and unpleasant, and they might describe themselves as feeling weary or restless. Boredom is "experience without qualities."[17] People try to escape from experiences of boredom if they can. Sometimes boredom is mild, as when someone finds a game or a lecture boring. But sometimes the experience is so unpleasant that people engage in odd or self-destructive activities to alleviate boredom, sometimes explicitly naming relief from boredom as their goal.[18] Boredom is often linked to decadent indulgence, thrill seeking, destructive sexual behavior, and violence. Hence there is a certain paradox: boredom often involves weariness and lethargy, but it can also inspire frenetic activity.

theological reflection on boredom, see Michael L. Raposa, *Boredom and the Religious Imagination* (Charlottesville: University of Virginia Press, 1999).

16. Until 1981 an average of one study on boredom was published each year, but since then psychological research into boredom has increased markedly. See R. P. Smith, "Boredom: A Review," *Human Factors and Ergonomics in Manufacturing* 23 (1981): 329–340 and William L. Mikulas and Stephen J. Vodanovich, "The Essence of Boredom," *Psychological Record* 43 (1993): 3–12. Nonetheless, as a comparative study of recent literature observes, the psychological study of boredom has yet to arrive at a consensus about what exactly boredom is, and this lack of consensus has hindered the development of tools to measure it. See Stephen J. Vodanovich, "Psychometric Measurement of Boredom: A Review of the Literature," *Journal of Psychology* 137 (2003): 569–95.

17. Goodstein, *Experience without Qualities.*

18. Lars Svendsen's recent book on the philosophy of boredom was inspired by "the boredom-related death of a close friend" and his growing conviction that boredom is a serious problem in today's culture. After the death of his friend, he writes, "Being bored was no longer merely an innocent pose or a minor infliction. . . . I believed that this experience was not restricted to a close circle of friends but rather indicated a serious problem regarding *meaning* in our contemporary culture as a whole. To investigate the problem of boredom is to attempt to understand who we are and how we fit into the world at this particular point in time. The more I thought about it, the more boredom seemed to be seminal for understanding contemporary culture. We live in a culture of boredom" (Svendsen, *A Philosophy of Boredom*, 7).

There is a strong subjective dimension to boredom. The same situations, activities, or people that bore one person might not bore another, or even the same person in a different context or at a different age. Similarly, while boredom is often linked to the absence of change, new experiences do not always ameliorate boredom, nor does the repetition of old and familiar experiences necessarily engender it.

Although it is a negative psychological phenomenon, the sheer fact of boredom is not seen as necessarily implying anything about the moral character of the bored person in the way that something like envy would. In fact, boredom is sometimes praised as being characteristic of superior individuals, whose greater aesthetic, intellectual, and/or moral sophistication renders much of what is sought by others banal and uninteresting.[19] According to this view, boredom is a badge of honor that marks off the elite from the masses and that provides a goad toward ever-greater creativity. Nonetheless, while boredom is sometimes seen as positive, it is more typical to infer negative conclusions about someone's character from the fact of boredom, as in the saying "boredom is the product of a boring mind." Some might praise being habitually bored as a superior state of being, but most people regard habitual boredom as undesirable, unattractive, and indicative of questionable character. For example, parents might attempt to dissuade their daughter from marrying a man who was habitually bored.

The sheer diversity of the phenomena associated with boredom raises the question of whether our concept of boredom is too broad. Being bored of playing cards and being bored of life are so different that it is plausible to conclude that our concept of boredom conflates experiences that are different in kind, and not just in degree. Many have therefore distinguished between boredom that arises in particular situations and more general existential boredom.[20] However, one of the striking things about boredom is

19. Byron typifies the elitist interpretation of boredom: "Society is now one polish'd horde, Form'd of two mighty tribes, the *Bores* and *Bored*" (*Don Juan* XIII.95).

20. For example, Lars Svendsen distinguishes between situative and existential boredom. He writes, "While situative boredom contains a longing for something that is desired, existential boredom contains a longing for any desire at all" (Svendsen, *A Philosophy of Boredom*, 42).

Similarly, Jerome Neu distinguishes between endogenous and reactive boredom: "There is boredom from within [endogenous boredom], which tends to color the whole of life, and there is reactive boredom, which seems to arise as a response to more particular objects." Jerome Neu, "Boring from Within: Endogenous versus Reactive Boredom" in *A Tear Is an Intellectual Thing: The Meanings of Emotion* (Oxford: Oxford University Press, 2000), 97.

that we all seem to know what it is even though we struggle to define it. One would expect that if certain experiences of boredom were different *in kind* from each other, our efforts to communicate with each other would reflect this radical difference. But that is not the case. Instead, we talk about finding a conversation boring in the same way that we talk about finding our lives boring. While it is certainly possible that our linguistic habits obscure the truth about boredom, on the surface they strongly suggest that all experiences of boredom share a common psychological structure. Consequently, accounts of boredom that can make sense of the phenomenology of boredom without appealing to equivocal meanings have a stronger claim to cogency.

The Structure of Boredom

Some propose that boredom is a psychological consequence of an absence of meaning.[21] However, when people speak about an "absence of meaning" in the context of boredom, no matter the literal implications of their words, they do not actually seem to be talking about the cognitive signification or the ultimate objective importance of some particular reality (e.g., a boring conversation) or even human life in its totality. They are talking about something very different, something more related to whether they as individuals feel engaged with the fact of the world and of their lives.

When people say, "Life is meaningless to me," it does not exclude the possibility that they have strong intellectual commitments about life in fact being full of meaning. For example, religious persons might say, "Life is meaningless to me," or perhaps the more nuanced, "Life *seems* meaningless to me," even though they would also acknowledge that life has some intrinsic worth and goodness. They are expressing something other than the literal meaning of their words, and the gist of what they *mean* by these words seems similar to what bored nihilists mean by them. It is possible to imagine a nihilist saying in a cheerful way, "Life is meaningless to me," because life is going well and full of absorbing interests, and so, despite the intellectual assessment that life has no meaning, the nihilist is cheerful—perhaps even relishing the irony of the situation. It is only when those absorbing interests run dry that the same nihilist might say, "Life is meaningless to me," in a different sense.

21. Lars Svendsen defends this view in his book.

Focusing on the cognitive dimension of boredom, therefore, obscures the greater relevance of desire. A worldview devoid of a sense of life's ultimate significance or purpose might well engender boredom, but it does not do so infallibly. Conversely, a worldview that sees abundant meaning in everything does not make an individual immune. Boredom is about desire, not cognition. When people say that they find life boring, they are not saying that they have come to the conclusion that life as such has no meaning, no significance, and no purpose. What they are saying is that nothing engages them about life. Their deeper desires somehow fail to latch on to anything that presents itself to their consciousness. Hence Leo Tolstoy describes boredom as the desire for desires.[22] Those who are bored might still desire certain things (food, drink, companionship, etc.), but they do not find such desires or even their satisfaction fully engaging. These lesser desires might fix on definite objects, but a deeper desire continues to search restlessly for something other than what is available. Modern literature presents innumerable characters who dedicate themselves to seeking out the most exquisite sensual and aesthetic pleasures and yet, even in the midst of their enjoyment, find themselves bored.

Aquinas's account of *acedia* provides his closest approximation to what might be interpreted as an account of boredom. However, as discussed in chapter 6, *acedia* is best understood not as boredom itself, but as a cause of boredom. But even acknowledging its imperfect applicability, Aquinas's account of *acedia* can be mined for some fresh perspectives on the problem of boredom. Two points are particularly suggestive. First, Aquinas defines *acedia* as a spiritual sorrow that especially involves the will, and that also involves "a certain disgust of working" (*quoddam taedium operandi*).[23] Second, he holds that *acedia* is a vice opposed to the theological virtue of charity and—very strikingly—to the joy that proceeds from charity.[24] These points prove illuminating when applied to the phenomenology of boredom, in conjunction with other aspects of his account of emotion.

Working within the context of Aquinas's anthropology, boredom might be described as the emotion that ensues when the will finds nothing it desires and nothing worth seeking. Rattling around in its cage, the will finds

22. See *Anna Karenina*, V.8.

23. *ST* I-II 84.4; *ST* II-II 35.1–2; *De malo* 11.1.

24. *ST* II-II 35.2.

no particular good apprehended by the intellect worthy of its infinite desires.[25] Nonetheless, the will cannot help desiring even though it finds nothing worthy of desire, and this fruitless straining is unpleasant—a spiritual pain or spiritual sorrow that may overflow into the passions, a kind of disgust in the face of what the world offers, or rather fails to offer. For Aquinas, desire is the affection that describes the will's movement toward a particular good, and joy is the affection that results when the will rests in that good. In his vocabulary, then, boredom would be the affection that results when the will neither moves toward any particular good nor rests in anything. Boredom is the non-space between desire and joy: the will stuck in neutral, or spinning its wheels.

This interpretation of boredom accounts for many aspects of its phenomenology. It explains its peculiar combination of lethargy and hyperactivity. It makes sense that the will's inability to find a desire worth endorsing might lead to either fatigue or frenetic activity, depending on the circumstances. In some cases, the fruitless straining of boredom might cause exhaustion; in others, it might lead to a manic pursuit of unsatisfying desires in the illusory hope that somehow their satisfaction will alleviate the will's deeper restlessness. If loneliness is what happens when we do not feel loved, boredom is what happens when we have nothing *to* love.

It also explains an aspect of boredom that has not yet been discussed: its apparent incompatibility with joy.[26] Boredom can coexist with all sorts

25. There are some striking similarities here with Schopenhauer's interpretation of boredom. For Schopenhauer, "the empty longing for a new desire is languor, boredom." It inevitably results when finite desires are satisfied but the will continues to desire something more. Such empty desiring is painful: "[W]hen at last all wishes are exhausted, the pressure of will itself remains, even without any recognized motive, and makes itself known with terrible pain as a feeling of the most frightful desolation and emptiness." But unlike Aquinas, Schopenhauer holds that there is no intrinsic good and so nothing could possibly satisfy the will, and in consequence boredom is inevitable. See Arthur Schopenhauer, *The World as Will and Representation*, trans. E. F. Payne (New York: Dover Publications, 1966), §52, 260; §65, 364; §58, 319–320; and Reginster, "Nietzche's 'New Happiness,'" 19–25.

Others also resign themselves to the conclusion that life simply involves a significant amount of boredom, because they conclude that life is just intrinsically boring in many respects. That seems to be the conclusion of Lars Svendsen, for instance: his "solution" to boredom is to accept that there is no solution. He writes, "Boredom has to be accepted as an unavoidable fact, as life's own gravity. This is no grand solution, for the problem of boredom has none" (Svendsen, *Boredom*, 154).

26. An article by Michael Hanby also argues for an essential opposition between boredom and joy. See Michael Hanby, "The Culture of Death, the Ontology of Boredom, and the Resistance of Joy," *Communio* 31 (2004): 181–99.

of desires and intense pleasures, but it cannot coexist with joy. It is not possible to imagine an individual who is bored and joyful at the same time. (Those who understand joy in a way substantially different from Aquinas might at least concede that a certain kind of joy—the kind of joy we most value—is incompatible with boredom.) It is striking that, on the whole, works of modern literature that take up the theme of boredom are unabashedly joyless—except in those rare instances where the author is also trying to sketch a way out.[27] If boredom is the will spinning its wheels, the incompatibility of boredom and joy makes perfect sense: joy occurs when the will is resting in some good, and boredom implies that the will has nothing to rest in.

Why, then, can the same objects or activities seem to inspire joy and then become boring? This seemingly odd phenomenon follows naturally from the juxtaposition of infinite desire with a finite intellect. Our desires are infinite: there are no limits to the magnitude of the good that the will desires. Consequently, the will cannot rest in finite goods when they are perceived as finite and limited. However, because our apprehension of the world is limited and imperfect, it often happens that the limitations of finite goods are not fully before our conscious awareness. Sometimes we cannot see around to the other side of a finite good, and because its goodness exceeds our cognitive capacity, it *seems* infinite.

For example, we sometimes set ourselves on some objective, investing enormous time and energy. But then we reach our goal, and though we might feel some brief joy, we find ourselves strangely disappointed. What has happened? According to this interpretation of boredom, our finite minds often fail to grasp the limits of finite goods vis-à-vis our desire for infinite good. We might know intellectually that a certain good is finite and limited, but our imperfect knowledge of it (and perhaps a dose of self-deception) makes it possible for us to think that it will satisfy our desires. But once this finite good is attained, its limitations rapidly become apparent. The infinite can-

27. Walker Percy deserves special mention for his portrayal and analysis of boredom: in many ways, his novels, and especially his nonfiction book *Lost in the Cosmos,* offer a diagnosis of the modern experience of boredom and then try to show a way out. He seems to start in wonder and then goes from there: "Why is it that no other species but man gets bored? Under the circumstances in which a man gets bored, a dog goes to sleep" (Percy, *Lost in the Cosmos,* 71). The reflections on boredom given here are indebted to him in many ways, not least because his writings alerted me to the anthropological significance of boredom.

not be satisfied with the finite. Our illusions are shattered, we become bored with this finite good, and we start to direct ourselves to another objective. Each time this process repeats itself with a finite good as its object, we find ourselves, having been burned so many times before, less and less optimistic that the next objective will satisfy. Unless the cycle is interrupted, we become more and more bored with life—more closed in on ourselves, and less interested in wasting the effort to act on desires that would require us to move outside ourselves. The best we start to hope for is a life filled with experiences that are intense enough to occasionally distract us from our habitual boredom. Often these experiences must become more and more intense to alleviate the boredom, because otherwise their limitations would be obvious, and thus unable to sustain the will's interest.[28] In this way, a character trait comes to be formed from discrete experiences of boredom. To the extent that these discrete experiences of boredom involve defective voluntary choices, this character trait can be called a vice. Otherwise, it is simply an affective deformation—the result, perhaps, of not knowing the way through a maze of boring options to something authentically interesting, or some other psychological challenge.

Boredom and God

For many, God is part of the problem of boredom, not its solution. The practices of religion are boring, and the idea of living according to a set of divine commandments is oppressive and stultifying—except possibly from the outside, where they can be interesting in the way that viewing an ancient building or living among a primitive tribe can be interesting.[29] But only God can capture the will's enduring interest, because God is the only infinite good. Hence Aquinas's opposition of *acedia* to charity and joy: only charity, the love of God for himself and the love of others in God, can generate enduring joy. Faith and hope in God charges the finite world with the in-

28. The most intense forms of boredom seem to gravitate toward intense pleasure that so absorbs conscious awareness that the self—along with all its insatiable desires—is forgotten. This intense pleasure is a sort of counterfeit joy. The intensely bored cannot stop desiring joy, but they cannot find it either: the counterfeit joy of intense pleasure is the best they can manage. But unlike its counterfeit, authentic joy involves full self-awareness and the experience of the self as resting in something that fully engages it.

29. I am particularly thinking of Walker Percy's detached nuclear physicist observing a corn dance in New Mexico. Taking a break from working on the Manhattan Project in Los Alamos, he watches with great interest. See *Lost in the Cosmos*, 127–40.

finite. Finite goods become intentionally infinite from the perspective of the acting person, because they are seen to exist in an ordered relationship to the divine. By being grasped in their relationship to their Creator, even finite goods can be suitable objects for the will's infinite desires and thus cause joy. As Aquinas puts it, "Created goods only excite spiritual joy to the extent that they are referred to the divine good, from which spiritual joy properly arises."[30] Without charity, however, the will is condemned to restless, futile striving: sooner or later, finite goods lose their charm, and the vice of *acedia* inevitably fills the vacuum.[31]

This account of God and boredom puts Augustine's introduction to the *Confessions* in a new light:

> "You are great, Lord, and highly to be praised: great is your power and your wisdom is immeasurable." Man, a little piece of your creation, desires to praise you, a human being "bearing his mortality with him," carrying with him the witness of his sin and the witness that you "resist the proud." Nevertheless, to praise you is the desire of man, a little piece of your creation. You stir man to take pleasure in praising you, because you have made us for yourself, and our heart is restless until it rests in you.[32]

Looking back over his life, Augustine is able to name the restlessness that had once characterized his life and the rest that has come to supplant it. According to this analysis of boredom, it seems evident that his restlessness is boredom, and his subsequent rest is his will resting in the divine good through charity.

Yet this view of God as the way out of boredom leaves some unanswered questions. Many people who dedicate themselves to the love of God and neighbor nonetheless experience boredom. In fact, discussion of *acedia* originates among hermits and monks who struggled with boredom in their daily lives. Moreover, many without faith in God seem to experience enduring joy. So if God is the solution to boredom, why do some who love God still struggle to overcome it, and why are others who do not believe in God seemingly immune to it?

First, there are many explanations for the fact of bored hermits. Although

30. *ST* II-II 9.4 ad 1.

31. For Aquinas, the principal torment of the damned might well be boredom, since the absence of charity is their defining characteristic.

32. Augustine, *Confessions*, trans. Henry Chadwick (Oxford: Oxford University Press, 1992), I.1.

the divine good is infinite, our minds cannot fully grasp it. We see through a glass darkly (1 Corinthians 13:12), and so God cannot fully captivate our wills. Moreover, we often fail to perceive that finite and limited goods can take on infinite value because of their relationship to the divine. It is only when we perceive how even finite goods are charged with the infinite that the infinite desires of our wills can seek them and rest in them.

Furthermore, the presence of theological charity does not guarantee the avoidance of boredom. It is acts of theological charity, and not the sheer *habitus* of charity, that give the will something to rest in, thus generating joy and warding off boredom. Therefore, if persons in possession of theological charity do not draw on the inner resource of theological charity in their actions, or do so only in a minimal sort of way, they are unlikely to escape some experience of boredom. On the other hand, those who exercise a certain creativity, and tend toward spontaneous, positive acts of charity, are likely to experience more joy and less boredom. Unlike boredom, whose tendency is inward, as though the will wants to shrink into nothingness in order to cease causing affliction, charity's tendency is outward to God and our neighbor in God. Hence, the more the outward thrust of charity finds new expressions, the more the experience of boredom will be avoided.

From these considerations, it follows that those who are not sufficiently engaged with loving God and neighbor, as well as those who are caught up in finite goods in ways disconnected from charity, are likely to end up bored sooner or later. It also sheds new light on a seeming fact of the phenomenology of boredom: that the multiplication of material goods and sensual pleasures tends to eviscerate the enjoyment of them. Being overwhelmed with finite goods can overload our minds, making it harder to perceive their connection to the infinite, and thus making them less likely to provide rest for the will, and more likely to generate boredom, even for those in possession of theological charity. Hence the traditional emphasis in Christian spirituality on detachment from worldly goods in order to grow in the spiritual life: oversaturation with the good things of this world makes it harder to appreciate their sacramental role of pointing us to God. Instead of being an aid to spiritual growth, creation becomes a threat to it, jeopardizing our appreciation not only of God but also of creation itself. This analysis helps to explain the strong correlation between secularization and boredom. Since secularization severs the finite from the infinite, it makes the world less interesting and inevitably leads to an increase in boredom. The accumulation of material goods can exacerbate the problem, because the sensory overload of real but limited goods can make it difficult to perceive how the created world opens to the infinite.

Second, while explicit faith in God provides the intellectual grounding for a deeper appreciation of finite goods, it is not strictly necessary to avoid boredom. There is nothing to rule out agnostics or atheists from perceiving finite goods as intrinsically related to the infinite—which in fact they are—even if they do not affirm that they are created by God. Furthermore, the presence of theological charity cannot be ruled out simply because someone is an agnostic or atheist, at least according to many common interpretations of Christ's teachings.[33] In any case, theological charity is necessary to avoid boredom over the long haul, but it is not necessary to avoid boredom absolutely.

Friendship and human love would seem to provide the most obvious way out of boredom, both for those with faith in God and those without it, because, in the visible creation, the human person is the most intrinsically interesting object toward which the will might be directed. The human person is created in the image and likeness of God and, even more, has the capacity to share in God's own life through grace, and so the human person approximates the infinite, even if very imperfectly. Moreover, our wills are most easily directed toward objects that are known through the senses, objects that we can see and touch. Consequently, active love of other human persons provides the easiest way out of boredom, because, of anything in the visible creation, other human persons are most able to satisfy the infinite desires of the will.[34] Friendship and all forms of reciprocal human love

33. In his book on the theology of Christian faith, Avery Dulles offers an excellent treatment of how one might interpret the witness of both Scripture and Christian tradition about the necessity of faith in a way that allows for the salvation of non-Christians and thus their possession of the theological virtues (Dulles, *Assurance of Things Hoped For,* 256–73). While the affirmation of the possibility of salvation of nonbelievers is more common now than in earlier periods of Christianity, even some early Christians such as Justin Martyr and Clement of Alexandria affirmed the possibility of salvation of non-Christians (59).

34. When are people boring? People become boring when they are seen as the sum of their natural talents and abilities, because even the most impressive talents and abilities are finite and eventually become boring. The only thing about us that is infinite is the intrinsic goodness of our being, especially our imaging of God (cf. Genesis 1:24) and our potential to share in God's life through divine grace. When this intrinsic goodness is perceived, people are not boring, and even those who are otherwise boring become interesting.

provide a particularly privileged mode of moving beyond ourselves and achieving the self-transcendence paradoxically necessary for happiness.[35] The experience of beauty also provides a way out of boredom because it awakens a desire for something more, and also, at the same time, gives us a proleptic experience of rest by inspiring hope that the infinite good seemingly promised by beauty will eventually be ours.

Boredom is not simply a matter of failing to perceive God's presence, or the infinite goodness of each human person, or the world as beautiful. These failures of perception often lead to boredom, but boredom is cast out decisively only by charity. So those closest to God stand the greatest chance of avoiding boredom. One of the perennially captivating features of the saints is that they often do seemingly boring things and yet are not bored.[36] We should expect as much, since the saints presumably perceive better than anyone else that the finite is charged with the infinite and love both all the more—and thus all the more perfectly manifest charity's necessary consequence of joy, which, as Léon Bloy has said, is "the most infallible sign of God's presence."

35. Cf. *Gaudium et Spes* 24.

36. George Lamb singles out St. Simeon the Stylite, who lived for many years as a hermit on top of a pillar in fifth-century Syria, as worthy of admiration—an unusual judgment—for his conquest of boredom. He writes, "If we could say no more about him than that he faced boredom, wrestled with it, did not succumb to it—did not descend from his pillar—but conquered it and remained up there, *doing nothing,* then I think that would be sufficient to make him a worthwhile study and counterblast to the present day." George Lamb, "St. Simeon Stylites," in *Saints for Now,* ed. Claire Booth Luce (New York: Sheed and Ward, 1952).

Conclusion

The inner logic of Aquinas's account of emotion can be difficult to penetrate. He can be maddeningly discreet about his theological agenda.[1] He also incorporates so many previous authors in his writings that it is sometimes hard to figure out exactly what he thinks. As Bonnie Kent observes, in his attentiveness to innumerable authorities (Jewish, Christian, Islamic, and pagan), Aquinas is "very much like a host laboring to produce congenial, fruitful conversation among guests deeply at odds with each other."[2] Furthermore, the range and complexity of his thought requires a grasp of his entire philosophy and theology—which is immense—for a complete understanding of one particular feature. Lastly, there seems to have been little precedent for either his profoundly positive evaluation of emotion or the central place he assigns it within his anthropology and ethics. As a result of these interpretative difficulties, Aquinas's views on emotion have often been misunderstood, even among Thomists.[3] The same characteristics

1. In his essay on the setting of the *Summa,* after noting the relatively poor reception of the *Prima secundae* and suggesting that Aquinas's Dominican confreres failed to understand its significance to his theological project, Leonard Boyle affirms, "One could argue, finally, that the relationship between the parts of the *Summa* is not as clear as it might be in the various prefaces, and that Thomas profitably could have been more forthright regarding his intentions when, in the *Summa theologiae,* he wrote what I may now venture to call his one 'Dominican' work, and made what I have suggested was his own very personal contribution to a lopsided system of theological education in the order to which he belonged" (Boyle, "Setting of the *Summa,*" 91).

2. She continues: "Like all good hosts, he conceals how hard he must work to ensure that conflicts are defused and the party goes well. Sometimes Thomas repeats, approvingly, the words of an authority while giving them a meaning rather different from what the author intended. (One would need a knowledge of the history of ethics independent of the 'history' offered by the *Summa* to recognize such distortions.) Sometimes he sounds as if he agrees wholeheartedly when he actually agrees only with significant reservations. And sometimes his reservations become clear only later in the *Summa,* so that his earlier statements appear, retrospectively, in an altogether different light" (Kent, "Habits and Virtues," 116).

3. For example, in the foreword to a book about John Capreolus, a fifteenth-century commentator on Aquinas, Servais Pinckaers praises his defense of Aquinas's system of the virtues at a time when it was not popular, which Pinckaers sees as laying the foundation for a contem-

that make Aquinas difficult, however, also make for a very rich treatment of emotion. After seven hundred years, it remains philosophically interesting and, given some recent developments, even prescient.[4]

At present, there is no dominant theory of emotion in any discipline. However, the psychology and philosophy of emotion is undergoing a promising renewal, often welcoming rather than rejecting the pre-Cartesian contributions of ancient and medieval thinkers. In addition, many Christians are working to incorporate theology into clinical psychology and pastoral counseling (although as yet little is being done to construct a contemporary theology of emotion). All of these considerations suggest that Aquinas's account of emotion is more relevant than ever. Few, if any, would maintain

porary renewal of moral theology. At the same time, he notes that Capreolus does not seem to grasp fully the place of natural inclinations in Aquinas. Pinckaers writes: "Even so, we perceive a weakness in Capreolus's argument. Though he firmly establishes the necessity of *habitus* to determine faculties to their acts, he does not seem to see that *habitus* are rooted in the natural inclinations to goodness and truth which are components of our spiritual faculties and which assure their development. He writes in conclusion: '. . . a habitless power [*potentia non habituate*, a term not found in St. Thomas and which seems to indicate a tendency to habitude] is not more inclined to an act that is morally good than to one that is morally evil; nor is it inclined to acting pleasurably or easily or readily; rather it remains an indistinct potentiality to this and that object, and similarly to a good and an evil act, and similarly again to a certain way of operating and its opposite . . . [*Defensiones Theologiae Divi Thomae Aquinatis*, III.23.3].' It seems therefore that for Capreolus the entire determination of acts comes from *habitus*, which increases their necessity in a morality based on virtues, but takes away their natural root. On this point one might wonder whether Capreolus is influenced by the theory of freedom of indifference that holds for the radical indetermination of the will in its action, notably in regard to natural inclinations, onto which, in St. Thomas's account, the *habitus* are grafted."

See Servais Pinckaers, "Capreolus's Defense of St. Thomas's Teaching on the Virtues," trans. Mary Thomas Noble, in John of Capreolus, *On the Virtues*, trans. Kevin White and Romanus Cessario (Washington, D.C.: The Catholic University of America Press, 2001), xviii–xix. See also John of Capreolus, *Defensiones Theologiae Divi Thomae Aquinatis*, III.23–40, in John of Capreolus, *On the Virtues*, esp. 1–51, 247–64.

4. Contemporary scholars who publish about Aquinas's account of emotion almost invariably find themselves in sympathy with some of its features, even if they also voice serious reservations. For example, Peter King observes: "Aquinas's account of the nature and structure of the passions as psychological phenomena is as fine a piece of philosophical analysis as the Middle Ages has to offer. And, apart from its historical merits, I have tried to argue that his theory is attractive in its own right. His emphasis on faculty psychology and scientific taxonomy is a more sophisticated philosophical approach to psychological inquiry than that found in the early modern period, bearing remarkable similarities to contemporary questions and accounts being developed in cognitive science. The subtlety and penetration of Aquinas's analysis of the passions is unparalleled, and the questions he addresses are still philosophically pressing and acute. His discussion deserves to be taken seriously by anyone concerned with the issues he examines, not just by those with primarily historical or systematic interests" (King, "Aquinas on the Passions," 376–77).

that his account as it stands could fill the current vacuum. However, once integrated with modern science and post-Freudian psychology, its inclusive methodology, systematic depth, and holistic approach might provide the basis for a new vision of the human person, culled from millennia of anthropological reflection and yet thoroughly accessible today. Still a gracious host, Aquinas continues to reward those who engage him in conversation, and his writings on emotion deserve a wider readership.

Bibliography

I. Works of Thomas Aquinas

A. Latin

Aquinas, Thomas. *Compendium theologiae*. Vol. 42. Rome: Leonine, 1979.

———. *De anima*. Vol. 24, 1. Rome: Leonine, 1996.

———. *De malo*. Vol. 23. Rome: Leonine, 1982.

———. *De potentia*. Rome: Marietti, 1965.

———. *De veritate*. Vol. 22. Rome: Leonine, 1972–76.

———. *De virtutibus*. Vol. 24, 2. Rome: Leonine, 1996.

———. *Expositio in orationem dominicam*. In *Opuscula theological*, vol. 2, 219–35. Edited by R. M. Spiazzi. 2nd ed. Rome: Marietti, 1953.

———. *Sententia libri De anima*. Vol. 45, 1. Rome: Leonine, 1984.

———. *Sententia libri Ethicorum*. Vol. 47, 1–2. Rome: Leonine, 1969.

———. *Sententia super Metaphysicam*. Rome: Marietti, 1926.

———. *Scriptum super libros Sententiarum*. Vols. 7–11. Paris: Vivès edition, 1889.

———. *Summa contra gentiles*. Vols. 13–15. Rome: Leonine, 1918–30.

———. *Summa theologiae*. Vols. 4–12. Rome: Leonine, 1888–1906.

———. *Super librum Dionysii De divinis nominibus*. Rome: Marietti, 1950.

———. In P.-M. Gils, "Textes inédits de S. Thomas: Les premières rédactions du *Scriptum super Tertio Sententiarum*," *Revue des sciences philosophiques et théologiques* 46 (1962): 460.

B. English Translations

Aquinas, Thomas. *Commentary on Aristotle's Nicomachean Ethics*. Translated by C. I. Litzinger. Notre Dame, Ind.: Dumb Ox Books, 1993.

———. *Compendium theologiae*. Translated by Cyril Vollert. St. Louis: Herder, 1947.

———. *The De Malo of Thomas Aquinas*. Translated by Richard Regan. Edited by Brian Davies. Oxford: Oxford University Press, 2001.

———. *The Disputed Questions on Truth*. Translated by Robert W. Schmidt. 3 vols. Chicago: Henry Regnery, 1954.

———. *Disputed Questions on the Virtues*. Translated by E. M. Atkins. Cambridge: Cambridge University Press, 2005.

———. *Summa theologiae*. 3 vols. Translated by the English Dominicans. New York: Benzinger Brothers, 1947.

———. *Summa theologiae*. Latin and English. 61 vols. Edited by Thomas Gilby. New York: McGraw-Hill, 1964–80.

II. Ancient and Medieval Sources

Albert the Great. *Opera omnia*. Edited by A. Borgnet. Vol. 9. Paris: Vivès, 1890–99.

———. *De bono*. Edited by C. Feckes. In *Opera Omnia*. Vol. 28. Münster: Aschendorff, 1951.

———. *Opera omnia*. Edited by Institutum Alberti Magni Coloniense. Münster: Aschendorff. 1951–.

Alexander of Hales. *Summa theologiae*. Vols. 1–4. Quaracchi, Florence: Collegium S. Bonaventurae, 1924–48.

———. *Glossa in quatuor libros Sententiarum Petri Lombardi*. Vols. 12–15. Quaracchi, Florence: Collegium S. Bonaventurae, 1951–57.

———. *Quaestiones disputatae "antequam esset frater."* Vol. 19–20. Quaracchi, Florence: Collegium S. Bonaventurae, 1960.

Aristotle. *The Complete Works of Aristotle*. Edited by Jonathan Barnes. 2 vols. Princeton, N.J.: Princeton University Press, 1984.

Augustine. *Confessions*. Translated by Henry Chadwick. Oxford: Oxford University Press, 1992.

———. *The City of God against the Pagans*. Translated by R. W. Dyson. Cambridge: Cambridge University Press, 1998.

Bonaventure. *Commentaria in quatuor libros Sententiarum Magistri Petri Lombardi*. Quaracchi, Florence: Collegium S. Bonaventurae, 1882–89.

Hilary of Poitiers. *De Trinitate*. CCSL 62–62A. Edited by P. Smulders. Turnhout, Belgium: Typographi Brepols, 1979–80.

Jerome. *Commentariorum in Matheum*. Edited by D. Hurst and M. Adriaen. Turnhout, Belgium: Typographi Brepols, 1969.

John of Capreolus. *On the Virtues*. Translated by Kevin White and Romanus Cessario. Washington, D.C.: The Catholic University of America Press, 2001.

John Damascene. *Saint John of Damascus: Writings*. Translated by Frederic H. Chase Jr. The Fathers of the Church 37. New York: Fathers of the Church, 1958.

John of La Rochelle. *Tractatus de divisione multiplici potentiarum animae*. Edited by Pierre Michaud-Quantin. Paris: J. Vrin, 1964.

Nemesius of Emesa. *De natura hominis*. Edited by G. Verbeke and J. R. Moncho. Leiden: Brill, 1975.

Peter Lombard. *Magistri Petri Lombardi Sententiae in IV libris distinctae*. Grottaferrata (Rome): Editiones Collegii S. Bonaventurae ad Claras Aquians, 1971–81.

III. Other Sources

This section of the bibliography includes as many significant secondary sources on Aquinas's account of emotion as could be identified in recent academic literature, in order to give a comprehensive overview of the scholarship on this topic. Consequently, some redundant sources have been listed for the sake of completeness.

Aertsen, Jan A. "The Convertibility of Being and Good in St. Thomas Aquinas." *New Scholasticism* 59 (1985): 449–70.

———. *Medieval Philosophy and the Transcendentals: The Case of Thomas Aquinas*. New York: E. J. Brill, 1996.

———. "Thomas Aquinas on the Good: The Relation between Metaphysics and Ethics." In *Aquinas' Moral Theory: Essays in Honor of Norman Kretzmann*, 235–53. Edited by S. MacDonald and E. Stump. Ithaca, N.Y.: Cornell University Press, 1999.

Alvira, Tomás. *Naturaleza y libertad: Estudio de los conceptos tomistas de voluntas ut natura y voluntas ut ratio.* Publicaciones de la Facultad de Filosófica 44. Pamplona, Spain: Ediciones Universidad de Navarra, 1985.

Arintero, John. *The Mystical Evolution.* 2 vols. Translated by Jordan Aumann. St. Louis: Herder, 1949.

Arnold, Magda B. *Emotion and Personality.* 2 vols. New York: Columbia University Press, 1960.

———. "The Internal Senses—Functions or Powers? Part II." *The Thomist* 26 (1963): 15–34.

Aroca, F. "Los estados prepasionales." *Ciencia Tomista* 26 (1936): 196–212.

Ashmore, Robert. "Aquinas and Ethical Naturalism." *New Scholasticism* 49 (1975): 76–86.

Aumann, Jordan. "Thomistic Evaluation of Love and Charity." *Angelicum* 55 (1978): 534–56.

Aumann, Jordan, and Conrad W. Baars. *The Unquiet Heart: Reflections on Love and Sexuality.* Staten Island, N.Y.: Alba House, 1991.

Baars, Conrad W. *Feeling and Healing Your Emotions.* Plainsfield, N.J.: Logos International, 1979.

———. "Anger and Forgiveness." In *I Will Give Them a New Heart: Reflections on the Priesthood and the Renewal of the Church,* 73–85. Staten Island, N.Y.: Alba House, 2008.

———. "Morality and the Christian Anthropology of Thomas Aquinas." In *I Will Give Them a New Heart: Reflections on the Priesthood and the Renewal of the Church,* 215–46. Staten Island, N.Y.: Alba House, 2008.

Bader-Saye, Scott. "Thomas Aquinas and the Culture of Fear." *Journal of the Society of Christian Ethics* 25 (2005): 95–108.

Baker, Richard R. "The Thomistic Theory of the Passions and Their Influence upon the Will." Ph.D. diss., University of Notre Dame, 1941.

Barad, Judith A. "Aquinas on the Role of Emotion in Moral Judgment and Activity." *The Thomist* 55 (1991): 397–413.

Barbado, F. M. "La physionomie, le tempérament et la caractère, d'après Albert le Grand et la science moderne." *Revue thomiste* 36 (1931): 90–127.

Bartolomei, T. "Natura e forme del sentimento sensibile e spirituale." *Divus Thomas* (Piacenza) 47 (1944): 236–66.

Barzaghi, Giuseppe. "La «passio tristitiae» secondo S. Tommaso. Un esempio di analisi realista." *Sacra Doctrina* 36 (1991): 56–71.

Batten, R. J. Introduction, notes, and appendices to *Summa theologiae.* Vol. 34, *Charity.* New York: McGraw-Hill, 1966.

Bedford, Errol. "Emotions." *Proceedings of the Aristotelian Society* 57 (1957): 281–304.

Bednarksi, Felix. "Vis concupiscibilis et irascibilis in luce psychologiae «profundi»." In *De homine: Studia hodiernae anthropologiae.* Congressus Thomisticus Internationalis, 2:60–64. Bibliotheca Pontificiae Academiae Romanae S. Thomae Aquinatis 8–9. Rome: Officium Libri Catholici, 1970–72.

———. "La psychoanalyse de l'aggressivité à la lumière de la psychosynthèse de saint Thomas d'Aquin." *Angelicum* 58 (1981): 389–419.

Ben-Ze'ev, Aaron. "Emotions Are Not Mere Judgments." *Philosophy and Phenomenological Research* 68 (2004): 450–57.

Benz, Hubert. "Lust (*delectatio*) und Freude (*gaudium*) bei Thomas von Aquin." *Bochumer Philosophisches Jarbuch für Antike und Mittelalter* 7 (2002): 1–23.

Beyer, Gerald J. "The Love of God and Neighbour according to Aquinas: An Interpretation." *New Blackfriars* 84 (2003): 116–32.

Blais, Gérard. *Petit traité pratique des passions humaines*. 5th ed. Sherbrooke, Quebec: Éditions Paulines, 1967.

Blanco, Guillermo. "El concepto de pasión en Santo Tomás." *Sapientia* 2 (1948): 128–46.

Bobik, Joseph. "Aquinas on Friendship with God." *New Scholasticism* 60 (1986): 257–71.

———. "Aquinas on *Communicatio,* the Foundation of Friendship and Caritas." *Modern Schoolman* 64 (1988): 1–18.

Boganelli, E. "Alcuni aspetti della psicologia e fisiologia delle passioni secondo S. Tommaso." *Bolletino Filosofico* 1 (1935): 56–68.

Bond, Leo. "A Comparison between Human and Divine Friendship." *The Thomist* 3 (1941): 54–94.Bonino, Serge-Thomas, ed. *Surnaturel: A Controversy at the Heart of Twentieth-Century Thomistic Thought*. Naples, Fla.: Sapientia Press, 2009.

Bouchard, Charles. "Recovering the Gifts of the Holy Spirit in Moral Theology." *Theological Studies* 63 (2002): 539–58.

Boyle, Leonard E. "The Setting of the *Summa theologiae* of Saint Thomas." In *Facing History: A Different Thomas Aquinas,* 65–91. Louvain-La-Neuve: Fédération Internationale des Instituts d'Études Médiévales, 2000.

———. "The 'Summa confessorum' of John of Freiburg and the Popularization of the Moral Teaching of St. Thomas and Some of His Contemporaries." In *Facing History: A Different Thomas Aquinas,* 37–64.Louvain-La-Neuve: Fédération Internationale des Instituts d'Études Médiévales, 2000.

Bradley, Denis J. M. *Aquinas on the Twofold Human Good: Reason and Human Happiness in Aquinas's Moral Science*. Washington, D.C.: The Catholic University of America Press, 1997.

———. "'To Be or Not to Be?': Pasnau on Aquinas's Immortal Human Soul." *The Thomist* 68 (2004): 1–39.

Brennan, Robert Edward. "The Passions and Actions of Man." In *Thomistic Psychology: A Philosophical Analysis of the Nature of Man,* 147–68. New York: Macmillan, 1941.

———. "The Thomistic Concept of Imagination." *New Scholasticism* 15 (1941): 149–62.

Brock, Stephen L. *Action and Conduct: Thomas Aquinas and the Theory of Action.* Edinburgh: T & T Clark, 1998.

Brown, Montague. “St. Thomas Aquinas on Human and Divine Forgiveness.” *Saint Anselm Journal* 6 (2009): 1–8.

Brungs, Alexander. *Metaphysik der Sinnlichkeit: Das System der Passiones Animae bei Thomas von Aquin.* Halle/Saale, Germany: Hallescher Verlag, 2002.

———. “Die *passiones animae.*” In *Thomas von Aquin: Die Summa theologiae,* 198–222. Edited by Andreas Speer. Berlin: Walter de Gruyter, 2005.

Bullet, Gabriel. *Vertus morales infuses et vertus morales acquises selon saint Thomas d'Aquin.* Fribourg: Éditions universitaires, 1958.

Burns, J. Patout. “The Concept of Satisfaction in Medieval Redemption Theory.” *Theological Studies* 36 (1975): 285–304.

Butera, Giuseppe. “On Reason's Control of the Passions in Aquinas's Theory of Temperance.” *Medieval Studies* 68 (2006): 133–60.

Calveras, José. *La afectividad y el corazón según Santo Tomás.* Barcelona: Editorial Librería Religiosa, 1951.

Cannon, Walter B. “The Interrelations of Emotions as Suggested by Recent Physiological Researches.” *American Journal of Psychology* 25 (1914): 252–82.

———. *Bodily Changes in Pain, Hunger, Fear and Rage: An Account of Recent Researches into the Function of Emotional Excitement.* New York: Appleton, 1915.

———. “The James-Lange Theory of Emotions: A Critical Examination and an Alternative Theory.” *American Journal of Psychology* 39 (1927): 106–24.

Canti, Stanislas. *Treatise on the Soul.* Translated by H. DuLac and W. Baumgaertner. St. Paul, Minn.: College of St. Thomas, 1951. French original: *Précis de psychologie thomiste.* Quebec: Éditions de L'Université Laval, 1948.

Casey, John. “Sloth.” *New Blackfriars* 81 (2000): 77–89.

Cates, Diana Fritz. “Taking Women Seriously: Thomas Aquinas and Audre Lorde on Anger.” In *Aquinas and Empowerment: Classical Ethics for Ordinary Lives,* 47–88. Edited by Simon G. Harak. Washington, D.C.: Georgetown University Press, 1996.

———. *Choosing to Feel: Virtue, Friendship, and Compassion,* esp. 16–48, 91–130. Notre Dame, Ind.: University of Notre Dame Press, 1997.

———. “The Virtue of Temperance (IIa IIae, qq 141–170).” In *The Ethics of Aquinas,* 321–39. Edited by Stephen J. Pope. Washington, D.C.: Georgetown University Press, 2002.

———. *Aquinas on the Emotions: A Religious-Ethical Inquiry.* Washington, D.C.: Georgetown University Press, 2009.

Centi, T. “Valore del trattato tomistico sulle passioni.” *Sapienza* 13 (1961): 395–410.

Cessario, Romanus. *The Godly Image: Christ and Salvation in Catholic Thought from Anselm to Aquinas.* Petersham, Mass.: St. Bede's Publications, 1990.

———. *The Moral Virtues and Theological Ethics.* Notre Dame, Ind.: University of Notre Dame Press, 1991.

———. *Christian Faith and the Theological Life.* Washington, D.C.: The Catholic University of America Press, 1996.

———. “The Theological Virtue of Hope (IIa IIae, qq. 17–22).” In *The Ethics of Aquinas,* 232–43. Edited by Stephen J. Pope. Washington, D.C.: Georgetown University Press, 2002.

———. *The Virtues, Or, the Examined Life*. New York: Continuum, 2002.

Chardonnens, Denis. *L'homme sous le regard de la providence: Providence de Dieu et condition humaine selon l'*Exposition littérale sur le livre de Job *de Thomas d'Aquin,* esp. 185–98. Bibliothèque thomiste 50. Paris: J. Vrin, 1997.

Charland, Louis C. "The Natural Kind Status of Emotion." *British Journal of the Philosophy of Science* 53 (2002): 511–37.

Chenu, Marie-Dominique. *Toward Understanding Saint Thomas*. Translated by A.-M. Landry and D. Hughes. New York: Macmillan, 1968.

———. "Les passions vertueuses: L'anthropologie de saint Thomas." *Revue philosophique de Louvain* 72 (1974): 11–18.

———. "Body and Body Politic in the Creation Spirituality of Thomas Aquinas." In *Western Spirituality: Historical Roots, Ecumenical Routes,* 193–214. Edited by Matthew Fox. Santa Fe, N.M.: Bear and Company, 1981.

Christoph, P. Markus. "Justice as an Infused Virtue in the *Summa Theologiae* II-II and Its Implications for Our Understanding of the Moral Life." Ph.D. diss., University of Fribourg, 2010.

Congar, Yves M.-J. "Le traité de la force dans la 'Somme Théologique.'" *Angelicum* 51 (1974): 331–48.

Coerver, Robert Florent. *The Quality of Facility in the Moral Virtues*. Washington, D.C.: The Catholic University of America Press, 1946.

Conway Morris, Simon. *Life's Solution: Inevitable Humans in a Lonely Universe*. Cambridge: Cambridge University Press, 2003.

Coolman, Boyd Taylor. "The Salvific Affectivity of Christ According to Alexander of Hales." *The Thomist* 71 (2007): 1–38.

Cornelius, Randolph R. "Magda Arnold's Thomistic Theory of Emotion, the Self-Ideal, and the Moral Dimension of Appraisal." *Cognition and Emotion* 20 (2006): 976–1000.

Corvez, Maurice. Introduction, notes, and appendices to *Somme Théologique*. Vol. 1, *Les passions de l'âme*. Edition Revue des jeunes. Paris: Désclée, 1949.

Cottier, Georges. "«Libido» de Freud et «appetitus» de saint Thomas." In *L'anthropologie de saint Thomas,* 91–123. Edited by N. A. Luyten. Fribourg: Éditions Universitaires, 1974.

———. *Le désir de Dieu: Sur les traces de saint Thomas*. Paris: Parole et Silence, 2002.

Crosby, John F. "Is All Evil Really Only Privation?" *Proceedings of the American Catholic Philosophical Association* 75 (2001): 197–210.

———. "Doubts about the Privation Theory That Will Not Go Away: Response to Patrick Lee." *American Catholic Philosophical Quarterly* 81 (2007): 489–505.

Cross, Richard W. "Aquinas on Psychology." *Journal of Psychology and Christianity* 17 (1998): 306–20.

Crowe, Frederick E. "Complacency and Concern in the Thought of St. Thomas." *Theological Studies* 20 (1959): 1–39, 198–230, 343–82.

Cunningham, Francis L. B. *The Indwelling of the Trinity: A Historico-Doctrinal Study of the Theory of St. Thomas Aquinas*. Dubuque, Iowa: Priory Press, 1955.

———, ed. "The Passions of Man." In *The Christian Life*. Dubuque, Iowa: Priory Press, 1959. 78–111.

Damasio, Antonio. *The Feeling of What Happens: Body, Emotion and the Making of Consciousness*. London: Vintage, 1999.

———. "Emotions and Feelings: A Neurobiological Perspective." In *Feelings and Emotions: the Amsterdam Symposium*, 49–57. Edited by Antony S. R. Manstead, Nico Frijda, and Agneta Fischer. Cambridge: Cambridge University Press, 2004.

D'Arcy, Eric. Introduction and notes to *Summa theologiae*. Vol. 19, *The Emotions*. New York: McGraw-Hill, 1967.

———. Introduction and notes to *Summa theologiae*. Vol. 20, *Pleasure*. New York: McGraw-Hill, 1975.

Davies, Brian. *The Thought of Thomas Aquinas*. Oxford: Clarendon Press, 1992.

———, ed. *Thomas Aquinas: Contemporary Philosophical Perspectives*. Oxford: Oxford University Press, 2002.

Deely, John. "Animal Intelligence and Concept Formation." *The Thomist* 35 (1971): 43–93.

Deferrari, Roy J., M. Inviolata Barry, and Ignatius McGuiness. *A Lexicon of St. Thomas Aquinas*. Washington, D.C.: The Catholic University of America Press, 1948.

Deigh, John. "Cognitivism in the Theory of Emotions." *Ethics* 104 (1994): 824–54.

Del Cura, Angel. "Voluntad y apetito sensitivo en el hombre." *Estudios filosóficos* 12 (1963): 439–67; 13 (1964): 5–40.

De Letter, Prudentius. "Hope and Charity in St. Thomas." *The Thomist* 13 (1950): 204–48, 325–52.

Dell'Olio, Andrew J. *Foundations of Moral Selfhood: Aquinas on Divine Goodness and the Connection of the Virtues*. New York: Peter Lang, 2003.

De Lubac, Henri. *Surnaturel: études historiques*. Paris: F. Aubier, 1946.

Denifle, H., and A. Chatelain. *Chartularium universitatis parisiensis*. Paris: Frairs Delalain, 1889.

De Sousa, Ronald. *The Rationality of Emotion*. Cambridge: M.I.T. Press, 1987.

———. "Emotion." Online *Stanford Encyclopedia of Philosophy*. Accessed June 2007.

DeYoung, Rebecca Konyndyk. "Power Made Perfect in Weakness: Aquinas's Transformation of the Virtue of Courage." *Medieval Philosophy and Theology* 11 (2003): 147–80.

———. "Resistance to the Demands of Love: Aquinas on the Vice of *Acedia*." *The Thomist* 68 (2004): 173–204.

Di Noia, J. Augustine. "Imago Dei–Imago Christi: The Theological Foundations of Christian Humanism." In *Proceedings of the International Congress on Christian Humanism in the Third Millennium: The Perspective of Thomas Aquinas: 21–25 September 2003*, 19–30.Vatican City: Pontificia Academia Sancti Thomae Aquinatis, 2004.

Dixon, Thomas. *From Passions to Emotions: The Creation of a Secular Psychological Category*, esp. 26–61. Cambridge: Cambridge University Press, 2003.

Dobler, Emil. "Zwei syrische Quellen der theologischen Summa des Thomas von Aquin. Nemesios von Emesa und Johannes von Damaskus: Ihr Einfluss auf die anthropologischen Grundlagen der Moraltheologie (S. Th. I-II. qq. 6–17; 22–48)." S.T.D. diss., University of Fribourg, 2000.

Dodds, Michael. *The Unchanging God of Love: Thomas Aquinas and Contemporary Theology on Divine Immutability.* 2nd ed. Washington, D.C.: The Catholic University of America Press, 2008.

Donohoo, Lawrence J. "The Nature of Desire: St. Thomas Aquinas's Primary Account of Appetite." S.T.L. thesis, Dominican House of Studies, Washington, D.C., 1989.

Drost, Mark P. "Intentionality in Aquinas' Theory of the Emotions." *International Philosophical Quarterly* 31 (1991): 449–60.

———. "In the Realm of the Senses: Saint Thomas Aquinas on Sensory Love, Desire, and Delight." *The Thomist* 59 (1995): 47–58.

Dulles, Avery. *The Assurance of Things Hoped For: A Theology of Christian Faith.* New York: Oxford University Press, 1994.

Duroux, Benoit. *La psychologie de la foi chez s. Thomas d'Aquin.* Tournai, Belgium: Declée, 1963.

Eardley, P. S. "Thomas Aquinas and Giles of Rome on the Will." *Review of Metaphysics* 56 (2003): 835–62.

Eisen Murphy, Claudia. "Virtues and Vices of the Passions: An Analysis of Thomas Aquinas's Moral Psychology." Ph.D. diss., Cornell University, 1998.

———. "Aquinas on Our Responsibility for Our Emotions." *Medieval Philosophy and Theology* 8 (1999): 163–205.

Ekman, Paul, and Richard J. Davidson, eds. *The Nature of Emotion: Fundamental Questions.* New York: Oxford University Press, 1994.

Elders, Leo. *The Ethics of Aquinas: Happiness, Natural Law, and the Virtues,* esp. 93–133. Frankfurt am Main: Peter Lang, 2005.

Erb, Heather McAdam. "Interior peace: *Inchoatio vitae aeternae.*" In *Wisdom's Apprentice: Thomistic Essays in Honor of Lawrence Dewan, O.P.,* 260–81. Edited by Peter A. Kwasniewski. Washington, D.C.: The Catholic University of America Press, 2007.

Feingold, Lawrence. *The Natural Desire to See God according to St. Thomas Aquinas and His Interpreters.* Naples, Fla.: Sapientia Press, 2010.

Fierro, Patricia Astorquiza. "Amor y Virtud: Reflexiones respecto a la doctrina tomista del amor." *Proceedings of the International Congress on Christian Humanism in the Third Millennium: The Perspective of Thomas Aquinas: 21–25 September 2003,* 294–308.Vatican City: Pontificia Academia Sancti Thomae Aquinatis, 2004.

Flannery, Kevin. *Acts Amid Precepts: The Aristotelian Logical Structure of Thomas Aquinas's Moral Theory.* Washington, D.C.: The Catholic University of America Press, 2001.

Floyd, Shawn D. "Aquinas on Emotion: A Response to Some Recent Interpretations." *History of Philosophy Quarterly* 15 (1998): 161–75.

———. "Aquinas on Temperance." *Modern Schoolman* 77 (1999): 35–48.

Forschner, Maximilian. "Amor est causa timoris: Thomas von Aquin über das Gefühl der Angst." In *Traditio Augustiniana: Studien über Augustinus und seine Rezeption,* 175–91. Edited by A. Zumkeller and A. Krümmel. Geburtstag, Würzburg: Augstinus-Verlag, 1994.

Fortenbaugh, W. W. *Aristotle on Emotion.* 2nd ed. London: Duckworth, 2002.

Fostor, Kenelm. Introduction, notes, and appendices to *Summa theologiae.* Vol. 9, *Angels.* New York: McGraw-Hill, 1968.

Frede, Dorothea. "Aquinas on *Phantasia.*" In *Ancient and Medieval Theories of Intentionality,* 155–83. Edited by Dominik Perler. Leiden: Brill, 2001.

Frijda, Nico H. *The Emotions.* Cambridge: Cambridge University Press, 1986.

———. "Emotions and Actions." In *Feelings and Emotions: the Amsterdam Symposium,* 158–73. Edited by Antony S. R. Manstead, Nico Frijda, and Agneta Fischer. Cambridge: Cambridge University Press, 2004.

Gaine, Simon Francis. *Will There Be Free Will in Heaven?* London: T & T Clark, 2003.

Gallagher, David. "Thomas Aquinas on the Will as Rational Appetite." *Journal of the History of Philosophy* 29 (1991): 559–84.

Gardair, J. M. *Les passions et la volonté.* Paris: P. Lethielleux, 1892.

Gardeil, H.-D. *Introduction to the Philosophy of St. Thomas Aquinas.* Vol. 3, *Psychology.* Translated by J. A. Otto. St. Louis: B. Herder, 1956. French original: *Initiation à la philosophie de s. Thomas d'Aquin: Psychologie.* Paris: Éditions du Cerf, 1954.

Gardiner, H. M., Ruth Clark Metcalfe, and John G. Beebe-Center. *Feeling and Emotion: A History of Theories,* 106–18. New York: American Book Company, 1937.

Garrigou-Lagrange, Réginald. *Christian Perfection and Contemplation according to St. Thomas Aquinas and St. John of the Cross.* Translated by M. T. Doyle. St. Louis: Herder, 1939.

———. *The Three Ages of the Interior Life.* 2 vols. Translated by Sr. M. Timothea Doyle. St. Louis: Herder, 1947.

———. *Reality: A Synthesis of Thomistic Thought,* 282–83. St. Louis: Herder, 1950. Unabridged French original: *La synthèse thomiste,* 433–41. Bibliothèque française de philosophie 3. Paris: Désclée de Brouwer, 1947.

Gasson, J. A. "The Internal Senses—Functions or Powers? Part I." *The Thomist* 26 (1963): 1–14.

Gauthier, René Antoine. *Magnanimité: l'idéal de la grandeur dans la philosophie païenne et dans la théologie chrétienne.* Paris: J. Vrin, 1951.

Geach, Peter. *The Virtues.* Cambridge: Cambridge University Press, 1977.

Gigante, Mario. "Thélésis e Boúlesis in San Tommaso." *Asprenas* (Naples) 26 (1979): 265–73.

Gilby, Thomas. Introduction, notes, and appendices to *Summa theologiae.* Vol. 28, *Law and Political Theory.* New York: McGraw-Hill, 1966.

———. Introduction, notes, and appendices to *Summa theologiae.* Vol. 43, *Temperance.* New York: McGraw-Hill, 1968.

Gillon, L.-B. "Genèse de la théorie thomiste de l'amour." *Revue thomiste* 46 (1946): 322–29.

Gilson, Etienne. *The Christian Philosophy of St. Thomas Aquinas,* 236–48, 271–86, 333–50. Translated by L. K. Shook. New York: Random House, 1956. French original: *Le thomisme: Introduction à la philosophie de saint Thomas d'Aquin.* 5th ed. Paris: J. Vrin, 1948.

Glenn, Mary Michael. "A Comparison of the Thomistic and Scotistic Concept of Hope." *The Thomist* 20 (1957): 27–74.

Goldie, Peter. *The Emotions.* Oxford: Clarendon Press, 2000.

———. "Emotion." *Philosophy Compass* 2 (2007): 928–38.

———. *The Oxford Handbook of the Philosophy of Emotion.* Oxford: Oxford University Press, 2009.

Goodstein, Elizabeth S. *Experience without Qualities: Boredom and Modernity.* Stanford, Calif.: Stanford University Press, 2005.

Gondreau, Paul. *The Passions of Christ's Soul in the Theology of St. Thomas Aquinas.* Münster: Aschendorff Verlag, 2003.

———. "The Humanity of Christ, the Incarnate Word." In *The Theology of Thomas Aquinas,* 252–76. Edited by Rik Van Nieuwenhove and Joseph Wawrykow. Notre Dame, Ind.: University of Notre Dame Press, 2005.

———. "The Passions and the Moral Life: Appreciating the Originality of Aquinas." *The Thomist* 71 (2007): 419–50.

———. "St. Thomas Aquinas, the Communication of Idioms, and the Suffering of Christ in the Garden of Gethsemane." In *Divine Impassibility and the Mystery of Human Suffering,* 214–45. Edited by James F. Keating and Thomas Joseph White. Grand Rapids, Mich.: Eerdmans Press, 2009.

Gordon, Robert M. *The Structure of Emotions: Investigations in Cognitive Philosophy.* Cambridge: Cambridge University Press, 1987.

Goris, Harm. "Steering Clear of Charybdis: Some Directions for Avoiding 'Grace Extrinsicism' in Aquinas." *Nova et Vetera* 5 (2007): 67–79.

Gratsch, Edward J. "The Passions" and "The Cardinal Virtues of Fortitude and Temperance." In *Aquinas' Summa: An Introduction and Interpretation,* 89–102, 191–204. New York: Alba House, 1985.

Greenspan, Patricia. "Emotions, Rationality, and Mind/Body." In *Thinking about Feeling: Contemporary Philosophers on Emotion,* 125–34. Edited by Robert C. Solomon. New York: Oxford University Press, 2004.

Griffiths, Paul. *What Emotions Really Are: The Problem of Psychological Categories.* Chicago: University of Chicago Press, 1997.

Gudaniec, Arkadius. "Amore come *complacentia boni* in Tomasso d'Aquino." In *Proceedings of the International Congress on Christian Humanism in the Third Millennium: The Perspective of Thomas Aquinas: 21–25 September 2003,* 497–504. Vatican City: Pontificia Academia Sancti Thomae Aquinatis, 2004.

Guindon, André. "La crainte honteuse selon Thomas d'Aquin." *Revue thomiste* 69 (1969): 589–623.

———. "L'influence de la crainte sur la qualité humaine de l'acte selon Thomas d'Aquin." *Revue thomiste* 72 (1972): 33–57.

———. *La pédagogie de la crainte dans l'histoire du salut selon Thomas d'Aquin.* Tournai-Montréal: Desclée-Bellarmin, 1975.

Haldane, John, and Patrick Lee. "Aquinas on Human Ensoulment, Abortion and the Value of Life." *Philosophy* 78 (2003): 255–78.

Hall, Pamela M. *Narrative and the Natural Law: An Interpretation of Thomistic Ethics.* South Bend, Ind.: University of Notre Dame Press, 1994.

Hanby, Michael. "The Culture of Death, the Ontology of Boredom, and the Resistance of Joy." *Commnio* 31 (2004): 181–99.

Harak, G. Simon. "The Passions, the Virtues, and Agency: Modern Research and Thomistic Reflection." *Logos* 8 (1987): 31–44.

———. *Virtuous Passions: The Formation of Christian Character.* New York: Paulist Press, 1993.

Harvey, John F. "The Nature of the Infused Virtues." *Proceedings of the Tenth Annual Convention of the Catholic Theological Society of America* (1955): 172–221.

Hatzimoysis, Anthony. *Philosophy and the Emotions.* Royal Institute of Philosophy Supplement 52. Cambridge: Cambridge University Press, 2003.

Hause, Jeffrey. "Thomas Aquinas and the Voluntarists." *Medieval Philosophy and Theology* 6 (1997): 167–82.

———. "Aquinas on the Function of Moral Virtue." *American Catholic Philosophical Quarterly* 81 (2007): 1–20.

Heath, Thomas. Introduction, notes, and appendices to *Summa theologiae.* Vol. 35, *Consequences of Charity.* New York: McGraw-Hill, 1972.

Heidegger, Martin. *The Fundamental Concepts of Metaphysics: World, Finitude, Solitude.* Translated by William McNeill and Nicholas Walker, 59–167. Bloomington: Indiana University Press, 1995.

Hibbs, Thomas. "Against a Cartestian Reading of *Intellectus* in Aquinas." *Modern Schoolman* 66 (1988): 55–69.

Hill, William J. Introduction, notes, and appendices to *Summa theologiae.* Vol. 33, *Hope.* New York: McGraw-Hill, 1966.

———. *Knowing the Unknown God,* 111–61. New York: Philosophical Library, 1971.

Houser, R. E. "The Virtue of Courage (IIa IIae, qq. 123–140)." In *The Ethics of Aquinas,* 304–20. Edited by Stephen J. Pope. Washington, D.C.: Georgetown University Press, 2002.

Hughes, Louis M. "Charity as Friendship in the Theology of Saint Thomas." *Angelicum* 52 (1975): 164–78.

Hughes, W. D. Introduction, notes, and appendices to *Summa theologiae.* Vol. 23, *Virtue.* New York: McGraw-Hill, 1969.

Hume, David. *A Treatise of Human Nature.* Critical edition. Edited by David F. Norton and Mary J. Norton. Oxford: Clarendon Press, 2007.

Ignatius of Loyola. *The Spiritual Exercises.* Translated by David Fleming. St. Louis: Institute of Jesuit Studies, 1978.

Inagaki, Ryosuke Bernard. "*Habitus* and *Natura* in Aquinas." In *Studies in Medieval Philosophy,* 159–75. Edited by John Wippel. Washington, D.C.: The Catholic University of America Press, 1987.

Inglis, John. "Aquinas's Replication of the Acquired Moral Virtues: Rethinking the Standard Philosphical Interpretation of Moral Virtue in Aquinas." *Journal of Religious Ethics* 27 (1999): 3–27.

Irwin, Terence. *The Development of Ethics: A Historical and Critical Study.* Vol. 1, *From Socrates to the Reformation,* 434–652. Oxford: Oxford University Press, 2007.

Jacob, P. Josef. *Passiones. Ihr Wesen und ihre Anteilnahme an der Vernuft nach dem hl. Thomas von Aquin.* St. Gabrieler Studien 17. Mödling bei Wien, Austria: St. Gabriel-Verlag, 1958.

Jacobi, Klaus. "*Vis irascibilis*—die Kraft für schwierige Vorhaben: Untersuchungen zu Handlungstheorie und Anthropologie bei Thomas von Aquin." In *Entwicklungslinien mittelalterlicher Philosophie*, 135–52. Edited by Gerhard Leibold and Winfried Löffler. Vorträge des 5. Kongresses der Österreichischen Gesellschaft für Philosophie. Wien: Hölder-Pichler-Tempsky, 1999.

James, Susan. *Passion and Action: The Emotions in Seventeenth-Century Philosophy.* Oxford: Clarendon Press, 1997.

James, William. "What Is an Emotion?" *Mind* 19 (1884): 188–205.

Jenkins, John I. *Knowledge and Faith in Thomas Aquinas*, 154–59. New York: Cambridge University Press, 1997.

John of the Cross. *Collected Works of John of the Cross.* Translated by Kieran Kavanaugh and Otilio Rodriguez. Washington, D.C.: Institute of Carmelite Studies, 1964.

John Paul II. *Theology of the Body.* Boston: Pauline Books and Media, 1997.

Johnson, Mark. "St. Thomas and the «Law of Sin.»" *Recherches de théologie et philosophie médiévales* 67 (2000): 80–95.

Jones, L. Gregory. "The Theological Transformation of Aristotelian Friendship in the Thought of St. Thomas Aquinas." *New Scholasticism* 61 (1987): 373–99.

Jordan, Mark D. "Aquinas's Construction of a Moral Account of the Passions." *Freiburger Zeitschrift für Philosophie und Theologie* 33 (1986): 71–97.

———. "Ideals of *Scientia moralis* and the Invention of the *Summa theologiae.*" In *Aquinas' Moral Theory: Essays in Honor of Norman Kretzmann*, 79–97. Edited by S. MacDonald and E. Stump. Ithaca, N.Y.: Cornell University Press, 1999.

Kahn, Journet D. "A Thomistic Theory of Emotion." Ph.D. diss., University of Notre Dame, 1957.

Kambouchner, Denis. "Passions." In *Dictionnaire d'éthique et de philosophie morale*, 1081–87. Edited by M. Canto-Sperber. Paris: Presses Universitaires de France, 1996.

Keaty, Anthony. "Thomas's Authority for Identifying Charity as Friendship: Aristotle or John 15?" *The Thomist* 62 (1998): 581–601.

Keenan, James F. "Proposing Cardinal Virtues." *Theological Studies* 56 (1995): 709–29.

———. "Towards an Inclusive Vision for Moral Theology. Part I: A Look into the Past." *Pacifica* 12 (1999): 249–64.

———. "The Virtue of Prudence (IIa IIae, qq. 47–56)." In *The Ethics of Aquinas*, 116–30. Edited by Stephen J. Pope. Washington, D.C.: Georgetown University Press, 2002.

Keller, M.-Joseph and M.-Benoît Lavaud. "La charité comme amitié d'apres saint Thomas." *Revue thomiste* 34 (1929): 445–75.

Kelly, Anthony J. "The Gifts of the Spirit: Aquinas and the Modern Context." *The Thomist* 38 (1974): 193–231.

Kenny, Anthony. *Action, Emotion and Will.* London: Routledge and Kegan Paul, 1963.

———. Introduction, notes, and appendices to *Summa theologiae.* Vol. 22, *Dispositions for Human Acts.* New York: McGraw-Hill, 1964.

———. *Aquinas on Mind.* New York: Routledge, 1993.

Kent, Bonnie. "Transitory Vice: Thomas Aquinas on Incontinence." *Journal of the History of Philosophy* 27 (1989): 199–223.

———. *Virtues of the Will: The Transformation of Ethics in Late Thirteenth Century.* Washington, D.C.: The Catholic University of America Press, 1995.

———. "Habits and Virtues." In *The Ethics of Aquinas,* 116–30. Edited by Stephen J. Pope. Washington, D.C.: Georgetown University Press, 2002.

———. "Rethinking Moral Dispositions: Scotus on the Virtues." In *The Cambridge Companion to Duns Scotus,* 352–76. Edited by Thomas Williams. Cambridge: Cambridge University Press, 2003.

Kerr, Fergus. "Charity as Friendship." In *Language, Meaning, and God,* 1–23. Edited by Brian Davies. London: Geoffrey Chapman, 1987.

———. *Immortal Longings.* Notre Dame, Ind.: University of Notre Dame Press, 1997.

———. *After Aquinas.* Oxford: Blackwell, 2002.

King, Peter. "Scholasticism and the Philosophy of Mind: The Failure of Aristotelian Psychology." In *Scientific Failure,* 109–38. Edited by T. Horowitz and A. Janis. Lanham, Md.: Rowman and Littlefield, 1993.

———. "Aquinas on the Passions." In *Thomas Aquinas: Contemporary Philosophical Perspectives,* 353–84. Edited by Brian Davies. New York: Oxford University Press, 2002. Originally in *Aquinas' Moral Theory: Essays in Honor of Norman Kretzmann,* 101–32. Edited by S. MacDonald and E. Stump. Ithaca, N.Y.: Cornell University Press, 1999.

———. "Late Scholastic Theories of the Passions: Controversies in the Thomist Tradition." In *Emotions and Choice from Boethius to Descartes,* 229–58. Edited by Henrik Lagerlund and Mikko Yrjönsuuri. Studies in the History of the Philosophy of Mind 1. Dordrecht: Kluwer, 2002.

Klingseis, Rupert. "Moderne Theorie über das Unbewußte bei Thomas von Aquin." *Divus Thomas* (Fribourg) 7 (1929): 147–83, 279–300; 8 (1930): 40–59, 129–206, 381–405.

Klubertanz, G. P. "Une théorie sur les vertus morales *naturelles* et *surnaturelles.*" *Revue thomiste* 42 (1959): 565–75.

Knuuttila, Simo. "Medieval Theories of the Passions of the Soul." In *Emotions and Choice from Boethius to Descartes,* 49–83. Edited by Henrik Lagerlund and Mikko Yrjönsuuri. Studies in the History of the Philosophy of Mind 1. Dordrecht: Kluwer, 2002.

———. *Emotions in Ancient and Medieval Philosophy,* 239–55. Oxford: Oxford University Press, 2004.

Kretzmann, Norman. "Warring against the Law of My Mind: Aquinas on Romans 7." In *Philosophy and the Christian Faith,* 172–95. Edited by T. V. Morris. Notre Dame, Ind.: University of Notre Dame Press, 1988.

———. "Philosophy of Mind." In *The Cambridge Companion to Aquinas,* 128–59. Edited by Norman Kretzmann and Eleonore Stump. Cambridge: Cambridge University Press, 1993.

———. "Aquinas on God's Joy, Love, and Liberality." *Modern Schoolman* 72 (1995): 125–48.

———. "The Metaphysics of Providence: Aquinas's Natural Theology in *Summa contra gentiles* III." *Medieval Philosophy and Theology* 9 (2000): 104–26.

Kuhn, Reinhard. *The Demon of Noontide: Ennui in Western Literature.* Princeton, N.J.: Princeton University Press, 1976.

Kutter, Peter. *Die menschlichen Leidenschaften.* Stuttgart-Berlin: Kreuz-Verlag, 1978.

Labourdette, M.-M. "La vie théologale selon saint Thomas: L'affection dans la foi." *Revue thomiste* 60 (1960): 364–80.

———. *Cours de théologie morale: Les actes humains* (*Summa theologiae* I-II, 6–48). Toulouse, France: Dominican Province of Toulouse, 1963–64.

Laghi, Matteo. "Passio et 'passione' nella letteratura tomista: Riflessioni in merito allo Status Quaestionis." *Divus Thomas* (Piacenza) 103 (2000): 59–92.

Lalor, Juvenal. "The Passions." In *Summa Theologica,* 3:3220–35. Translated by the Fathers of the English Dominican Province. New York: Benzinger Brothers, 1948.

Laporte, Jean-Marc. *Les structures dynamiques de la grâce: grâce médicinale et grâce élevante selon Thomas d'Aquin.* Montreal: Bellarmin, 1973.

Lazarus, Richard. *Emotion and Adaptation.* New York: Oxford University Press, 1991.

Lee, Patrick. "The Relation between Intellect and Will in Free Choice according to Aquinas and Scotus." *The Thomist* 49 (1985): 321–42.

———. "The Goodness of Creation, Evil, and Christian Teaching." *The Thomist* 64 (2000): 239–70.

———. "Evil as Such Is a Privation: A Reply to John Crosby." *American Catholic Philosophical Quarterly* 81 (2007): 469–88.

Leget, Carlo. "Moral Theology Upside Down: Aquinas' Treatise *de passionibus animae* Considered through the Lens of Its Spatial Metaphors." In *Jaarboek Thomas Instituut 1999,* 101–26. Utrecht: Thomas Instituut, 2000.

———. "Martha Nussbaum and Thomas Aquinas on the Emotions." *Theological Studies* 64 (2003): 558–81.

Leighton, Stephen. *Philosophy and the Emotions: A Reader.* Petersborough, Ont., Canada: Broadview Press, 2003.

Le Rochelec, J. "La théorie des passions chez saint Thomas." *Revue des philosophie* 22 (1913): 306–14.

Levering, Matthew. "Natural Law and Natural Inclinations: Rhonheimer, Pinckaers, McAleer." *The Thomist* 70 (2006): 155–201.

Levi, A. *French Moralists: The Theory of the Passions 1585 to 1649,* 1–39. Oxford: Clarendon Press, 1964.

Lisska, Anthony J. "Medieval Theories of Intentionality: From Aquinas to Brentano and Beyond." In *Analytical Thomism: Traditions in Dialogue,* 147–70. Edited by Craig Paterson and Matthew S. Pugh. Burlington, Vt.: Ashgate, 2006.

Loughlin, Stephen. "Similarities and Differences between Human and Animal Emotion in Aquinas's Thought." *The Thomist* 65 (2001): 45–65.

———. "The Complexity and Importance of *timor* in Aquinas' *Summa Theologiae.*" In *Fear and Its Representations in the Middle Ages and Renaissance,* 1–16. Edited by Anne Scott and Cynthia Kosso. Tempe: Arizona Center for Middle Ages and Renaissance Studies Publications, 2002.

———. "Thomas Aquinas and the Importance of Fasting to the Christian Life." *Pro Ecclesia* 17 (2008): 343–61.

Lumbreras, Pedro. *De actibus humanis (In I-II, 6–48).* Rome: Officium Libri Catholici, 1950.

———. "Sfondo psicologico della morale di San Tommaso." *Sapienza* 9 (1957): 405–18.

———. *Psicología de las pasiones. Santo Tomás y los clásicos.* Madrid: Ediciones Studium, 1958.

Macdonald, Paul A., Jr. "Direct Realism and Aquinas's Account of Sensory Cognition." *The Thomist* 71 (2007): 343–78.

MacDonald, Scott, ed. *Being and Goodness: The Concept of the Good in Metaphysics and Philosophical Theology.* Ithaca: Cornell University Press, 1991.

MacIntyre, Alasdair. *After Virtue.* 2nd ed. Notre Dame, Ind.: University of Notre Dame Press, 1984.

———. *Whose Justice? Which Rationality?* Notre Dame, Ind.: University of Notre Dame Press, 1988.

Madigan, Kevin. *The Passions of Christ in High-Medieval Thought: An Essay on Christological Development.* New York: Oxford University Press, 2007.

Maguire, Daniel C. "*Ratio Practica* and the Intellectualistic Fallacy." *Journal of Religious Ethics* 10 (1982): 22–39.

Malloy, Christopher J. "Thomas on the Order of Love and Desire: A Development of Doctrine." *The Thomist* 71 (2007): 65–87.

Mañero, Salvador. "Sobre las mútuas influencias de las pasiones y del voluntario libre." *Revista de Filosofía* 7 (1949): 401–32.

Mangeau, Pierre-Paul. "La passion dans l'âme et dans l'appétit." *Laval théologique et philosophique* 5 (1949): 9–24.

Mansfield, Richard K. "Antecedent Passion and the Moral Quality of Human Acts According to St. Thomas." In *Virtues and Virtue Theory: Proceedings of the American Catholic Philosophical Association* 71, edited by Michael Baur (1997): 221–31.

Mansini, Guy. "*Duplex amor* and the Structure of Love in Aquinas." In *Thomistica,* 137–96. Edited by E. Manning. Leuven, Belgium: Peeters, 1995.

———. "*Similitudo, Communicatio,* and the Friendship of Charity in Aquinas." In *Thomistica,* 1–26. Edited by E. Manning. Leuven, Belgium: Peeters, 1995.

———. "Understanding St. Thomas on Christ's Immediate Knowledge of God." *The Thomist* 59 (1995): 91–124.

Manzanedo, Marcos F. "La clasificación de las pasiones o emociones." *Studium* 23 (1983): 357–78.

———. "La naturaleza de las pasiones o emociones." *Studium* 23 (1983): 47–69.

———. "La pasiones en relación a la razón y a la voluntas." *Studium* 24 (1984): 289–315.

———. *Las pasiones o emociones según santo Tomás.* Filosofia 8. Madrid: Instituto Pontificio de Filosofia "Santo Tomás," 1984.

———. "El amor y sus causas." *Studium* 25 (1985): 41–69.

———. "Propiedades y efectos del amor." *Studium* 25 (1985): 423–43.

———. "El odio según Santo Tomás." *Studium* 26 (1986): 3–27.

———. "El deseo y la aversión según Santo Tomás." *Studium* 27 (1987): 187–233.

———. "La delectación y sus causas." *Studium* 28 (1988): 265–95.

———. "Efectos y propiedades de la delectación." *Studium* 29 (1989): 107–39.

———. "La moralidad de la delectación." *Studium* 30 (1990): 113–34.

———. "El dolor y sus causas." *Studium* 31 (1991): 63–97.

———. "Efectos y propiedades del dolor." *Studium* 31 (1992): 505–40.

———. "La esperanza y la desperación." *Studium* 33 (1993): 79–108.

———. "El temor según Santo Tomás." *Studium* 34 (1994): 85–130.

———. "La audacia según Santo Tomás." *Studium* 34 (1994): 437–53.

———. "La ira: efectos, propiedades y remedios." *Studium* 35 (1995): 401–30.

———. "La ira y sus causas." *Studium* 35 (1995): 85–107.

Marmo, Constantino. "Hoc autem etsi potest tollerari: Egidio Romano e Tommaso d'Aquino sulle passioni dell'anima." In *Documenti e studi sulla tradizione filosofica medievale,* 2:281–315. Spoleto, Italy: Centro italiano di studi sull'alto Medioevo, 1991.

Massara, L. "La «delectatio» dans la psychologie de Saint Thomas d'Aquin." *Archives de Philosophie* 27 (1964): 186–205.

Mattison, William C., III. "Thomas and Damasio in Dialogue." *Journal of Faith and Science Exchange* 1 (1997): 57–63.

———. "Examining the Role of the Emotions in the Moral Life: Thomas Aquinas and Neuropsychology." In *Theology and the Social Sciences,* 277–92. Edited by Michael Barnes. Maryknoll, N.Y.: Orbis Books, 2001.

———. "Christian Anger? A Contemporary Account of Virtuous Anger in the Thomistic Tradition." Ph.D. diss., University of Notre Dame, 2002.

———. "Virtuous Anger? From Questions of *Vindicatio* to the Habituation of Emotion." *Journal of the Society of Christian Ethics* 24 (2004): 159–79.

———. "Interpretation of Jesus' Prohibition on Anger (Mt 5:22): The Person/Sin Distinction from Augustine to Aquinas." *Theological Studies* 68 (2007): 839–64.

Mauro, Letterio. *«Umanità» della passione secondo Tommaso d'Aquino.* Firenze: Felice Le Monnier, 1974.

———. "Le passioni nell'antropologia di san Tommaso." In *Tommaso d'Aquino nel suo settimo centenario: atti del Congresso Internazionale.* Vol. 5, *L'agire morale,* 337–43. Naples: Edizioni Domenicane Italiane, 1977.

May, William E. "Contemporary Perspectives on Thomistic Natural Law." In *St. Thomas Aquinas and the Natural Law Tradition: Contemporary Perspectives,* 113–56. Edited by John Goyette, Mark S. Latkovic, and Richard S. Myers. Washington, D.C.: The Catholic University of America, 1994.

McAleer, G. J. "The Politics of the Flesh: Rahner and Aquinas on *Concupiscentia.*" *Modern Theology* 15 (1999): 355–65.

———. *Ecstatic Morality and Sexual Politics: A Catholic and Antitotalitarian Theory of the Body.* New York: Fordham University Press, 2005.

McEvoy, J. "Amitié, attirance et amour chez S. Thomas d'Aquin." *Revue philosophique de Louvain* 91 (1993): 383–408.

McGuiness, Joseph Ignatius. "The Distinctive Nature of the Gift of Understanding." *The Thomist* 3 (1941): 217–78.
McKay, Angela M. "The Infused and Acquired Virtues in Aquinas' Moral Philosophy." Ph.D. diss., University of Notre Dame, 2004.
———. "Prudence and Acquired Moral Virtue." *The Thomist* 69 (2005): 535–55.
Meier, Matthias. "Die Lehre des Thomas von Aquino «De passionibus animae» in quellenanalytischer Darstellung." In *Beiträge zur Geschichte der Philosophie des Mittelalters*. Vol. 11. Münster-Westfalia: Aschendorff, 1912.
Melina, Livio. "Desire for Happiness and the Commandments in the First Chapter of Veritatis splendor." Translated by Margaret Harper McCarthy. In *Veritatis Spendlor and the Renewal of Moral Theology*, 143–60. Edited by J. A. Di Noia and Romanus Cessario. Huntington, Ind.: Our Sunday Visitor, 1999.
———. "La prudenza secondo Tommaso d'Aquino." *Aquinas* 49 (2006): 381–93.
Meyer, Michel. "Le problème des passions chez Saint Thomas d'Aquin." *Revue Internationale de Philosophie* 48 (1993–94): 363–74.
———. *Philosophy and the Passions: Toward a History of Human Nature*, 81–89. Translated by Robert F. Barsky. University Park: Pennsylvania State University Press, 2000.
Michel, Alain. "La joie spirituelle." *Revue des études latines* 76 (1999): 270–85.
Milhaven, John Giles. *Good Anger*. Kansas City, Mo.: Sheed and Ward, 1989.
Miner, Robert. *Thomas Aquinas on the Passions: A Study of* Summa Theologiae *1a2ae 22–48*. Cambridge: Cambridge University Press, 2009.
Mirkes, Renée. "Aquinas on the Unity of Perfect Moral Virtue." *American Catholic Philosophical Quarterly* 71 (1997): 589–605.
———. "Aquinas's Doctrine of Moral Virtue and Its Significance for Theories of Facility." *The Thomist* 61 (1997): 189–218.
Monahan, William B. *The Psychology of St. Thomas Aquinas and Divine Revelation*. Worcester-London: E. Baylis and Son, 1935.
Moncher, Frank. "A Psychotherapy of Virtue: Reflections on St. Thomas Aquinas' Theology of Moral Virtue." *Journal of Psychology and Christianity* 20 (2001): 332–41.
Mongeau, P. "La passion dans l'âme et dans l'appétit." *Laval théologique et philosophique* 4 (1949): 9–24.
Mongillo, Dalmazio. "La struttura del 'De iustitia': Summa theologiae II-II qq. 58-122." *Angelicum* 48 (1971): 355–77.
Moran, Dermot. *Introduction to Phenomenology*. London: Routledge, 2000.
Morgott, Franciscus (de Paola). *Die Theorie der Gefühle im System des hl Thomas*, 1863–64. Eichstätt, Germany: Jahres-Bericht über das Bischöfliches Lyceum zu Eichstätt.
Mulchahey, M. Michèle. *"First the Bow Is Bent in Study": Dominican Education before 1350*. Toronto: Pontifical Institute of Mediaeval Studies, 1998.
Muñoz, Jesús. *Psychologia philosophica*. Santander, Spain: Sal Terrae, 1961.
Nault, Jean-Charles. "Acedia: Enemy of Spiritual Joy." *Communio* 31 (2004): 236–58.
———. *La saveur de Dieu: l'acédie dans le dynamisme de l'agir*. Paris: Les Éditions du Cerf, 2006.

Neu, Jerome. “Boring from Within: Endogenous versus Reactive Boredom.” In *A Tear Is an Intellectual Thing: The Meanings of Emotion*, 97–107. Oxford: Oxford University Press, 2000.

Nicolas, Jean-Hervé. *Synthèse domatique: De la Trinité à la Trinité*. Fribourg: Éditions Universitaires, 1985.

———. “Les dons du Saint-Spirit.” *Revue thomiste* 92 (1992): 141–52.

Noble, Henri-Dominique. “La nature de l’émotion selon les Modernes et selon Saint Thomas.” *Revue des sciences philosophiques et théologiques* 2 (1908): 225–45, 466–83.

———. “Les émotions.” *Revue des sciences philosophiques et théologiques* 1 (1908): 312–26.

———. “L’état agréable.” *Revue des sciences philosophiques et théologiques* 4 (1910): 661–77.

———. “Le plaisir et la joie.” *Revue des sciences philosophiques et théologiques* 5 (1911): 689–707.

———. “L’évolution des états affectifs.” *Revue de philosophie* (1911): 281–315.

———. “La connaissance affective.” *Revue des sciences philosophiques et théologiques* 7 (1913): 637–62.

———. *L’éducation des passions*. Paris: P. Lethielleux, 1919.

———. “La nature de la passion d’après S. Thomas.” *Divus Thomas* (Piacenza) 28 (1925): 651–68; 29 (1926): 55–76.

———. “Comment la passion enjôle la volontè.” *Divus Thomas* (Piacenza) 29 (1926): 635–63.

———. “La passion et la sensation.” *Divus Thomas* (Piacenza) 29 (1926): 447–60.

———. “Les diverses passions.” *Divus Thomas* (Piacenza) 29 (1926): 259–78.

———. “La responsabilité passionnelle.” *Revue des sciences philosophiques et théologiques* 20 (1926): 635–63.

———. “Le péché de passion.” *Revue thomiste* 35 (1930): 329–53.

———. “Le tempérament passionnel d’après saint Thomas.” *Revue thomiste* 35 (1930): 97–127.

———. “La moralité de la passion.” *Revue des sciences philosophiques et théologiques* 25 (1931): 259–75.

———. “La passion au service de la conscience morale.” *Divus Thomas* (Piacenza) 34 (1931): 28–38.

———. *Les passions dans la vie morale*. 2 vols. Paris: P. Lethielleux, 1931–32.

———. “Passions.” *Dictionnaire de Théologie Catholique* 11 (1932): 2211–41.

Nussbaum, Martha C. *Upheavals of Thought: The Intelligence of Emotions*. Cambridge: Cambridge University Press, 2003.

Oatley, Keith. *Best Laid Schemes: The Psychology of the Emotions*. Cambridge: Cambridge University Press, 1992.

O’Brien, T. C. Introduction, notes, and appendices to *Summa theologiae*. Vol. 26, *Original Sin*. New York: McGraw-Hill, 1965.

———. Introduction, notes, and appendices to *Summa theologiae*. Vol. 27, *Effects of Sin, Stain and Guilt*. New York: McGraw-Hill, 1974.

O'Callaghan, John. "Aquinas' Rejection of Mind, Contra Kenny." *The Thomist* 66 (2002): 15–59

O'Connor, Edward D. Introduction, notes, and appendices to *Summa theologiae*. Vol. 24, *The Gifts of the Spirit*. New York: McGraw-Hill, 1973.

O'Meara, Thomas F. "Virtues in the Theology of Thomas Aquinas." *Theological Studies* 58 (1997): 254–85.

O'Neil, Charles J. "Is Prudence Love?" *Monist* 58 (1974): 119–39.

Osborne, Thomas M. "The Augustinianism of Thomas Aquinas's Moral Theory." *The Thomist* 67 (2003): 279–305.

———. "Perfect and Imperfect Virtues in Aquinas." *The Thomist* 71 (2007): 39–64.

Otten, A. "Die Leidenschaften." *Jahrbuch für Philosophie und spekulative Theologie* 1 (1887): 113–36, 196–223, 391–402; 2 (1888): 413–43, 559–87.

Panaccio, Claude. "Aquinas on Intellectual Representation." In *Ancient and Medieval Theories of Intentionality*, 185–201. Edited by Dominik Perler. Leiden: Brill, 2001.

Pascal, Blaise. *Pensées*. Translated by A. J. Krailsheimer. Rev. ed. New York: Penguin, 1995.

Pasnau, Robert. *Thomas Aquinas on Human Nature: A Philosophical Study of Summa theologiae Ia 75–89*. Cambridge: Cambridge University Press, 2002.

Peghaire, Julien. "A Forgotten Sense, the Cogitative, according to St. Thomas Aquinas." *Modern Schoolman* 20 (1943): 123–40, 210–29.

Peindador, A. "Responsabilidad moral del acto pasional." *Miscelanea Comillas* 6 (1951): 181–222.

Percy, Walker. *Lost in the Cosmos: The Last Self-Help Book*. New York: Farrar, Strauss, Giroux, 1983.

Pesch, Otto H. *Thomas von Aquin: Grenze und Grösse mittelalterlicher Theologie*. Eine Einführung. 2nd ed. Mainz: Matthias-Grünewald-Verlag, 1989.

Pestana, Mark Stephen. "Second Order Desires and Strength of Will." *Modern Schoolman* 72 (1996): 173–82.

Peters, R. S. "Emotion and the Category of Passivity." *Proceedings of the Aristotelian Society* 62 (1961–62): 117–42.

Petruzelis, N. "Le passioni nel pensiero di Tommaso d'Aquino, di R. Descartes e di Spinoza." *Rassegna di Scienze Filosofiche* 25 (1972): 253–86, 381–405.

Pfürtner, Stephanus. *Triebleben und sittliche Vollendung: Eine moralpsychologische Untersuchung nach Thomas von Aquin*. Studia friburgensia, N.S. 22. Fribourg: Universitätsverlag, 1958.

Pieper, Josef. *The Four Cardinal Virtues: Prudence, Justice, Fortitude, and Temperance*. Notre Dame, Ind.: University of Notre Dame Press, 1966.

———. *Faith, Hope, Love*. San Francisco: Ignatius Press, 1997.

Pinckaers, Servais. "La nature verteuse de l'espérance." *Revue thomiste* 58 (1958): 405–42, 623–644.

———. "Virtue Is Not a Habit." Translated by Bernard Gilligan. *Cross Currents* 12 (1962): 65–81.

———. "Les passions et la morale." *Revue des sciences philosophiques et théologiques* 74 (1990): 379–91. Also published in *The Pinckaers Reader*.

———. "L'Instinct et L'Esprit au couer de l'éthique chrétienne." In *Novitas et veritas vitae: Aux sources du renouveau de la morale chrétienne,* 213–23. Edited by C.-J. Pinto de Oliveira, Fribourg: Éditions universitaires, 1991. Also published in *The Pinckaers Reader.*

———. *The Sources of Christian Ethics.* Translated by Mary Thomas Noble. Washington, D.C.: The Catholic University of America Press, 1995.

———. *The Pursuit of Happiness—God's Way.* Translated by Mary Thomas Noble. New York: Alba House, 1998.

———. *Morality: The Catholic View.* Translated by Michael Sherwin. South Bend, Ind.: St. Augustine's Press, 2001.

———. "Capreolus's Defense of St. Thomas's Teaching on the Virtues." Translated by Mary Thomas Noble. In John of Capreolus, *On the Virtues,* xi–xxvi. Translated by Kevin White and Romanus Cessario. Washington, D.C.: The Catholic University of America Press, 2001.

———. "The Role of Virtue in Moral Theology." Translated by Mary Thomas Noble. In *The Pinckaers Reader: Renewing Thomistic Moral Theology,* 288–303. Edited by John Berkman and Craig Steven Titus. Washington, D.C.: The Catholic University of America Press, 2005.

———. *Passions et Vertu.* Paris: Éditions Parole et Silence, 2009.

Pitcher, George. "Emotion." *Mind* 74 (1965): 326–46.

Plé, Albert. "St. Thomas Aquinas and the Psychology of Freud." *Dominican Studies* 5 (1952): 1–34. Unrevised French original: "Saint Thomas d'Aquin et la psychologie des profondeurs." *Vie spirituelle Supplement* 82 (1951): 402–34.

———. Introduction, notes, and appendices to *Somme Théologique.* Vol. 2, *Les passions de l'âme.* Paris: Éditions du Cerf, 1986.

Pomplun, Trent. "Impassibility in St. Hilary of Poitiers's *De Trinitate.*" In *Divine Impassibility and the Mystery of Human Suffering,* 187–213. Edited by James F. Keating and Thomas Joseph White. Grand Rapids, Mich.: Eerdmans Press, 2009.

Pope, Stephen J., ed. *The Ethics of Aquinas.* Washington, D.C.: Georgetown University Press, 2002.

Porter, Jean. "Natural Desire for God: Ground of the Moral Life in Aquinas." *Theological Studies* 47 (1986): 48–68.

———. "Perennial and Timely Virtues: Practical Wisdom, Courage and Temperance." In *Changing Values and Virtues,* 60–68. Edited by Dietmar Mieth and Jacques Pohier. Edinburgh: T & T Clark, 1987.

———. *The Recovery of Virtue: The Relevance of Aquinas for Christian Ethics.* Louisville, Ky.: Westminster/John Knox Press, 1990.

———. "The Subversion of Virtue: Acquired and Infused Virtues in the Summa theologiae." *Annual of the Society of Christian Ethics* 12 (1992): 19–41.

———. "The Virtues Reformulated." In *Moral Action and Christian Ethics,* 167–200. New York: Cambridge University Press, 1995.

———. "Recent Studies in Aquinas's Virtue Ethics: A Review Essay." *Journal of Religious Ethics* 26 (1998): 191–215.

———. "The Virtue of Justice (IIa IIae, qq. 58–122)." In *The Ethics of Aquinas,*

272–86. Edited by Stephen J. Pope. Washington, D.C.: Georgetown University Press, 2002.

Prinz, Jesse. "Embodied Emotions." In *Thinking about Feeling: Contemporary Philosophers on Emotion,* 44–58. Edited by Robert C. Solomon. New York: Oxford University Press, 2004.

Purkiss, M. Ubeda. "Desarrollo histórico de la doctrina sobre las emociones." *Ciencia Tomista* 43 (1953): 433–86; 44 (1954): 35–68.

Putallaz, François-Xavier. *Insolente liberté: controversies et condamnations au XIIIe siècle.* Paris: Cerf, 1995.

Prügl, Thomas. "Tristitia: Zur Theologie der *passiones animae* bei Thomas von Aquin." In *Die Einheit der Person: Beiträge zur Anthropologie des Mittelalters,* 141–56. Edited by Martin Thurner. München: Geburtstag, 1998.

Quinto, Riccardo. "*Timor* e *timiditas:* Note di lessicografia tomista." *Rivista di filosofia neoscholastica* 77 (1985): 387–410.

———. "Per la storia del trattato tomistico de passionibus animae: il timor nella letteratura teologica tra il 1200 e il 1230 ca." In *Recherches de théologie ancienne et médievale.* Supplementa 1, *Thomistica,* 35–87. Edited by E. Manning. Leuven, Belgium: Peeters, 1995.

Rahner, Karl. "The Theological Concept of Concupiscentia." In *Theological Investigations,* vol. 1. Baltimore, Md.: Helicon Press, 1961.

Raposa, Michael L. *Boredom and the Religious Imagination.* Charlottesville: University of Virginia Press, 1999.

Reginster, Bernard. "Nietzche's 'New Happiness': Longing, Boredom, and the Elusiveness of Fulfillment." *Philosophic Exchange: Annual Proceedings* 37 (2007): 16–40.

Reid, John Patrick. Introduction, notes, and appendices to *Summa theologiae.* Vol. 21, *Fear and Anger.* New York: McGraw-Hill, 1968.

Reilly, George Cajetan. "The Psychology of Saint Albert the Great Compared with That of Saint Thomas." Diss., The Catholic University of America, 1934.

Ricken, Freido. "Aristotelische Interpretationem zum Trakat *De Passionibus Animae* (*Summa Theologiae* I II 22–48) des Thomas von Aquin." In *Die Einheit der Person: Beiträge zur Anthropologie des Mittelalters,* 125–40. Edited by Martin Thurner. München: Geburtstag, 1998.

Rist, John M. *Augustine: Ancient Thought Baptized.* Cambridge: Cambridge University Press, 1994.

Roberts, Robert C. "Thomas Aquinas on the Morality of Emotions." *History of Philosophy Quarterly* 9 (1992): 287–305.

———. *Emotions: An Essay in Aid of Moral Psychology.* Cambridge: Cambridge University Press, 2003.

Rocca, Gregory P. *Speaking the Incomprehensible God: Thomas Aquinas on the Interplay of Positive and Negative Theology.* Washington, D.C.: The Catholic University of America Press, 2004.

Rorty, Amélie Oksenberg, ed. *Explaining Emotions.* Berkeley and Los Angeles: University of California Press, 1980.

———. "From Passions to Emotions and Sentiments." *Philosophy* 57 (1982): 159–72.

———. "Enough Already with Theories of Emotion." In *Thinking about Feeling: Contemporary Philosophers on Emotion*, 269–78. Edited by Robert C. Solomon. New York: Oxford University Press, 2004.

Rota, Michael. "The Moral Status of Anger: Thomas Aquinas and John Cassian." *American Catholic Philsophical Quarterly* 81 (2007): 395–418.

Royo, Antonio, and Jordan Aumann. *The Theology of Christian Perfection.* Dubuque, Iowa: Priory Press, 1962.

Ryan, Thomas. "Comparison and Evaluation of the Moral Significance of Emotions in Aquinas, the Manualists and Catholic Moral Theology 1960–1990." Ph.D. diss., University of Notre Dame Australia, Fremantle, Western Australia, 1999.

———. "Aquinas' Integrated View of Emotions, Morality, and the Person." *Pacifica* 14 (2001): 55–70.

———. "Positive and Negative Emotions in Aquinas: Retrieving a Distorted Tradition." *Australasian Catholic Record* 78 (2001): 141–52.

———. "Revisiting Affective Knowledge and Connaturality in Aquinas." *Theological Studies* 66 (2005): 49–68.

Sabelli, Mary Veronica. "St. Thomas Aquinas on Whether the Human Soul Can Have Passions." In *Proceedings of the International Congress on Christian Humanism in the Third Millennium: The Perspective of Thomas Aquinas: 21–25 September 2003*, 667–74. Vatican City: Pontificia Academia Sancti Thomae Aquinatis, 2004.

Sacchi, Mario E. "La terapéutica del dolor y la tristeza según Santo Tomás." *Psychologica* (Buenos Aires) 2 (1979): 85–104.

Sarot, Marcel. "God, Emotion and Corporeality: A Thomist Perspective." *The Thomist* 58 (1994): 61–92.

Schmid, Karl. *Die menschliche Willensfreiheit in ihrem Verhältnis zu den Leidenschaften nach der Lehre des hl. Thomas von Aquin.* Engelberg, Switzerland: Verlag der Stiftsschule, 1925.

Schockenhoff, Eberhard. "The Theological Virtue of Charity (IIa IIae, qq. 23–46)." In *The Ethics of Aquinas*, 244–58. Edited by Stephen J. Pope. Washington, D.C.: Georgetown University Press, 2002.

Schopenhauer, Arthur. *The World as Will and Representation.* Translated by E. F. Payne. New York: Dover Publications, 1966.

Schumacher, Bernard. *A Philosophy of Hope: Josef Pieper and the Contemporary Debate on Hope.* Translated by D. C. Schindler. New York: Fordham University Press, 2003.

Schwartz, Daniel. *Aquinas on Friendship.* Oxford: Clarendon Press, 2007.

Sciuto, Italo. "Le passioni dell'anima nel pensiero di Tommaso d'Aquino." In *Anima e corpo nella cultura medievale*, 73–93. Edited by C. Casagrande and S. Vecchio. Florence: Edizioni del Galluzzo, 1999.

Scrutton, Anastasia. "Emotion in Augustine of Hippo and Thomas Aquinas: A Way Forward for the Im/possibility Debate?" *International Journal of Systematic Theology* 7 (2005): 169–77.

Selman, Francis. "The Emotions." In *Aspects of Aquinas*, 112–35. Dublin: Veritas Publications, 2005.

Sertillanges, A.-D. "L'Appétit sensitif: Les passions." In *S. Thomas d'Aquin,* 2:203–05. 2 vols. Les grand philosophes. Paris: Félix Alcan, 1910.

Shanley, Brian. "Aquinas on Pagan Virtue." *The Thomist* 63 (1999): 553–77.

———. *The Thomist Tradition,* esp. 151–78. Dordrecht: Kluwer Academic Publishers, 2002.

Sherwin, Michael. *By Knowledge and By Love: Charity and Knowledge in the Moral Theology of Thomas Aquinas.* Washington, D.C.: The Catholic University of America Press, 2005.

———. "Aquinas, Augustine, and the Medieval Scholastic Crisis concerning Charity." In *Aquinas the Augustinian,* 181–204. Edited by Michael Dauphinais, Barry David, and Matthew Levering. Washington, D.C.: The Catholic University of America Press, 2007.

———. "Infused Virtue and the Effects of Acquired Vice: A Test Case for the Thomistic Theory of Infused Cardinal Virtues." *The Thomist* 73 (2009): 29–52.

Shockenhoff, Eberhard. *Bonum hominis: Die anthropologischen und theologischen Grundlagen der Tugendethik des Thomas von Aquin.* Tübinger theologische Studien 29. Mainz: Matthias-Grünewald-Verlag, 1987.

———. "Die Rolle und Funktion der menschlichen Leidenschaften im Aufbau und Tugend." In *Bonum hominis: Die anthropoligischen und theologischen Grundlagen der Tugendethik des Thomas von Aquin,* 172–201. Tübinger theologische Studien 29. Mainz: Matthias-Grünewald-Verlag, 1987.

Siewerth, Gustav. *Die menschliche Willensfreiheit: Texte zur thomistischen Freiheitslehre mit einer Einführung.* Düsseldorf: L. Schwann, 1954.

Simonin, H.-D. "Autour de la solution thomiste du problem de l'amour." *Archives d'histoire doctrinale et littéraire du moyen âge* 6 (1931): 174–274.

Sokolowski, Robert. "Intentionality." In *Introduction to Phenomonology,* 8–16. Cambridge: Cambridge University Press, 2000.

Solomon, Robert C. "Emotions and Choice." *Review of Metaphysics* 28 (1973): 20–41.

———. "What Is a 'Cognitive Theory' of the Emotions?" In *Philosophy and the Emotions,* 1–18. Edited by Anthony Hatzimoysis. Royal Institute of Philosophy Supplement 52. Cambridge: Cambridge University Press, 2003.

———, ed. *What Is an Emotion? Classic and Contemporary Readings.* 2nd ed. New York: Oxford University Press, 2003.

———, ed. *Thinking about Feeling: Contemporary Philosophers on Emotion.* New York: Oxford University Press, 2004.

———. "Emotions in Continental Philosophy." *Philosophy Compass* 1 (2006): 413–31.

Sorabji, Richard. "From Aristotle to Brentano: The Development of the Concept of Intentionality." In *Oxford Studies in Ancient Philosophy.* Supplement vol. 1991, *Aristotle and the Later Tradition,* 227–59. Edited by H. Blumenthal and H. Robinson. Oxford: Clarendon Press, 1991.

———. *Emotion and Peace of Mind: From Stoic Agitation to Christian Temptation.* Gifford Lectures. Oxford: Oxford University Press, 2003.

Spacks, Patricia Meyer. *Boredom: The Literary History of a State of Mind.* Chicago: University of Chicago Press, 1995.

Spohn, William. "Notes on Moral Theology 1990: Passions and Principles." *Theological Studies* 52 (1991): 69–87.

Stagnitta, Antonio. *L'anthropologia in Tommaso d'Aquino: saggio di ricerca comparata sulle passioni e abitudini dell'uomo.* Naples: E.D.I. Editrice, 1979.

———. "Tommaso d'Aquino e i precorrimenti da sistema: La psicologia. Le passion dell'uomo come tendenze istintive ed affettive (pulsioni)." *Angelicum* 62 (1985): 531–64.

———. *La fondazione medievale della psicologia. Struttura psicologia dell'etica tomista e modelli scientific contemporaeni. Passioni, frustrazioni e depression, virtù.* Bologna: ESD, 1993.

Stévaux, A. "La doctrine de la charité dans les Commentaires des *Sentences* de Saint Albert, de Saint Bonaventure et de Saint Thomas." *Ephemerides Theologiae Louvaniensis* 24 (1948): 59–97.

Stock, Michael. "Thomistic Psychology and Freud's Psychoanalysis." *The Thomist* 21 (1958): 125–45.

Stocker, Michael L. "Some Considerations about Intellectual Desire and Emotions." In *Thinking about Feeling: Contemporary Philosophers on Emotion*, 135–48. Edited by Robert C. Solomon. New York: Oxford University Press, 2004.

Stocker, Michael L., and Elizabeth Hegeman. *Valuing Emotions.* Cambridge: Cambridge University Press, 1996.

Stump, Eleonore. *Aquinas.* New York: Routledge, 2003.

Stump, Eleonore, and Norman Kretzmann. "Being and Goodness." In *Thomas Aquinas: Contemporary Philosophical Perspectives*, 295–323. Edited by Brian Davies. New York: Oxford University Press, 2002.

Sutter, Timothy. Introduction, notes, and appendices to *Summa theologiae.* Vol. 11, *Man.* New York: McGraw-Hill, 1970.

Svendsen, Lars. *A Philosophy of Boredom.* Translated by John Irons. London: Reaktion Books, 2005.

Svorcik, Constantin. "Die Theorie der Gefühle (passiones) nach dem hl. Thomas von Aquin." *Studien und Mitteilungen aus dem Benediktiner und Cistercienser Orden* 23 (1902): 16–30, 243–59.

Sweeney, Eileen. "Restructuring Desire: Aquinas, Hobbes, and Descartes on the Passions." In *Meeting of the Minds: The Relations between Medieval and Classical Modern European Philosophy*, 215–33. Edited by Stephen F. Brown. Turnhout, Belgium: Brepols, 1998.

Taylor, Gabriele, and Sybil Wolfram. "Virtues and Passions." *Analysis* 31 (1970–71): 76–83.

Terruwe, Anna A. *Psychopathic Personality and Neurosis.* Translated by Conrad W. Baars. New York: P. J. Kenedy and Sons, 1958.

———. *The Neurosis in the Light of Rational Psychology.* Translated by Conrad W. Baars. New York: P. J. Kenedy and Sons, 1960.

Terruwe, Anna A., and Conrad W. Baars. *Loving and Curing the Neurotic: A New Look at Emotional Illness.* New Rochelle, N.Y.: Arlington House, 1972.

———. *Healing the Unaffirmed.* Staten Island, N.Y.: Alba House, 1976.

———. *Psychic Wholeness and Healing.* Staten Island, N.Y.: Alba House, 1981.

Terzis, George N. "Human Flourishings: A Psychological Critique of Virtue Ethics." *American Philosophical Quarterly* 31 (1994): 333–42.

Te Velde, Rudi A. *Participation and Substantiality in Thomas Aquinas.* New York: E. J. Brill, 1995.

Tittley, Rémi. "La Douleur Sensible Est-Elle une Passion Corporelle ou une Passion Animale Selon Saint Thomas d'Aquin?" Diss., University of Montreal, 1967.

Titus, Craig Steven. *Resilience and the Virtue of Fortitude: Aquinas in Dialogue with the Psychosocial Sciences.* Washington, D.C.: The Catholic University of America Press, 2006.

———. "Passions in Christ: Spontaneity, Development, and Virtue." *The Thomist* 73 (2009): 53–87.

Torrell, Jean-Pierre. *Saint Thomas Aquinas.* Vol. 1, *The Person and His Work.* Translated by Robert Royal. Washington, D.C.: The Catholic University of America Press, 1996.

———. *Le Christ en ses mysteres: La vie et l'oeuvre de Jésus selon saint Thomas d'Aquin.* Vol. 2. Paris: Desclée, 1999.

———. "La vision de Dieu «per essentiam» selon saint Thomas d'Aquin." In *Recherches Thomasiennes: Études Revues et Augmentées,* 177–97. Paris: Librairie Philosophique J. Vrin, 2000.

———. "Saint Thomas d'Aquin et la science du Christ: une relecture des Questions 9–12 de la Tertia Pars de la «Somme de théologie»." In *Recherches Thomasiennes: Études Revues et Augmentées,* 198–213. Paris: Librairie Philosophique J. Vrin, 2000.

———. "Nature et grâce chez Thomas d'Aquin." *Revue thomiste* 101 (2001): 167–202.

———. *Saint Thomas Aquinas.* Vol. 2, *Spiritual Master,* esp. 244–65. Translated by Robert Royal. Washington, D.C.: The Catholic University of America Press, 2003.

———. *Aquinas's* Summa: *Background, Structure, and Reception.* Washington, D.C.: The Catholic University of America Press, 2005.

Uffenheimer-Lippens, Elisabeth. "Rationalized Passion and Passionate Rationality: Thomas Aquinas on the Relation between Reason and the Passions." *Review of Metaphysics* 56 (2003): 525–58.

Voll, Urban. "The Vice of Acedia." S.T.D. diss., Dominican House of Studies, Washington, D.C., 1964.

Wadell, Paul J. "An Interpretation of Aquinas' Treatise on the Passions, the Virtues, and the Gifts from the Perspective of Charity as Friendship with God." Ph.D. diss., University of Notre Dame, 1985.

———. *The Primacy of Love: An Introduction to the Ethics of Thomas Aquinas.* Mahwah, N.J.: Paulist Press, 1992.

Wallace, William A. "Appetition and Emotion." In *The Modeling of Nature: Philosophy of Science and Philosophy of Nature in Synthesis,* 174–80. Washington, D.C.: The Catholic University of America Press, 1996.

Wang, Stephen. "Aquinas on Human Happiness and the Natural Desire for God." *New Blackfriars* 88 (2007): 322–34.

Wawrykow, Joseph. *God's Grace and Human Action: "Merit" in the Theology of Thomas Aqinas.* Notre Dame, Ind.: University of Notre Dame Press, 1995.

———. "Hypostatic Union." In *The Theology of Thomas Aquinas*, 222–51. Edited by Rik Van Nieuwenhove and Joseph Wawrykow. Notre Dame, Ind.: University of Notre Dame Press, 2005.

Weil, Howard Gil. *The Dynamic Aspect of Emotions in the Philosophy of St. Thomas Aquinas*. Rome: Angelicum, 1966.

Weinandy, Thomas G. "The Beatific Vision and the Incarnate Son: Furthering the Discussion." *The Thomist* 70 (2006): 605–15.

Weisheipl, James. *Friar Thomas d'Aquino*. 2nd ed. Washington, D.C.: The Catholic Unversity of America Press, 1983.

Wenzel, Siegfried. *The Sin of Sloth: Acedia in Medieval Thought and Literature*. Chapel Hill: University of North Carolina Press, 1967.

Westberg, Daniel. "Did Aquinas Change His Mind about the Will?" *The Thomist* 58 (1994): 41–60.

———. *Right Practical Reason: Aristotle, Action, and Prudence in Aquinas*. Oxford: Clarendon Press, 1994.

———. "Emotion and God: A Reply to Michael Sarot." *The Thomist* 60 (1996): 109–21.

White, Kevin. "The Passions of the Soul (IaIIae, qq. 22–48)." In *The Ethics of Aquinas*, 103–15. Edited by Stephen J. Pope. Washington, D.C.: Georgetown University Press, 2002.

White, Thomas Joseph. "The Voluntary Action of the Earthly Christ and the Necessity of the Beatific Vision." *The Thomist* 69 (2005): 497–534.

Williams, A. N. *The Ground of Union: Deification in Aquinas and Palamas*. Oxford: Oxford University Press, 1999.

Williams, Bruce. "The Capital Vices in Contemporary Discourse." *Angelicum* 84 (2007): 29–47.

Wippel, John F. "The Condemnations of 1270 and 1277 at Paris." *Journal of Medieval and Renaissance Studies* 7 (1977): 169–201.

———. "Metaphysical Foundations for Christian Humanism in Thomas Aquinas." In *Proceedings of the International Congress on Christian Humanism in the Third Millennium: The Perspective of Thomas Aquinas: 21–25 September 2003*, 101–18. Vatican City: Pontificia Academia Sancti Thomae Aquinatis, 2004.

Van Nieuwenhove, Rik, and Joseph Wawrykow, eds. *The Theology of Thomas Aquinas*. Notre Dame, Ind.: University of Notre Dame Press, 2005.

Zajonc, Robert B. "On the Primacy of Affect." *American Psychologist* 39 (1984): 117–23.

Ziermann, Bernhard. *Die menschlichen Leidenschaften: Summa theologica II 22–48*. Die deutsche Thomas-Ausgabe 10. Heidelberg: F. H. Kehrle, 1955.

Zimmerman, Albert. "Zur Unterscheidung des sinnlichen Strebevermögens gemäss Thomas von Aquin." In *Aristotelisches Erbe im arabisch-lateinischen Mittelalter*, 43–52. Berlin: Walter de Gruyter, 1986.

———. "Gedanken des Thomas von Aquin über *Defectus Naturalis* und *Timor*." In *Thomas von Aquin*, 43–52. Edited by Albert Zimmerman. Miscellanea Mediaevalia 19. Berlin: Walter de Gruyter, 1988.

Znidar, Ivana. "Die Lehre des Thomas von Aquin von der Angst." Ph.D. diss., Cologne, 1986.

Index of Citations

General Index

The Logic of Desire: Aquinas on Emotion was designed and typeset in Meta Serif
with Meta display type by Kachergis Book Design of Pittsboro, North Carolina.
It was printed on 50-pound Natural and bound by Versa Press of East Peoria, Illinois.